Environmental Racism in the United States and Canada

Environmental Racism in the United States and Canada

Seeking Justice and Sustainability

Bruce E. Johansen

BLOOMSBURY ACADEMIC
NEW YORK • LONDON • OXFORD • NEW DELHI • SYDNEY

BLOOMSBURY ACADEMIC
Bloomsbury Publishing Inc
1385 Broadway, New York, NY 10018, USA
50 Bedford Square, London, WC1B 3DP, UK
29 Earlsfort Terrace, Dublin 2, Ireland

BLOOMSBURY, BLOOMSBURY ACADEMIC and the Diana logo
are trademarks of Bloomsbury Publishing Plc

First published in the United States of America by ABC-CLIO 2020
Paperback edition published by Bloomsbury Academic 2024

Copyright © Bloomsbury Publishing Inc, 2024

Cover photo: A member of the Menominee Indian Tribe at Standing Rock Indian Reservation, North Dakota, November 25, 2016. (ZUMA Press, Inc./Alamy Stock Photo)

All rights reserved. No part of this publication may be reproduced or transmitted in any form or by any means, electronic or mechanical, including photocopying, recording, or any information storage or retrieval system, without prior permission in writing from the publishers.

Bloomsbury Publishing Inc does not have any control over, or responsibility for, any third-party websites referred to or in this book. All internet addresses given in this book were correct at the time of going to press. The author and publisher regret any inconvenience caused if addresses have changed or sites have ceased to exist, but can accept no responsibility for any such changes.

A catalog record for this book is available from the Library of Congress.

ISBN: HB: 978-1-4408-6402-5
PB: 979-8-7651-1529-9
ePDF: 978-1-4408-6403-2
eBook: 979-8-2160-8050-3

To find out more about our authors and books visit www.bloomsbury.com and sign up for our newsletters.

Contents

Preface ix

Chapter 1	**Background**	1
	What Is Environmental Justice?	1
	Types of Environmental Discrimination	6
	Perpetrators and Victims	11
	Challenges and Solutions	18
	Future Outlook	23
Chapter 2	**Unifying Themes**	29
	Introduction	29
	Mining: Mother Earth or Mother Lode?	30
	Lead, Lead Everywhere: Flint, Michigan's Water Crisis in Context	37
	The Political Economy of Lead Poisoning and Other Water Quality Issues	50
	Canadian Tar Sands: From Treaty Forest to Moonscape	62
	Pipelines and Protests	73
	"Cowboys" vs. "Indians": Racial Stereotyping and Agent Orange in Vietnam	78
	Farmworkers: Toxicity as an Occupational Hazard	89
	Extermination of the Buffalo as Environmental Warfare	103
	Environmental Racism and the Demise of an Ice World	113
Chapter 3	**Cases: United States East**	131
	Introduction	131
	Houston, Texas: Segregation, Sewage, and Environmental Racism	133

	Anniston, Alabama: A Plague of PCBs	138
	Dickson, Tennessee: Environmental Racism's "Poster Child"	143
	A 100 Percent Chance of Pig-manure Showers in North Carolina	147
	Bridgeport, Connecticut: A Spreading Web of Toxins	154
	Chester, Pennsylvania: Unwilling Capital of Hazmat	158
	South Chicago: Life and Death in the "Toxic Doughnut"	162
	Race, Class, and Toxicity at Love Canal	166
	North Carolina: Protesting Unwelcome Toxic Dumps	172
	Donald Trump, Hurricane Maria, and Puerto Rico	177
	Triana, Alabama: Dumped On, Ceaselessly	184
	Malathion and the Rosebud Sioux in Mission, South Dakota	187
	Houston, Texas: Always Awaiting the Next Flood	190
	Akwesasne: Land of the Toxic Turtles	195
	The Toxics Plantation: Life and Death in Louisiana's "Cancer Alley"	204
	The Demographics of Death in New Orleans: Race, Class, and Hurricane Katrina	212
Chapter 4	**Cases: United States West**	219
	Introduction	219
	Montana's Gros Ventre and Assiniboine: Gold Mining and Cyanide Poisoning	222
	The Mothers of East Los Angeles Stand Down a Toxic Incinerator—and More	227
	Pueblo, Colorado: The Toxic Legacy of the "Pittsburgh of the West"	233
	Richmond, California: The Greens vs. Big Oil	238
	Alaska's Pebble Mine: Corporate Gold vs. Natives' Salmon	243
	Alaska Natives: Swamped by Warming	249
	The Point Hope Eskimos: An Atomic Harbor and a Nuclear Dump as a Neighbor	254
	"The Most Bombed Nation on Earth"	260
	Utah's Goshute Asked to House Waste Uranium—but Were Denied	263
	The Laguna Pueblo and Anaconda's Jackpile Uranium Mine	267
	The Navajos' Nuclear Legacy	272

	The Largest Uranium Spill in the United States	278
	Hunting Grounds to Dumping Grounds	285
	The Moapa Paiute: Good-Bye Toxic Ash: Solar In, Coal Power Out	289
Chapter 5	Cases: Canada	295
	Introduction	295
	Grassy Narrows, Ontario: The Continuing Toxic Toll of Mercury	297
	The Aamjiwnaang of Ontario: Immersed in a Toxic Bath	302
	Dumping on Blacks in Africville, Nova Scotia	306
	British Columbia: Native Canadians vs. Mining's "New Prosperity"	311
	The Crees: Hydro Quebec's Electric Dreams	317
	The Lubicon Cree: Land Rights and Resource Exploitation	330
	The Dene: Killed by the "Money Rock"	335
	The Inuit: Mother's Milk Is Toxic	339
	Who Is Liable for Ruining a Culture? The Inuit Sue the United States of America	346

Selected Bibliography   353

Index   361

Preface

Environmental Racism in the United States and Canada: Seeking Justice and Sustainability traces the relationship between environmental discrimination, race, and class. The idea for the book originated with ABC-CLIO's editorial board. It is directed at anyone who has an interest in social justice and environmental issues, but it is especially designed for high school students in advanced placement courses as well as college undergraduates. Readers will receive an enhanced understanding of how poor and minority people are affected by environmental crises ranging from chemical pollution to floods spawned by hurricanes made worse by climate change.

Environmental racism and the pursuit of justice against it intertwines ecology with issues of race and class, involving poor, often racial minority communities whose residents are subjected to a disproportionate level of many kinds of toxicity, while being denied ecological benefits such as clean water and air, as well as sustainable use of resources for a decent and dignified standard of living.

This work is organized into five background essays, which provide an overview of the subject, followed by case studies grouped by regions in the United States and Canada, including the eastern half of the United States, the western half of the United States, and Canada. We have extended the scope to Canada because quite a number of environmental law and racism issues (often those involving Inuit and other indigenous peoples) stem from there. Some of these are quite important on a global basis, for example, the toll that persistent organic pollutants (POPs) have been taking on the Inuit. Often they can't eat fish or seals, staples in their traditional diet. Eating food flown in from lower latitudes is not only culturally out of character, but very expensive. Inuit mothers cannot breast-feed their babies because toxins such as dioxin biomagnify up the food chain (their effects increase exponentially at each step). The Canadian Inuit have taken a lead role globally in measures such as the Stockholm Convention, which outlaw many POPs.

The background essays and case studies are mainly contemporary, but also include some historic accounts from as early as the nineteenth century.

CHAPTER ONE

Background

What Is Environmental Justice?

Environmental racism and the pursuit of justice against it intertwines ecology with issues of race and class, involving poor, often racial minority communities whose residents are subjected to a disproportionate level of many kinds of toxicity, while being denied ecological benefits such as clean water and air, as well as sustainable use of resources for a decent and dignified standard of living. Benjamin Chavis, an activist in both environmental and civil rights, has said that "environmental racism is racial discrimination in environmental policy-making and enforcement of regulations and laws, the deliberate targeting of communities of color for toxic waste facilities, the official sanctioning of the presence of life-threatening poisons and pollutants for communities of color, and the history of excluding people of color from leadership of the environmental movement" (Chavis, 1987). In a worldwide context, "environmental racism" also has been used to describe the movement of polluting industries, with their toxicity, from affluent nations to the Third World. Thus in the last century the worst air quality in the world has moved from urban areas such as New York City and London to such cities as Beijing and New Delhi.

Environmental racism and the environmental justice that addresses it unite human and civil rights with acute ecological crises. The road through this thicket is paved with human stories fraught with suffering and death—human agony inflicted by several types of cancer and many other maladies borne usually by poor, nonwhite people who are already ailing, stuck at the bottom in a world increasingly laced with growing income inequity from all manner of pollution that is a by-product of modern industry. As a scholarly pursuit, environmental racism and justice can be traced to the 1970s. "In Indian Country," however, writes Zoltán Grossman in *Unlikely Allies: Native American and White Communities Join to Defend Rural Lands* (2017, 103), "the environmental justice movement could be traced back to 1492—with the arrival of a certain Italian interested in mining gold."

Robert D. Bullard has defined environmental justice as "the fair treatment and meaningful involvement of all people regardless of race, color, national origin or income with respect to the development, implementation, and enforcement of environmental laws, regulations, and policies." Bullard said that fair treatment should be defined in a way that inflicts no single racial, ethnic, or socioeconomic group with a disproportionate share of pollution from industrial, municipal, and commercial operations. "Simply put," wrote Bullard, "environmental justice demands that everyone (not just the people who can 'vote with their feet' and move away from threats or individuals who can afford lawyers, experts, and lobbyists to fight on their behalf) is entitled to equal protection and equal enforcement of our environmental, health, housing, land use, transportation, energy, and civil rights laws and regulations" (Bullard et al., 2007).

Environmental racism also has been defined as "the disproportionate burden of environmental problems on people of color" (Gottlieb, 2005). The primary goal of environmental justice scholarship has been to document the correlation between polluting industries and environmental health, involving the economics and politics of race and class and proximity to injury. It afflicts economically deprived people of all races, because poor whites, as well as poor people of color, end up in run-down houses near chemical plants, or find themselves on floodplains without insurance as hurricanes roll in. Environmental justice is what socially conscious people are doing (or would like to do) about these inequities.

The sheer ubiquity of toxic effluent in communities of color may be increasing even as programs such as the U.S. Environmental Protection Agency's Superfund program (which contained more than 1,300 sites in 2018) seeks to cleanse some of them. Coal-fired power plants that supply cities often are sited in rural areas, often within sight of poor nonwhite communities whose residents rely on easily polluted wells for water. Consider Walnut Tree, a mainly African American town near Duke Energy's Belews Creek Steam Station in North Carolina. Margaret Talbot wrote in the *New Yorker*, "For years, coal ash from the station . . . fell like snow over the town's modest houses and backyard vegetable gardens. Kids wrote their names in the ash that blanketed their parents' cars and corroded the paint" (Talbot, 2018, 41). The people were stuck, unable to move, their homes unsalable amid the toxic ash fall. David Hairston, a local activist, said, "A lot of these people can't afford to move. The resale value is no good" (Talbot, 2018, 41).

Environmental racism has become evident in many ways, including toxicity-provoked diseases suffered by people who cannot afford to live anywhere except adjacent to present or former factory sites that emit damaging pollutants, as well as housing and job sites in low areas of cities subject to heavy rain (often during hurricanes). Environmental racism began to be recognized as a subject of discourse in politics, the news media, and among academics during the 1970s, with the development of a more general environmental consciousness that was spurred by a realization that the effluvia of industry often threatened healthy life.

Association of race and class with environmental degradation began within months of the first Earth Day (in 1970), with the Council of Environmental Quality's "Annual Report to the President" in 1971. Following protests along these lines in Warren County, North Carolina, the United Church of Christ assembled a report emphasizing the relationship. In 1979, Robert D. Bullard, a sociologist at Texas Southern University and one of the earliest academics to develop a specialty in environmental racism, described the efforts of an African American community to defeat the siting of a hazardous waste landfill near their neighborhood. In this case, the suburb was mainly upper middle class.

Many such sites have been "orphaned"—abandoned by corporate creators that have gone bankrupt or simply can't be found. Dawn Chapman, a resident near the West Lake Landfill complex in a Missouri suburb of St. Louis, was described in the *New Yorker* (Talbot, 2018, 46) as having founded Just Moms to publicize the perils of local life. "The smell is unbearable," she said. Parts of the ground collapsed, releasing smoke and steam. West Lake was first listed as a Superfund site in 1990. Very little had changed by 2018, even after almost three decades of assessments and debates within the agency (Talbot, 2018, 46).

Few places define environmental racism as precisely as Uniontown, Alabama, 30 miles west of Selma, home of the Arrowhead Landfill, into which, for 18 months beginning in July 2009, hundreds of railcars a day poured more than 4 million tons of coal ash laced with arsenic, lead, and several other heavy metals. Uniontown's 2,400 residents are more than 90 percent black. The ash had come from a coal-burning power plant in Roane County, Tennessee, 300 miles north. The population of Roane is roughly 90 percent white. An accident at the power plant had spilled the ash into a nearby watershed. The remaining ash was exported to

Uniontown, where residents feared it would also pollute their water, especially around ranks of trailer homes that nearly surround the dump, where, as Ian MacDougall wrote in *Harper's*, "The odor was inescapable. What began as the smell of manure [from a nearby meat-processing plant] ripened into the fetor of something dead and mildewed" (MacDougall, 2018, 43).

During the 1990s, environmental racism and justice became a subject of symposia and publications in several academic fields. In 1992, for example, the *National Law Journal* published a special issue titled "Unequal Environmental Protection" that dissected legal doctrines that reinforce maintenance of double standards and differential treatment during environmental crises of whites as compared to people of color. The American Bar Association (ABA) established a Special Committee on Environmental Justice, which, during 2004, issued a report titled "Environmental Justice for All: A Fifty State Survey of Legislation, Policies, and Initiatives," with the stated goal of identifying legal measures of all types (policies, statutes, initiatives, etc.) that states have enacted or declared in support of goals supporting environmental justice. Between 1993 and 2004, the ABA found that 30 states had made some attempt to legally define and deal with the issue.

The toll of environmental racism has been exceptionally well documented. Benjamin Chavis's *Toxic Wastes and Minority Communities*, published by the United Church of Christ (1985), remains a seminal document in the field of environmental justice. It revealed "the widespread presence of uncontrolled toxic waste sites in racial and ethnic communities throughout the United States." Flint, Michigan, was among the cities cited as an example of environmental racism—in 1985, by Paul Mohai, founder of the Environmental Justice Program at the University of Michigan, discussing Flint as an example of the deadly impact of noxious industrial waste inflicted on Michigan's poor.

Once people began looking for it, environmental racism (and the need to address it in the context of civil and human rights) turned up everywhere. A 2002 study conducted in Southern California, titled "Environmental Justice and Regional Inequality," demonstrated that Asians, Latinos, and African Americans in the region experience a lifetime cancer risk from airborne toxins that, even when controlled for income, is nearly 50 percent greater than the risk their white counterparts face. The same study found that Native American reservations frequently have been targeted for toxic waste disposal and other environmental health hazards.

The factual basis for a relationship between race, class, and exposure to hazardous waste sites also has been very well documented by many academics. For example, in 2017 Robin Saha, associate professor at the University of Montana, who teaches Environmental Justice Issues and Solutions, was working on *Burning Vulnerable Communities: Trash, Sludge and Biomass Incineration in Communities of Color and Low-Income Communities*; as well as *Who's in Danger? Race, Poverty and Chemical Disasters* (Environmental Justice and Health Alliance for Chemical Policy Reform, Coming Clean, and Center for Effective Government).

"I have used two basic approaches in this research," Saha said. "One involves the development and application of accurate and reliable methods for assessing environmental inequalities, particularly in the distribution of environmental hazards such as polluting industrial facilities. As part of this research agenda, I have helped enhance the capacity of various public interest organizations that work on environmental health and justice issues to conduct credible analytical studies of their own and use them to advocate for related policy reforms" (Saha, 2017). Saha's work has established that "people of color and people living in poverty, especially poor children of color, are significantly more likely to live in these hazardous . . . zones than whites and people with incomes above the poverty line [and that] the health and safety of communities of color and people in poverty are severely and unequally impacted by living in close proximity to hazardous pollution sources and dangerous chemical facilities" (Saha, 2017).

Further Reading

Bullard, Robert D., Paul Mohai, Robin Saha, and Beverly Wright. *Toxic Wastes and Race at Twenty: 1987–2007: A Report Prepared for the United Church of Christ Justice & Witness Ministries.* 2007. http://www.ucc.org/environmental-ministries_toxic-waste-20

Chavis, Benjamin F., Jr. "Toxic Wastes and Race in the United States." United Church of Christ Commission for Racial Justice, 1985, 1987. https://www.nrc.gov/docs/ML1310/ML13109A339.pdf

Gottlieb, Robert. *Forcing the Spring: The Transformation of the American Environmental Movement.* New York: Island Press, 2005.

Grossman, Zoltán. *Unlikely Allies: Native American and White Communities Join to Defend Rural Lands.* Seattle: University of Washington Press, 2017.

MacDougall, Ian. "Empty Suites: Defamation Law and the Price of Dissent." *Harper's*, January 2018, 43–51.

Saha, Robin. Faculty web page. University of Montana. 2017. https://hs.umt.edu/evst/people/default.php?s=Saha

Talbot, Margaret. "Dirty Politics: Scott Pruitt's E.P.A. Is Giving Even Ostentatious Polluters a Reprieve." *The New Yorker*, April 2, 2018, 38–51.

Types of Environmental Discrimination

Environmental discrimination involves a broad spectrum of damage to human health inflicted by corporate emissions, resulting in air and water pollution that limits many minority people's access to clean resources. Across the United States and Canada, poor, usually nonwhite people find themselves living near oil refineries, toxic waste dumps, and other sources of pollution. Another type of discrimination involves delays in emergency response to natural disasters, most notably hurricanes (such as Katrina in New Orleans and Maria in Puerto Rico). Political inaction also figures into environmental discrimination, inhibiting long-range solutions to all of these problems.

Superfund sites are densely clustered in low-income, mainly minority neighborhoods in sizable U.S. urban areas that are prone to flooding. One site discussed in our case studies section that shares many of these attributes is Houston, Texas, which contains a dozen of the 327 Superfund sites that are notable for their vulnerability to flooding. Two of the case studies featuring the eastern United States describe toxicity and flooding in Houston. One of these case studies describes Houston's risk of flooding generally, while the other focuses specifically on perils posed by flooding resulting from Hurricane Harvey in 2017. Other clusters of flood-prone Superfund sites occur in Florida, New Jersey, and California. Nationwide, according to a report by the Associated Press, "More than 800,000 homes are situated near flood-prone toxic sites . . . largely in low-income, heavily minority neighborhoods" (Associated Press, 2017, 5-A).

The toxic toll on people can sometimes seem to be an overwhelming and inescapable part of everyday life in our time. Lead, especially, appears in the narrative of environmental racism with unrelenting regularity, from the water pipes of Flint, Michigan, to the inner-city garden soil of Omaha, Nebraska, and many places in between. Sociologist Robert D. Bullard has described consistent siting of toxic incinerators and waste dumps in and near Latino and African American communities: "Institutional racism influences local land use, enforcement of environmental regulations, industrial facility siting, economic vulnerability, and where people of color live, work, and play. Environmental racism is just as real as the racism that exists in housing, employment, and education. . . . Discrimination is a manifestation of institutional racism. Even today, racism permeates nearly every social institution" (Bullard, 1993, 25). "It is unlikely that this nation will ever achieve lasting solutions to its environmental problems unless it

Background

also addresses the system of racial injustice that helps sustain the existence of powerless communities forced to bear disproportionate environmental costs" (Bullard, 1993, 22).

Many of these stories are urban, but a surprising number are rural. Nearly 40 percent of the Superfund sites slated for cleanup by the Environmental Protection Agency in the United States are on or near Indian reservations, often out of sight and out of mind of the majority of society. Words such as "sacrifice areas" have been used to describe these places and peoples. Winona LaDuke, a well-known environmental activist, did the math indicating that every U.S. nuclear weapons test that was conducted on land during the twentieth century occurred on land that was guaranteed to indigenous peoples by treaty (LaDuke, 1993, 99), more than 600 on Shoshone land alone (Waugh, 2010).

Native American lands have long been purposefully used as dumping grounds for all manner of pollutants from mine tailings to industrial waste. The U.S. military during World War II made a policy of dumping its most hazardous wastes on or near Indian reservations on the assumption that the land was far from population centers and otherwise relatively worthless. The International Tribunal of Indigenous People and Oppressed Nations convened in 1992, the 500th anniversary of Columbus's first landing, to examine the history of criminal activity against indigenous groups in the United States. The organization published a "Significant Bill of Particulars" outlining grievances indigenous peoples had with the United States, including allegations that the United States "deliberately and systematically permitted, aided, and abetted, solicited and conspired to commit the dumping, transportation, and location of nuclear, toxic, medical, and otherwise hazardous waste materials on Native American territories in North America and has thus created a clear and present danger to the health, safety, and physical and mental well-being of Native American People" ("Environmental Racism," n.d.).

Environmental racism has reached extreme proportions, in many cases involving indigenous peoples throughout North America when governmental agencies earmarked their homelands for nuclear testing. These agencies seemed to have forgotten (or never even realized) that indigenous peoples existed at all—as in Alaska during the 1950s, when the Atomic Energy Commission (AEC) seriously considered blasting open a harbor along the Alaskan coast with nuclear weapons, or in regions of the U.S. West that were used as atomic test ranges within range of Pueblos, Navajos, Shoshones, and many others. In all of these cases plans were canceled or testing stopped after copious protests.

At a personal level, these are horror stories—Navajo and Laguna Pueblo uranium miners dying of lung cancer, their lives replicated on the Dene Nation of the Yukon; black neighbors of giant hog farms in North Carolina, whose homes are routinely sprayed with pig manure mist; Akwesasne Mohawks who can no longer eat fish from the St. Lawrence River; and Inuit mothers who can no longer breastfeed their infants because their bodies harbor dioxins and PCBs. The toll is often worldwide, as with generations of Vietnamese and U.S. Vietnam War veterans who have been cursed with the legacy of dioxin-laced Agent Orange; farmworkers who face the toll of the same chemicals in their daily lives from the tomato fields of Florida to the table-grape harvests of California.

Some of these stories are historical. What, for example, does the slaughter of the buffalo on the Great Plains of North America in the nineteenth century tell us about wars of ethnic "cleansing" (the more honest word is "extermination") in later centuries? It was an early example of "total war" that exterminated peoples by removing their economic base—much as Agent Orange was being used to destroy the nourishing farms and forests of Vietnam to deny the Viet Cong shelter. Another historical account details plans to blast a harbor on Eskimo land on Alaska's North Slope with atomic bombs. This plan was reality, not *Dr. Strangelove*. The plan was shelved after strenuous protests by the Eskimos and many environmentalists.

Some of these stories are being told in the future tense. One example is Alaska's Pebble Mine—again, on Native American lands, where industrialists want to replace some of the world's richest salmon runs, which have sustained Native peoples for many centuries, with one of Earth's largest gold mines and attendant toxic mining waste. President Barack Obama stalled that plan, but Scott Pruitt, Donald Trump's former Environmental Protection Agency secretary, had revived it as of this writing.

Some of the place names where toxic events have taken place have entered our popular language as metaphors for pollution: Love Canal (near Niagara Falls, New York), for example. Many, many more live in searing local memory, such as Anniston, Alabama, where more than $700 million in damage was done to human health by PCB contamination.

Benjamin K. Sovacool, writing in *Nature* (2017, 433), made a case that disaster recovery is often undertaken in a manner that entrenches elites and penalizes impoverished poor and minority communities that "already bear the brunt of natural catastrophes." He asserted that "rebuilding efforts must not increase disparities. . . . We can no longer assume that disaster-recovery efforts sufficiently involve, protect and empower those most in need." One of Sovacool's main examples was recovery from Hurricane Katrina in New Orleans after it struck in 2005.

> In Louisiana, recovery efforts after Hurricane Katrina in 2005 enabled private companies to capture public housing. Homes owned or occupied predominantly by poor evacuees were declared a nuisance, marked for demolition and resold at cut-throat rates. When the federal government allocated billions of dollars to the Army Corps of Engineers to fix, upgrade and rehabilitate levees and flood walls, this served only to entrench, rather than eliminate, vulnerability among some poor communities. To hasten repairs after Katrina, environmental and air-pollution standards were relaxed: hazardous wastes were not properly stored and open burning was allowed. Clean-up efforts concentrated toxic pollution and debris in particular landfills or alongside communities of colour. Sediment left in the wake of floodwaters contained high levels of arsenic, raising its concentrations in soils at playgrounds and schools in minority neighborhoods. Although some long-term restoration planning is worthy of praise, there is plenty to criticize. The rebuilding of canals and roads further eroded environmental buffers (such as wetlands) crucial to future storm-surge mitigation. (Sovacool, 2017, 433)

The state of Michigan, often a source of environmental crises of all types concerning people of color, also became a center of study for environmental racism. The University of Michigan's School of Natural Resources convened a major conference during 1990 on environmental racism. Out of this conference and many other activities grew a consensus that racism played a major role in exposure to environmental hazards, but so did class and gender. The term "environmental inequity" came into use as a counterpart to inequity of wealth. All of this aided study of how and why people of modest means have been subjected to environmental hazards in the types of work they do, the siting of their housing, the intentional location of toxic waste dumps in or near their communities, and discrimination in provision of urban services, such as waste removal. All of this adds up to a greater incidence of many illnesses, greater personal suffering, and shorter lifespans.

The toxicity of air, water, and soil in poor and minority communities inflicts a catalogue of health maladies on the people who live in them. Radiation poisoning has been associated with high incidences of several kinds of cancers, as well as miscarriages and birth defects. For lead and mercury, common maladies include profound effects on children's growth rates, behavior, and intelligence, including learning disabilities, problems with attention and fine motor coordination, and violent behavior. Dioxins (TCDDs—as in Agent Orange) "are carcinogenic in humans and can cause immune-system alterations; reproductive, developmental, and nervous system effects; endocrine disruption, altered lipid metabolism; liver damage; and skin lesions" (Schecter et al., 2001, 436). Everyday effects of many of these toxins also include bronchitis, irregular heartbeat, nervous disorders, thyroid disorders, immune-deficiency diseases, liver and prostate cancers, reproductive abnormalities, liver disease, hypertension, speech impediment, hearing impairment, stroke, anemia and other blood disorders, diabetes, kidney disease, urinary tract disorders, and skin rashes.

Like other persistent organic pollutants, effects of PCBs may be transferred from generation to generation. They also biomagnify up the food chain in an exponential manner, doing more damage at each step along the way. An Inuit mother who breastfeeds her infant is merely one step up this toxic chain from the flesh of the fish or seals that she eats; the baby is another. Each is passing along a potent toxic cocktail. The three most common contaminants that researchers found in Inuit mothers' breast milk were three pesticides (dieldrin, mirex, and DDE) and two industrial chemicals, PCBs and hexachlorobenzene.

A study by the United Church of Christ, edited by Robert D. Bullard, dean of the School of Public Affairs at Texas Southern University in Houston, sketched a comprehensive picture of just how dangerous being nonwhite and poor can be to health. In 19 of the 50 states, the study said, blacks were at least twice as likely as whites to live in neighborhoods with dangerous air pollution. Due to exposure to pollution, African Americans are 20 percent more likely to suffer from asthma and three times more likely to die from asthma-related causes than whites. Bullard said that "environmental racism is a process designed to eliminate Black and Brown people" (Gilbert, 2015).

Further Reading

Associated Press. "327 Superfund Sites Face Flood Risks and Toxic Trouble." *Omaha World-Herald*, December 24, 2017, 5-A.

Bullard, Robert D., ed. "Anatomy of Environmental Racism and the Environmental Justice Movement." *Confronting Environmental Racism: Voices from the Grassroots*. Boston: South End Press, 1993.

"Environmental Racism." Revolvy, n.d. Accessed October 17, 2017. https://www.revolvy.com/main/index.php?s=Environmental%20racism

Gilbert, Peter. "Environmental Justice Summit Links Racism, Environmental Destruction." *Mundo Obrero (Workers World)*, October 20, 2015. https://

www.workers.org/2015/10/20/environmental-justice-summit-links-racism-environmental-destruction/

LaDuke, Winona. "A Society Based on Conquest Cannot Be Sustained: Native Peoples and the Environmental Crisis." In *Toxic Struggles: The Theory and Practice of Environmental Justice*, ed. Richard Hofrichter. Philadelphia: New Society Publishers, 1993, 98–106.

Schecter, Arnold, Le Cao Dai, Olaf Papke, Joelle Prange, John D. Constable, Muneaki Matsuda, Vu Duc Thao, and Amanda L. Piskac. "Recent Dioxin Contamination from Agent Orange in Residents of a Southern Vietnamese City." *Journal of Occupational and Environmental Medicine* 43, no. 5 (May 2001): 435–443.

"Siting of Hazardous Waste Landfills and Their Correlation with Racial and Economic Status of Surrounding Communities." Washington, D.C.: General Accounting Office, 1983. RCED-83-168. Published: June 1, 1983. Publicly released: June 14, 1983. http://www.gao.gov/products/RCED-83-168

Sovacool, Benjamin K. "Don't Let Disaster Recovery Perpetuate Injustice." *Nature* 549 (September 27, 2017): 433.

Waugh, Charles. "'Only You Can Prevent a Forest': Agent Orange, Ecocide, and Environmental Justice." *Interdisciplinary Studies of Literature and the Environment* 17, no. 1 (2010): 113–132. http://digitalcommons.usu.edu/english_facpub/791

Perpetrators and Victims

One may be driving in a picturesque rural area, far from the smokestacks usually associated with city life, and run head-on into a Superfund site. Examples abound, sea to shining sea. To cite only one of many: zinc and lead were mined within the jurisdiction of the Quapaw Indian Reservation in Picher, Oklahoma, until 1967, when, according to a retrospective by Terri Hansen on the Indian Country Today Media Network, "mining companies abandoned 14,000 mine shafts, 70 million tons of lead-laced tailings, 36 million tons of mill sand and sludge, as well as contaminated water, leaving residents with high lead levels in blood and tissues. Cancers skyrocketed, and 34 percent of elementary-school students suffered learning disabilities" (Hansen, 2013). The companies had names that few people recognize today: NL Industries, Blue Tee Corp., Gold Field Mining LLC, Doe Run Resources Corp., Eagle Picher Industries Inc., Childress Royalty Co., Asarco, Inc., and others. Combined, the companies left behind the largest environmental disaster in Oklahoma history. The area was designated as the Tar Creek Superfund site in 1983, but Picher initially was skipped for remediation and assigned to a special environmental hell: too toxic to clean up. Instead, the federal government offered a rock-bottom buyout that paid people to leave town.

Experts have argued over whether owners of hazardous waste–bearing industries and disposal sites deliberately target minority communities to make what they regard as "sound" (that is, profitable) business decisions because land there is cheap, as lack of political resistance allows easy access to ghettos, barrios, and Indian reservations. With the rise of environmental consciousness and organizing efforts, however, people in these communities have been resisting their designation as dumps for a technologically advanced affluent (and effluent) culture.

In the meantime, the fossil-fuel economy degrades the lands of Native peoples across the continent, a graphic example being the Crees of Alberta, whose homelands have been so scarred by the mining and processing of tar sands that they resemble a moonscape. The perpetrators of this environmental disaster read like a who's who of fossil fuels (see Table 1).

The oil industry mines and refines sand-laced oil tar that requires more energy to manufacture than will be produced by its use, thereby doubling the impact on the climate of a warming Earth.

This book's very brief annotated history of environmental racism/justice reveals just how pervasive it is, continent-wide—and how well documented it has become, in a barrage of reports with a staggering array of statistics proving a rather evident theorem: if you are nonwhite and poor, it is very likely that you live with pollution, and that it is making you sick.

Even as at Love Canal or in Flint, Michigan, environmental racism becomes a household word and mass media focus on immensely egregious, astounding, and sometimes fatal examples of pollution, more often than not, minority and poor white communities bear the burden of life-shortening pollution in silence, as part of daily life.

Scholars and journalists began to trace this pattern in 1978 with the discovery of 22,000 tons of toxic waste at Love Canal, New York, which was being spread by the City of Niagara Falls, the Hooker Chemical Company (later part of Occidental Chemical Corp.), as well as the Niagara Power and Development Company. Hooker was especially prominent in this disaster, as it used the site to dump 21,800 short tons of chemical waste used to make dyes, perfumes, and solvents for rubber and synthetic resins. The pollution was so pervasive that an entire neighborhood was evacuated and destroyed.

At about the same time, mothers in Akwesasne, in upstate New York, were discovering that their breast milk was toxic. The Mohawk Nation was learning that the fish from the St. Lawrence River on which they and their ancestors had subsisted for centuries was unsafe to eat because of

Table 1 Tar Sands Reserves, 2018

Rank	Company	Reserves (in millions of barrels)
1	Suncor Energy	10,935.35
2	Canadian Natural Resources (CNRL)	6,867.53
3	Cenovus Energy	5,613.97
4	ConocoPhillips	5,520.38
5	ExxonMobil	4,844.35
6	Shell	3,670.18
7	PetroChina	3,225.71
8	Athabasca Oil Corporation	3,162.50
9	MEG Energy	2,973.10
10	OSUM	2,776.40
11	Total	2,575.16
12	Laricina Energy	2,293.82
13	Sunshine Oilsands	2,048.86
14	Imperial Oil	1,694.29
15	CNOOC	1,655.91
16	BP	1,271.27
17	Marathon Oil	1,232.01
18	Devon Energy	1,206.83
19	Husky Energy	1,110.44
20	Chevron	1,089

Source: "List of Tar Sands Companies," 2018.

leaching from General Motors industrial dumps near their reservation. Also during the same time period, across the country, Navajo uranium miners began to die in large numbers of lung cancer in Arizona and New Mexico, provoked by uranium mining at more than 500 sites by the Kerr-McGee Company and many others.

The name "Warren County, North Carolina" is usually not recognized by many general readers, although events there played a major role in the recognition of environmental racism and justice as a social, political, and legal movement. It is one of the poorest predominantly black counties in the state, which drew national attention for protesting the construction of a polychlorinated biphenyl (PCB) disposal landfill. More than 6,000 truckloads of PCBs were deposited there by the Ward PCB Transformer Company of Raleigh, North Carolina, and others, despite public outcry—and despite the fact that these toxins were knowingly poisoning lives in a majority black community.

Robert D. Bullard, who has written many books and articles on the subject of environmental racism for three decades, said that pollution in vulnerable communities is "business as usual in the United States. . . . When will this madness stop?" (Krajicek, 2016). The backyards of poor, minority communities host municipal landfills, sewage treatment plants, hazardous waste sites, illegal chemical dumps, garbage transfer stations, incinerators, and smelters with regularity. (The cases sections of this book describe a number of them in detail, but this is only a sampling.) "I think this denial has persisted for so many years because when people think of civil rights, they think of voting, they think of education, they think of housing. . . ." Bullard says. "Now we have the environmental justice movement, converging environmental rights with civil rights. But it's taken two decades for those two movements to come together" (Krajicek, 2016).

Defining environmental racism using Census ethnic categories can be problematic. Economic class also plays a powerful part in environmental "racism." Barbara Alice Mann, a professor in the Honors College at the University of Toledo (Ohio), points out that over time fewer and fewer people in any given city or neighborhood fit a single category.

> For each example you give, a thousand more could be evoked. By the way . . . I'm annoyed by the US Census categories for Toledo, because "white" is just one, big, lying lump. We have an infinite variety of folks in Toledo who get lumped together as "white," including a lot of [American] Indians, who fought hard in the early twentieth century not to be listed as "Black" (the only "other" category then), and who are now relentlessly presented as "white." Also, all the Middle Easterners here are listed as "white," as are the Macedonians (yes, we have a Macedonian community), and everyone else. However, Greeks here are NOT listed as "white," for reasons I cannot fathom. Thus, the black/white demographics of Toledo are quite misleading. Toledo has the greatest ethnic diversity outside of New York City, last I checked. (Mann, personal communication, 2017)

Professor Mann is part Jewish and part Seneca and lives in Toledo's inner city. I have heard the same characterization for the Rainier Valley and Beacon Hill neighborhoods in Seattle, an area that much out-of-town popular imagination may stereotype as "white."

Although environmental racism is most evident in pollution, it's also at work in global warming. In a sprawling city with many types of geographical locations (Los Angeles, for example), "Asian, Black, and Hispanic residents are more likely to live in hotter parts of the city than White residents because of a complicated range of factors like green spaces, elevation, prevailing winds and proximity to the ocean. Lack of green spaces in some neighborhoods, for example, can exacerbate the heat-island effect, a phenomenon in which cities are as much as 22 degrees Fahrenheit warmer than less built-up environments because of their impervious, heat-absorbing surfaces," Kendra Pierre-Louis and Nadja Popovich observed in the *New York Times* (2018). Many poorer people, such as agricultural, construction, and other outdoor workers, are more vulnerable to hotter weather than the more affluent, who more often work in air-conditioned offices that waste heat, intensifying the urban heat-island effect. People who work outside often have no choice as to the time of day when they are employed, exposing them during the hottest hours. At home, they also are less likely to have access to air conditioning.

"Just as with any other facet of society, physical environments are not exempt from institutional racism that also affects environmental decisions, actions and policies, which results in continued racial disadvantages and public health disparities," according to a 2012 NAACP report titled *Coal Blooded: Putting Profits Before People*. This report found that communities of color disproportionately encounter toxic work conditions, environmental hazards, and polluted neighborhoods. The report, which examined 378 coal-fired plants in the United States, indicated that 75 of those plants earned an environmental justice grade of F. Four million people lived within three miles of these plants, and their average per capita income was only $17,500. Of those 4 million people, 53 percent were people of color. The same report also found that 2 million people with an average annual per capita income of $14,626 lived within three miles of the 12 worst-polluting plants. Approximately 76 percent of these residents were people of color. As is so often the case, danger from pollution goes up as income goes down (*Coal Blooded*, 2019).

A report by the Environmental Justice and Health Alliance for Chemical Policy Reform, Coming Clean, and the Center for Effective Government also focused on connections between race and chemical disasters. The report, published during 2014, *Who's in Danger: A Demographic Analysis of Chemical Disaster Vulnerability*, "shows that more than 134 million Americans live within danger zones around 3,433 chemical facilities." The report also found that 3.8 million live within "fence-line" areas or zones that present greater danger, thus leaving residents near those areas less time to evacuate in an event of a chemical crisis. In regard to black and Latino communities dwelling in these areas, the study showed that the "percentage of blacks in the fence-line zones is 75 percent greater than for the U.S. as a whole, while the percentage of Latinos in the fence-line zones is 60 percent greater than for the U.S. as a whole" (*Coal Blooded*, 2019).

Keith Rushing, writing in the *Huffington Post* (2015), described a University of Michigan study indicating that "minorities on average are exposed to 38 percent higher levels of nitrogen dioxide—which is produced by cars and construction equipment—than whites. The findings show that the exposure of increased nitrogen oxide is linked to asthma and heart attacks. According to the Centers for Disease Control, from 2001 to 2009, the greatest rise in asthma rates (a 50 percent increase) was among black children. In 2011, the asthma rate for African-Americans was 47 percent higher than it was for whites."

According to the NAACP report, "African Americans are suffering the worst. Blacks are hospitalized for asthma at more than three times the rate of whites. Between 2001 and 2009 asthma rates in Black children increased almost 50 percent, according to the Centers for Disease Control, with higher exposure to environmental pollutants listed as one of the causes. Whether you choose to call it a 'disproportionate burden of environmental risks and harms,' as the Environmental Protection Agency did in 2004, or 'environmental racism'—the term preferred by community advocates—the problem is real, and it's not getting any better."

Government response to hurricanes has shown an acute bias. This work contains profiles of environmental racism that tainted treatment after Katrina in New Orleans (2005), as well as Harvey (in eastern Texas) and Maria (in Puerto Rico and the Virgin Islands), both during 2017. If you were black, brown, and poor (or "white" and poor), you were more likely to be living in a flooded area where most of the damage was done. You were also more likely to experience significant delays in relief efforts. As social activist Naomi Klein wrote, following Katrina, "What does #BlackLivesMatter, and the unshakable moral principle that it represents, have to do with climate change? And with environmental racism, for that matter? Everything. Because we can be quite sure that if wealthy white Americans had been the ones left without food and water for days in a giant sports stadium after Hurricane Katrina, even [President] George W. Bush would have gotten serious about climate change" (Miller, 2017, 161; Klein, 2014).

The same analysis has been applied to tainted water in Flint, Michigan. "I see what's happening in Flint [Michigan, with lead-tainted water] as the classic case and a poster child for environmental racism," Robert D. Bullard said. "This is a man-made disaster. It did not have to happen. And it

Background

basically tells us that the state of Michigan believes that the residents of Flint don't deserve equal protection. They don't deserve the same rights that would be enforced if they were not largely poor and majority African American" (Krajicek, 2016).

Bullard said that the politics of environmental racism haven't changed since economist William J. Kruvant described the pattern in 1975: "Disadvantaged people are largely victims of middle- and upper-class pollution because they usually live closest to the sources of pollution—power plants, industrial installations, and in central cities where vehicle traffic is heaviest. Usually they have no choice. Discrimination created the situation, and those with wealth and influence have political power to keep polluting facilities away from their homes. Living in poverty areas is bad enough. High pollution makes it worse" (Krajicek, 2016).

Further Reading

Coal Blooded: Putting Profits Before People. National Association for the Advancement of Colored People (NAACP), 2019.

Hansen, Terri. "Major Environmental Disasters in Indian Country." Indian Country Today Media Network, October 8, 2013. http://indiancountrytodaymedianetwork.com/2013/10/08/7-major-industrial-environmental-disasters-indian-country-151661

Klein, Naomi. "Why #BlackLives Matter Should Transform the Climate Debate." *The Nation*, December 12, 2014. Accessed March 22, 2017. https://www.thenation.com/article/what-does-blacklivesmatter-have-do-climate-change/

Krajicek, David J. "7 Toxic Assaults on Communities of Color Besides Flint: The Dirty Racial Politics of Pollution." Alternet. January 23, 2016. https://www.alternet.org/environment/7-toxic-assaults-communities-color-besides-flint-dirty-racial-politics-pollution

"List of Tar Sands Companies." Banking on Climate Change: Fossil Fuel Finance Report Card 2017. Rainforest Action Network, San Francisco, 2018. https://www.ran.org/list-tar-sands-companies/

Mann, Barbara Alice. Personal communication, November 7, 2017.

Miller, Todd. *Storming the Wall: Climate Change, Migration, and Homeland Security.* San Francisco: City Lights/Open Media Series, 2017.

"NAACP Report Condemns Environmental Racism." *Philadelphia Tribune*, December 25, 2012. http://www.phillytrib.com/news/naacp-report-condemns-environmental-racism/article_ed34835d-4f6a-50b0-a936-bd96de2fa4b2.html

Pierre-Louis, Kendra, and Nadja Popovich. "Nights Are Warming Faster Than Days. Here's Why That's Dangerous." *New York Times*, July 11, 2018.

https://www.nytimes.com/interactive/2018/07/11/climate/summer-nights-warming-faster-than-days-dangerous.html

Rushing, Keith. "Black Futures Must Involve Environmental Justice." *Huffington Post*, March 2, 2015. https://www.huffingtonpost.com/keith-rushing/black-futures-must-involv_b_6772204.html

Swift, James A. "It's Not Just Flint: Environmental Racism Is Slowly Killing Blacks across America." *The Grio*, January 24, 2016. http://thegrio.com/2016/01/24/flint-water-environmental-racism-blacks/

Challenges and Solutions

Part of any solution to environmental racism will be to redistribute the flow of waste so that it is fairly shared across boundaries of race and class. That's only part of the problem, however. The broader solution is to reduce the amount of waste flowing into landfills and other dumps, everywhere. Efforts to dramatically reduce the amount of waste (especially toxic waste) produced by our "affluent society" should become a technological imperative. Everyone will benefit.

Society also must come to understand the burden that waste disposal places on poor and nonwhite communities, and why people have been organizing against it. This is not merely a story of passive human suffering. It is also an instructive story of resistance, of people uniting to claim their right to a cleaner, decent life from the ground up. Throughout our stories a constant drumbeat of human resistance pulses. The Mothers of East Los Angeles have been uniting people of several ethnicities in their predominantly Latino barrio, rising up in readiness, galvanizing their neighbors, to stave off a hazardous-waste incinerator. A local coalition won multimillion-dollar settlements for damage done by toxic chemicals in Anniston, Alabama. Inuit mothers appealed to the world to stop the toxification of their homeland—and won a ban on many persistent organic pollutants, including PCBs and dioxins that were banned worldwide in the Stockholm Convention. It is, however, a long road back. Toxic chemicals do not simply wash away. They are insidious, and pervasive, and incredibly difficult to remove from the food chain.

Across North America, many hazmat sites are now slowly being cleansed, all because of popular pressure expressed by local people in such initiatives as the U.S. Environmental Protection Agency's Superfund program. As of September 2017, the EPA had identified 1,342 sites as part of its Superfund program National Priorities List (NPL), all areas requiring cleanup because they have been contaminated by hazardous wastes that pose risks to human health and to the environment generally. The program was created in 1980, after the U.S. Congress enacted the Comprehensive Environmental Response, Compensation, and Liability Act (CERCLA), which required the then decade-old EPA to work with responsible parties in local communities, as well as scientists, researchers, contractors, and state, local, Native American tribal, and federal authorities first to identify hazardous waste sites, then to test conditions, write cleanup plans, and finally decontaminate the sites. Many of these are case studies of environmental racism and consequent environmental justice.

Some governmental officials and agencies have become involved as well. Governor James McGreevey of New Jersey during 2004 signed an executive order that required all state government executive bodies in that state that make decisions affecting environmental quality and public health to support environmental equity for low-income people and people of color to mitigate exposure to environmental hazards. The order also established an environmental justice advisory council across state agencies under the aegis of the state Department of Environmental Protection, with channels of access for citizens seeking claims related to health risks based on income level and race.

Pervasive environmental racism begins to crumble on a local basis when people organize and challenge siting of environmentally harmful projects. In April 1998, for example, after strenuous local protests, the Nuclear Regulatory Commission denied a license to a uranium enrichment plant that impacted the African American communities of Forest Grove and Center Springs, Louisiana. Thomas Linzey sketched the pervasive nature of toxicity there for *In These Times* (2016): "In the United States alone, 4 billion pounds of toxic chemicals—including 72 million pounds of known carcinogens—are released into the atmosphere each year from 20,000 industrial polluters. On top of that, 2 trillion pounds of livestock waste—laced with antibiotics, hormones, and chemicals—are dumped into waterways and applied to land, not to mention the 11 million citizens who live within one mile of a federal Superfund site. Currently, 80,000 industrial chemicals are in use, with more than 700 of those chemicals now found within every human body. Each year, 1,800 new chemicals are introduced."

To resist such chemical pollution, Linzey urged people to adopt "bills of rights" to protect their right to a clean environment. As a case study for his advocacy of local environmental bills of rights, Linzey described local organizing efforts in Tamaqua Borough, Pennsylvania, home to about 7,000 people in the Schuylkill region, who confronted a state plan that would have dumped PCB-laced river dredge into abandoned deep mines. The people of Tamaqua Borough were reacting in the context of a century of environmental abuse that has been blamed for abnormally high cancer rates in the area.

The people of Tamaqua Borough engaged in a popular uprising on behalf of their environmental health and their children's rights to a cleaner environment after they decided that without pressure government at all levels was going to ignore them. "Consent of the governed" was producing no results, so they adopted a local law that banned the dumping of PCB-laced dredge, along with a local, environmentally centered bill of rights, emphasizing that they valued clean air and water over the rights claimed by corporations that sought space to dump toxic dredge in their community. They asserted rights that state and federal governments said they did not possess. Without such assertion, the people of Tamaqua Borough said, they would be forced to forfeit their rights to life, liberty, and happiness.

Linzey wrote, "They didn't stop there. Understanding that protecting the people of Tamaqua required protecting the natural environment upon which the human race depends, they adopted a law that recognized ecosystems within the Borough—groundwater, streams, and rivers specifically—as having legally enforceable, independent rights to be free from toxic dredge" (Linzey, 2016).

Similar themes echoed in other communities across the United States' industrial Midwest. Protesters knew their work was having an impact when corporations that sought to impose waste facilities tried to silence local actions with lawsuits. Jim Motavalli wrote in *E-Magazine* (1998):

> Two prominent activists, Terri Swearingen, who fought tirelessly against a giant waste incinerator in East Liverpool, Ohio, winning the Goldman Environmental Prize for her work, and Phyllis Glazer, whose work is widely credited with helping close a toxic injection well in Winona, Texas, were hit with lawsuits by the companies involved. Such suits, designed to quiet crusaders, are known as SLAPPs, or Strategic Lawsuits Against Public Participation. It's not a coincidence that both SLAPPed activists are women, as are most of the people profiled in this special issue. Ask them why this is and you'll get a variety of answers, but the most common one is that women are nurturers who feel most deeply about building a future for their children and their community.

Friends and neighbors in minority communities across the United States often have found themselves making common cause to evict dumping of organochlorine chemicals from their communities. In so doing, they often have found themselves coming together, becoming organized, sharing strategy and tactics, and speaking out against several forms of racism. In this process, leaders have arisen. One such leader was Mildred Bahati McClain, executive director of the group People of Color and Disenfranchised, who described herself as a "mother, grandmother and a steward of my community" (Johansen, 1993, 128). McClain, who lives in Savannah, Georgia, also is a singer who has enthralled many audiences. McClain said of her childhood: "I grew up in Savannah smelling the stench from the Union Camp Paper Company thinking the [pollution] was a natural part of life. My mother's friends who lived near Union Camp were always complaining of headaches, bad skin rashes, kidney problems and severe cases of asthma. . . . I am frustrated because we are clearly being discriminated against. Many think we are crying wolf, but I ask you to come to our neighborhoods and see for yourself. You will be in shock" (Johansen, 1993, 128).

McClain became a major organizer of resistance to organochlorine-manufacturing plants in minority communities, notably in the southern regions of the United States. Along the way, she and her supporters have made some political points regarding racism as well. McClain tells the following story about a meeting in New Orleans:

> On Sunday morning . . . several Cherokee Indians were treated miserably in a Shoneys restaurant. They were ignored and then received only partial and reluctant service. When this was made known to those attending the conference, participants quickly organized a march involving over 200 people. We went to the restaurant to demand an apology. In a very moving meeting, the tearful manageress apologized and said it would never happen again. It felt really good on that march. We had Native Americans, African Americans, Asian Americans, Hispanic Americans and White Americans marching together. It felt like a microcosm of what we had to do. Just after we got back to the hotel, the heavens opened. Native Americans saw this as a "cleansing." (Johansen, 1993, 284)

Many advocates advise several steps to help protect minority communities that also may be applied anywhere. The United Church of Christ (UCC) report urged concentration on the "Dirty Dozen" (the most dangerous persistent organic pollutants because of their toxicity, endurance in the food chain, and the fact that many of them "bioaccumulate" (increase in potency exponentially) at each step along the food chain (Bullard et al., 2007, xv). This effect is most dramatic (as described in this volume) in the Arctic, where Inuit mothers cannot breastfeed their infants. Before they were banned by the Stockholm Convention, PCBs, dioxins, and other POPs were riding prevailing winds into the Arctic from industries at lower latitudes, and bioaccumulating up the food chain among life on both land and in seawater. Humans are at the top of the food chain. While production of these POPs has declined drastically, they are very slow to degrade and remain in the food chain essentially indefinitely.

The UCC report also advocated alliances between mainstream (e.g., white-led) environmental groups and others that advance minority interests, advising that local organizers increase efforts to diversify mainstream environmental organizations. "There must be a serious and sustained effort to redress the utter lack of diversity within the mainstream environmental movement," authors of the report wrote (Bullard et al., 2007). "While a few environmental organizations took seriously the challenges put forward at the First National People of Color Environmental Leadership Summit in 1991, the overall lack of diversity at the staff, board and program levels remains staggering," the report said (Bullard et al., 2007). The report also advocated increased cooperation between various minority organizations on environmental justice issues.

The UCC report also urged Congress to reinstate taxes on fossil-fuel companies for the EPA Superfund. It urged attention to the fact that a large proportion of people of color live on or near Superfund sites. For example: nearly 40 percent of these sites involve American Indian lands, while they make up about 1 percent of the U.S. population (Bullard et al., 2007, 2).

The legal system provides a formidable challenge to the resolution of environmental racism. The idea that the United States' environmental laws, regulations, and policies are not applied uniformly, resulting in some individuals, neighborhoods, and communities being exposed to elevated health risks, gained traction in many fields during the 1990s. In 1992, staff writers from the *National Law Journal* uncovered glaring inequities in the way the federal EPA enforces its laws. The authors wrote: "There is a racial divide in the way the U.S. government cleans up toxic waste sites and punishes polluters. White communities see faster action, better results and stiffer penalties than communities where blacks, Hispanics and other minorities live. This unequal protection often occurs whether the community is wealthy or poor" (Lavelle and Coyle, 1992, S1–S2).

Despite all of this new bureaucracy, activism, media reports, and so on, the basic situation of many people who face environmental racism at street level has not changed much since the term was coined 50 years ago. Local organizing, which is described in detail in the U.S. and Canadian case studies of this volume, have provoked cancellation of some projects. Overall, however, racial and income equity biases in the placement of industries that pollute have been very stable.

Similarly, patterns of discrimination have persisted largely unchanged (except where local organized resistance has challenged it) for several decades despite considerable attention among academics and activists, mass media reports, and unsuccessful lawsuits. "These findings raise serious questions about the ability of current policies and institutions to adequately protect people of color and the poor from toxic threats," wrote Bullard. "Thus, it does not appear that existing environmental, health and civil rights laws and local land use controls have been adequately applied or adapted to reducing health risks or mitigating various adverse impacts to families living in or near toxic 'hot spots'" (Bullard et al., 2007, xii, xv).

Further Reading

Bullard, Robert D., Paul Mohai, Robin Saha, and Beverly Wright. *Toxic Wastes and Race at Twenty: 1987–2007: A Report Prepared for the United Church of Christ Justice & Witness Ministries.* 2007. http://www.ucc.org/environmental-ministries_toxic-waste-20

Johansen, Bruce E. *The Dirty Dozen: Toxic Chemicals and the Earth's Future.* Westport, CT: Praeger, 2003.

Lavelle, Marianne, and Marcia Coyle. "Unequal Protection." *National Law Journal*, September 21, 1992, pp. S1–S2.

Linzey, Thomas. "'We've Broken the Planet': A Case for Liberation Ecology and the Rights of Nature." *In These Times*, June 16, 2016. http://inthesetimes.com/rural-america/entry/19222/linzey-celdf-community-rights-13-breaking-the-planet

Motavalli, Jim. "Toxic Targets: Polluters That Dump on Communities of Color Are Finally Being Brought to Justice." 1998. E-Magazine. http://www.ejnet.org/ej/Estory.html

Future Outlook

One very important solution to environmental racism and its economic inequities will be to realize that a sustainable earth is good for all races and classes, since we all share the same environment, and what pollutes one part of it eventually contaminates everything (Ash et al., 2013, 616). In an unexpected twist on environmental racism, one study indicates that racial segregation correlates with high pollution *regardless* of race. Many U.S. cities that are more racially divided have higher levels of pollution than those that are less segregated. As a result, both whites and minorities who live in less integrated communities are exposed to higher levels of pollution than those who live in more integrated areas.

"Over the past decade, more researchers have focused on the correlation between segregation and broad pollution exposure," wrote Kendra Pierre-Louis, a professor of environmental health at the University of California, Berkeley, in the *New York Times* (2018). "Residents of a city like Memphis, they have found, are exposed to more pollution than those living in a city like Tampa, Fla., which is less racially divided." However, middle-class blacks are still afflicted with higher levels of pollution than low-income whites. "In more segregated cities, communities of color and the poor might be less able to have civic engagement power and influence land-use decision making," said Dr. Rachel Morello-Frosch, professor of environmental health science at the University of California, Berkeley (Morello-Frosch et al., 2002, 149). "They have less ability to resist when decisions are made about polluting activities," she said.

In 1977, Sidney Howe, director of the Human Environment Center, argued that class, as well as race, played a role in disproportionate exposure to toxicity. He was among the first to use the phrase "environmental justice" to describe ways to address this imbalance. Also during the 1970s, workers in areas that suffered from toxic exposure, such as the Latino United Farm Workers, made environmental justice part of their practical, daily, work-related campaigns. By the 1980s, African American farmworkers (who faced the same pesticides as Latinos in the West) also were organizing around environmental issues. Black people also faced problems with lead poisoning in many inner cities, from the Detroit area (including Flint, Michigan) to Omaha, Nebraska, as well as many others.

Another way of solving these problems in the future will be to legally recognize ways in which race and class reinforce environmental racism, something that our legal system has not faced. Having surveyed a large number of cases across North America, it is very difficult *not* to notice a pattern in which all these elements combine with biases of race and class to afflict minority and poor people with degraded health and shortened lives—even while legally defined "intent" has not been recognized in the court systems of the United States and Canada. There seems to be a certain synergy at work here: people of color are more likely than most to be impoverished (although this is certainly not always the case), and cost is a consideration in companies' calculation of potential profit and loss. The siting of a chemical plant or dump in any given area often damages already low property values, accelerating a downward spiral. This is most likely in minority neighborhoods, but may afflict poor whites as well.

Events in Warren County, described in the text that follows, provided the first test of the Civil Rights Act of 1964 as a vehicle to obtain redress. That strategy has failed in the courts, which have generally required proof of intent to do harm that is absent in this and other cases. Even though intent is not required for obvious harm to occur, the courts have generally refused to hold polluting corporations legally responsible and financially liable without it. Similarly, the law of genocide requires proof of intent (as, for example, the Nazis provided with the Jews during the Holocaust). Even in the absence of legally defined intent to do harm, the dangerous legacy of hazardous synthetic chemical wastes, contaminated manufacturing sites, and polluting industries has fallen disproportionately on poor, nonwhite communities in the United States. Communities of color are disproportionately burdened by neighboring hazardous waste sites, incinerators, petrochemical plants, lead contamination, dirty air, and contaminated drinking water.

Even after the courts had turned back several environmental justice suits based on Title VI of the 1964 Civil Rights Act because of an inability to prove intent, the EPA in 2002 created an Office of Civil Rights (OCR) to "enforce federal civil rights laws that prohibit discrimination against members of the public by recipients of EPA funds, and [protect] employees and applicants for employment from discrimination" (Swift, 2016). The OCR turned out to be something of a bureaucratic front, however. "Out of 298 complaints filed across 22 years," wrote James A. Swift in *The Grio* (2016), "the OCR has never made a finding of discrimination—in fact, more than half of the complaints never lead to investigations at all and were instead rejected for various reasons." Many people who were protesting various environmental insults generally gave up on it. Even without legal support, traces of a case do exist that some siting of environmentally damaging activity has been undertaken with intent. In 1986, the Center of Third World Organizing reported that more than 2 million tons of radioactive uranium tailings had been dumped on Native American lands.

As the legal system must change, so the basics of accounting must recognize linkages to the environment, recognizing pollution as a taxable debit on the "bottom line," bringing the accounting system into congruence with environmental principles. This necessity has already been recognized in theory under the rubric of "green accounting." Such an accounting system looks at environmental costs as real debits, not "externalities." It also looks at property values (including property taxes) in a world in which the real estate market takes sea-level rise seriously, one of many changes that will be required to fully address climate change. The total picture adds up to a world in which we no longer ignore the use of the atmosphere as common property, a free good that can be despoiled at will. To address global warming at its roots, we will be forced to address the tragedy of the commons. Until then, do not buy real estate investment trusts based in Florida. Watch insurance bills, especially those that reflect risks of coastal flooding. Insurance companies are very attuned to climate change. It's their business to avoid (and profit from) perils.

A 1992 study by the *National Law Journal*, "Unequal Protection," uncovered significant disparities in the way the U.S. Environmental Protection Agency enforces laws. This must change. The study found abundant evidence of a racial divide when the U.S. government cleans up toxic waste sites and punishes polluters. White communities see faster action, better results, and stiffer penalties compared with communities where blacks, Latinos, and other minorities make up most of the population. In 1994, President Bill Clinton issued an executive order that required federal agencies to develop environmental justice strategies to address the disproportionate human health and environmental effects of their programs on minority and low-income populations. The U.S. Environmental Protection Agency after that (until Donald Trump's appointment of Scott Pruitt as EPA director in 2016) developed programs that coordinated environmental justice advocacy across all government agencies, providing mandatory consideration of issues involving pollution and racism.

Nick Chiles wrote in the *Atlanta Black Star* that:

> Environmental racism is made possible by extreme segregation. Eight out of every 10 African-Americans live in neighborhoods where they are in the majority. While residential segregation decreases for most racial and ethnic groups with additional education, income and occupational status, [this] does not hold true for African-Americans. African-Americans, no matter what their educational or occupational achievement or income level, are exposed to higher crime rates, less effective educational systems, high mortality risks, more dilapidated surroundings and greater environmental threats because of their race. (Chiles, 2015)

Future solutions to environmental racism also must recognize and cope with the endurance of pollution, and adjust legal doctrines to compensate generations into the future. Only then will pollution become so expensive that market forces will cease to tolerate it. One stark example of this toxic endurance has been provided in the Arctic, where Inuit homelands were poisoned by synthetic chemicals such as PCBs (polychlorinated biphenyls) and dioxins. It is, however, a long road back. These chemicals are still embedded in the Arctic food chain (as they are in many similarly polluted places further south) to a degree that diplomacy cannot quickly solve. Another example is provided by the continuing effects of the defoliant Agent Orange, which was used to deny the Viet Cong cover in jungles during a war that is now half a century in the past. Today, three generations later, it is still producing deformations in the children of both the Vietnamese farmers and the U.S. Army troops who were soaked with it. A future legal system must provide compensation for these victims.

Similarly, with regard to the rapid warming of the Arctic, the laws of geophysics—most notably thermal inertia—guarantee that until the proportion of carbon dioxide and other greenhouse gases in the atmosphere starts to decline worldwide, rapidly warming temperatures will continue to heat the atmosphere for at least 50 years after our energy sources change from fossil fuels to renewables. The world has yet to confront a fundamental issue that some scientists now call the question of "unburnable carbon," which estimates how much oil, natural gas, and coal will have to remain in the ground to avoid catastrophic global warming.

The atmosphere is warming for all of us, and persistent organic pollutants have become common in the entire food chain. Minorities and poor people are afflicted first and worst, but their cries for justice should be a warning to everyone. Such knowledge must become an important part of everyday conversation, supported by successful litigation. The rewards of the economy must become congruent with a sustainable environment.

Further Reading

Ash, Michael, James K. Boyce, Grace Chang, and Helen Scharber. "Is Environmental Justice Good for White Folks? Industrial Air Toxics Exposure in Urban America." *Social Science Quarterly* 94, no. 3 (September 2013): 616–636.

Chiles, Nick. "8 Horrifying Examples of Corporations Mistreating Black Communities with Environmental Racism." *Atlanta Black Star*, February 12, 2015. http://atlantablackstar.com/2015/02/12/8-horrifying-examples-of-corporations-mistreating-black-communities-with-environmental-racism/

Coal Blooded: Putting Profits Before People. National Association for the Advancement of Colored People (NAACP), 2019.

Morello-Frosch, Rachel, Manual Pastor Jr., Carlos Porras, and James Sadd. "Environmental Justice and Regional Inequality in Southern California: Implications for Future Research." *Environmental Health Perspectives* 110 (suppl. 2) (April 2002): 149–154.

Pierre-Louis, Kendra. "Dr. King Said Segregation Harms Us All; Environmental Research Shows He Was Right." *New York Times*, February 3, 2018. https://www.nytimes.com/2018/04/03/climate/mlk-segregation-pollution.html

Swift, James A. "It's Not Just Flint: Environmental Racism Is Slowly Killing Blacks across America." *The Grio*, January 24, 2016. http://thegrio.com/2016/01/24/flint-water-environmental-racism-blacks/

CHAPTER TWO

Unifying Themes

Introduction

While sections that follow describe specific cases and places, this one develops more general themes in environmental racism and justice that span the continent, or also inflict American-made environmental maladies on other peoples.

One important example of exported toxicity has been the fate of Vietnamese people and U.S. soldiers who served in the Vietnam War (1964–1975) and were cursed with the legacy of dioxin-laced Agent Orange. The toll of the synthetic chemicals used in that war has now spread to several succeeding generations in both countries. Eighteen million gallons of Agent Orange were sprayed over vast tracts of Southeast Asian forests between 1962 and 1971 in concentrations up to 1,000 times as potent as dioxin-based herbicides sold over the counter in the United States. Soon after spraying of Agent Orange and other herbicides began during the late 1960s, reports increased of deformed births in unusually large numbers. Areas sprayed with Agent Orange later reported very high incidences of certain birth defects: anencephaly (absence of all or parts of the brain), spina bifida (a malformed vertebral column), and hydrocephaly (swelling of the skull). The Saigon newspaper *Tin Sang* published descriptions of "monster babies" born to mothers in areas that had been sprayed (Johansen, 1972, 4).

Our narrative then focuses on farmworkers who face the toll of the same chemicals in their daily lives from the tomato fields of Florida to the table-grape harvests of California. Exposure to toxic chemicals has become an occupational hazard for those who pick and process our food.

In the United States, lead, especially, appears in the narrative of environmental racism with unrelenting regularity, from the water pipes of Flint, Michigan, to the inner-city garden soil of Omaha, Nebraska, and many places in between. An essay titled "Lead, Lead Everywhere: Flint, Michigan's Water Crisis in Context" describes the unifying theme of ubiquitous lead poisoning in many U.S. urban areas.

Phrases such as "sacrifice areas" and "sacrifice zones" have been used to describe Native American places and peoples. It is a supreme historical irony that Native peoples whose "original instructions" have helped all of us understand the concept of Earth as mother have been subjected to some of North America's worst pollution caused by mining that regards "Mother Earth" as a "mother lode."

Humankind's urge to dominate nature extends beyond mining. The intentional extermination of animals such as the Plains buffalo during the nineteenth century was designed to alter the environment and to destroy the indigenous economic base. The Great Plains Indian conflicts were early examples of "total war" that defeated indigenous peoples by obliterating their economic base—much as Agent Orange later was used to destroy foliage in Vietnam.

In our time, "Canadian Tar Sands: From Treaty Forest to Moonscape" takes the reader to the prairies of Alberta, where Mother Earth is being consumed in an intensifying search for subsurface hydrocarbons to the point that it is now useless for any other purpose. Finally, "Environmental Racism and the Demise of an Ice World" describes how the intensifying storms of a warming world are wiping some villages off the map.

Further Reading

Johansen, Bruce. "Ecomania at Home; Ecocide Abroad." University of Washington *Daily*, May 24, 1972, 4.

Mining: Mother Earth or Mother Lode?

To many Native Americans—those with a naturalistic philosophy—mining is the ultimate insult, a rape of Mother Earth transformed into mother lode, thus the number and intensity of protests by indigenous peoples against mining across Turtle Island, the Iroquois name for North America. The mining of uranium is the most notably odious; it is such a natural breach that Navajo cosmology warns against it. Mercantile capitalism has no such qualms about mining. It is, in fact, the very basis of a system that survives and thrives by making and selling things, thus the germ of conflict: Native American homelands contain vast stores of exploitable natural resources that corporations find useful and profitable, often available from governments at prices far below market value—or so they were until the "other" started talking back.

The catalog of mining and its toxic legacy on Native American lands is vast. Many Native peoples across North America have organized against mining on their homelands, notably in Alaska, where the world's largest sockeye salmon run could be imperiled by the proposed Pebble Mine, the largest gold and copper strip mine on Earth, which has the potential to produce as much as 80 billion pounds of copper. A permit for that mine was denied in 2014 by the U.S. Environmental Protection Agency (EPA), but mining companies are challenging it. With the election of Donald Trump in 2016 and his appointment of Scott Pruitt to head the Environmental Protection Agency, the Pebble Mine was back in play.

In Wisconsin, copper, zinc, and sulfide mining are being proposed, and they are being resisted by Native peoples. Silver mining in Mexico is poisoning indigenous children. Coal strip mining is an important issue for Hopis and Navajos, whose shepherds have lost many of their sheep to the toxic plumes of the Four Corners Power Plant.

The Quapaw Tribe's Toxic Mining Mess

We begin our toxic journey with the Quapaw in Oklahoma, whose homeland is now nearly uninhabitable. On March 25, 2013, the Quapaw sued the U.S. federal government for $75 million, alleging failure to clean up the nation's largest lead and zinc mine, which had produced millions of tons of ore. Much of the reservation's water had become polluted. Bullfrog Films and director Matt Myers made a documentary film on the Quapaws' pursuit of justice, released in 2011. The film, simply titled *Tar Creek*, provides a searing portrait of human and natural damage wrought on a 1,188-square-mile area in northeastern Oklahoma now known as the Tar Creek Superfund site, where residents are still seeking relief from acidic mine water in creeks, lead poisoning of children, and sinkholes that swallow backyards of contaminated houses.

With very little editorial comment—none is required—*Tar Creek* describes the demise of the Native American and European American communities that supplied the materials basic to two world wars. The Quapaws, whose homeland once encompassed much of Arkansas, were removed to a small tract of land during the 1830s; whites later moved in around them. The Quapaws, once a nation of at least 35,000 people, were reduced to about 150, mainly by smallpox and other diseases. They were recovering when the mining ruined their new homeland.

Following the mining, mountainous piles of "chat" (mine tailings) remained; local waters infused with sulfur ran rust-red. No one told the residents that the enormous piles of chat caused developmental difficulties for the children who played on them. Families laid out picnics on the chat piles, and fathers built sandboxes filled with the gray sandy material that was poisoning their children.

Tar Creek follows a tale of bureaucratic ineptitude. The federal government initially spent $138 million replacing soil around many houses, an average of $70,000 per house in an area where the homes themselves averaged $58,000 in value. All told, the remediation effort did very little to address the systemic problems caused by leaks from the chat piles and massive water pollution. One report estimated that 50 large trucks would have been required around the clock for 40 years to clear the chat piles—and then where would they dump it?

The film followed people's responses as the government conducted a slow-motion buyout in which very few people received anything close to what they would need to start over elsewhere. The camera pans a dead landscape largely bereft of animal, fish, and bird life as human communities slowly disintegrate. One resident compared his community's fate to Rachel Carson's *Silent Spring*. He is wrong, in a sense, because this environmental apocalypse—miles of prairie turned into permanent wasteland—is worse than anything described in Carson's book.

By mid-2014, parts of the 1,188-square-mile Tar Creek Quapaw toxic mining site, most notably areas called the Catholic Forty and Chat Base 11 North, were being cleaned up as part of the first Superfund project by the Quapaw tribal government, cooperating with state and local environmental agencies. "We completed the first cleanup less expensively and better than previous efforts," said Quapaw chairman John Berrey. "Our goal is to make this land useful and productive again. We live here and we care about the outcomes, so we are very pleased to have these two new agreements in place" ("Quapaw Take Lead," 2014). Roughly 72,000 tons of contaminated material had been removed from the Catholic Forty by 2014—the start of a lifetime of decontamination to come.

Wisconsin's Mining Maladies

Early in the nineteenth century, Native peoples on mineral-rich lands in Wisconsin, Michigan, and Minnesota were forced off their homelands. Four treaties signed during the 1850s removed 19 million acres of land from Native control as well as 100 billion board feet of timber, 150 billion tons of iron ore, and 13.5 billion pounds of copper. Mining on these lands provided early profits for U.S. Steel under the control of J. P. Morgan. For half a century, beginning in the 1890s, iron mines in the Lake Superior area shipped more than 4 billion tons of iron ore to steel mills in the United States (Gedicks, 1993). After World War II, the focus of mining moved to other countries (including Canada, Australia, Venezuela, and Brazil), as the iron-ore mining region near Lake Superior sank into a deep depression.

During the 1970s, miners again focused their attention on this area as the Phelps Dodge Corporation sought a copper-extraction contract from the Lac du Flambeau Chippewa. The company expected speedy approval by the tribal council, but its members, knowing the history of the area, were skeptical. The council hired Charles J. Lipton, a lawyer and expert in minerals-contract negotiation, who told them that "no company that I have seen in recent times would dare to suggest such terms now to a developing nation overseas" (Gedicks, 1993). The contract required the tribe (if it was to be a partner) to pay the company $250,000 (worth about $1 million in 2014) to explore its lands for copper; Lipton advised the tribe to decline the offer.

Mike Wiggins Jr., chairman of the 2,000-member Bad River tribe, looked at the conflict as a "clash of cultures." However, he said, "you have to see life from the eyes of a sturgeon. . . . Rivers and streams are the lifeblood of the Earth" (Pogash, 2013, 4-A). While many members of the tribe believe that the mine will foul their river and the Earth with mercury, asbestos, sulfuric acid, and arsenic, a representative of the mining company "envisioned reclaimed land becoming an ATV park or a long shooting range, [with] people and fish swimming in the mine-made lake" (Pogash, 2013, 4-A).

In 1976, Exxon announced the discovery of one of the world's largest potential zinc and copper deposits near the 200-member Sokaogon Chippewa's 1,900-acre reservation near Mole Lake in northeastern Wisconsin. The tiny Indian band soon found itself facing off with the world's largest energy corporation. The tribe had an annual budget of $1,200; Exxon's energy reserves exceeded $1.3 trillion (Gedicks, 1993).

Deciding that such a mine would ruin their homeland and way of life, the Sokaogon Chippewa decided to resist. The tribe decided that Exxon would be legally vulnerable as it sought permits in areas that threatened their wild rice harvest. They allied with non-Indians across northern Wisconsin in the Wisconsin Resources Protection Council. After a decade of struggle, the smallest, poorest Indian tribe in Wisconsin leveraged this support into an environmental movement that forced Exxon to withdraw.

By mid-1992, however, Exxon returned, as the prices of both copper and zinc had risen substantially. The estimated value of the deposit had risen from $4.6 billion in 1984 to $7.6 billion in 1992 (Gedicks, 1993). The environmental movement also had been weakened by widespread Republican victories in Wisconsin, including the election of Governor Tommy Thompson. Even so, on December 14, 1992, Phelps Dodge withdrew from an anticipated partnership with Exxon in the mining venture.

Also in the mid-1970s, the Kennecott Copper Corporation (a subsidiary of Rio Tinto Zinc, the largest mining company in the world) announced plans to open a small open-pit copper mine in Grant, one mile southwest of Ladysmith, Wisconsin. The Lac Courte Oreilles Chippewa reservation was adjacent to the proposed mine site. Neither Kennecott nor the Wisconsin Department of Natural Resources consulted with this tribe or others, contending that their treaty rights were irrelevant despite contrary opinions in several legal proceedings. The state approved the mine in March 2003.

Native Americans in northern Wisconsin are combining with neighboring non-Indians to fight a proposal to dig what could become the world's largest iron-ore mine near an area in which Native peoples exercise their treaty rights to hunt, fish, and gather wild rice. The political movement that has grown out of resistance to mining in this area, which calls itself the Watershed Alliance to End Environmental Racism, went head-to-head with energy-industry lobbyists in the Wisconsin statehouse over a proposed mining moratorium. Opposition to mining intensified as Wisconsin residents discovered what the mining wastes could do to the Earth from which they wrest their lives. Metallic sulfides, combined with air and water, can create sulfuric acid as well as residues of several toxic metals, including mercury, lead, and arsenic.

Northern Wisconsin has been a toxic hot spot for at least a quarter century. In 1992, the Environmental Protection Agency published *Tribes at Risk: The Wisconsin Comparative Risk Project,* describing how the Ojibwe as well as other Native American nations in northern Wisconsin had been afflicted by an unusual number of illnesses and chronic health problems after eating fish, deer, and other wildlife contaminated with industrial pollutants like airborne polychlorinated biphenyls (PCBs), mercury, and other toxins deposited on land and water (EPA, 1992).

Dan Kaufman (2014), writing in the *New York Times*, sketched what is at stake in far northern Wisconsin's Penokee Hills: "The $1.5 billion mine would initially be close to four miles long, up to a half-mile wide and nearly 1,000 feet deep, but it could be extended as long as 21 miles. In its footprint lies the headwaters of the Bad River, which flows into Lake Superior, the largest freshwater lake in the world and by far the cleanest of the Great Lakes. Six miles downstream from the site is the reservation of the Bad River Band of Lake Superior Chippewa, whose livelihood is threatened by the mine."

Plans for the mine call for the dumping of waste into a 350-acre waste pond that would reach, in some locations, to within 15 feet of the water table, raising fears that sulfuric acid and heavy metals would leach into local water supplies. Not only are these waters used for bathing, drinking, and cooking, but they also sustain the local Chippewa with fish as well as wild rice, a cash crop as well as a sacred part of Sokaogon Chippewa religious life. Native Americans in the area realized that if the mine is constructed, their drinking water and their harvest could become inedibly toxic. One mining executive, having been challenged on the quality of water in the tailing ponds, said he would be happy to drink it himself. "Pour him a tall one!" headlined the Indian Country Today Media Network (August 2014).

The conflict over sulfide mining in Wisconsin had begun in 1975, when the Exxon Minerals Company located one of the largest zinc–copper sulfide deposits in North America adjacent to the Mole Lake Sokaogon Chippewa reservation near Crandon, Wisconsin. Company plans anticipated the extraction of roughly 50 million tons of sulfide ore over the life of the mine, about 30 years. This volume of waste could fill Egypt's Great Pyramid about 10 times. Mine supporters have maintained that new technologies will mitigate the spread of sulfide by-products from the mine wastes, but few people in the area bought the company's argument.

On March 11, 2013, Republican governor Scott Walker signed into law a "streamlined" permit process that eliminated several environmental regulations to speed the development of new mines. The law reduced the number of public hearings required for approval of the open-pit mine proposal and required speedy state responses to environmental impact statements. This law also allowed miners to dump millions of tons of waste into the Bad River watershed, stating that "a significant adverse impact on wetlands is assumed to be necessary" (Pogash, 2013, 4-A). Democrats called the bill "a giveaway to an out-of-state corporation of Wisconsin's lands and waters" that enables a slow poisoning of Walker's people with pollutants that would be tantamount to genocide. To Walker, the bill was a vehicle to "create sustainable jobs for generations" (Hughes, 2013). Gogebic Taconite's (GTAC) executives and other supporters of the proposed mine have given about $15 million to Governor Walker, as well as Wisconsin Republican legislators, 600 times their donations to the mine's opponents (Kaufman, 2014).

Having lobbied its mine proposal for several years, pouring several million dollars into its campaign in exploratory expenses and political contributions, in February 2015, Gogebic Taconite suddenly closed its office in Hurley, Wisconsin, and pulled out of the area, leaving behind a galvanized opposition that had united Native Americans and whites who heretofore had agreed on little else; an Ashland County Board that had tempered its initial support with regulations of prospective noise, damage to roads, dust, and pollution; and Wisconsin's governor, Scott Walker, with a $700,000 GTAC donation in his political coffers.

No one was saying that anything was final. The company was reacting in part to a petition by the Wisconsin Federation of Tribes requesting that the EPA use the Clean Water Act (as it had to stop the Pebble Mine in Alaska) against GTAC's proposal. "It's unfortunate that the federal requirements for mitigating wetlands make it cost-prohibitive for Gogebic to move forward at this time. We remain committed to working with companies interested in creating quality, family-supporting jobs in Wisconsin," Walker said. "We will continue to investigate the possibility of pursuing a permit to mine the Upson site [in Iron County] but cannot justify maintaining an office in Hurley without a prospect of immediate action," Gogebic added. Opponents of the mine were not declaring victory. "Mines are like vampires; they're very hard to kill. The mineral deposit [that attracted GTAC] isn't going away," said Rich Eggleston, a member of Citizens Concerned, about the proposed Penokee Mine (Pember, 2015).

Further Reading

EPA (U.S. Environmental Protection Agency). *Tribes at Risk: The Wisconsin Comparative Risk Project.* Washington, D.C.: EPA, 1992. https://grist.org/climate-energy/when-did-republicans-start-hating-green-when-it-started-helping-blacks/

Gedicks, Al. *The New Resource Wars: Native and Environmental Struggles Against Multinational Corporations.* Boston: South End Press, 1993.

Huff, Andrew. 2000. "Gold Mining Threatens Communities." The Progressive Media Project, July 11, 2000. https://archive.org/stream/140J.D.Spencer TheAmericanCivilWarInTheIndianTerritory/Amerikan%20History%20 encyklopedia_djvu.txt

Hughes, Pam. "Bad River Band Establishes Legal Defense Fund to Stop Proposed Iron-Ore Mine." Indian Country Today Media Network, March 19, 2013.

http://indiancountrytodaymedianetwork.com/2013/03/19/bad-river-band-establishes-legal-defense-fund-stop-proposed-iron-ore-mine-148251

Johansen, Bruce E. "Exxon vs. Chippewas in Wisconsin." *Native Americas* 15, no. 1 (1998): 6.

Kaufman, Dan. "The Fight for Wisconsin's Soul." *New York Times*, March 29, 2014. http://www.nytimes.com/2014/03/30/opinion/sunday/the-fight-for-wisconsins-soul.html

Pember, Mary Annette. "Racism & Violent Threats: Wis. [Wisconsin] Mining War Gets Uglier and Scarier." Indian Country Today Media Network, July 17, 2013. https://www.indianz.com/News/2013/07/17/mary-pember-racism-surfaces-in.asp

Pember, Mary Annette. "A Bad River Win; Gogebic Taconite Putting Wisc. [Wisconsin] Mine on Hold." Indian Country Today Media Network, March 3, 2015. http://indiancountrytodaymedianetwork.com/2015/03/03/bad-river-win-gogebic-taconite-putting-wisc-mine-hold-159434

Pogash, Carol. "Governor, Chippewas Battle over Mine." *USA Today*, September 9, 2013, 4-A.

"Pour Him a Tall One! Mining Exec Insists He'd Drink Water from Tailings Pond." Indian Country Today Media Network. August 7, 2014. http://indiancountrytodaymedianetwork.com/2014/08/07/pour-him-tall-one-mining-exec-insists-hed-drink-water-tailings-pond-156294

"Quapaw Take Lead in Tar Creek Superfund Site Cleanup in Oklahoma, Kansas." Indian Country Today Media Network. June 4, 2014. http://indiancountrytodaymedianetwork.com/2014/06/04/quapaw-take-lead-tar-creek-superfund-site-cleanup-oklahoma-kansas-155155

Lead, Lead Everywhere: Flint, Michigan's Water Crisis in Context

The poisoning of Flint, Michigan's water supply, beginning in 2014, was not subtle. "From the start, the people of Flint, Mich., knew something was wrong with the water coming out of their taps," wrote Parul Sehgal in the *New York Times* (2018). "It was brown and orange, visibly full of particles, frothy and foul-smelling. Their hair started falling out, and showers left their bodies burning with red welts. Their plants and pets began to die. On a hot day, children playing in the spray of a water hydrant were streaked with coffee-colored liquid." Flint's lead toxicity received copious national media attention as it occurred and was very ably described in books afterward, such as Anna Clark's *The Poisoned City: Flint's Water and the American Urban Tragedy* (2018) and Mona Hanna-Attisha's *What the Eyes Don't See: A Story of Crisis, Resistance, and Hope in an*

American City (2018). Hanna-Attisha was the Flint pediatrician who assembled proof that the toxic water was poisoning children.

Flint's poisoned water flowed brown from the tap, smelling rotten and tasting metallic. For example, LeeAnne Walters's family developed skin rashes and mysterious aches, and they lost hair. One of the children stopped growing. The water had turned brown. When she showed bottles of it to officials, they refused to believe it had come from her kitchen tap (Peplow, 2018). As in Walters's case, officials refused to believe users' reports, even after citizens mobilized to test lead in the water themselves, finding levels averaging 2,000 parts per billion, ranging as high as 13,000 (the legal limit is 15 ppb).

The crisis that afflicted Flint is only one very dramatic example of lead poisoning in U.S. urban areas. Every so often a crisis involving its insidious (and sometimes deadly) effects breaks into the headlines, but in many places it is so common as to be unremarkable—in the air, in the soil, in the water, concentrating in older, poor, and nonwhite neighborhoods, stripping years from many people's lives.

The U.S. Environmental Protection Agency has been so slow to update and enforce lead standards in paint and dust that the Ninth District Federal Appeals Court in San Francisco on December 27, 2017, ordered it to get to work on them, a rare legal move that, according to a *New York Times* account, "amounts to a sharp rebuff of President Trump and Scott Pruitt, the EPA administrator" (Friedman, 2017). More than 40 years after lead paint was banned in homes, the EPA was asking for six more years to update its regulations, which by then were 21 years old. The court gave it three months.

"This is going to protect the brains of thousands of children across the country," said Eve C. Gartner, a staff attorney for Earthjustice who helped argue the case on behalf of groups pushing for tougher standards. "It's going to mean that children that otherwise would have developed very elevated blood lead levels will be protected from the damage associated with that, assuming EPA follows the court order," she said. The court ruling said, "Indeed EPA itself has acknowledged that 'lead poisoning is the number one environmental health threat in the U.S. for children ages 6 and younger,' and that the current standards are insufficient." It added, "The children exposed to lead poisoning due to the failure of EPA to act are severely prejudiced by EPA's delay" (Friedman, 2017).

Origins of Flint's Water Crisis

One very well-publicized instance of lead exposure in urban water occurred in Flint, Michigan, peaking in 2016. It was unusual only in the amount of attention paid to it. The context (children in a largely black urban area being toxified by routine exposure to lead) happens very frequently. In Flint, however, the situation assumed a uniquely human dimension as parents, having discovered that their children were drinking poison, quickly switched to bottled water.

Authorities in Flint had failed to address the lead crisis in Flint's water for two years as toxic residues built up in people's bodies, and many of these officials lost their jobs as the world watched. Internal reports in the federal government indicated that the Environmental Protection Agency had ample evidence to warn residents of Flint, Michigan, that their water was toxic several months before it did so, meanwhile allowing dangerous levels of lead to accumulate in their bodies. Arthur A. Elkins Jr., inspector general at the EPA, said that the federal government was responsible for the situation in Flint, failing in its oversight role. The EPA possessed enough information as early as June 2015. The agency also knew that the water was tainted over and above federal standards. Test results indicated that action was necessary (Bosman, 2016).

The Michigan state government's own reports (in this case by a task force appointed by Governor Rick Snyder) indicated how authority at all levels had failed the public interest in Flint. Though it avoids the word "racism," the report clearly identifies the pivotal role that poverty and environmental racism have played in Flint's water crisis. "Flint residents, who are majority black or African-American and among the most impoverished of any metropolitan area in the United States, did not enjoy the same degree of protection from environmental and health hazards as that provided to other communities," the report said. The Flint water system was under state control and the state did not order local officials to treat the water in such a way that lead leaching from pipes and plumbing fixtures would be reduced to safe levels.

The same task force, which included two state legislators, two medical doctors, and a water expert, advised the state to provide long-term health care for residents of the city who had been poisoned, as well as replacement of the lead-laden pipes in Flint and other urban areas in Michigan that were the primary cause of the water's contamination. All of this would have been enormously expensive and therefore, in reality, probably would require a long time. Such neglect is not unique to Flint, nor to Michigan. For years, minority and poor communities have been suffering from environmental degradation at a much greater rate than most people across the United States—witness the poorest neighborhoods of New Orleans after Hurricane Katrina and the breach of levees in that city, as well as several communities across West Virginia that have suffered chemical spills in recent years. Washington, D.C. also experienced a lead contamination crisis about 10 years before Flint's. "Most of these disasters could have been avoided or mitigated by aggressive government action," wrote the *Times* ("Racism at the Heart of Flint's Crisis," 2016).

Environmental Racism as Policy

Even as Flint's water was poisoning them with lead, some Flint residents who had failed to pay their water bills were faced with foreclosure of their homes. Jacey Fortin wrote in the *New York Times* (2017) that "the city had mailed 8,002 letters billing residents for $5.8 million worth of unpaid sewer and water bills, demanding payment by May 19, 2017." The city also began to file liens for seizure of homes if bills remained unpaid after March, 2018. The city had extended its usual six-month deadline during the height of the water crisis in 2016, but did not forgive the bills, which, when updated, included two years of overdue charges.

Racism seemed embedded in the official response to Flint's water-contamination crisis. One Flint official who used racial slurs in reference to black victims of lead poisoning was forced to resign in 2017. Philip Stair, 63 at the time, who worked at the Genesee County Land Bank, a government organization, as a sales manager developing abandoned properties in Flint, used the slur to describe blacks who "don't pay their bills," as he attempted to explain Flint's water crisis. The Genesee County Land Bank had become the largest landowner in Flint due to foreclosures of homes mainly previously owned by poor, black residents. Tainted water has done nothing to support home values in Flint.

Stair's remark was secretly recorded by Chelsea Lyons, a journalist and activist working with Truth Against the Machine, which described itself as "an independent media organization that covers 'stories the corporate media is ignoring on a local, national and international scale.'" In the same recording, Stair also referred to some Flint residents as "derelict" and "deadbeats" (Fortin, 2016). Stair did not respond to a request for comment from Lyons, but she told MLive, an online news outlet based in Michigan, that the Genesee County Land Bank was "a disaster," in part because of the tax foreclosures that made so much land available to the bank in the first place. Michele Wildman, executive director of the Land Bank, fired Stair after she heard the recording. She had arrived at work to find protesters at her door and Stair's resignation letter on her desk. "I am deeply sorry for what I said and those I offended," his letter said. "I do not know how I can face my friends and co-workers" (Fortin, 2016). Wildman said the bank might start staff "cultural competency training."

Even after filters were delivered in 2016, subsequent tests revealed that some of Flint's tap water was still not fit to drink or to use in food preparation. Even with filtration, at 150 parts per billion, the lead content still was 10 times safe levels. "Residents and advocates have expressed outrage over the government's failure to protect Flint's children, something many of them say would not have happened if the city were largely white," Abby Goodnough reported (2017). "Adding to their injury, they say, are the harsh conditions of poverty that have already placed obstacles in their young lives." At the same time, many were turning their attention to the future, when the effects of consuming lead-laced water for months may be all too evident.

Flint pediatrician Mona Hanna-Attisha and colleagues collected evidence of high lead levels in Flint children's blood, forcing once-reluctant officials to take action to prevent continued, profound effects on children's growth, behavior, and intelligence, including learning disabilities, problems with attention and fine motor coordination, and violent behavior. At the same time, black and poor people in Flint were receiving evidence that officials couldn't have cared less, until they were caught in the dull glare of publicity.

Emails released by Michigan governor Rick Snyder described a Flint resident who said that a state nurse had told her in January 2015, when her son's blood lead tested at an elevated level, "It is just a few IQ points. . . . It is not the end of the world" (Goodnough, 2017).

Even fixes for Flint's toxic water had their own perils. Hanna-Attisha also worried about the effect of total trihalomethanes (TTHMs), chemical compounds introduced into Flint's water to kill bacteria with extra chlorine. These chemicals may increase miscarriage rates. Extra chlorine and TTHMs also may be related to rashes reported by Flint residents. The water crisis in Flint was further complicated by an outbreak of shigellosis, a bacterial gastrointestinal malady that spreads easily among people who do not wash their hands.

Health department officials in Genesee County, where Flint is the largest city, said there has been an increase in the illness, with severe diarrhea, fever, nausea, vomiting, cramps, and stools laced with mucus and blood. Cases of shigellosis surged in Flint when people avoided handwashing because of tainted water. The disease spreads via accidental ingestion of fecal matter, which can be washed away with clean, soapy water, something that was in short supply in Flint, where the water was not only laced with lead, but often rusty and emanating a foul odor. Many people were avoiding the water not only for bathing, but cooking as well (Hauser, 2016).

By April 2014, after it began drawing water from the Flint River, the city's drinking water contained enough lead to qualify as toxic waste under EPA guidelines, 19 times as corrosive as water from Lake Huron, its previous (and more expensive) source. Supervisors at General Motors noticed that the water was corroding its assembly-line machinery, and quit using it.

After the switch back to Lake Huron water, the crisis in Flint could have been 90 percent corrected by using an anticorrosive additive (orthophosphate) that cost $100 a day, which would have stopped most of the leaching from the lead-laced pipes. The city declined to use the additive on cost grounds. Instead, leaching of lead continued and Flint's water became discolored, as well as toxic.

By late in 2017, water pipes leading to 5,200 homes in Flint had been replaced, but Mayor Karen Weaver, who had been elected on a pledge to cleanse the water supply, was facing recall as many residents charged incompetence. She said her opponents were driven by racism (she is black) and sexism. Flint remained in a long-term malaise, its population about half of what it had been when the automobile industry was booming, with 40 percent of its 97,000 residents in poverty. Mitch Smith reported in the *New York Times* (2017): "Life and politics remain upended here by the water. Many Flint residents, including Ms. Weaver, still use bottled water to drink and to brush their teeth, even though tests show the tap water is improving. 'We don't trust,' said Ms. Weaver, a psychologist who had never before held elected office. 'Something that's difficult to re-establish is trust, when you've been lied to at every level of government.'"

Lead's Effects on Fetal Deaths and Fertility Rates in Flint

During the years after Flint's water crisis, scientists continued to reveal just how damaging it had been. Research health economists Daniel Grossman and David Slusky disclosed, according to a report in the *Detroit Free Press*, that babies in Flint born during the period when Flint's water was most toxic weighed an average of almost 150 grams less than those born in Michigan as a whole (Matheny, 2017). Fertility rates decreased by 12 percent among women in Flint who drank the water, as fetal death rates rose by 58 percent after April 2014. The researchers used Census tract data to compare rates in Flint to the rest of Michigan between 2008 and 2015. Their research shows that problems spiked in April 2014—when Flint's city government, seeking to save money, switched from Detroit's water system to the polluted Flint River, without using anticorrosive compounds, causing lead to leach into pipes carrying the water. Michigan governor Rick Snyder colluded with state health officials to withhold this information from Flint residents for 15 months, even after Marc Edwards, a Virginia Tech researcher, and Miguel Del Toral of the EPA told state and federal officials that they were concerned about the lead level. At about the same time, Hanna-Attisha's own research showed children's blood lead levels were rising in Flint (Matheny, 2017).

By late in 2017, state health officials reported that the number of reported Legionnaire's disease (a severe respiratory infection) cases had risen to 91, 12 of which had been fatal, while Flint River water was being used. During 2016, Flint switched back to water from the Great Lakes Water Authority, but the city's pipes were still corroding. Fifteen state and local officials were indicted on criminal charges, including manslaughter in some cases. These included Nick Lyon, Michigan Department of Health and Human Services director, and Michigan's chief medical executive, Eden Wells, as well as Liane Shekter-Smith, the fired head of the Michigan Department of Environmental Quality's drinking water unit (Matheny, 2017).

A Dissenting View

Hernán Gómez and Kim Dietrich, both of whom are experts in toxicology and environmental health, dissented from the widespread characterization of Flint's water as "poisoned." They wrote that during the middle 1970s, children in the United States had an average blood lead level of 14 micrograms per deciliter. Following bans of lead in gasoline and paint, that level fell to 0.84 by 2014. At that time, the Centers for Disease Control and Prevention established a reference level of 5 micrograms per deciliter as a reference point intended to identify children at higher risk and set off communitywide prevention activities. They said that Flint's children were tested at an average of about half that level.

"This [level] does not suggest that a child needs medical treatment. In fact, the CDC recommends medical treatment only for blood lead levels at or above 45 micrograms per deciliter. Not a single child in Flint tested this high," they said (2018). From 2006 to 2015, the proportion of of Flint children who were tested above the reference level fell to 3.7 percent from 11.8 percent, according to their analysis. By comparison, 14 percent of children in Highland Park, Michigan, as well as 8.8 percent of children in Detroit, and 8.1 percent in Grand Rapids surpassed the CDC reference level.

Flint's Water Crisis After Five Years

Five years after Flint's water was switched to the Flint River, initiating its crisis, many residents retained a powerful skepticism of its quality. While the state of Michigan insists that lead and copper levels no longer exceed dangerous levels, demand for bottled water remained strong in 2019. The city had replaced about half of the 15,000 service lines containing lead or galvanized steel and pledged to finish all of them in 2019. Even so, Flint's mayor, Karen Weaver, who was elected on a pledge to clean up the water, was advising residents to drink only filtered or bottled water. Weaver and many other Flint residents have heard too many reassurances. "On April 25, 2014," the *New York Times* reported, "a group of smiling officials . . . stood in front of television cameras, held their glasses aloft, and toasted the switch to the city's new water source, the Flint River. 'Here's to Flint!' Dayne Walling, the mayor, said, taking a gulp of river water." Within days, the water "smelled terrible, tasted like metal, and seemed to give [people] skin rashes." People marched on City Hall with bottles of rust-colored water, but were told all was well. "We don't trust," said Mayor Weaver. "Trust was broken on every single level of government" (Smith et al., 2019, A-13).

Omaha, Nebraska: ASARCO's Leaded Legacy

An ASARCO lead smelter and associated industries that immersed much of North Omaha's black community in lead has been dismantled, but its toxic legacy remains in local soil as far as 2.5 miles from its former site, affecting more than 65,000 people, 240 childcare facilities, and 20 Omaha public schools with 11,725 students (Omaha Lead, n.d.). The smelter began operation on about 23 acres on the west bank of the Missouri River north of downtown Omaha during the early 1870s and fully closed in 1996, having toxified residential properties, childcare facilities, schools, and other residential-type properties across at least 8,840 acres. In 1999, the EPA removed and replaced contaminated soils at childcare facilities and properties where children had elevated blood lead levels. In 2002, the removal action expanded to include additional heavily contaminated properties.

The American Smelting and Refining Company, Inc. (ASARCO) operated a lead refinery at 500 Douglas Street for more than 125 years. Aaron Ferer & Sons Company, later called Gould Electronics, Inc., also operated a lead battery recycling plant at 555 Farnam Street for many years. Both plants routinely released lead-laden particulates into the atmosphere from

Unifying Themes

several smokestacks that were spread over a wide area, depending on wind speed and direction.

Soil had been removed at about 13,000 residences in the polluted area by the end of 2015, but not at many others. Only some lead contamination was deemed eligible for "remediation." "For example," said EPA internal documents, the agency "does not have authority to address soil contamination from emissions of lead containing gasoline, indoor lead-based paint, or lead pipes." Thus, only about 14,000 of 42,000 properties contaminated at 450 ppm or more were accepted as eligible. Even so, exposure to lead from ineligible sources can contribute to elevated blood lead levels in children (Omaha Lead, n.d.). Later, lead was located by private testing at homes well outside the Superfund site's boundaries. In addition, commercial and industrial properties were excluded (Omaha Lead, n.d.). Thus, the limited definition of the Superfund site was more of a bureaucratic convenience than a reality.

After the EPA closed its Omaha Lead file in 2016, it provided $42 million to the City of Omaha and $6 million to the Douglas County Health Department for access with owner consent to other properties for the testing of soil, exterior lead-based paint, and interior dust at no cost to the property owner. The Douglas County Health Department continued to compile data from health care providers on blood lead levels in children to help the EPA to evaluate the effectiveness of the lead cleanup work, as well as conduct education and outreach to health care providers to increase awareness of lead's health effects.

As of late 2017, the city of Omaha had obtained access to several additional residential properties and was planning to begin cleanup there. The cooperative agreement included a database at www.omahalead.org. By the end of 2017, soil from more than 42,000 sites in Omaha's Superfund site had been tested for lead contamination, and 14,065 were found to have dangerous levels. All but 975 had been addressed, usually by removing and replacing one foot of soil and sod. The EPA has reimbursed the city for the work. In the meantime, the percentage of children with dangerous ("elevated") lead levels in their blood had declined from about 33 percent in 1998 to less than 2 percent in 2015 (Nohr, 2018, 1-A, 2-A).

Lead in East Chicago, Indiana

Stephanie King, a single mother of five, is one of more than a thousand mainly poor, most often black residents of East Chicago who found in 2016 that their living spaces and the bodies of their children contained "staggering" levels of debilitating lead. The lead levels were so high in her apartment and those nearby that they could not be cleaned up. Residents were evicted and their apartments demolished. To cope with the contamination, Ms. King adopted a grim routine:

> Mopping with bleach twice a day and sweeping even more often to remove any dirt her family might have tracked inside. She has a haunted look, and for good reason. Ms. King and other residents of the West Calumet Housing Complex here learned recently that much of the soil outside their homes contained staggering levels of lead, one of the worst threats to children's health. Ms. King's 3-year-old son, Josiah, has a worrisome amount of lead in his blood, according to test results she received last week. Like about 1,100 other poor, largely black residents of West Calumet, including 670 children, she is scrambling to find a new home after Mayor Anthony Copeland of East Chicago announced last month that the residents had to move out and that the complex would be demolished. (Goodnough, 2016)

The apartment complexes to be demolished had been built adjacent to a huge United States Steel smelter, and on top of a location that previously had housed a smaller smelter. Residents in East Chicago found themselves compared to the people in poor and mainly black areas of Flint, Michigan, who at about the same time found themselves drinking water with high levels of lead, caused by an aging system of lead-lined pipes. The intensity and extent of the contamination came as a shock to residents of the complex, even though it had been designated as a Superfund site in 2009. Many residents asked why neither the state nor the EPA made public just how toxic their soil had become, much less what government agencies would do to remedy the situation.

The city's East Chicago Housing Authority's sudden decision to demolish the complex, as well as to close a neighboring elementary school, contradicted a previously announced plan by the EPA (announced during 2012) to remove the contaminated soil without evicting residents.

Robert A. Kaplan, the EPA's acting regional administrator for the Great Lakes region, said that for many years, cleanup efforts focused on the former smelting plant and not on nearby neighborhoods. In 2008, as the EPA sought Superfund status for the plant and the surrounding area, tests of several dozen yards at and near the housing complex found some "hot spots," Kaplan said, but also soil with lead under a level of concern. The EPA did remove soil from the hot spot areas nearest to the former smelter and did so again in 2011 after limited testing. The EPA had begun suing companies that were responsible for the contamination as early as 2009, and by the time its cleanup plan was ready three years later, it was prepared to remove all lead- and arsenic-contaminated soil from the housing complex. Delays and agencies working at cross-purposes postponed testing until 2014, and it was 2016 until test results locating specific contamination sites were made public.

By the time the city closed the apartment complex and school, the EPA had been warning West Calumet residents to avoid the soil for a decade, with public notices and community meetings, even as delays caused in part by problems with contractors kept the agency from actually removing the suspect soil. Hot spots discovered during preliminary testing had not created a sense of urgency partly because a federal assessment of the Superfund site, released in 2011, concluded that "breathing the air, drinking tap water or playing in soil" in the area "is not expected to harm people's health" (Goodnough, 2016). After the EPA released the arsenic and lead data to city officials, Mayor Copeland decided to call for demolition of the housing complex regardless of the EPA's soil-removal plan. "I cannot multiply this enough times, to tell you the irreparable damage that can happen to your child," Copeland told residents of the complex at a meeting on August 3, 2016. "I do not see how you can remove tons and tons of dirt and don't aggravate the problem" (Goodnough, 2016).

In the meantime, several hundred children were tested for lead, and many were found to have elevated levels in their blood. Jennifer O'Malley, a spokeswoman for the Indiana State Department of Health, said that since early July, 474 residents of the housing complex and surrounding neighborhoods had been screened for lead in a month and a half, and that 29, including 19 children younger than 8, had elevated levels in their blood. In a July 14 letter to the EPA, however, Mayor Copeland said that preliminary tests had found that "hundreds of children suffer from excessive levels of lead in their blood" (Goodnough, 2016). Abby Goodnough reported in the *New York Times* (2017) that Shantel Allen had said tests had shown that all five of her children, who ranged in age from 2 to 10 in 2017, had toxic levels of lead in their blood. She said she had been told that her yard had some of the highest lead and arsenic levels in the area. "They show all the signs and symptoms of lead poisoning—they vomit randomly, have headaches," said Ms. Allen, who said she had retained a lawyer. "Nobody's given us any advice other than give them foods high in iron."

Lead may have been outlawed in paint decades ago, but its presence continues to poison children in major U.S. cities, such as New York City, where, in 2018, the *New York Times* reported that young people living in City Housing Authority projects were carrying the highest lead levels of anyone in the urban area. The levels, high enough to cause permanent damage, were higher than those found in the bodies of factory and construction workers. The CHA houses 400,000 people in New York City (Goodman et al., 2018, A-1).

Lead-Laced Water in Newark, New Jersey

By 2017, after initial denials, officials in Newark, New Jersey, which is predominantly nonwhite, admitted that water from both of its water-treatment plants was contaminated with lead at toxic levels. At first, the city had argued that the contamination was restricted to lead-lined pipes in small parts of the city, as they distributed filters to customers served by them. Later, by 2018, tests revealed that a significant proportion of homes in Newark were receiving lead-contaminated water. By that time, Mayor Ras Baraka and other officials were no longer maintaining that most of Newark's water was "absolutely safe to drink" (Leyden, 2018, A-23). By July 2018, tests had disclosed that more than half of residents served by the Paquannock treatment plant had been drinking water with lead levels that exceeded 15 parts per billion. A smaller proportion of residents served by the Wanaque plant were receiving lead-laced water, but one sample tested at 182 parts per billion.

The federal standard of 15 parts per billion is based on "old, old science," said Jennifer Lowry, a toxicologist at Children's Mercy Hospital in Kansas City, who is also chairwoman of the American Academy of Pediatrics' Council on Environmental Health. "We know so much more now" (Leyden, 2018, A-23). Lowry is one of many medical and environmental specialists who believe that 15 parts per billion may damage children's mental and physical development. That position has been upheld by the Centers for Disease Control. According to Lowry, "A health-based standard would certainly be below five [ppb]" (Leyden, 2018, A-23).

Further Reading

Bosman, Julie. "EPA Waited Too Long to Warn of Flint Water Danger, Report Says." *New York Times*, October 20, 2016. https://www.nytimes.com/2016/10/21/us/epa-waited-too-long-to-warn-of-flint-water-danger-report-says.html

Clark, Anna. *The Poisoned City: Flint's Water and the American Urban Tragedy*. New York: Metropolitan Books, 2018.

Fortin, Jacey. "Official in Flint Who Used a Racial Slur Against Black Residents Resigns." *New York Times*, June 6, 2016. https://www.nytimes.com/2017/06/06/us/flint-bills-racism-resignation.html

Fortin, Jacey. "In Flint, Overdue Bills for Unsafe Water Could Lead to Foreclosures." *New York Times*, May 4, 2017. https://www.nytimes.com/2017/05/04/us/flint-water-home-foreclosure.html

Friedman, Lisa. "EPA Wanted Years to Study Lead Paint Rule. It Got 90 Days." *New York Times*, December 27, 2017. https://www.nytimes.com/2017/12/27/us/epa-lead-paint.html

Gómez, Hernán, and Kim Dietrich. "The Children of Flint Were Not 'Poisoned'" *New York Times*, July 22, 2018. https://www.nytimes.com/2018/07/22/opinion/flint-lead-poisoning-water.html

Goodman, J. David, Al Baker, and James Glann. "Housing Agency Battled Findings of Lead Hazards." *New York Times*, November 19, 2018, A-1, A-16–17.

Goodnough, Abby. "Their Soil Toxic, 1,100 Indiana Residents Scramble to Find New Homes." *New York Times*, August 30, 2016. https://www.nytimes.com/2016/08/31/us/lead-contamination-public-housing-east-chicago-indiana.html

Goodnough, Abby. "Flint Weighs Scope of Harm to Children Caused by Lead in Water." *New York Times*, January 29, 2017. https://www.nytimes.com/2016/01/30/us/flint-weighs-scope-of-harm-to-children-caused-by-lead-in-water.html

Hanna-Attisha, Mona. *What the Eyes Don't See: A Story of Crisis, Resistance, and Hope in an American City.* New York: One World, 2018.

Hauser, Christine. "Flint Hit with Bacterial Illness as Residents Shun City Water." *New York Times*, October 4, 2016. https://www.nytimes.com/2016/10/05/us/flint-hit-with-bacterial-illness-as-residents-shun-city-water.html

Leyden, Liz. "Newark's Water Crisis Might Be Worse Than It Realized." *New York Times*, December 4, 2018, A-23.

Matheny, Keith. "Study: Flint Water Killed Unborn Babies; Many Moms Who Drank It Couldn't Get Pregnant." *Detroit Free Press*, Sept. 21, 2017. http://www.freep.com/story/news/local/michigan/flint-water-crisis/2017/09/20/flint-water-crisis-pregnancies/686138001/

Nohr, Emily. "EPA Superfund Site: Omaha Makes Strides on Lead Contamination." *Omaha World-Herald*, January 20, 2018, 1-A, 2-A.

Omaha Lead. National Priority List. Superfund. Environmental Protection Agency, n.d. Accessed October 10, 2017. https://www.epa.gov/superfund/national-priorities-list-npl-sites-state#NE

Peplow, Mark. "The Flint Water Crisis: How Citizen Scientists Exposed Poisonous Politics." *Nature* 559 (July 6, 2018): 180. https://www.nature.com/articles/d41586-018-05651-7

"The Racism at the Heart of Flint's Crisis." *New York Times*, March 25, 2016. https://www.nytimes.com/2016/03/25/opinion/the-racism-at-the-heart-of-flints-crisis.html

Sehgal, Parul. "Toxic History, Poisoned Water: The Story of Flint." *New York Times*, July 3, 2018. https://www.nytimes.com/2018/07/03/books/review

-poisoned-city-anna-clark-what-eyes-dont-see-mona-hanna-attisha-flint-water-crisis.html

Smith, Mitch. "Flint Mayor, Ushered in to Fix Water Crisis, Now Faces Recall." *New York Times,* November 7, 2017. https://www.nytimes.com/2017/11/06/us/flint-mayor-karen-weaver-recall-water.html

Smith, Mitch, Julie Bosman, and Monica Davey. "Five Years After a Crisis, Flint's Residents Doubt the Water Is Any Safer." *New York Times,* April 26, 2019, A-13.

Stamm, Alan. "Flint Book Author Anna Clark of Detroit Tells Why 'an Apology Was in My Voice.'" *Deadline Detroit,* July 1, 2018. http://www.deadlinedetroit.com/articles/20099/flint_book_author_anna_clark_works_to_cut_through_the_numbness_and_fatigue#.WzywD35JlcA

The Political Economy of Lead Poisoning and Other Water Quality Issues

Lead toxicity is not uncommon in the United States' 53,000 public drinking-water systems. Official testing standards are not accurate, as the number of problematic systems rises and as aging infrastructure that is more than a hundred years old decays. Even though lead was banned in drinking water during the middle 1980s, aging pipes that were manufactured out of lead, have lead soldering (or both) have been leaching. The EPA danger level for lead in drinking water (15 parts per billion) is not related to health effects, but to an assumption that 90 percent of homes with lead in water will fall on the "safe" side of the standard. The standard is, therefore, rather worthless for purposes of gauging toxicity. When homes are tested for lead, sample sizes are often so small (less than 100 in large systems) that results mean very little, until a crisis with political ramifications and media attention compel more testing, as in Flint, Michigan, during 2015 and 2016.

"We have a lot of threats to the water supply," said Dr. Jeffrey K. Griffiths, a professor of public health at Tufts University and a former chairman of the EPA's Drinking Water Committee. "And we have lots of really good professionals in the water industry who see themselves as protecting the public good. But it doesn't take much for our aging infrastructure or an unprofessional actor to allow that protection to fall apart" (Wines and Schwartz, 2016).

Problems with Testing and Detection

One member of the Water Committee, Yanna Lambrinidou, an adjunct assistant professor of science and technology studies at Virginia Tech

University (who led a team of experts that compiled the first detailed reports on the scope of Flint's lead contamination), argued that the existing testing standards do not go far enough. She cited a report by the American Water Works Association, which found unacceptable lead-contamination levels in as many as 70.5 percent of water systems across the United States.

Lead has caused problems in Sebring, Ohio's water pipes, for example. The town had been using chemicals to reduce corrosion in its leaded pipes. When the additive was eliminated, lead levels spiked, but five months went by before officials told pregnant women to stop drinking the water. Similarly, Washington, D.C. changed its formula for disinfecting water in 2001, after which lead levels rose rapidly in some areas to 20 times the federal safety standard. Notice was not served to residents for three years, after which water pipes serving 17,600 homes were removed and replaced. A *New York Times* survey indicated that in addition to Sebring and Washington, D.C., problems with lead have occurred in Durham and Greenville, North Carolina (2006), Columbia, South Carolina (2005), and Jackson, Mississippi (2015), among others (Wines and Schwartz, 2016).

"Over the last decade we've learned that the testing routines did not detect true risk from lead, that there are forms of lead that we're not testing for and that testing was too infrequent," said Griffiths, the former chairman of the EPA's Drinking Water Committee. "It's hard to see how the status quo in lead testing for water is adequately serving the public" (Wines and Schwartz, 2016). The Drinking Water Committee has called for strengthening of programs that reduce corrosion of lead pipes. It has also called for a testing standard that is based more on health effects.

In addition, lead is only one of several pollutants in drinking water. It is well known and easily tested. Others (such as the herbicide Atrazine in areas with intensive agriculture, such as cities in the Midwest) may pose problems in the future. The *Times* survey said that "many potentially harmful contaminants have yet to be evaluated, much less regulated. Efforts to address shortcomings often encounter pushback from industries like agriculture and mining that fear cost increases, and from politicians ideologically opposed to regulation" (Wines and Schwartz, 2016).

State and federal capacity to monitor drinking-water quality also has been declining; less testing usually means lower rates of detection. In 2013, the U.S. Association of State Drinking Water Administrators reported that federal officials had slashed drinking water grants, 17 states had cut drinking water budgets by more than a fifth, and 27 had cut spending on full-time employees. The reductions were impeding states' ability to protect public water safety and health. Republican state legislatures and the U.S. Congress are reducing regulatory scope and enforcement funding, often with the rationale that enforcing regulations poses problems for businesses. The reduction in enforcement comes at a time when many jurisdictions lack accurate maps that show where pipes that contain lead have been laid.

The EPA's Water Committee under President Barack Obama also proposed rules requiring governments to release water-quality test results to affected residents in a timely manner. These proposals were dropped once Donald Trump was elected president and Scott Pruitt was named to head the agency. The same group the Trump administration installed also was considering dumping another "Obama era" recommendation that all lead pipes be replaced, at a cost ($5,000 per pipe, by one estimate), that would consume between $16.5 billion and $50 billion nationwide), a small fraction of the $384 billion in deferred maintenance the EPA had said in 2016 would be needed by 2030 to maintain water safety in the United States.

By 2017, water-quality improvements that require regulations were at a standstill. Erik D. Olson, head of the health and environment program at the Natural Resources Defense Council, said: "You think our roads and bridges aren't being fixed? The stuff underground is just totally ignored. We're mostly living off the investment of our parents and grandparents for our drinking water supply" (Wines and Schwartz, 2016). A small number of cities had tapped local resources in the face of federal and state cuts. Lansing, Michigan, less than 60 miles from Flint but with a more affluent tax base, by 2017 had rebuilt more than 14,000 miles of leaded pipe at a cost of about $41 million.

Lead Poisoning Tied to Race and Income Levels

Lead toxicity is very common in the United States, especially in older neighborhoods populated mainly by nonwhite, poor people where water is carried in leaded pipes, houses contain leaded paint that was manufactured before it was banned, and lead remains in soil from smelters and industrial plants that have been closed. It is, as such, a tax upon the living from a time when its toxicity was not fully understood.

Lead occurs naturally in the Earth's crust, but human exposure is usually most intense through residual effects of mining, smelting, and recycling, as well as use of lead in paint, gasoline, and aviation fuel. More than three-quarters of global lead consumption results from the manufacture of lead-acid batteries for motor vehicles. Lead is, however, also used in many other products, such as pigments, paints, solder, stained glass, lead crystal glassware, ammunition, ceramic glazes, jewelry, toys, and in some cosmetics and traditional medicines.

The World Health Organization has found that poor and nonwhite people worldwide are more frequently exposed than the more affluent. This is also true in U.S. urban areas. According to WHO, "Lead is a cumulative toxicant that affects multiple body systems and is particularly harmful to young children. Lead in the body is distributed to the brain, liver, kidney and bones. It is stored in the teeth and bones, where it accumulates over time. Human exposure is usually assessed through the measurement of lead in blood. Lead in bone is released into blood during pregnancy and becomes a source of exposure to the developing fetus. There is no known level of lead exposure that is considered safe. Lead exposure is preventable" ("Lead Poisoning," 2013).

Usually, the only way to correct problems is to remove the source—replace the soil or the pipes. Such changes are usually very time-consuming and costly. Here we will consider effects of lead in soil (Omaha, Nebraska) and water (Flint, Michigan), both of which afflicted primarily black communities. Work to remove lead from the environment concentrates on exposure of children because, according to WHO, they absorb four to five times as much lead as adults from any given source. Children, not realizing its harmful effects, may pick at and eat old, peeling leaded paint in houses. "Young children are particularly vulnerable to the toxic effects of lead and can suffer profound and permanent adverse health effects, particularly affecting the development of the brain and nervous system. Lead also causes long-term harm in adults, including increased risk of high blood pressure and kidney damage. Exposure of pregnant women to high levels of lead can cause miscarriage, stillbirth, premature birth and low birth weight, as well as minor malformations" ("Lead Poisoning," 2013).

Lead at low levels is a silent killer, but at higher concentrations, according to WHO, it affects the brain and the central nervous system, provoking coma, convulsions, and eventually, at high doses, death. Not everyone dies, but children who remain alive may sustain behavioral disorders, including mental retardation. Low levels of toxicity display no obvious symptoms and once were considered safe, but even these can produce reduced intelligence quotient (IQ), as well as other behavioral changes, including antisocial behavior and reduction of attention span, all of which reduce educational performance. Other long-term, low-level effects, according to WHO, include anemia, hypertension, renal impairment, immune system toxicity, and toxicity to reproductive organs. The most destructive long-term effect is that "the neurological and behavioral effects of lead are believed to be irreversible" ("Lead Poisoning," 2013).

Lead was banned in paint and other consumer goods made and sold in the United States after 1978; however, lead paint in old buildings is still a very common source of contamination. Lead dust can remain on surfaces even after they have been stripped or painted over. Food grown in soil laced with lead even decades after a source has been demolished may cause levels of harmful toxicity, especially in children. Canned goods may have been soldered with lead, and imported toys may contain lead. Water pipes in older parts of cities, often those that house minority and poor people, also may have been soldered with lead. Leaded paint and gasoline is still a problem in many countries, to a degree that the World Health Organization has organized a Global Alliance to Eliminate Lead Paint.

Abby Goodnough and Diantha Parkerjan wrote in the *New York Times* (2016), "Low levels of lead exposure usually have no obvious or immediate symptoms, which means it can go undetected. But over time, even low levels of lead in blood can have profound effects on the brain and nervous system. Lower intelligence, difficulty in paying attention and with fine motor skills, and lower academic achievement have all been connected to elevated lead levels. Some studies have also linked lead exposure to violent behavior, and higher crime rates that can span at least two generations."

Once inflicted, lead poisoning cannot be reversed or cured, so remediation begins with prevention. A diet rich in vitamin C, calcium, and iron can cause lead to be absorbed less rapidly, however. Chelation therapy also may help with injections of chemicals that bind with lead so that some of it will be excreted in urine. This therapy will not reverse lead poisoning that has already taken place, usually to the nervous system and brain.

Anyone with a risk of lead exposure should be tested, beginning in infancy. Many urban areas in the United States and Canada have a history of industry begun in the nineteenth century that used lead, leaving residues that remain in soil. In Baltimore, for example, testing by Maryland state authorities between 1993 and 2005 revealed that 65,000 children were carrying dangerously high levels of lead in their bodies. Even though the number of children with lead poisoning has been falling in Chicago, in 2015, 60,000 were found to have experienced reduced test scores in math and reading that very likely were related to it (Goodnough and Parkerjan, 2016). Blood tests may not fully indicate the extent of lead exposure because it quickly leaves the blood to become absorbed by other parts of the body, especially bones (including teeth), as well as vital organs.

The level at which lead poses a danger has been reduced over recent years. The CDC (Centers for Disease Control) uses a standard of

5 micrograms per deciliter to classify children with elevated blood lead levels, half the level it had used before 2012. The standard is a matter of political convenience (and compromise), not a medical indicator. Actually, the only level of true safety of lead in a child's blood is *zero*. Even very low levels may impede cognitive function and produce other adverse effects. The CDC recommends chelation therapy when a child's blood lead level exceeds 45 micrograms per deciliter.

Professor Marc Edwards of Virginia Tech, who was instrumental in exposing damaging lead levels in Flint, Michigan, documented high levels of lead in blood samples taken from children in Washington, D.C. between 2000 and 2003, which he associated with contaminated drinking water. Edwards in 2013 said that Washington, D.C. women also suffered an abnormally high rate of miscarriages as well as spontaneous abortions during that same time period. Edwards's findings contradicted a report that the U.S. Environmental Protection Agency had published nine years earlier stating that Washington, D.C.'s water was safe to drink.

Water Quality: Toledo's "Green Slime"

Aside from lead, the measurement of water quality is largely unknown territory, with the EPA having compiled a list of more than 100 chemicals that are usually neither tested, nor regulated. Cities that are largely poor and minority have no way to even scratch the surface. Beyond that, some water carries potentially dangerous microbes and viruses. Watercourses that are used for human consumption include estrogen mimics that leach from birth control pills and other pharmaceuticals. The Platte River, which supplies part of Omaha's supply (along the Missouri River), is also home to fish with two sets of sex organs caused by estrogen mimics flushed down toilets in the Denver metropolitan area.

During 2014, Toledo, Ohio, shut down its drinking water supply for three days, after a toxin generated by an algae-like bacteria called microcystin clogged intake valves from Lake Erie. The "green slime," as the mass of rapidly reproducing algae is locally known, is a product of fertilizer runoff from agricultural areas around the lake, and it has become a regular visitor to Toledo's shoreline every late summer and early autumn in recent years. It can cause liver damage in humans and has killed some animals that drank large amounts of Lake Erie water. By late summer 2017, residents were being warned not to bathe in (much less drink) the bright-green water, satellite photos of which were going viral on the Internet.

Much of the algae is fed by massive amounts of nitrates from fertilizers that wash from farms into largely land-locked western Lake Erie. Even removing the nitrates can cause problems: "Researchers were long unaware that removing nitrates from finished water can leave behind a toxic byproduct, nitrosamines, the cancer-causing chemical found in cooked bacon," according to a report in the *New York Times* (Wines and Schwartz, 2016).

Local activists in Toledo framed water quality, including the "green slime," as a broader environmental justice issue for the city's poor and nonwhite communities. Keith Jordan, development director for JLJ Vision Outreach, said that along the Maumee River shoreline, "Urban residents are often most vulnerable. They also represent the communities that will be hit hardest by climate change and algal blooms. . . . Ohio lawmakers must take immediate action to ensure the health and safety of area residents" (Henry, 2017).

Toledo city councilman Peter Ujvagi said that scientific data indicate that most of the problem stems from farm runoff in northwest Ohio. He added that the Trump administration's plan to gut budgets for the U.S. Environmental Protection Agency, the National Oceanic and Atmospheric Administration, and other agencies with major roles in Great Lakes research is "a travesty." "We can't let our elected officials turn their backs on our natural resources," Ujvagi said. Lucas County commissioner Carol Contrada asserted a human right to clean water. "Water is really what's made civilizations flourish," she said (Henry, 2017).

Nick Mandros, northwest Ohio policy coordinator for the Ohio Environmental Council, said: "A river holds a connection to a community. Toxic algae will continue to threaten drinking water until we get serious about it" (Henry, 2017). One of the local activists who keeps up the pressure is Mike Ferner, a former Toledo City Council member, Vietnam-era veteran, author, and peace activist. He sometimes gets a little theatrical, pouring the green slime into the fountain in front of the government building downtown, as he keeps the issue on the front burner, asking why Toledo is being forced to clean up the mismanagement of agribusiness out of town.

The toxic algae that is fouling the water in minority and poor neighborhoods of Toledo has become a problem in many other areas, as illustrated by John Flesher and Angeliki Kastanis in an account for the Associated Press:

> Competing in a bass fishing tournament two years ago, Todd Steele cast his rod from his 21-foot motorboat—unaware that he was being poisoned. A thick, green scum coated western Lake Erie. And Steele, a semipro angler, was sickened by it. Driving home to Port Huron, Michigan, he felt

lightheaded, nauseous. By the next morning he was too dizzy to stand, his overheated body covered with painful hives. Hospital tests blamed toxic algae, a rising threat to U.S. waters. "It attacked my immune system and shut down my body's ability to sweat," Steele said. "If I wasn't a healthy 51-year-old and had some type of medical condition, it could have killed me." He recovered, but Lake Erie hasn't. Nor have other waterways choked with algae that's sickening people, killing animals and hammering the economy. (Flesher and Kastanis, 2017)

The problem over a few years had gone from an occasional nuisance to a severe, widespread hazard, as increasing fertilizer runoff from farms has poured into many lakes and rivers. It was not unique to one area, as toxic blobs have fouled waterways from Chesapeake Bay to the Snake River in Idaho, as well as to reservoirs in California's Central Valley. Florida beaches were closed when algae blooms oozed from Lake Okeechobee. Oxygen-starved "dead zones" caused by algae decay have increased thirtyfold since 1960, "causing massive fish kills . . . a trend likely to accelerate with global warming" (Flesher and Kastanis, 2017).

In large parts of Florida's southeastern and southwestern coasts, a toxic algal "red tide" killed millions of fish during the summer of 2018. All of these events have been exacerbated by warmer water and farm and phosphorus runoff, as well as leakage from sewer systems. In 2018, Lake Superior, which has more than 2,700 miles of shoreline, became the site of the largest masses of green, oozing algae ever detected in the Great Lakes. "We believe it to be the largest, most intense bloom yet," said Robert Sterner, the director of the Large Lakes Observatory at the University of Minnesota Duluth. Sterner said that Lake Superior "is one of the fastest-warming lakes on earth." Donald M. Anderson, a senior scientist at the Woods Hole Oceanographic Institution, said that scientists have been finding algal blooms in many places they have not previously appeared. "The fresh water problem has exploded in the United States," he said (Hauser, 2018).

Authorities have often relied on farmers to voluntarily curtail runoff, but this approach has not reduced the amount of toxic algae in the water. As the U.S. Department of Agriculture has spent more than $29 billion in the United States to stem the algae since 2009 (as the "green slime" on Lake Erie has grown worse), calls are growing for legal restrictions on use of fertilizers in both the United States and Canada. More than $51 million has been spent to change farming practices in western Lake Erie's watershed, which includes Toledo, on a small fraction of farms, to no avail. "We've had decades of approaching this issue largely through a voluntary framework," said Jon Devine, senior attorney for the Natural Resources Defense Council. "Clearly the existing system isn't working." The toxic algae bloom shut off water in Toledo and nearby areas to 400,000 people in 2014. The next year, the "green slime" covered 300 square miles, an area as large as New York City. The amount of toxic algae in the waters of western Lake Ontario has doubled in two decades, according to researcher Laura Johnson of Ohio's Heidelberg University (Flesher and Kastanis, 2017).

By 2017, the life of the green slime at Toledo's lakeside was extending into late autumn, an indication of warmer-than-usual water temperatures as well as the increasing amount of nitrates (fertilizer) and municipal sewer overflows that feed the algae. The mayor of Toledo asked President Donald Trump for help from the federal government to clean up the lake and declare the western end impaired (e.g., a disaster area), as the coverage of the slime grew, extending to the Canadian coast of Lake Ontario to the north. "Some [people] have taken to stockpiling bottled water in the summer months when algae blooms blanket the western end in the shallowest of the Great Lakes. Store shelves were emptied of bottled water . . . when algae pushed into a river that flows through downtown Toledo into the lake," wrote John Seewer of the Associated Press in the *Toronto Star*. "There is something very wrong with our country when our rivers and lakes turn green," Toledo mayor Paula Hicks-Hudson wrote in a letter to Trump. "As I look out my office at a green river, I can tell you one thing: the status quo is not working" (Seewer, 2017). Trump did not reply.

The decline in oxygen levels that afflicts Lake Erie is part of a worldwide trend, as described by Denise Breitburg and colleagues in *Science* (2018). "This oxygen loss, or deoxygenation, is one of the most important changes occurring in an ocean increasingly modified by human activities that have raised temperatures, carbon-dioxide levels, and nutrient inputs and have altered the abundances and distributions of marine species," they wrote. In the open oceans, deoxygenation has been intensified by rising acidity provoked by carbon dioxide absorption, as well as the injection of nutrients from agriculture and sewage that are predominant in Lake Erie around Toledo, as well as other inland bodies of water.

The decline in oxygen levels has intensified since the 1950s, due nearly entirely to human activities, from increasing emissions of carbon dioxide and other greenhouse gases and overload of nitrogen-based fertilizers. All of these activities combine along coastlines at the mouths of major rivers (such as the Mississippi in the United States and the Ganges in India and Bangladesh) to produce oxygen-starved "dead zones."

"Oxygen is fundamental to biological and biogeochemical processes in the ocean," wrote Breitburg and colleagues (2018). "Its decline can cause major changes in ocean productivity, biodiversity, and biogeochemical cycles. Analyses of direct measurements at sites around the world indicate that oxygen-minimum zones in the open ocean have expanded by several million square kilometers and that hundreds of coastal sites now have oxygen concentrations low enough to limit the distribution and abundance of animal populations and alter the cycling of important nutrients."

Pollution of Lake Erie was a major reason for an unusual initiative on Toledo's ballot on February 26, 2018. The ballot issue asked voters whether Lake Erie, which supplies water to parts of Ohio, New York, and Michigan, as well as Ontario (including the cities of Cleveland, Buffalo, and Toronto) should be protected by a "bill of rights" "to exist, flourish, and naturally evolve" (Williams, 2018, A-8). The ballot issue was a result not only of the green slime, but also invasive fish, runoff laced with fertilizer and animal manure, and fouling of Toledo's drinking water. Its approval (61 to 39 percent) may provoke legal challenges that could begin to define an important doctrine in environmental law: can a body of water be protected from pollution by a guarantee of its "rights"? At present, no precedent exists, although the White Earth Band of Ojibwe has granted its wild rice legal rights, including "the right to pure water" (Williams, 2018, A-8).

As 2019 wore on, there was more potentially bad news for Toledo's green slime, and similar growths elsewhere. If the U.S. Constitution could use some help at improving Lake Erie, perhaps rice husks can come to the rescue. When rice husks were heated to 250° C and treated with hydrochloric acid, then added to water samples, 70 to 95 percent of microcystins were removed from the water within 40 minutes, according to a study by scientists at the University of Toledo. "Therefore, treated RH [rice husks] enables rapid and efficient removal of MCs [microcystins] from water and they can be recycled for use as a raw material. Overall, treated RH can contribute to mitigation of environmental and health effects caused by MCs and reduce concerns for toxic waste disposal" (Dilrukshika et al., 2019).

"Delivering safe water is critical, and finding an economically viable solution to deliver safe water to people all over the world is going to be really important. The ability of this simple material to be powerful enough to address this issue is impressive," said Dr. Jon Kirchhoff, Distinguished University Professor and chair of the Chemistry and Biochemistry Department at the University of Toledo (Linkhorn, 2019).

Two Wells in Winona, Texas

Phyllis Glazer, who owns the 2,200-acre Blazing Saddles Ranch in Winona, about 100 miles east of Dallas, where she has horses, donkeys, zebras, and emus, never planned to become an environmental activist. She had never planned to spend most of her inheritance protecting her land and that of her neighbors from an enormous toxic dump run by Gibraltar Chemical's subsidiary American Ecology (how Orwellian a name!), a deep-well injection site for hazardous wastes, from what she called "2,200 acres of environmental liability." From 1981, when the site opened, to 1997, when it closed, trucks from all over the region lined up to dump hundreds of tons of toxic material down the narrow, one-mile-deep twin shafts, where it supposedly was held in an impermeable rock formation. But the safety of such wells is in question.

According to a report from the Virginia-based Center for Health, Environment and Justice, "Supporters of deep wells say there are no documented examples of groundwater contamination from leaking underground wells. This is false." The report goes on to list cases of just such failures in Alabama, Florida, Louisiana, and North Carolina (Motavalli, 1998). In 2006, Tammy Cromer-Campbell published a book, *Fruit of the Orchard: Environmental Justice in East Texas*, describing how "residents were told that the company would plant fruit trees on the land left over from its ostensible salt-water injection well. Soon after the plant opened, however, residents started noticing huge orange clouds rising from the facility and an increase in rates of cancer and birth defects in both humans and animals" (Cromer-Campbell, 2006).

Phyllis Glazer didn't know anything about American Ecology, the hazardous waste dump, or its effects when she bought the ranch. Faced with a future of toxic maladies, however, Glazer organized Mothers Organized to Stop Environmental Sins (MOSES) to aid Winona's mostly poor black and Latino families as Winona crumbled and many of them became sick. Eventually, the operators of the dump pulled up stakes and departed, but the cost to residents' health was enormous. After that, American Ecology tried to crush Glazer and the rest of her family by suing them. The company failed at that as well, but in the process drained Glazer of nearly all her money. The people of Winona couldn't prove that the dump gave them cancer, lupus, respiratory problems, and other afflictions, illnesses that were running rampant in the community. Hud Clarke's 11-year-old daughter, Mandy, died of Hodgkin's disease, having gotten sick at age 8.

Anita Lamb, 39, had frequent migraine headaches, respiratory infections, osteoporosis, short-term memory loss, and anemia, as well as chronic lupus, "a serious ailment that attacks muscles and mucous membranes and is often seen in heavily polluted environments, in 1996." Lamb believes that "85 percent of what's wrong with me is because of that plant. The doctors won't say it's definitely because of exposure to chemicals, but that's what I believe. They should pay our medical bills, because we were damaged for the rest of our lives" (Motavalli, 1998). "When we hung our clothes on the line, they would smell like chemicals," said Charles Sharpe, a dignified septuagenarian and church elder. "And then we started getting sickness in our community. And people started dying, many of them younger than me." Sharpe, once 269 pounds, shriveled to 155 (Motavalli, 1998).

Property values plunged in Winona—no one could sell if they had wanted to. Glazer remained committed to the cause, however. "Winona is known as a black town and a poor town," she told Jim Motavalli of *E—The Environmental Magazine* (1998). "The people can't afford to pay their M.O.S.E.S. dues, but they bring me food and gave me a lot of support when things got really bad here. I've been shot at, had my animals killed. Trucks have tried to run me off the road. It's calmed down a bit since then."

Further Reading

Breitburg, Denise, Lisa A. Levin, Andreas Oschlies, Marilaure Grégoire, Francisco P. Chavez, Daniel J. Conley, Véronique Garçon, Denis Gilbert, Dimitri Gutiérrez, Kirsten Isensee, Gil S. Jacinto, Karin E. Limburg, Ivonne Montes, S. W. A. Naqvi, Grant C. Pitcher, Nancy N. Rabalais, Michael R. Roman, Kenneth A. Rose, Brad A. Seibel, Maciej Telszewski, Moriaki Yasuhara, and Jing Zhang. "Declining Oxygen in the Global Ocean and Coastal Waters." *Science* 359, January 5, 2018. https://doi.org/10.1126/science.aam7240. http://science.sciencemag.org/content/359/6371/eaam7240

Cromer-Campbell, Tammy, Fruit of the Orchard: Environmental Justice in East Texas. University of North Texas web page, 2006. https://untpress.unt.edu/catalog/3321

Dilrukshika, S. W. Palagama, Amila M. Devasurendra, David Baliu-Rodriguez, Jon R. Kirchhoff, and Dragan Isailovic. "Treated Rice Husk as a Recyclable Sorbent for the Removal of Microcystins from Water." *Science of the Total Environment* 666 (May 20, 2019): 1292–1300. https://www.sciencedirect.com/science/article/pii/S0048969719305200?via%3Dihub

Egan, Dan. *The Death and Life of the Great Lakes.* New York: W. W. Norton, 2017.

Flesher, John, and Angeliki Kastanis. "Toxic Algae Flourishes Despite Vast Sums Spent to Prevent It." *Los Angeles Times*, November 16, 2017. https://www.seattletimes.com/business/toxic-algae-flourishes-despite-vast-sums-spent-to-prevent-it-2/

Goodnough, Abby, and Diantha Parkerjan. "The Facts About Lead Exposure and Its Irreversible Damage." *New York Times*, January 29, 2016. https://www.nytimes.com/2016/01/30/us/lead-poisoning.html

Hauser, Christine. "Algae Bloom in Lake Superior Raises Worries on Climate Change and Tourism." *New York Times*, August 29, 2018. https://www.nytimes.com/2018/08/29/science/lake-superior-algae-toxic.html

Henry, Tom. "Algae Termed Environmental Justice Issue; Trump Plan Called 'Travesty'." *Toledo Blade*, March 23, 2017. http://www.toledoblade.com/Politics/2017/03/23/Algae-termed-environmental-justice-issue.html

"Lead Poisoning and Health: Fact Sheet." World Health Organization (WHO), United Nations. September 18, 2013. http://sdg.iisd.org/news/who-releases-lead-poisoning-and-health-fact-sheet/

Linkhorn, Tyrel. "Inexpensive Agricultural Waste Product Can Remove Microcystin from Water, New UToledo Research Finds." *Toledo Blade*, May 21, 2019. http://utnews.utoledo.edu/index.php/05_21_2019/inexpensive-agricultural-waste-product-can-remove-microcystin-from-water-new-utoledo-research-finds

Motavalli, Jim. "Toxic Targets: Polluters That Dump on Communities of Color Are Finally Being Brought to Justice." 1998. E-magazine. http://www.ejnet.org/ej/Estory.html

Seewer, John. "Lake Erie Algae Bloom Touching Shores of Ontario and Two U.S. States is the Largest in Years." *Toronto Star*, October 8, 2017. https://www.thestar.com/news/world/2017/10/08/lake-erie-algae-bloom-touching-shores-of-ontario-and-two-us-states-is-the-largest-in-years.html

Williams, Timothy. "Legal Rights for Lake Eire? Voters in Ohio City Will Decide." *New York Times*, February 18, 2018, A-8.

Wines, Michael, and John Schwartz. "Unsafe Lead Levels in Tap Water Not Limited to Flint." *New York Times*, February 8, 2016. https://www.nytimes.com/2016/02/09/us/regulatory-gaps-leave-unsafe-lead-levels-in-water-nationwide.html

Canadian Tar Sands: From Treaty Forest to Moonscape

Native peoples in Alberta who have taken a leading role in fighting mining of tar sands have found some of their homelands devastated to the point that the landscape has been compared to a moonscape. Native peoples in the United States also have taken a role in opposing the Keystone XL Pipeline, which is being proposed to carry tar sands oil from Alberta to the U.S. Gulf Coast for refining. Roads carrying equipment to the tar sands fields have been blocked, and several arrests have taken place on Nez Perce land in Idaho and the Lakotas' Pine Ridge reservation in South Dakota. Opposition to tar sands development and the Keystone XL has become robust because completion of the pipeline allows tar sands to be further developed, leading to higher greenhouse gas levels in the atmosphere. By 2013, one-third of Alberta's economy was tied in some way to the tar sands, including royalties worth more than $4 billion during its 2011–2012 fiscal year, before crashing oil prices caused the boom to be curtailed (Lizza, 2013, 47).

Stephen Harper, Canadian prime minister during the tar sands boom, had aggressively promoted tar sands development with plans for 10,000 miles of pipelines eastward and westward across the country as well as the better-known Keystone XL southward from the tar sands fields. By 2014, the Canadian federal Parliament, with Harper's backing, had revoked or annulled 70 environmental laws. In its 2013–2014 budget, the Canadian federal government allocated about $22 million to promote tar sands–based oil outside of Canada (Leslie, 2014, A-19). In 2014, Canadian oil producers expected their web of new pipeline capacity to nearly double the country's production of tar sands–based oil by 2025 from 3.5 million to 6 million barrels a day, mostly for export (Krauss and Austen, 2014, B-4).

By 2015 and 2016, Canadian voters revolted, electing Liberal Justin Trudeau and several left-leaning legislators, even in the usually conservative tar sands heartland of Alberta. Oil prices dropped as well, making tar sands mining less appealing financially, and so exploitation of the area slowed—but it did not stop. Indigenous opponents of both tar sands mining and the Keystone XL Pipeline also united with non-Native environmental groups to contend that the amount of fossil-fuel energy required to produce useful energy from tar sands exceeds that of conventional oil, contributing to greenhouse gas emissions. Tar sands have the consistency of very gritty peanut butter and are so viscous that they must be thinned (using fossil-fuel energy) to allow refining into usable fuel.

Junk Energy and the Creation of the "Moonscape"

Exploitation of tar sands at the surface requires a form of strip mining that scars the Earth in ways that will not be quickly or easily repaired. The opponents assert that tar sands are a relatively new form of fossil fuel—the last thing the Earth needs when carbon dioxide levels in the atmosphere have risen to more than 400 parts per million (ppm), more than 40 percent above peak preindustrial levels, with damage to the climate as well as rising seas and oceanic acidity. On a local level, many people worry about oil spills in fragile areas, such as the Nebraska Sand Hills, that could contaminate the Ogallala Aquifer in an area where water is scarce. This aquifer supplies 78 percent of public water and 83 percent of irrigation water in Nebraska, almost a third of the irrigation water used in the United States.

According to NASA, the Alberta fields, which were first mined in 1967, are "the world's largest tar sands deposit, with a capacity to produce 174.5 billion barrels of oil—2.5 million barrels of oil per day for 186 years"

("Athabasca Oil Sands," 2011). (The United States as a whole consumes 15 million to 20 million barrels of oil per day.) Environmental activist Bill McKibben has called tar sands mining and the Keystone XL the "fuse to the biggest carbon bomb on the planet" (Tollefson, 2013). "Saying that the tar sands are not necessarily worse than coal is like saying that drinking arsenic is not necessarily worse than drinking cyanide," said geophysicist Raymond Pierrehumbert of the University of Chicago. He said that fully developing the tar sands could by itself, even if we suddenly stopped burning coal, "warm the planet an additional 3.6 degrees Fahrenheit by century's end—an amount that climate scientists warn could be catastrophic" (Koch 2014).

Tar sands are a mixture of clay and sand with bitumen, a thick, low-grade form of petroleum similar to asphalt. According to Thomas Homer-Dixon, who teaches global governance at the Balsillie School of International Affairs, "Tar sands production is one of the world's most environmentally damaging activities. It wrecks vast areas of boreal forest through surface mining and subsurface production. It sucks up huge quantities of water from local rivers, turns it into toxic waste and dumps the contaminated water into tailing ponds that now cover nearly 70 square miles" (Homer-Dixon, 2013).

Also, wrote Homer-Dixon (2013), "bitumen is junk energy. A joule, or unit of energy, invested in extracting and processing bitumen returns only four to six joules in the form of crude oil. In contrast, conventional oil production in North America returns about 15 joules. Because almost all of the input energy in tar sands production comes from fossil fuels, the process generates significantly more carbon dioxide than conventional oil production." According to NASA, oil sands refining produces the equivalent of 86 to 103 kilograms of carbon dioxide for every barrel of crude oil produced. By comparison, 27 to 58 kilograms of carbon dioxide are emitted in the conventional production of a barrel of crude oil. By 2012, the mining and refining of tar sands in Canada consumed as much natural gas as Canada was using for home heating (Kolbert, 2007, 49). The gas is used to produce synthetic oil and by-products, such as gasoline. Tar sands require about 15 to 40 percent more energy in manufacture compared to conventional crude oil.

Carol Berry of the Indian Country Today Media Network described the environmental damage of tar sands mining to Indigenous peoples' lands in Alberta (2012):

> If you can imagine the bleak landscape of the moon, you can envision the desolate, 54,000-square-mile tar sands of northern Alberta.... "It's literally

a toxic wasteland—bare ground and black ponds and lakes—tailings ponds—with an awful smell," said Warner Nazile . . . [an activist] from British Columbia and member of the Wet'suwet'en First Nation. The mining is "despoiling an area roughly the size of England." . . . University of Alberta scientists "found indications that contamination from the tailings ponds was polluting a huge aquifer that ultimately flows into the Arctic Ocean," Nazile said. Two aboriginal communities downstream from the oil sands have experienced higher-than-average rates of cancer and other health problems, he added.

James Hansen, former senior climate scientist at NASA and author of *Storms of My Grandchildren,* described the impact of tar sands mining: "Canada's tar sands, deposits of sand saturated with bitumen, contain twice the amount of carbon dioxide emitted by global oil use in our entire history. If we were to fully exploit this new oil source, and continue to burn our conventional oil, gas and coal supplies, concentrations of carbon dioxide in the atmosphere eventually would reach levels higher than in the Pliocene era, more than 2.5 million years ago, when sea level was at least 50 feet higher than it is now. That level of heat-trapping gases would assure that the disintegration of the ice sheets would accelerate out of control. Sea levels would rise and destroy coastal cities. Global temperatures would become intolerable. Twenty to 50 percent of the planet's species would be driven to extinction. Civilization would be at risk. . . . If this sounds apocalyptic, it is" (Hansen, 2012).

The concentration of carbon dioxide in the atmosphere has risen from 280 ppm to slightly more than 410 ppm over the past 160 years, as of 2017. The tar sands contain enough carbon—240 gigatons—to add 120 ppm to that total. Tar shale, similar to tar sands found mainly in the United States, contains at least an additional 300 gigatons of carbon. If we turn to these dirtiest of fuels, instead of finding ways to phase out our addiction to fossil fuels, there is no hope of keeping carbon concentrations below 500 ppm—a level that would, as Earth's history shows, leave our children a climate system that is out of their control.

The Ruination of Native Lands in Alberta

In late August 2013, in the midst of the debate over the environmental effects of tar sands, a large toxic waste spill, the largest of its kind in North America, rolled over indigenous lands in northern Alberta. The *Toronto Globe and Mail* reported that "the substance is the inky black colour of oil, and the treetops are brown. . . . Across a broad expanse . . .

the landscape is dead. It has been poisoned by a huge spill of 9.5 million litres of toxic waste from an oil and gas operation in northern Alberta, the third major leak in a region whose residents are now questioning whether enough is being done to maintain aging energy infrastructure" ("Every Tree," 2013).

"Every plant and tree died," Dene Tha' First Nation chief James Ahnassay told the *Toronto Globe and Mail* ("Every Tree," 2013). The Dene Tha' said that the spill ran along a trapline (animal-harvesting area) about half a mile from its reserve, a mile from the same people's fishing grounds in the Zama River, where its members fish. The 103-acre spill sprang from a breach in a pipeline owned by the Apache Corporation near Alberta's far northern border. Company representatives said that it was salty water tainted with a small amount of oil and that no people were harmed.

Such a spill is not a one-time event. A 1,000-person Beaver Lake indigenous community near Lac La Biche (in northern Alberta) now lives with a moonscape all the time and has been nearly surrounded by oil sands extraction, as its hunting and fishing range has been laced by 600 miles of roads. In 2008, the Beaver Lake Cree Nation filed suit against the governments of Alberta and Canada alleging breach of treaty rights. The defendants fought to have the suit dismissed (as "frivolous") but failed as the Court of the Queen's Bench upheld the community's standing in court in a ruling by Justice Beverley Browne. The governments appealed, and on April 30, 2013, the Alberta Court of Appeal again upheld their right to sue. The suit claims co-management rights under the treaty.

British Columbia photographer Garth Lenz said, "I'd heard about the tar sands but I hadn't been, so I went there and spent a couple of days and was pretty much flabbergasted by the scale of the devastation and the impacts. I had photographed industrial devastation all over, including some of the most massive clear-cuts on the planet, right in British Columbia and in Chile and Patagonia, so I'd seen that massive industrialization of the landscape on a huge, huge scale," he said. "But I was completely unprepared for what I found. Because this is just completely off-the-grid crazy—the scale is unbelievable" ("Athabasca Oil Sands," 2011).

Lenz pointed out that the development harms fish and caribou that indigenous peoples in the area rely on. "It's the complete eradication of an ecosystem," Lenz said. "I mean, the forest is clear-cut, the wetlands are drained and dredged, the soil is dug up, replaced by massive mines and toxic ponds which you can see from outer space" ("Athabasca Oil Sands," 2011). Chief Bill Erasmus of the Yellowknife Northwest Territories in northern Canada said: "Our people, in some areas, can no longer eat the fish. . . . Our people can no longer drink the water. Water levels are decreasing. Where I'm from, it's never been like that before" (Capriccioso, 2011).

In 2014, a report by the Joint Oil Sands Monitoring Program alleged that dams holding back wastewater from oil sands mining waste were seeping 6.5 million liters (or 1.7 million gallons) daily into the Athabasca River's groundwater, including bitumen, arsenic, cadmium cyanide, phenols, naphthenic acids, and other metals. "In short, [the study] highlights past studies identifying tailings ponds as significant sources of groundwater contamination, and brings to light that groundwater contaminated by leaking tailings ponds is almost certainly flowing into the Athabasca River," said William Donahue, a freshwater science specialist based in Edmonton (Nikiforuk, 2014).

After several decades of tar sands extraction and refining, the tailings piles of northern Alberta had grown behind earthen dams 11 miles long that now encircle several lakes of toxic sludge. The accumulating waste has spawned a battle over who will pay for a cleanup that could cost an estimated $22 billion. "At issue is how, and by extension when, the ponds must be returned to a natural state," wrote Kevin Orland for Bloomberg News. As industry seeks more time, environmentalists assert that the problem has intensified for 50 years, as waste piles up. By 2017, the tailings ponds covered 97 square miles and held 340 billion gallons of mining waste (Orland, 2018).

Blockade by the Nez Perce

The Nez Perce hosted Lewis and Clark in 1805 and later, in 1877, led the U.S. Army on a months-long chase over some of the roughest landscape in North America. In 2013, the fighting spirit of the Nez Perce again was marshaled by transport through their lands of huge loads destined for Alberta's tar sands fields. On August 5, 2013, more than 200 Nez Perce intercepted a convoy of trucks destined for the oil sands fields of Alberta, forming a blockade that was broken up by police, who arrested 30 people, including chairman Silas Whitman and six members of the tribe's executive council.

In 2013, as in 1877, the Nez Perce didn't appreciate being pushed around, and they quickly put events into context. "The development of American corporate society has always been—and it's true throughout the world—on the backs of those who are oppressed, repressed, or depressed," Silas Whitman, chairman of the Tribal Executive Committee, told the *New York Times*. "We couldn't turn the cheek anymore." After their meeting, the Nez Perce leaders decided to face arrest as a group

(Johnson, 2013). Whitman, 72 years of age at the time, was one of several Nez Perce arrested at the barricade as police dismantled it. The blockade lasted four nights.

"Lights! Lights!" they shouted as amber-colored flashers on a pilot truck came into view in the darkness just after midnight along Highway 12 on the Nez Perce reservation. The Indian Country Media Network reported that "a rush of more than 200 tribal members and others—from grandmothers to children—followed, all determined to stop a football-field-sized mega-load from passing through their sacred lands," erecting wooden barriers, as "police cruisers idling in the darkness nearby flipped on their headlights and rooftop light bars and rolled to within yards of the blockade. It was an eerie blue-and-red strobe-lit standoff: Tribal members sang and drummed and whooped, while state and tribal police faced them, arms crossed. Looming behind the police came the mega-load, its cylindrical face appearing as an enormous ghostly moon, swathed in a white tarp" (Taylor, 2013). The trucks they stopped were carrying a 23-foot-tall, 322-ton water evaporator hooked onto a diesel truck front and back, 243 feet long.

Early in 2013, the Nez Perce Executive Council adopted a position opposing transportation of very large (mega-load) mining equipment through its land along 780 miles of Highway 12. Such shipments have become common there. "They will also be traveling really close to our creation story," said McCoy Oatman, chairman of the Nez Perce Executive Committee. "It's called 'The Heart of the Monster.' It's essentially the birthplace of the Nez Perce people. It [the route] runs dangerously close to that site, and that's pretty significant for us" ("Nez Perce Victory," 2013).

The protests paid off. The Nez Perce also joined with Idaho Rivers United, an environmental group, and took the matter to Boise's federal district court, where Chief Judge B. Lynn Winmill stopped further transport of mega-loads until the Nez Perce and the U.S. Forest Service assessed their environmental impact. The Nez Perce believe that their scenic route was being turned into an industrial corridor as federal and state officials ignored them. In September 2013, the Forest Service closed the Nez Perce route to mega-loads and required consultation with the tribe in the future. "The closure order is effective immediately and is in place until the agency agrees to lift it, mostly likely when forest officials complete a study on the impacts the shipments could have on the river corridor," the Associated Press said. "The agency has also vowed to consult with tribal officials on the impact to treaty rights and cultural values" ("Nez Perce Victory," 2013).

Indigenous Protests Spread Across the Continent

Protests of the mega-loads soon spread beyond the Lakota and Nez Perce. The Ho-Chunk (Winnebago) Tribal Council adopted a resolution against all sand mining on their lands in 2012. The sand was to be used for fracking. Such operations have been spreading across North America, and Native Americans have taken a leading role in resisting some of them. Water is used in very large amounts at high pressure to fracture shales, releasing the gas, in combination with a "fracking cocktail [that] includes acids, detergents and poisons that are not regulated by federal laws but can be problematic if they seep into drinking water" (Brantley and Meyendorff, 2013). Methane release can create the risk of explosion.

Native people at Umatilla and the Confederated Tribes of Warm Springs in northern Oregon also protested the passage through their lands of a 45-ton mega-load (18 feet tall, 22 feet wide, and 376 feet long) bound for Alberta's tar sands fields in early December 2013. About 70 people carrying signs reading "Hands Off Our Planet! Stop the Tar Sands" swarmed the mega-load and impeded its path. "This has gone too far. Our children are going to die from this," some of them said in an online video posted by Portland Rising Tide. "If we don't stop this now . . . [future generations] are going to ask, 'Where were you? Where was our tribe?'" (Dadigan, 2013). A few locked their bodies to the huge truck. The mega-load forced the protesters aside but was later stopped by snow and ice near Pendleton, Oregon. Several activists were arrested on charges of disorderly conduct after police removed the locks.

Alberta's Lubicon Lake Cree Nation protested fracking as well as tar sands mining on and near their lands, the latter with a blockade on unceded territory of a road northeast of Peace River in late 2013. The Calgary-based oil and gas company Penn West Petroleum Ltd., whose site was being dismantled, filed suit to dismantle the Lubicons' blockade. "The judge denied [us] the opportunity to raise any of the constitutional issues and arguments for the Lubicon," said Garrett Tomlinson with the Lubicon Lake Nation. "More time must be provided for both sides to be heard" (Troian, 2014). Some of the Lubicon argued that lack of a treaty between their tribe and the Canadian government rendered any permits to Penn West null and void. The Lubicon Cree leadership itself is split, however, between a faction supporting Penn West and one opposing it.

The Lubicon Lake Nation's leadership argued that Canada has never entered into a treaty with them. They assert that lack of a treaty renders permits for oil and gas development on Lubicon lands issued to Penn West by Alberta null and void. Penn West has explored fracking between

Haig and Swan Lakes, areas where Lubicon Lake people are known to carry out traditional activities such as fishing and hunting. The Indian Country Today Media Network reported that a "dialogue among the Lubicon themselves may be difficult, since the people are actually divided into two bands. Chief Bernard Ominayak represents the Lubicon Lake Nation, whereas Chief Billy Joe Laboucan leads the Lubicon Band, a separate group that was federally recognized by Aboriginal Affairs and Northern Development Canada in February 2013. . . . The First Nation split during the mid-1990s, a breakup that some say was orchestrated by Aboriginal Affairs in order to undermine an unfinished land claim settlement with Chief Ominayak's group. Chief Ominayak and his council said that by supporting industry, Chief Laboucan's group is out to destroy the Lubicon lands, as are PennWest and the provincial government" (Troian, 2014).

"We have to stand up for Mother Earth. We have to stand up for our sacred water—for our children, our grandchildren, for the coming generations," said Lakota activist Debra White Plume as she was arrested at the White House on September 2, 2011, with 186 others protesting the Keystone XL Pipeline. Several of those arrested were Canadian Native people who also were protesting oil sands development on or near their homelands. White Plume said that leaks from the pipeline could desecrate the freshwater Ogallala Aquifer near her homeland in Pine Ridge, South Dakota, a violation of the 1868 Fort Laramie Treaty. "It is with great honor that I come here today to ask President Obama to stand with us for Mother Earth against Father Greed," White Plume said (Capriccioso, 2011).

When 68-year-old Canadian folksinger Neil Young devoted a tour to help the Athabasca Chipewyan First Nation's legal campaign to impede expansion of oil sands mining, Prime Minister Stephen Harper said that his "rockstar lifestyle made him unfit" to criticize it. In response, Young took the stage at a concert in Toronto with an audience of 2,700 on January 12, 2014, with song lyrics needling Harper as a party to genocide. David Ball of the Indian Country Today Media Network wrote that "the legendary Canadian musician substituted Harper's name into his song 'Pocahontas,' which describes massacres against Indigenous Peoples." The Chipewyan First Nation says that contamination of soil and water from tar sands mining is causing cancer rates among their people to rise rapidly. "In the street outside Massey Hall," wrote Bell, "dozens held a round dance—a fixture of the Idle No More movement that has swept the country over the past year" (Ball, 2014).

In addition to Toronto, Young's "Honor the Treaties" tour visited Winnipeg, Regina, and Calgary. "We made a deal with these people," Young said. "We are breaking our promise. We are killing these people. The blood of these people will be on modern Canada's hands, and it will be the result of not just a slow thing, but of a fast and horrific thing if this continues. Believe me, these people are not going to sit back and let modern Canada roll over them" (Ball, 2014).

A celebrity filmmaker arrived in tar sands country in Fort Chipewyan, Alberta, and met with members of the ACFN to discuss creating a documentary on the Alberta tar sands. On August 22, 2014, actor Leonardo DiCaprio met with *Black Swan* director Darren Aronofsky, both of whom received a blast of invective from a spokesman for the Canadian Association of Petroleum Producers, wrapped in Canadianismo: "Like Canadians, we are growing tired of the fad of celebrity environmentalists coming into the region for a few hours or a few days, and offering their ideas and solutions to developing this resource" ("Leo DiCaprio," 2014).

Further Reading

"Athabasca Oil Sands." NASA Earth Observatory, November 30, 2011. http://earthobservatory.nasa.gov/IOTD/view.php?id=76559&src=eoa-iotd

Ball, David. "Neil Young: Blood of First Nations People Is on Canada's Hands." Indian Country Today Media Network, January 14, 2014. http://indiancountrytodaymedianetwork.com/2014/01/14/neil-young-blood-first-nations-people-canadas-hands-153104

Berry, Carol. "Alberta Oil Sands Up Close: Gunshot Sounds, Dead Birds, a Moonscape." Indian Country Today Media Network, February 2, 2012. http://indiancountrytodaymedianetwork.com/article/alberta-oil-sands-up-close%3A-gunshot-sounds%2C-dead-birds%2C-a-moonscape-95444

Brantley, Susan L., and Anna Meyendorff. "The Facts on Fracking." *New York Times*, March 13, 2013. http://www.nytimes.com/2013/03/14/opinion/global/the-facts-on-fracking.html

Capriccioso, Rob. "Indigenous Oil Sands Protest Leads to White House Arrests." Indian Country Today Media Network. September 2, 2011. http://indiancountrytodaymedianetwork.com/article/indigenous-oil-sands-protest-leads-to-white-house-arrests-51420

Dadigan, Marc. "Umatilla Tribe Battles Mega-Loads Headed for Alberta Oil Sands." Indian Country Today Media Network, December 1, 2013. http://indiancountrytodaymedianetwork.com/2013/12/11/umatilla-tribe-battles-megaloads-headed-alberta-oil-sands-152657

"Emissions from Oil Sands Mining." NASA Earth Observatory, March 2, 2012. http://earthobservatory.nasa.gov/IOTD/view.php?id=77283&src=eoa-iotd

"'Every Tree and Plant Died': Massive Toxic Spill Guts Alberta." Indian Country Today Media Network, August 26, 2013. http://indiancountrytodayme

dianetwork.com/2013/08/26/toxic-wastewater-spill-alberta-kills-dene-tha-landscape-150968

Hansen, James. "Game Over for the Climate." *New York Times*, May 9, 2012. http://www.nytimes.com/2012/05/10/opinion/game-over-for-the-climate.html

Homer-Dixon, Thomas. "The Tar Sands Disaster." *New York Times*, March 31, 2013. http://www.nytimes.com/2013/04/01/opinion/the-tar-sands-disaster.html

Johnson, Kirk. "Fight over Energy Finds a New Front in a Corner of Idaho." *New York Times*, September 25, 2013. http://www.nytimes.com/2013/09/26/us/fight-over-energy-finds-a-new-front-in-a-corner-of-idaho.html

Koch, Wendy. "Would Keystone Pipeline Unload 'Carbon Bomb' or Job Boom?" *USA Today*, March 10, 2014. http://www.usatoday.com/story/news/nation/2014/03/01/keystonexls-myths-debunked/5651099

Kolbert, Elizabeth. "Unconventional Crude: Canada's Synthetic-Fuels Boom." *The New Yorker*, November 12, 2007, 46–51.

Krauss, Clifford, and Ian Austen. "Rocky Road for Canadian Oil." *New York Times*, May 13, 2014, B-1, B-4.

"Leo DiCaprio Tours Tar Sands, Joins Natives in ALS Ice Bucket Challenge." Indian Country Today Media Network, August 26, 2014. http://indiancountrytodaymedianetwork.com/2014/08/26/leo-dicaprio-tours-tar-sands-joins-natives-als-ice-bucket-challenge-156602

Leslie, Jacques. "Is Canada Tarring Itself?" *New York Times*, March 31, 2014. A-19.

Lizza, Ryan. "The President and the Pipeline." *The New Yorker*, September 16, 2013. 38–51.

"Nez Perce Victory: U.S. Forest Service Forbids Mega-Loads along Highway 12." Indian Country Today Media Network, September 20, 2013. http://indiancountrytodaymedianetwork.com/2013/09/20/nez-perce-victory-us-forest-service-forbids-mega-loads-along-highway-12-151372

Nikiforuk, Andrew. "Large Dams of Mining Waste Leaking into Athabasca River: Study." Indian Country Today Media Network, February 26, 2014. http://indiancountrytodaymedianetwork.com/2014/02/26/large-dams-mining-waste-leaking-athabasca-river-study-153749?page=0%2C2

Orland, Kevin. "340 Billion Gallons of Sludge Spur Environmental Fears in Canada." Bloomberg News, January 16, 2018. https://www.bloomberg.com/news/articles/2018-01-16/340-billion-gallons-of-sludge-spur-environmental-fears-in-canada

Taylor, Kevin. "Nez Perce Leaders Stand Firm on Frontlines of Mega-Load Transport." Indian Country Today Media Network, August 9, 2013. http://indiancountrytodaymedianetwork.com/2013/08/09/nez-perce-leaders-stand-firm-frontlines-mega-load-transport-150809

Tollefson, Jeff. "Climate Science: A Line in the Sands." *Nature* 500 (August 8, 2013): 136–137. https://www.nature.com/news/climate-science-a-line-in-the-sands-1.13515

Troian, Martha. "Court Tells Lubicon Lake Cree in Alberta to Stop Blocking Fracking Activities." Indian Country Today Media Network, February 6,

2014. http://indiancountrytodaymedianetwork.com/2014/02/06/court-tells-lubicon-lake-cree-alberta-stop-blocking-fracking-activities-153435

Pipelines and Protests

Protests against the Dakota Access pipeline at Standing Rock during 2016 were the best known of many pipeline protests that pitted Native peoples against oil and gas interests. They have been acts of cathartic, communal expression and shared outrage against the defilement of Mother Earth by a way of thinking that regards nature as a vending machine: mother lode vs. Mother Earth. Judith LeBlanc, a member of the Caddo Nation of Oklahoma and director of the Native Organizers Alliance, which trains social activists in Indian Country, described the sense of common cause shared by protesters:

> At Standing Rock, our love and commitment to the land, to our people, and to all the people of Mother Earth, made us much stronger when we were facing rubber bullets, when we were being hosed down [in freezing weather], and watching drones flying overhead. It's harder in some ways to resist brutality with love, but it builds a core strength that can never be defeated. That's the kind of moral resistance that people are yearning for. They are yearning for unity and a sense of humanity that will give us the strength necessary to survive very difficult conditions. If we're going to change the system, if we're going to have economic and racial justice, it's going to take resistance driven by compassion. . . . Coming together showed the world we were willing to do whatever it took to protect Mother Earth and the sacred, not just for ourselves, but for everyone on the planet. . . . At the high point [at Standing Rock], 10,000 of us were bound together by a common belief. (LeBlanc, 2018 213–214)

Aside from the delicious historical irony of a "cowboy-Indian" alliance, common cause among Native Americans and environmentally aware European Americans (especially against such projects as the Keystone XL and Dakota Access pipelines) is quite logical. Both groups have common interests in maintaining a sustainable home. Their alliance tied Trans-Canada into political and legal knots in Nebraska over the Keystone XL.

Opposition to Canada's Trans Mountain Pipeline

Protests also built in 2018 throughout Canada and the Pacific Northwest against expansion of a 700-mile-long Kinder Morgan Trans

Mountain pipeline project planned to carry 890,000 barrels a day of Alberta tar sands oil to an export terminal in Burnaby, near Vancouver, B.C., then to ports around the Pacific Rim. The new pipeline would triple the existing capacity of the Trans Mountain Pipeline along the same route, allowing increased exports of Alberta tar sands oil.

On March 10, 2018, about 5,000 people took to the streets in Vancouver to protest the oil pipeline expansion. "We cannot stand by anymore," said Will George of the Tsleil-Waututh Nation, spokesman for the Protect the Inlet movement. "It is going to be like Standing Rock," where several thousand "water protectors" rallied against the Dakota Access Pipeline in North Dakota during 2016. "The similarity is [that] we are standing up to protect our water. And we are going to do this in a peaceful way," George said. "It is going to mark a day in history; it will be a massive mobilization" (Mapes, 2018). The Canadian federal government approved the pipeline in November 2016.

The pipeline is opposed by the province of British Columbia as well as the largest cities on the lower B.C. mainland: Vancouver, Burnaby, and Victoria. "All hell is going to break loose," said Murray Rankin, a member of Parliament representing the city of Victoria since 2012. "This is only the beginning, this is just the start, this is Ground Zero, day one. And it is going to go on for a very long time" (Mapes, 2018). Washington State tribes, state agencies, and environmental groups also rallied against the pipeline because it would increase oil-tanker traffic by 700 percent across northern Puget Sound.

Jan Hasselman, staff attorney at EarthJustice's Northwest office in Seattle, who was the lead attorney for the Standing Rock Sioux against the Dakota Access Pipeline, said: "We are undergoing a cultural shift with a growing awareness that the benefits of fossil fuel projects simply aren't worth the cost. Momentum is building as the same fight plays out in British Columbia, with more people, and government agencies joining the side of indigenous people" (Mapes, 2018).

"Our spiritual leaders today are going to claim back Burnaby Mountain," Reuben George of the North Shore's Tsleil-Waututh Nation said before the crowd marched to the steady beat of drums and chants in opposition to the project. "It's going to take gatherings such as this . . . [to] make sure the environment is not laid to waste and taken away from future generations. This is what we stand for today," George said. According to an account by Nick Eagland in the *Vancouver Sun* (2018), "The peaceful march ended outside Kinder Morgan's Burnaby tank farm, where First Nations began construction of a wood-frame 'Watch House' along the pipeline route. The building is expected to be completed by Monday and will serve as a base for project opponents on the mountain."

A smaller pro-pipeline rally (about 250 people) also was held in Vancouver the same day. Supporters wore "I ♥ Oil & Gas" shirts and carried placards bearing messages such as "I'll fight to lay pipe" and "Bring jobs, not lawsuits." "Crude oil in Canada is what pays the rent for us as a country," said Stewart Muir of Resource Works Society, a nonprofit funded by the Business Council of British Columbia (Eagland, 2018). The company plans to complete the $7.4 billion project in December 2020.

"It's the ongoing proverbial battle between oil vs. water," said Grand Chief Stewart Phillip, an Okanagan aboriginal leader and president of the Union of B.C. Indian Chiefs, a political advocacy organization representing 118 bands and First Nations within British Columbia. Phillip was one of several hundred people who were arrested in 2014 when they tried to block test drilling by Kinder Morgan.

On May 29, the Canadian federal government announced plans to buy the Trans Mountain pipeline for 4.5 billion Canadian dollars (U.S. $3.46 billion), with plans to begin expansion during the summer of 2018, regardless of local and provincial opposition in British Columbia, and placing Justin Trudeau's government firmly in support of Canada's oil industry. "The Trans Mountain expansion project is of vital interest to Canada and Canadians," Bill Morneau, the federal finance minister, told reporters after a special cabinet meeting in Ottawa to discuss the deal. "Our government's position is clear: It must be built and it will be built." Aurore Fauret, the Canadian tar sands campaign coordinator of the environmental group 350.org, said that Kinder Morgan had "abandoned this project because people organized all across the country to stop it, and we'll do it again." She said that Trudeau "had an opportunity to walk away from pipeline politics and get on with the real work of leading Canada, and the world, in a 100 percent renewable energy revolution, but instead he's opted to ignore science, Indigenous rights, and the voices of people across Canada and bailed out a dangerous, unwanted pipeline with public money" (Austin, 2018).

Just a few weeks after Trudeau's government bought the Trans Mountain project, Canada's Federal Court of Appeal on August 30, 2018 halted it, ordering a new review by the National Energy Board to incorporate consultations with First Nations peoples who have adamantly opposed the pipeline for several years. It was unclear whether an amended proposal might be appealed, or approved by the court at a later date after it is amended.

A Brewing Confrontation in Oregon

Don Gentry, chairman of the Klamath Tribes, and Emma Marrismarch, 18, author of *Rambunctious Garden: Saving Nature in a Post-Wild World*, described another brewing confrontation in Oregon for the *New York Times* (2018):

> Each spring and fall in the old days, Chinook salmon swam up the Klamath River, crossing the Cascade Mountains, to Upper Klamath Lake, 4,000 feet above sea level. For millenniums, the Klamath, Modoc and Yahooskin Band of Snake Indians fished salmon from the lake and the river. The Klamath had agreements with the downriver tribes—the Karuk, Hoopa and Yurok among them—to let fish pass so that some could swim all the way back to their spawning grounds. After dams were built on the river starting in 1912, the salmon were blocked. Today the only "c'iyaals hoches" (salmon runs) are enacted by the Klamath Tribes, whose members carry carved cedar salmon on a 300-mile symbolic journey from the ocean to the traditional spawning grounds to bring home the spirit of the fish.

The dams on the Klamath River will be demolished in 2020, according to plans (in 2018), one of the largest river restorations in North America. According to Gentry and Marrismarch, "There's a threat to the dream of a revitalized river—a project that would put a newly unobstructed Klamath at risk of contamination while simultaneously contributing to climate change, desecrating grave sites and trampling the traditional territory of the Klamath people. If you've read anything at all about the protests near the Standing Rock Sioux Reservation in North Dakota, you might be able to guess what that threat is. It's a pipeline" (2018).

The 36-inch-wide Pacific Connector Gas Pipeline, planned for 229 miles between Malin and Coos Bay, Oregon, will bore underneath the Klamath River near Klamath Falls, connecting with the Ruby Pipeline carrying natural gas from Wyoming to a very large export terminal for shipment to Pacific Rim countries, a huge potential energy market.

The pipeline's owner, Pacific Connector Gas Pipeline LP, and the developer of the export terminal, Jordan Cove Energy Project LP, are both owned by the Pembina Pipeline Corporation, which is based in the Canadian tar sands country in and near Calgary, Alberta. The company asserts a familiar corporate position that the new pipeline will provide jobs and taxes to some of Oregon's most impoverished counties, while disturbing nothing.

Twice during the Obama presidency, the Federal Energy Regulatory Commission ruled that the pipeline was not in the public interest, saying that the companies had failed to demonstrate that the benefits outweighed the project's negative impacts. In March 2017, however, Gary Cohn, director of the National Economic Council (who resigned in March 2018), sought to reopen the case, saying, "The first thing we're going to do is we're going to permit an LNG (Liquid Natural Gas) export facility in the Northwest." By that time, President Donald Trump had appointed four of the Federal Energy Regulatory Commission's five members, so approval seemed likely.

"As far as the Klamath people are concerned," Gentry and Marrismarch wrote, "this pipeline is a bad idea even if the price of gas were predicted to skyrocket. The Klamath people oppose this project because it puts at risk their watersheds, forests, bays, culture, spiritual places, homes, climate and future." They continued (2018): "The 95-foot-wide gash through the tribes' ancestral territory that pipeline construction would require would be likely to unearth long-buried ancestors and pulverize sites of cultural importance. Construction would strip shade from streams and pollute them with sediment, harming fish central to the Klamath's traditions and way of life. If the pipeline catches fire or leaks, the Klamath River and its fish will be put at risk. The track record of fossil fuel pipelines suggests such a calamity is only a matter of time."

An analysis by Oil Change International, which researches clean energy, said that the proposed pipeline would transport enough natural gas to emit 2.2 million metric tons of carbon dioxide, methane, and nitrous oxides, and would become the state's single largest source of these greenhouse gases. The Klamath, Yurok, and Karuk tribes have joined hundreds of landowners, conservation groups, and other citizens in a suit to stop the pipeline, an alliance much like that in Nebraska against the Keystone XL and in Canada against the Trans Mountain Project.

Further Reading

Austin, Ian. "Canadian Government to Buy Kinder Morgan's Trans Mountain Pipeline." *New York Times*, May 29, 2018. https://www.nytimes.com/2018/05/29/world/canada/canada-oil-pipeline.html

Eagland, Nick. "Deep Divide Between Anti- and Pro-Pipeline Rallies in Metro Vancouver." *Vancouver Sun*, March 19, 2018. http://vancouversun.com/news/local-news/live-hundreds-protest-kinder-morgan-pipeline-expansion-in-burnaby

Gentry, Don, and Emma Marrismarch. "The Next Standing Rock? A Pipeline Battle Looms in Oregon." *New York Times*, March 8, 2018.

Johansen, Bruce E. "Dakota Conflict the Latest of Many." *Omaha World-Herald*, December 13, 2016. http://www.omaha.com/opinion/bruce-e-johansen

-dakota-conflict-the-latest-of-many/article_4aaf6af6-3892-5d04-bf60-4c2ee49e46a5.html
LeBlanc, Judith. "Lead with Love." *Together We Rise: The Women's March: Behind the Scenes at the Protest Heard Around the World.* New York: HarperCollins, 2018.
Mapes, Lynda V. "'Like Standing Rock': Trans Mountain Pipeline-Expansion Opponents Plan B.C. Protest." *Seattle Times*, March 8, 2018. https://www.seattletimes.com/seattle-news/environment/like-standing-rock-trans-mountain-pipeline-expansion-opponents-plan-b-c-protest/?utm

"Cowboys" vs. "Indians": Racial Stereotyping and Agent Orange in Vietnam

At the time of the first Earth Day, in the spring of 1970, the United States was pouring dioxin (an active ingredient of Agent Orange) on the jungles of Vietnam, Laos, and Cambodia, in an attempt to defoliate the countryside and deny Viet Cong insurgents places to hide from aerial bombing. The guerrillas were said to be "fish" in a verdant "sea" that would be stripped bare of vegetative cover by defoliants. Between 1962 and 1971, at least 12 percent of southern Vietnam's land area was doused liberally with nearly 18 million gallons of 2,3,7,8-tetrachlorodibenzo-p-dioxin, the most potent of dioxin's many varieties (Schecter et al., 2001, 435).

As pilots joked that they were "cowboys" to the Vietnamese "Indians," U.S. armed forces dropped more bombs (measured by weight) on Vietnam than it dropped in the entire Pacific theater during World War II. By 1971, more than 600 pounds of bombs *per person* had been rained on Vietnam. Between 12 percent (U.S. figure) and 43 percent (a National Liberation Front figure) of South Vietnam's land area was sprayed at least once with defoliants, usually Agent Orange (Johansen, 1972, 4).

Before it was called Operation Ranch Hand, the dioxin-spraying campaign had been known as Operation Hades. Given a half-century of aftereffects, that name may have been more appropriate. The dioxin was sprayed not only on jungles, but also on farms in parts of South Vietnam that were controlled by the National Liberation Front, a deliberate attempt to cripple food production. Many farmers were exposed to very high levels of the toxic herbicide. Denial of dioxin's effects was widespread. According to a history of Project Ranch Hand, "Herbicide scientist E.J. Kraus [who invented dioxin] needed to prove the safety of his herbicide to humans, so he ingested half a gram of 2,4-D daily for three weeks" (Waugh, 2010). Ezra Jacob Kraus (March 19, 1885–February 28, 1960), a U.S. botanist and horticulturalist, died before widespread use of dioxin made it a health issue.

Eighteen million gallons of Agent Orange were sprayed over vast tracts of Southeast Asian forests between 1962 and 1971 in concentrations up to 1,000 times as potent as dioxin-based herbicides now sold over the counter in the United States (Johansen, 2003, 26). Large areas of the countryside became unfit for human habitation during the war, and for several years thereafter. As noncombatants fled poisoned, defoliated, and bombed-out rural areas, the population of Saigon, now Ho Chi Minh City, increased tenfold between 1954 (when the war began with French intervention) and 1970, from 300,000 to 3 million people (Johansen, 1972, 4).

Agent Orange was only one of several herbicides that the U.S. armed forces used to soak Vietnam's jungles in a toxic bath, but its horrendous effects on everyone who was exposed have made it the most infamous. Chemical companies could have made Agent Orange safer, but changing manufacturing methods would have reduced profits. At the time, no one warned troops (much less Vietnamese victims) of its long-range effects. Some troops even used 55-gallon barrels of Agent Orange as showers (Nguyen and Hughes, 2017). Soldiers sometimes used the empty 55-gallon drums as BBQ pits, as residue soaked into their food. The United States distributed films "showing civilians happily applying herbicides to their skin and passing through defoliated areas without concern. One prominent comic strip featured a character named Brother Nam, who explained that 'The only effect of defoliant is to kill trees and force leaves to wither, and normally does not cause harm to people, livestock, land, or the drinking water of our compatriots'" (Von Meding, 2017).

"Monster Babies"

Most of the herbicides, including Agent Orange, were applied without prior hazard testing. Agent Orange was applied in large amounts, often haphazardly, by troops taking part in Operation Ranch Hand, whose participants proclaimed, "Only we can prevent forests," an allusion to the U.S. Forest Service's Smokey the Bear's slogan, "Only you can prevent forest fires" (Johansen, 1972, 4). Samples collected between 1970 and 1973 documented elevated levels of TCDD in milk samples, as well as in fish and shrimp. Nursing mothers who had been heavy consumers of fish were found to have the highest levels in their blood (Schecter et al., 2001, 435).

Soon after spraying of Agent Orange and other herbicides began during the late 1960s, reports increased of deformed births in unusually large numbers. Areas sprayed with Agent Orange later reported very high incidences of certain birth defects: anencephaly (absence of all or parts of the brain), spina bifida (a malformed vertebral column), and hydrocephaly (swelling of the skull).

The Saigon newspaper *Tin Sang* published descriptions of "monster babies" born to mothers in areas that had been sprayed. The newspaper reported that one woman "reported that her newly pregnant daughter was caught in a chemical strike, and fainted, with blood coming out her mouth and nostrils, and later from her vulva. She was taken to a hospital where she was later delivered of a deformed fetus" (Johansen, 1972, 4). The same day (October 26, 1969), *Dong Nai*, another Saigon newspaper, published a photograph of a stillborn fetus with a duck-like face and an abnormally twisted stomach. A day later, the newspaper reported that a woman in the Tan An district who had been soaked with Agent Orange had given birth to a baby with two heads, three arms, and twenty fingers (Johansen, 1972, 4). Many other similar accounts were published before the South Vietnamese government shut down the newspapers for "interfering with the war effort" (Johansen, 1972, 4). The South Vietnam health ministry also began to classify accounts of deformed births as state secrets.

When these accounts were presented to U.S. Department of Defense officials, they were, at first, dismissed as unconfirmed enemy propaganda. When the accounts persisted and began to be more specific and numerous, the U.S. armed forces finally stopped using Agent Orange. The U.S. Air Force later found a "significant and potentially meaningful" relationship between type 2 diabetes and bloodstream levels of dioxins in its ongoing study of people who worked with the defoliant Agent Orange during the Vietnam War (Brown, 2000, A-14; Institute of Medicine, 1994).

Members of the U.S. armed services who were exposed to high levels of dioxins were found to be more prone to development of diabetes compared to those with lower levels of exposure. People with the highest exposure levels developed diabetes most rapidly. While it once dismissed reports of cancers caused by Agent Orange as groundless, three decades later the U.S. Army was giving a special medallion—the Order of the Silver Rose—to soldiers who had been afflicted.

Philip Jones Griffiths's photographic account, *Agent Orange: "Collateral Damage" in Vietnam* is a wrenching reminder of Agent Orange's human toll. Even 50 years later, Viet Thanh Nguyen and Richard Hughes described the generational legacy of Agent Orange in Vietnamese orphanages:

> Phan Thanh Hung Duc, 20, lies immobile and silent, his midsection covered haphazardly by a white shirt with an ornate Cambodian temple

design. His mouth is agape and his chest thrusts upward, his hands and feet locked in gnarled deformity. He appears to be frozen in agony. He is one of the thousands of Vietnamese victims of Agent Orange. Pham Thi Phuong Khanh, 21, is another such patient. She quietly pulls a towel over her face as a visitor to the Peace Village ward in Tu Du Hospital in Ho Chi Minh City, starts to take a picture of her enlarged, hydrocephalic head. Like Mr. Hung Duc, Ms. Khanh is believed to be a victim of Operation Ranch Hand, the United States military's effort during the Vietnam War to deprive the enemy of cover and food by spraying defoliants. . . . Pham Van Truc is another Vietnamese victim of Agent Orange. With his crippled, birdlike limbs and patches of scaly skin. . . . Perhaps Ms. Khanh does not want strangers to stare at her. Perhaps she feels ashamed. But if she does feel shame, why is it that those who should do not? (Nguyen and Hughes, 2017)

Agent Orange and Risk of Diseases

By mid-2001, the U.S. Department of Veterans Affairs was soliciting applications for compensation from Vietnam veterans with any of a large number of "presumptive disabilities": chloracne, Hodgkin's disease, multiple myeloma, non-Hodgkin's lymphoma, soft-tissue sarcoma, acute and subacute peripheral neuropathy, spina bifida, and prostate cancer ("Bulletin Board," 2001). The same request for claims asserted that diabetes mellitus soon would be included in its list of dioxin-induced pathologies.

The diseases that the U.S. Veterans Administration (VA) recognizes as associated with Agent Orange exposure expanded during the 1990s to include chloracne (a skin disorder), porphyria cutanea tarda, acute or subacute peripheral neuropathy (a nerve disorder), type 2 diabetes, and numerous cancers, including non-Hodgkin's lymphoma, soft-tissue sarcoma, Hodgkin's disease, multiple myeloma, prostate cancer, and respiratory cancers (including cancers of the lung, larynx, trachea, and bronchus). The VA later added chronic lymphocytic leukemia to this list (Environmental Agents, n.d.). Vietnamese people who were exposed to Agent Orange (and their offspring) probably suffer from at least as many ailments as U.S. veterans, although a complete tally has never been undertaken. Agent Orange "hotspots" in Vietnam have been described by Wayne Dwernychuk (2002, 2005).

At roughly the same time, a panel advising the U.S. Environmental Protection Agency, well stocked with industry representatives, was still arguing whether dioxin should be classified as carcinogenic for human beings. After ten years of work, during the summer of 2000, the EPA released a 3,000-plus-page *Draft Dioxin Reassessment* (EPA, 2000), which concluded that "TCDD (and possibly other closely related structural analogs, such as the chlorinated didenzofurans) are carcinogenic in humans and can cause immune-system alterations; reproductive, developmental, and nervous system effects; endocrine disruption, altered lipid metabolism; liver damage; and skin lesions" (Schecter et al., 2001, 436). The EPA study confirmed many other studies that had linked TCDD and other forms of dioxin to "cancer and cancer mortality at relatively high levels in chemical workers and in toxicity studies" (Fingerhut et al., 1991; Flesch-Janys et al., 1995, Flesch-Janys et al., 1998; Becher et al., 1998; Report on Carcinogenesis, 1998).

About 50,000 American veterans won $180 million in an out-of-court settlement over Agent Orange's effects, but many were never able to collect because the chemical's effects are long-term and often cannot be attributed to meet strict legal standards. Legal testimony indicates that the U.S. government and Agent Orange's manufacturer were well aware of its effects. The program ended three years before U.S. withdrawal from Vietnam in 1975. "Beginning in the mid-1970s," wrote Richard Alan-Leach in Z Magazine (2000), "Vietnam veterans who had sprayed the chemical began to complain of bronchitis, irregular heartbeat, nervous disorders, thyroid disorders, immune-deficiency diseases, liver and prostate cancers, and reproductive abnormalities of the kind that are now rife among the South Vietnamese."

In 2010, after decades of pressure from veterans' groups, the Department of Veterans Affairs added 14 diseases that could be attributed to Agent Orange–related diseases to its compensation list, as Congress allocated up to $13.3 billion for treatment and compensation. Only $12 million was allocated for treatment in Vietnam, a pittance against the need.

Effects of the chemicals sprayed on Vietnam have been spreading since the spraying stopped. "Canadian scientists located a heavily-defoliated valley located in the Central Highlands," wrote Alan-Leach. "Testing Vietnam's soil for dioxin residues, they found high rates of birth defects, deformities, and cancer. These maladies have been steadily increasing since the mid-1970s. Children living near the former U.S. military base at Bien Hoa have dioxin levels 50 times higher than children in Hanoi. Today, in South Vietnam, new generations of children continue to be born with spinal deformities, severe retardation, cerebral palsy, cleft palate, cataracts, club feet, and extra fingers or toes" (Alan-Leach, 2000).

Effects on Succeeding Generations

Men who sprayed Agent Orange in Vietnam between 1962 and 1971 were followed to determine whether exposure to dioxin affected their children. Nervous-system disorders were found to be widespread. Spontaneous abortions, birth defects, and developmental delays also were noted—paradoxically, men who received low doses of dioxin tended to father more children with these problems than those who had been exposed at higher levels (Wolfe et al., 1995). Newspaper reports more than 40 years later indicated that medical problems had been passed down to U.S. veterans' children and grandchildren (Liewer, 2016, 1-A, 5-A).

Dioxin levels remained very high for several decades in some areas of Vietnam that had been sprayed with Agent Orange more than three decades earlier (Schecter et al., 1992). Tests of people in the city of Bien Hoa (population 390,000), about 20 miles north of Ho Chi Minh City (formerly Saigon), in particular, showed dioxin readings 135 times higher than levels in Hanoi, which was not sprayed. Levels in Hanoi were measured at 2 to 3 parts per billion TCDD (roughly background level in today's world) while blood levels of 271 ppb were found in the blood of people living in Bien Hoa (Schecter et al., 2001, 435).

The research of Arnold Schecter (an environmental scientist at the University of Texas School of Public Health) and colleagues clearly indicated how residents of Bien Hoa—some of whom had not been born during the war—continued to acquire contamination. The dioxin first dumped in the area by U.S. armed forces was bioaccumulating up the food chain, from phytoplankton to zooplankton, and then to fish consumed by people whose progeny inherited the contamination and disorders attributed to it.

Human Effects on Vietnamese Children Decades Later

Thanh Xuan, a "peace village" near Hanoi, housed a hundred children who are retarded, some with stunted limbs or twisted spines. Most arrived at the "peace village" unable to walk, speak, or read. Across Vietnam, rates of birth defects, miscarriages, and other complications were still uncommonly high several decades after the spraying of Agent Orange had ended during 1971. Many of the deformed children in the "peace village" were born to parents who were sprayed during the war.

"If I wasn't here, I don't know what I would do," lamented Nguyen Kim Thoa, 15, sitting in her bedroom beneath a Britney Spears poster. A reporter described Thoa's delicate features, "wrapped in a shroud of spongy skin tumors and charcoal splotches sprouting bristles" (Verrengia and Tran, 2000). "I wasn't able to go to school at home," Thoa said. "The children always made fun of me. In their eyes, I was a freak. Here, I have friends and teachers who love me" (Verrengia and Tran, 2000). Thoa's father served in the Vietnamese Army between 1978 and 1980 along the Cambodian border, an area that was heavily sprayed during the war.

Hoang Dinh Cau, chairman of a national Vietnamese panel that investigates the war's ongoing health consequences, estimates that about 1 million Vietnamese people have been afflicted with dioxin poisoning, including 150,000 children. Thirty years after the war, some rice paddies that were abandoned after spraying have not been reclaimed, as "soaring forests with 1,000 different tree species shriveled, replaced by weedy meadows that livestock won't graze. Farmers call the new growth 'American grass'" (Verrengia and Tran, 2000).

In a sparsely decorated bedroom of a two-story concrete building, Bui Dinh Bi recalled his days with Communist forces in Quang Tri, in what was then called South Vietnam. During the early 1970s, after he was exposed to Agent Orange, Bui's skin lesions changed from mosquito-bite-like bumps to tumors of a type that covered his body thirty years later. Bui and his wife had eight children. The first was stillborn, and then the next five died in infancy. Their two surviving children grew up mentally retarded (O'Neill, 2000). Bui lived with 29 other veterans and 70 children in Friendship Village, near Hanoi, one of about a dozen similar communities that the Vietnamese government has established for veterans and children afflicted with dioxin toxicity.

The *Washington Post* reported in April 2000 that "Canadian researchers have found high levels of dioxins in children [who] were born long after the spraying ceased in 1971. The lingering contamination is so severe in some areas that if they were in the United States, they would be declared Superfund sites, requiring an immediate cleanup effort" (O'Neill, 2000).

About $100 million was allocated by Congress for environmental cleansing of Vietnam's Da Nang airport, only one of 28 "hot spots" that were contaminated in Vietnam (the chemicals were stored there). Only $20 million was allocated for victims' care in that country, a pittance against the need, considering that "Vietnamese soldiers, from both sides, with perfectly healthy children before going to fight, came home and sired offspring with deformities and horrific illnesses; villages repeatedly sprayed have exceptionally high birth-deformity rates" (Nguyen and Hughes, 2017).

Environmental Racism and Agent Orange: Context

The environmental justice movement in the United States was taking shape in the 1970s, recognizing that racism had forced peoples of color to endure a major portion of the world's environmental toxic burden. This burden extended to areas such as Vietnam, where U.S. armed forces subjected the lands and peoples to toxic exposure by Agent Orange. In addition, the troops who were drafted into the Vietnam War (especially those who served in front-line combat) included a higher ratio of Latinos and blacks than the general population, so they were more likely to suffer exposure to Agent Orange. Many of these troops had been involuntarily drafted and perceived their service as an extension of home-front racism. As they served, many inner cities were convulsed by civil rights demonstrations that doubled as antiwar rallies, and veterans of color often were chosen to lead the marches. As Herman Graham suggested in *The Brothers' Vietnam War*, the fact that the rate of African American casualties was disproportionately higher than their draft eligibility was not lost on them, and after Muhammed Ali refused his draft notice, fewer and fewer African American men saw service in the army as an acceptable means toward achieving equality and social justice at home (Graham, 2003, 135).

Stereotyping the Vietnamese as "Indians" allowed dehumanization that led even the top leaders of the army, such as General William Westmoreland, to think of the Vietnamese as less than human, and to regularly imagine Americans as "plac[ing] higher value on human life than [the Vietnamese]" (Berman, 1982, 76). "Just as repugnant, but perhaps more pertinent, given the environmental justice movement's roots in social justice for indigenous people," commented Charles Waugh (2010), "was the ubiquitous equation of the war effort with playing cowboys and Indians." Michael Yellow Bird asserted (2004, 43): "During the Vietnam War the United States often thought of Vietnam in images of the American West and cast the Vietnamese in the role of Indians. It was common for American soldiers to refer to enemy territory (free-fire zones) as 'Indian Country' and for American soldiers to brutally massacre Vietnamese while fantasizing they were killing Indians."

The terminology of the program even summoned up images of the Old West—"Ranch Hand," and "Trail Dust," which employed jeep-mounted and smaller, backpack-sized spray apparatuses for defoliation missions on the ground. Thinking of themselves as cowboys helped them establish a rationale for the mission: not only were they cleaning up "the ranch" by removing unwanted vegetation, they were taming the wild, assisting in the eradication of the "Indian" and the "Indian country" all at once (Waugh, 2010). To this day, some veterans of Ranch Hand still call each other "cowboys."

Yellow Bird illustrated racist Vietnamese-Indian associations with a reference to the March 16, 1968 massacre at My Lai, citing testimony by

Robert Johnson at the congressional War Crimes Hearings during April 1971. Representative Patsy Mink asked him: "You made a statement that in your opinion the My Lai massacre was the inevitable consequence of certain policies. Would you specify what policy you make reference to with regard to the killing of POWs?" Johnson replied, "First, the underlying rational policy, that is, that the only good gook is a dead gook. Very similar to the only good Indian is a dead Indian and the only good nigger is a dead nigger" (Citizens Commission, 1972, 50–51). William Calley, who was convicted for the massacre at My Lai, wrote in his memoir, *Body Count*: "We weren't in My Lai to kill human beings, really. We were there to kill ideology that is carried by—I don't know. Pawns. Blobs. Pieces of flesh. And I wasn't in My Lai to destroy intelligent men. I was there to destroy an intangible idea. To destroy communism. . . . I looked at communism as a southerner looks at a Negro, supposedly. It's evil. It's bad" (Calley and Sack, 1971, 104–105).

Likewise, as they dumped Agent Orange on Vietnam, pilots dehumanized the Vietnamese as the Ranch Hand program sprayed the land and people of Vietnam—environmental racism, *ipso facto*. And, by extension to the general context of environmental racism and justice, as Waugh observed (2010), "saying what the environmental justice movement has maintained all along, that the system of industrial capitalism in the United States has co-evolved with several forms of institutionalized racism, so that the two are at their historic cores inseparable." The Ranch Hand program reached its height in Vietnam just as the United States was celebrating its first Earth Day and President Richard Nixon, a supporter of the war, was signing the enabling legislation for the Environmental Protection Agency.

Charles Waugh wrote (2010): "The American war in Vietnam, after all, was not only the first declared war on the environment, but also the world's first planned ecocide, in which entire ecosystems were targeted and destroyed." "More than 40 years on," wrote Jason Von Meding in *Salon* during 2017, "the impact on their health has been staggering. . . this dispersion of Agent Orange over a vast area of central and south Vietnam poisoned the soil, river systems, lakes and rice paddies of Vietnam, enabling toxic chemicals to enter the food chain" (Von Meding, 2017). Some locations were sprayed three or four times. Effects intensified as time passed. The most evident health problem at first (for both Vietnamese people and American soldiers) was several forms of cancer. "But then," wrote Von Meding, "the children were born. It is estimated that, in total, tens of thousands of people have suffered serious birth defects—spina bifida, cerebral palsy, physical and intellectual disabilities and missing or deformed limbs. Because the effects of the chemical are passed from one generation to the next, Agent Orange is now debilitating its third and fourth generation" (Von Meding, 2017).

Arno Mayer of Harvard University wrote, "If crop destruction efforts are successful, they constitute a war measure primarily, if not exclusively, directed at children, the elderly, and pregnant and lactating women" (Alan-Leach, 2000). A half-century later, the toll of this war on the environment continues to spread.

Further Reading

Alan-Leach, Richard. "Agent Orange: Better Killing Through Chemistry." *Z Magazine*, November 2000. http://www.thirdworldtraveler.com/Environment/Agent_Orange.html

Becher, H., K. Steindorf, and D. Flesch-Janys. "Quantitative Cancer Risk Assessment for Dioxin Using an Occupational Cohort." *Environmental Health Perspectives* 106 (1998): 663–670.

Berman, Larry. *Planning a Tragedy: The Americanization of the War in Vietnam.* New York: Norton, 1982.

Brown, David. "Defoliant Connected to Diabetes." *Washington Post*, March 29, 2000, A-14. https://www.washingtonpost.com/archive/politics/2000/03/29/defoliant-connected-to-diabetes/281227f4-094f-44fd-b35e-212f825f6f8f/?utm_term=.e2ddaf8ca2cf

"Bulletin Board: Vietnam Veterans Benefit from Agent Orange Rules." *Indian Country Today*, May 16, 2001, D-4.

Calley, William, and John Sack. *Body Count: Lieutenant Calley's Story as Told to John Sack.* London: Hutchinson, 1971, 104–105.

Cecil, Paul Frederick. *Herbicidal Warfare: The Ranch Hand Project in Vietnam.* New York: Praeger, 1986, 1–2.

Citizens Commission of Inquiry, Eds. Statement of Robert B. Johnson, Captain, U.S. Army, West Point Class of 1965, *The Dellums Committee Hearings on War Crimes in Vietnam: An Inquiry into Command Responsibility in Southeast Asia.* New York: Vintage, 1972.

Dwernychuk, Wayne. "Dioxin Hot Spots in Vietnam." *Chemosphere* 60, no. 7 (August 2005): 998–999.

Dwernychuk, Wayne, Hoang Dinh Cau, Christopher T. Hatfield, Thomas G. Boivin, Tran Manh Hung, Phung Tri Dung, and Nguyen Dinh Thai. "Dioxin Reservoirs in Southern Viet Nam—A Legacy of Agent Orange." *Chemosphere* 47, no. 2 (April 2002): 117–138.

Environmental Agents Service, Department of Veterans Affairs. Agent Orange: Information for Veterans Who Served in Vietnam, General Information, n.d. Accessed October 20, 2017. http://www1.va.gov/agentorange/docs/AOIB10-49JUL03.pdf

Environmental Protection Agency, U.S. *EPA Draft Dioxin Reassessment.* 2000. https://cfpub.epa.gov/ncea/cfm/iris/recordisplay.cfm?deid=55265

Fingerhut, M. A., W. E. Halperin, D. A. Marlow, et al. "Cancer Mortality in Workers Exposed to 2,3,7,8-tetrachlorodibenzo-p-dioxin." *New England Journal of Medicine* 324 (1991): 212–218.

Flesch-Janys, D., J. Berger, P. Gurn, et al. "Exposure to Polychlorinated Dioxins and Furans (PCDD/F) and Mortality in a Cohort of Workers from a Herbicide-Producing Plant in Hamburg, Federal Republic of Germany." *American Journal of Epidemiology* 142 (1995): 1165–1175.

Flesch-Janys, D., J. Steindorf, P. Gurn, and H. Becher. "Estimation of the Cumulated Exposure to Polychlorinated dibenzo-p-dioxins/furans and Standardized Mortality Ratio Analysis of Cancer Mortality by Dose in an Occupationally Exposed Cohort." *Environmental Health Perspectives* 106 (1998): 655–662.

Graham, Herman, III. *The Brothers' Vietnam War: Black Power, Manhood, and the Military Experience.* Gainesville: Florida University Press, 2003.

Griffith, Philip Jones. *Agent Orange: "Collateral Damage" in Vietnam.* London: Trolley Books, 2004.

Institute of Medicine: *Committee to Review Health Effects in Vietnam Veterans of Exposure to Herbicides: Veterans and Agent Orange.* Washington, D.C.: National Academy Press, 1994.

Johansen, Bruce. "Ecomania at Home; Ecocide Abroad." University of Washington *Daily,* May 24, 1972, 4.

Johansen, Bruce E. *The Dirty Dozen: Toxic Chemicals and the Earth's Future.* Westport, CT: Praeger, 2003.

Liewer, Steve. "A Toxic Legacy." *Omaha World-Herald,* June 5, 2016, 1-A, 5-A.

Nguyen, Viet Thanh, and Richard Hughes. "The Forgotten Victims of Agent Orange." *New York Times,* September 15, 2017. https://www.nytimes.com/2017/09/15/opinion/agent-orange-vietnam-effects.html

O'Neill, Annie. "Damaged Lives: Vietnamese Veterans and Children: While World Leaders Debate the Effects of Agent Orange, a Multinational Project Reaches Out to People at the Center of the Storm." *Pittsburgh Post-Gazette,* November 5, 2000. http://old.post-gazette.com/magazine/20001105agentorange1.asp

Report on Carcinogenesis: TCDD. Bethesda, MD: National Institute of Environmental Health, National Toxicology Program, 1998.

Santillo, David. "World Chemical Supplies Contaminated with Toxic Chemicals." Greenpeace Listserve, March 19, 2000. Cited in Bruce E. Johansen. *The Dirty Dozen: Toxic Chemicals and the Earth's Future.* Westport, CT, 2003, 19.

Schecter, Arnold, Le Cao Dai, Olaf Papke, Joelle Prange, John D. Constable, Muneaki Matsuda, Vu Duc Thao, and Amanda L. Piskac. "Recent Dioxin Contamination from Agent Orange in Residents of a Southern Vietnamese City." *JOEM Journal of Occupational and Environmental Medicine* 43, no. 5 (May 2001): 435–443.

Schecter, A., O. Papke, M. Ball, D. C. Hoang, C. D. Le, Q. M. Nguyen, T. Q. Hoang, N. P. Nguyen, H. P. Pham, K. C. Huynh, D. Vo, J. D. Constable, and J. Spencer. "Dioxin and Dibenzofuran Levels in Blood and Adipose Tissue of Vietnamese from Various Locations in Vietnam in Proximity to Agent Orange Spraying." *Chemosphere* 25, no. 7–10 (1992): 1123–1128.

Verrengia, Joseph B., and Tini Tran. "Vietnam's Children Feeling Effects of Agent Orange." *Amarillo* [Texas] *Globe-News*, November 20, 2000. http://www.amarillonet.com/stories/112000/hea_agentorange.shtml

Von Meding, Jason. "Agent Orange, Exposed: How U.S. Chemical Warfare in Vietnam Unleashed a Slow-Moving Disaster." *Salon*, October 9, 2017. https://www.salon.com/2017/10/09/agent-orange-exposed-how-u-s-chemical-warfare-in-vietnam-unleashed-a-slow-moving-disaster_partner/

Waugh, Charles. "'Only You Can Prevent a Forest': Agent Orange, Ecocide, and Environmental Justice." *Interdisciplinary Studies of Literature and the Environment* 17, no. 1 (2010): 113–132. http://digitalcommons.usu.edu/english_facpub/791

Wolfe, W. H., J. E. Micalek, and J. C. Miner. "Paternal Serum Dioxin and Reproductive Outcomes Among Veterans of Operation Ranch Hand." *Epidemiology* 6, no. 1 (1995): 17–22.

Yellow Bird, Michael. "Cowboys and Indians: Toys of Genocide, Icons of American Colonialism." *Wicazo Sa Review* 19, no. 2 (2004): 43.

Farmworkers: Toxicity as an Occupational Hazard

Pesticides are created to kill undesired organisms and are toxic by nature. Farmworkers who mix and apply these poisons risk accidental poisoning, as well as lower-level, day-to-day exposure. Farm laborers suffer more illnesses and injuries than any other occupational group. A majority of them are black and Latino, who sustain dangerous and sometimes fatal risks to their health at poverty-level pay scales even after decades of advocacy for better compensation and working conditions by the United Farmworkers and other groups.

Each growing season, three great migrant streams follow a seasonal cycle and ripening crops north, then south, across the United States. One begins in Florida and extends north along the Atlantic Seaboard. Another originates in and near Texas and New Mexico, migrating through the middle of the continent and into the Pacific Northwest. The third migrant stream spans California, and reaches, in season, into Washington, Oregon, and Idaho. Even through much of the harvest has been mechanized in recent decades, migrant labor remains important in the harvest of major crops.

According to Pesticide Safety, an informational website (2017), risks to farmworkers' health from exposure to toxic herbicides and pesticides remain substantial, with acute (immediate) health effects including rash, eye irritation, nausea, dizziness, and vomiting, and headaches. In addition, acute effects may include seizures, difficulty with breathing, loss of consciousness, and eventually death from several of these. Chronic (long-term) effects can provoke several forms of cancer, hormonal and reproductive health problems, neurological disorders, birth defects, and infertility. Even low-level pesticide exposure over several years may lead to chronic health effects. Pesticide Safety observes, "Workers who perform hand labor tasks in areas that have been treated with pesticides face exposure from direct spray, drift or contact with pesticide residues on the crop or soil. Farmworker families can also be injured by pesticides when farmworker children play in treated fields; when workers inadvertently take home pesticide residues on their hair, skin or clothing; or when pesticides drift into residences, schools and other areas located near fields."

The short-term effects of pesticide exposure (rashes, headaches, stinging eyes, blisters, nausea, headaches, and breathing problems) may not seem life-threatening at first. The longer-term problems caused by prolonged exposure, including several types of cancer, birth defects to children, and neurological impairment (including Parkinson's disease), pose more serious issues. This is why near-term reports of exposure and its effects mean little. Farm work is short-term and mobile, so records at any one place are nearly useless. The U.S. Environmental Protection Agency has estimated that 10,000 to 20,000 farmworkers suffer pesticide poisoning per year (Pesticide Safety, 2017), but for reasons mentioned above, this number has little meaning.

A High-Risk Occupation

Edward Zuroweste, chief medical officer for Migrant Clinicians Network, who spent more than two decades treating farmworkers who worked in rural Pennsylvania, said he frequently treated farmworkers and their families who complained of intense headaches, nausea, and vomiting following pesticide exposure. Often, he said, these symptoms were misdiagnosed as routine flu or stress headaches. "It's a high-risk occupation to work among chemicals on a daily basis," Zuroweste said. "We're still putting billions of pounds of very dangerous chemicals on fields and orchards. Many of these pesticides have been proven to be carcinogenic and have been proven to cause birth defects" (Brown, 2017).

No national system exists to track the number of farmworkers injured or killed by pesticide and herbicide exposure. Even if such a system existed, tracking of such illnesses would be complicated by the fact that much of the exposure is low-level and long-term. While 30 states require reporting of pesticide poisoning, many workers, who lack health insurance, do not seek medical care until problems are acute. In addition to lack of insurance, many workers avoid reporting illnesses because they cannot speak English, or lack immigration certification or transport to medical facilities. Many also fear that reporting exposure will risk loss of their jobs.

The Pesticide Action Network, an advocacy group, captured the enduring agonies of farmworker life (2017) when it stated: "Farmworkers represent the backbone and marrow of our agricultural economy. Yet this group is one of the least protected from on-the-job harms—including exposure to pesticides. Decades after Edward R. Murrow's *Harvest of Shame* documentary and John Steinbeck's *The Grapes of Wrath*, farmworkers . . . still face many of the same deplorable conditions." In addition, farmworkers sometimes face wage theft as well as inadequate housing, extreme poverty, and restricted access to clean water, education, and health care. The cruelest irony of all is that they often cannot afford to buy the food that they harvest.

To protect both farmworkers and consumers, the Pesticide Action Network advocates "shifting away from reliance on hazardous pesticides— and toward agro-ecological farming" ("Farmworkers," n.d.). The same organization also supports a return to a smaller scale of localized farming and reduced dependence on "factory farms" controlled mainly by very large corporations that engage in monoculture (growth of one crop over very large areas), which requires heavy doses of pesticides and herbicides.

"Gradually, this needed shift is gaining momentum—from the ground up," said PAN. "'Local food economies' are growing, farmers are demanding more control of inputs and production on their own farms, and farmworkers are beginning to experience (and support) the safer and healthier working conditions resulting from sustainable farming" ("Farmworkers," 2017). The group also supports stronger federal regulations to protect farmworkers' rights, including safeguards against overuse and abuse of pesticides and herbicides.

Historical Protests of Pesticides

Pesticide exposure has been an issue among farmworkers for several decades. Some of the United Farmworkers' earliest demands when the union was founded during the 1960s concerned exposure to them. In rallies across the United States, César Chávez and other leaders organized grape boycotts and publicized the dangers of work in fields doused with toxic chemicals.

The table-grape boycott hit a peak in Seattle, for example, during the last half of 1969 and most of 1970, as supporters carried signs through grocery stores in the University District until they were "escorted" out by police. Boycott supporters were coached in picket-line etiquette: contact grocers where you shop (if they know you by name, that's a plus, explained a leaflet). "Explain that grape pickers in California and Arizona are struggling to gain contracts, living wages, and protection from pesticide poisoning. . . . Point out that you will not shop at this store anymore if you see grapes there. Explain that you will be talking to your neighbors" ("Grape Boycott," 1969). In Seattle, by May 1, 1970, A&P and 40 independent grocers had agreed not to sell grapes at a time when only 1.5 percent of California and Arizona table grapes were covered by UFW contracts ("Grape Boycott," 1969).

The UFW also opposed proposed laws that would have made strikes during harvest season (as well as protests of chemical exposure) illegal. The owners argued that crops were perishable and should be harvested without delay. In a speech, Chávez dismissed the proposed laws. The workers didn't work except during the harvest, he said. "What they are saying is that we can't strike at all. However perishable the crops may be, I maintain that the life of one worker is more perishable than all the damned grapes they can produce" (Hannula, December 21, 1969, n.p.).

A crowd at Seattle's Garfield High School, in the black community, rose to its feet, one of several standing ovations that Chávez received that evening. Chávez criticized the use of pesticides in the fields as a threat to workers' health, and urged members of the audience to contact members of Congress to protest purchase of grapes in large lots by the Defense Department. He said that the workers "put food on your tables all your life, and when all the work is done they don't have enough food on the table for themselves—and I think that's a sin" (Hannula, December 20, 1969, n.p.). Having attended a mass, Chávez, a devout Roman Catholic, had been asked about the power of prayer in the UFW's work. Prayer is powerful, he said, but "a lot of hard picketing is even more effective" (Hannula, December 21, 1969).

While in Seattle, Chávez also took part in a picket line at a University District Safeway store in December, with about 375 people, saying: "God knows we are not beasts of burden. We are not agricultural implements or rented slaves. We are men. We are men locked in a death struggle against this nation's largest corporate interests" ("Chávez," 1969, n.p.). The boycotters targeted Safeway as the largest grocery chain in Seattle and the biggest seller of nonunion grapes in the United States. Picketers also pointed out to shoppers that the UFW campaigned against use of pesticides in the fields.

Pesticide Use Accelerates under President Trump's EPA

Policies restricting chemical use on farm fields that had been ordered under President Barack Obama were annulled after the election of Donald Trump. The Trump presidency ushered in broad repeal of existing efforts to reduce workers' exposure to toxic chemicals. Both Scott Pruitt as the head of EPA (who resigned) and Sonny Perdue (as secretary of agriculture) were longtime advocates of corporate "freedom" to manufacture and use pesticides and herbicides. Pruitt arrived in his EPA post as the agency was conducting reviews of several pesticides in addition to chlorpyrifos, including glyphosate, atrazine, and neonicotinoids. Virginia Ruiz, who is director of occupational and environmental health for Farmworker Justice, said: "There are costs to poisoning communities and individuals. Farmworkers are not machines. . . . Douse them with chemicals and they are going to get sick" (Brown, 2017).

Effects of regulatory relaxation by the Trump administration reached ground level among farmworkers very quickly, as many reported increased incidence of illness. On May 5, 2017, at least 50 farmworkers near Bakersfield, California, came down with nausea, diarrhea, and vomiting after chemicals drifted over them from an adjacent field. At least one fainted, according to a report by the television news station Kern Golden Empire. "Anybody that was exposed, that was here today, we encourage them to seek medical attention immediately," warned Michelle Corson, public relations officer at Kern County Public Health (Philpott, 2017).

The chemical in use at the time was chlorpyrifos, a neurotoxic insecticide, for which a ban had been sought for several years by many public health experts, other scientists, and environmentalists. Preparations were being made to regulate it when Donald Trump won the 2016 U.S. presidential election. Shortly after Trump's election, DowDuPont, the chemical's manufacturer, donated $1 million to his inauguration (Branch and Lipton, 2018, F-4). After Trump appointed Pruitt to lead the Environmental Protection Agency, Pruitt brought regulation efforts to a halt in March 2017 and gave Dow AgroSciences a free hand to produce and sell chlorpyrifos, even as many farmworkers, a majority of whom are Latino, complained of numb lips, itchy skin, watery eyes, and headaches. The chemical also caused many workers to vomit and experience convulsions.

After Dow Chemical introduced chlorpyrifos in 1965, it became the most widely used insecticide in the United States, with about 6 million pounds used per year by 1996. One-sixth of that total is used in California on about 60 crops, including oranges, alfalfa, and almonds, to kill ants, moths, larvae, and worms. As an organophosphate, chlorpyrifos is a nerve agent similar in chemical structure to Sarin (which has been used as a nerve gas in warfare), but much less toxic. According to a report on California's KQED, "At high doses, nerve agents like chlorpyrifos cause symptoms like headaches, nausea, dizziness and disorientation. If larger doses are ingested, it can lead to vomiting, stomachaches, diarrhea and even death. By 2017, roughly 6 million pounds of the chemical were being spread on crops in the United States" (Branch and Lipton, 2018, F-4). "An increasing number of studies show correlations to neurological problems in children, among other issues," the *New York Times* reported in 2018, "but are their problems the result of chlorpyrifos? Dow says no" (Branch and Lipton, 2018, F-4).

Reports of farmworkers stricken with illnesses have become common in California. According to another KQED report, by Ted Goldberg (2017): "Two dozen people who work in agricultural fields in the Salinas and Watsonville areas were hospitalized after chemical drifts apparently made them ill during June 2017. The case [came] a week after 18 celery workers were rushed to the Salinas Valley Memorial Healthcare System emergency room, complaining of dizziness, nausea and stomach pain. On June 22, a crew of workers employed by the produce company Tanimura & Antle got sick about an hour into their shift with one of them vomiting, according to Bob Roach, an assistant agricultural commissioner in Monterey County."

The EPA ruling in favor of chlorpyrifos use provoked protests in farmworker communities throughout California, including a petition containing 167,000 signatures. The petition said: "Use of chlorpyrifos is particularly problematic in California, where more than one million pounds of the neurotoxic organophosphate pesticide are used each year, much of it in close proximity to schools and residences. . . . In the Monterey Bay Area, chlorpyrifos is most heavily used on wine grapes, brussel sprouts, and apple orchards. In 2016, the air monitor at the Salinas Airport registered average air levels of chlorpyrifos three times higher than the EPA's target risk level" (Bernstein, 2017). In other words, the chemical had become part of the general atmosphere in Salinas.

Alina Diaz, a social worker who also is vice president of Alianza Nacional de Campesinas, relayed an account from a migrant worker near

Ontario, New York, where migrants work with apples and other crops. "After toxic pesticides were sprayed on a cleared field nearby, a cloud . . . drifted to an adjacent field covering the woman and her fellow farmworkers with harmful chemicals. Even though they had been exposed to toxic pesticides, the field manager ordered them to continue working. The woman couldn't breathe." She told Diaz: "I don't care if I lose my job; I'm not going to die here like a roach. I am a human being, not an insect" (Brown, 2017). Nearly everyone who works in the fields has a horror story of being doused with pesticides by a low-flying aircraft, and not knowing what would come of it. Brian Brown, writing in an Earthjustice blog in 2017, relayed one such story:

> Mily Treviño-Sauceda recalls a day decades ago that still reduces her to tears. While working on a citrus farm in Blythe, California, a plane flew overhead and doused the field—and the people working on it—with pesticides. "I was up on the ladder when I heard a plane fly over," said Treviño-Sauceda, now 55. "Then everyone just started suffocating. I tried to run away but couldn't see or breathe. Everyone was covered with white dust and their eyes were itchy and watering." Thankfully, Treviño-Sauceda and her brothers and father who also worked in the fields had no serious short-term health problems, but not everyone remained unscathed. She remembers a pregnant woman who had to be rushed to the hospital to deliver her baby. While the baby survived, the mother did not.

Treviño-Sauceda joined the farmworker justice movement because of that experience, founding Líderes Campesinas, a women's group in California that allied with the National Farmworker Women's Alliance (Alianza Nacional de Campesinas). Both groups have been actively engaged in political lobbying that will help to protect farmworkers from the dangers of pesticides.

Members of Alianza as well as other allies and farmworkers marched in Washington, D.C., on July 15–16, 2013 to call on Congress to strengthen and finalize a federal safeguard called the Worker Protection Standard and, in turn, implement stronger protections for farmworkers from hazardous pesticides. Earthjustice estimates that 5.1 billion pounds of pesticides are applied to crops around the world every year. Between 1 and 2 million farmworkers in the United States have some of the highest exposure rates in the world (because pesticides are so intensively used).

The advocates' goals have been modest, "calling for the EPA to update the Worker Protection Standard to provide more frequent pesticide training for farmworkers, giving workers the information they deserve about the specific pesticides used in their line of work and potential exposure to their families. They're also asking the EPA to require safety precautions, protective equipment that would limit farmworkers' contact with pesticides, and medical monitoring of workers who handle neurotoxic pesticides" (Brown, 2017).

Following the poisoning incident near Bakersfield, the Migrant Clinicians Network restated its opposition to use of chlorpyrifos, after it had been used to spray a neighboring mandarin orchard the night before, close to a cabbage field where the afflicted farmworkers had been laboring. The clinicians said, "The EPA's initial assessment of the insecticide in response to the petition in 2014 and its updated assessment and review of scientific studies released last year found that chlorpyrifos was dangerous to human health, particularly to developing brains in utero and of young children. Despite the assessments, the EPA declined the petition to ban the chemical in March [2017]" ("Pesticide Poisoning," 2017).

Without a federal ban of chlorpyrifos, farmworkers in California appealed for a state-wide prohibition. The California Department of Pesticide Regulation decided to review the science on chlorpyrifos in 2017 before ruling on a ban. The EPA had banned chlorpyrifos for most home and garden uses in 2000. The United Kingdom banned its use on almost all crops, and the United States was preparing to do the same (beginning with a ban on apples and tomatoes) when Trump was elected. Rejecting the ban, Pruitt said, "By reversing the previous administration's steps to ban one of the most widely used pesticides in the world, we are returning to using sound science in decision-making—rather than predetermined results." The new policy allowed use of chlorpyrifos until 2022, "pending the agency's further scientific review" (McClurg, 2017). The chemical's effects had already been studied for several decades.

According to KQED's report, "California already had stricter rules related to its application than most states. For example, farmers must have a permit to apply the chemical; they must post a warning after they spray a field; and the state requires buffer zones between sprayed fields and human dwellings" (McClurg, 2017).

Effects of Chlorpyrifos

According to the National Pesticide Information Center, inhalation of chlorpyrifos may cause initial symptoms like "tearing of the eyes, runny nose, increased saliva and sweat production, nausea, dizziness and headache," followed by possible "muscle twitching, weakness or tremors, lack of coordination, vomiting, abdominal cramps, diarrhea, and pupil constriction with blurred or darkened vision." Chlorpyrifos is also an endocrine disrupter. Studies have found strong evidence to suggest that even at very low exposers, the chemical triggers effects among children ranging from lower IQ to higher rates of autism (Philpott, 2017). However, Dow AgroSciences, parent of Dow Chemical, which had contributed $1 million to Trump's inaugural committee, asserted that, used correctly, the chemical was safe.

Fernando Stein, president of the American Academy of Pediatrics, wrote in the *New York Times* (2017):

> Extensive epidemiologic studies associate pesticide exposure with adverse birth and developmental outcomes, including preterm birth, low birth weight, congenital abnormalities, pediatric cancers, neurobehavioral and cognitive deficits, and asthma. The evidence is especially strong linking certain pesticide exposure with pediatric cancers and permanent neurological damage. The agency's own calculations suggest that babies, children and pregnant women all eat much more chlorpyrifos than is safe. In fact, the EPA has estimated that "typical" exposures for babies are probably five times greater than its proposed "safe" intake and 11 to 15 times higher for toddlers and older children. This chemical is unambiguously dangerous and should be banned from use. We urge the EPA to reverse its decision and protect child health.

Research on chlorpyrifos has focused on how exposure influences the development of a fetus, not on the workers themselves, and it "shows that prenatal exposure can lead to preterm births, abnormal reflexes in newborns, pervasive attention problems, motor control deficiencies and lower IQ. Scientists have also noted that some young children who have been exposed to the chemical have conditions related to compromised lung function, like asthma" (McClurg, 2017). Dow Agrosciences said that it remained confident that "authorized uses of its product offer wide margins of protection for human health and safety." In a statement the company said, "Overall, more than 4,000 studies and reports have examined chlorpyrifos in terms of health, safety, and the environment. No pest-control product has been or continues to be more thoroughly evaluated" (McClurg, 2017).

The fumigant methyl bromide was most strongly associated with prostate cancer. Use of chlorinated pesticides, such as DDT, also has been associated by other studies with cancer among applicators who were more than 50 years of age. In 2013 men who had been exposed to certain pesticides, such as fonofos (which was removed from the market in 1998), as well as terbufos and malathion, were more likely to develop aggressive forms of prostate cancer (Bienkowski, 2017). This type of exposure to pesticides would be "unusually high," said lead author Dr. Jennifer Rusiecki, an assistant professor of medicine at Uniformed Services University in Maryland.

In addition to toxic chemicals that are applied in the fields, farmworkers also risk exposure to gasoline and diesel emissions, many solvents, dust, oils, and microbes at rates greater than for most people. However, exposure to pesticides is an important long-term problem later in life, Linda McCauley said. "Our entire pesticide regulatory system is built on neurotoxicity and poisonings," she said (Bienkowski, 2017). Personal protection equipment is not enough to protect farmworkers' health, said Nishelle Harriott, science and regulatory director of Beyond Pesticides, which advocates for phasing out harmful pesticides. "Long sleeve shirts, gloves are considered personal protective equipment," she said. "Those things wouldn't do much for someone breathing these chemicals in" (Bienkowski, 2017).

Pesticide Exposure Changes DNA

One major impediment to accurate reporting of pesticide and herbicide toxicity is that effects may take place over many years and affect workers in ways that are dangerous and systemic, but not part of any diagnosis immediately after a poisoning incident. For example, *Environmental Health News* reported in 2017 that "farmworkers who have a high pesticide exposure event—such as a spill—are more likely to experience molecular changes in DNA that may lead to certain cancers (such as prostate), according to a large U.S. study of pesticide applicators in Iowa and North Carolina" (Bienkowski, 2017).

This research was part of the Agricultural Health Study that was following the state of physical health for more than 57,000 pesticide applicators in Iowa and North Carolina. "This lines up perfectly with what the National Cancer Institute is doing on the markers that increase the risk of cancer. It's a timely, relevant study," said McCauley, dean and professor of Emory University's Nell Hodgson Woodruff School of Nursing. McCauley was not involved in the study. "There are changes that happen to the body before we kill the body. It's really sad how [farmworkers] are told 'don't worry, there's not a problem,' when they know that working around these chemicals cannot be healthy for them," she said (Bienkowski, 2017).

"Safe" Sulfur Reduces Children's Breathing Capacity

The Environmental Protection Agency generally considers elemental sulfur as safe, even though it may cause respiratory irritation to exposed farmworkers. While elemental sulfur can drift over residential areas close to fields where it is used, its effects on children had not been studied with any degree of precision until 2017, when a new study became the first to associate use of sulfur in agriculture with respiratory health problems in children living nearby.

The study was published August 14, 2017, in the journal *Environmental Health Perspectives*, where Rachel Raanan, a University of California Berkeley postdoctoral fellow, and colleagues found:

> Elemental sulfur, "the oldest of all pesticides," is the most heavily used agricultural pesticide in California and Europe. Sulfur is considered relatively safe and is used in both conventional and organic farming systems. Adverse respiratory effects have been reported in applicators and animals, but the effect on residential populations, and especially on children living in proximity to fields treated with elemental sulfur, is not known. . . . This study suggests that elemental sulfur use, allowed in both organic and conventional farming, in close proximity to residential areas, may adversely affect children's respiratory health. (Raanan et al., 2017)

Elemental sulfur is used to control pests and fungi. "Sulfur is widely used because it is effective and low in toxicity to people. It is naturally present in our food and soil and is part of normal human biochemistry, but breathing in sulfur dust can irritate airways and cause coughing," said Asa Bradman, a co-author of the study, who is an associate director of the Center for Environmental Research and Children's Health at UC Berkeley's School of Public Health. "We need to better understand how people are exposed to sulfur used in agriculture and how to mitigate exposures. Formulations using wettable powders could be a solution" (Israel, 2017).

The study examined lung function and asthma-related respiratory symptoms in several hundred children who lived near fields where sulfur had been applied. According to the study, "A 10-fold increase in the estimated amount of sulfur used within 1 kilometer of a child's residence during the year prior to pulmonary evaluation was associated with a 3.5-fold increased odds in asthma medication usage and a two-fold increased odds in respiratory symptoms such as wheezing and shortness of breath." The study also found that each 10-fold increase in the amount of elemental sulfur applied in the previous 12 months within a 1-kilometer radius of the home was associated with an average decrease of 143 milliliters per second (mL/s) in the maximal amount of air that the 7-year-old children could forcefully exhale in one second. For comparison, research has shown that exposure to maternal cigarette smoke is associated with a decrease of 101 mL/s after five years of exposure. "This study provides the first data consistent with anecdotal reports of farmworkers and shows that residents, in this case, children, living near fields may be more likely to have respiratory problems from nearby agricultural sulfur applications," said senior author Brenda Eskenazi, Berkeley professor at the School of Public Health (Israel, 2017).

The Huichols Live with Pesticides around the Clock

Exposure to toxic pesticides is one of the greatest risks faced by indigenous migrant workers in Mexico, where tobacco growers and other agricultural companies use them on an industrial scale. Many of the workers are denied safety equipment and access to showers and facilities to wash their clothes after having come into contact with pesticides. In addition, many of the workers live in the same pesticide-laced fields that they harvest, exposing them to contamination around the clock.

Each year, an estimated 170,000 field workers arrive in the valleys of Sinaloa during each planting season. Among these workers, roughly 5,000 have been found to suffer from toxic contamination as a result of the handling of, or prolonged exposure to, pesticides that are used in cultivation (Diaz-Romo and Salinas-Alvarez, n.d.).

Of the 35,000 agricultural laborers who worked in the San Quintin Valley of Baja California during 1996, 70 percent were indigenous people. The majority of the indigenous migrant workers who work in the agro-industrial fields of northern Mexico are Mixtecos, Triquis, and Zapotecs from Oaxaca; Nahuas, Mixtecos, and Tlapenecos from Guerrero; and Purhepechas from Michoacan. According to Estela Guzmán Ayala, women (34 percent) and children under 12 years of age (32 percent) constitute two-thirds of the indigenous labor force in the agricultural regions in northern Mexico (Diaz-Romo and Salinas-Alvarez, n.d.).

Ruth Franco, a doctor specializing in work-related health and coordinator of the Program for Day Laborers in Sinaloa, estimated that 25 percent of the 200,000 workers in the Sinaloa valleys during the 1995–1996 cycle were children between the ages of 5 and 14. In the fields where these children and their families work, observers asserted that "thousands of used containers and toxic residues that are generated by the annual use of upwards of 8 million tons of pesticides are criminally disposed of in *ad hoc* trash bins, channels, drains, incinerators, and recycled to storing drinking water" (Diaz-Romo and Salinas-Alvarez, n.d.).

One group of migrants includes between 15,000 and 20,000 Huichols, who inhabit the mountains of the Sierra Madre Occidental. Approximately 40 percent of all the Huichol families leave their communities in the dry season to find employment in the tobacco fields of the Nayarit coast. During the rainy season, the Huichols traditionally cultivate a combination of corn, chile, beans, squash, and amaranth. The Mexican government has made the traditional cycle difficult by promoting monocultural planting, distributing hybrid seeds of corn that require the use of pesticides and artificial fertilizers, and replacing the mixed seeds that traditionally were used by the Huichols and other indigenous agricultural peoples. The use of industrial-scale monocultural agriculture breaks down the indigenous traditions of cooperation while, at the same time, increasing malnutrition and alcoholism. The introduction of herbicides such as Paraquat and 2,4-D gradually destroys communal work, placing the health of cultivators and their families in danger (Diaz-Romo and Salinas-Alvarez, n.d.).

A report on the travails of the Huichols said: "To arrive at the tobacco fields the Huichols make a journey from the Sierras under subhuman conditions, arriving hungry and thirsty. The 'valuable and appreciated' human merchandise includes pregnant women, babies incapable of crying, mute from pain, who have recently been born to malnourished mothers or mothers with tuberculosis. Vulnerable elders and even the 'strong' men arrive at these centers in weak condition" (Diaz-Romo and Salinas-Alvarez, n.d.).

Favored workers are given purified water, while the remainder are forced to drink water from irrigation canals that draw from the pesticide-laced Santiago River, or local wells that also have been contaminated with the chemicals used in the tobacco fields. As they toil in the heat, the workers become drenched with sweat, allowing their bodies to absorb pesticide residues more easily. Nicotine in the tobacco also causes skin irritation and hives, called Green Tobacco Sickness. Child laborers are particularly susceptible to the effects of pesticides and the Green Tobacco Sickness (Diaz-Romo and Salinas-Alvarez, n.d.).

The harvesting families often spend the entire day and night in the fields, living and sleeping in boxes, or under blankets or sheets of plastic, beneath the strings of drying tobacco leaves, further exposing themselves to toxic chemicals and tobacco residues. Most have no potable water, drainage, or latrines. Occasionally, "The Huichols use the empty pesticide containers to carry their drinking water, without paying notice to the grave dangers that this represents, since the majority cannot read the instructions on the labels which may be written in English" (Diaz-Romo and Salinas-Alvarez, n.d.).

Further Reading

Bernstein, Dennis J. "Farmworkers Protest EPA's Pesticide Ruling." Consortiumnews.com, July 22, 2017. https://consortiumnews.com/2017/07/22/farmworkers-protest-epas-pesticide-ruling/

Bienkowski, Brian. "Study of Iowa, North Carolina Farmworkers Finds High Doses of Pesticides Can Potentially Impact DNA, Triggering Cancers Later in Life." Environmental Health News, February 16, 2017. https://www.ehn.org/researchers_find_pesticide_spills_accidents_may_alter_farmworkers_dna-2497137986.html

Branch, John, and Eric Lipton. "Dismissing Science." *New York Times*, December 27, 2018, F-4–F-5.

Brown, Brian. "Pesticides: The Workplace Hazard That the EPA Is Ignoring." Earthjustice, 2017. Accessed October 11, 2017. https://earthjustice.org/features/pesticides-the-workplace-hazard-the-epa-is-ignoring

"Chavez—December 19." University of Washington *Daily*, December 10, 1969. Seattle Civil Rights and Labor History Project. Special Section: Chicano Movement Newspaper Coverage 1968–79. http://depts.washington.edu/civilr/mecha_news.htm

Diaz-Romo, Patricia, and Samuel Salinas-Alvarez. "Migrant Workers and Pesticides. A Poisoned Culture: The Case of the Indigenous Huichols Farm Workers." *Abya Yala News: The Journal of the South and Meso-American Rights Center*, n.d. http://saiic.nativeweb.org/ayn/huichol.html

"Farmworkers." Pesticide Action Network, n.d. Accessed October 11, 2017. http://www.panna.org/frontline-communities/farmworkers

Goldberg, Ted. "Chemicals Sicken Two Dozen Central Coast Farmworkers in One Week." KQED Science, June 30, 2017. https://ww2.kqed.org/news/2017/06/30/chemicals-sicken-two-dozen-central-coast-farm-workers-in-one-week/

"Grape Boycott Store Visit." Leaflet, Seattle, 1969.

Hannula, Don. "Uhlman Again Backs Chávez, Gets Cheers." *Seattle Times*, December 20, 1969, n.p.

Hannula, Don. "From Chavez: A Spiritual Note." *Seattle Times*, December 21, 1969, C-1.

Israel, Brett. "Heavily Used Pesticide Linked to Breathing Problems in Farmworkers' Children." *Berkeley News*, August 14, 2017.

McClurg, Lesley. "Farmworkers Want Pesticide Banned in California After Trump EPA Refuses." KQED Science, October 9, 2017. https://ww2.kqed.org/futureofyou/2017/10/09/farmworkers-want-common-pesticide-banned-in-calif-after-trump-epa-refuses/

"Pesticide Poisoning of Farmworkers: Bakersfield." Migrant Clinicians Network. May 19, 2017. http://www.migrantclinician.org/blog/2017/may/pesticide-poisoning-farmworkers-bakersfield.html

Pesticide Safety. Farmworker Safety. 2017. https://www.farmworkerjustice.org/content/pesticide-safety

Philpott, Tom. "Trump's EPA Greenlights a Nasty Chemical. A Month Later, It Poisons a Bunch of Farmworkers." *Mother Jones,* May, 2017 http://www.motherjones.com/environment/2017/05/california-farm-workers-just-got-poisoned-nasty-pesticide-greenlghted-trump/

Raanan, Rachel, Robert B. Gunier, John R. Balmes, Alyssa J. Beltran, Kim G. Harley, Asa Bradman, and Brenda Eskenazi. "Elemental Sulfur Use and Associations with Pediatric Lung Function and Respiratory Symptoms in an Agricultural Community (California, USA)." *Environmental Health Perspectives* 125, no. 8 (August 2017). https://ehp.niehs.nih.gov/ehp528/

Stein, Fernando. "A Pesticide and the EPA." *New York Times*, November 2, 2017. https://www.nytimes.com/2017/11/01/opinion/pesticide-epa.html

Extermination of the Buffalo as Environmental Warfare

The United States surged westward across the North American continent during the nineteenth century, propelled by a relatively new form of environmental warfare that destroyed Native peoples' economic base, including the buffalo culture of the Great Plains. Within a few decades, dozens of Native American nations were reduced to poverty, without buffalo, and restricted to reservations where they were dependent on the U.S. government. The spread of several devastating diseases (such as smallpox) and alcoholism sped the conquest, as did technical innovations such as improved weapons of war and the railroad.

General Phil Sheridan of the U.S. Army viewed slaughter of the buffalo as a weapon in the U.S. Army's arsenal against the last remaining independent Native Americans: "I would not seriously regret the total disappearance of the buffalo from our western prairies, in its effect upon the Indians, regarding it rather as a means of hastening their dependence upon products of the soil [e.g., as farmers]," Sheridan said (Morris, 1992, 343). At one point, Sheridan suggested that buffalo poachers be given medals with a dead buffalo engraved on one side and a discouraged-looking Indian on the other (Morris, 1992, 343). Sheridan, never a man to mince words, remarked that buffalo hunters had done more to defeat the Indians than the entire regular United States Army.

Buffalo (Bison) Culture: History and Origins

On the high plains of North America, the buffalo was basic to Native American economic life and culture well into the nineteenth century. When European-American settlement began to encroach on the area early in that century, an estimated 30 million buffalo lived in a large area from present-day Texas in the south to northern Alberta. East and west, buffalo ranged from present-day New York State to Alabama and Mississippi, to Idaho and eastern Oregon.

John Fire Lame Deer, a Brulé spiritual leader, recalled that, culturally, "The buffalo was part of us, his flesh and blood being absorbed by us until it became our own flesh and blood. Our clothing, our tipis, everything we needed for life came from the buffalo's body. It was hard to say where the animal ended and the man began" (Hedren, 2011, 92). Major Irving Richard Dodge was riding with the Third Cavalry in 1871 when he observed, "The whole country appeared one mass of buffalo" (Hedren, 2011, 94). In 1876, another soldier said, "As far as the eye could reach on both sides of our route . . . somber, superb buffalos were grazing in thousands! The earth was brown with them" (Hedren, 2011, 94).

Most native peoples worked nature into their rituals and customs because their lives depended on the bounty of the land around them. Where a single animal comprised the basis of a native economy (such as the salmon of the Pacific Northwest or the buffalo on the Great Plains), strict cultural sanctions came into play against killing of such animals in numbers that would exceed their natural replacement rate. On the Plains, the military societies of the Cheyenne, Lakota, and other peoples enforced rules against hunting buffalo out of season, and against taking more animals than people could use. Many Plains societies had special police who maintained discipline before and during communal buffalo hunts. An individual who began the hunt early could be severely punished.

Native peoples on the Plains used nearly every part of the buffalo in their every-day cultural economies. In addition to the meat that was eaten fresh or preserved as jerky, buffalo hides were tanned and used as tipi covers, moccasin tops, shirts, leggings, dresses, and other clothing, bedding, bags, and pouches. Rawhide was used for moccasin soles, shields, rattles, drums, saddles, bridles, and other horse tack, as well as snowshoes. Buffalo horns were fashioned into cups, spoons, and other eating utensils, toys, and rattles. The bones became knives, arrowheads, shovels, hoes, war clubs, and ceremonial objects, while buffalo hair was used in headdresses and ropes. Buffalo tails became fly brushes; while the bladder could be fashioned into a watertight canteen. Buffalo chips were sometimes used as fuel when wood was unavailable.

Buffalo Hunt Customs and Protocols

Before they acquired horses, Native bands sometimes hunted buffalo by herding them over "jumps," cliffs that were nearly invisible to the stampeding animals until they were crowded over the edge by others behind them, after which they would be killed with arrows. Following such a stampede, the hunters and their wives worked quickly to preserve the meat, often by drying it in the sun to make jerky. In the heat of summer, when buffaloes were usually hunted, undressed meat could spoil within a day.

Before they acquired horses from the immigrating Europeans, the traveling range of Plains Native peoples was limited. Many of them lived east of the areas that they later utilized as buffalo-hunting ranges. The Lakota, Nakota, and Dakota (called Sioux by the immigrants), for example, lived mainly in present-day Minnesota, where they pursued a mixed agriculture, raising corn and other crops, and hunting buffalo when they came within a range that could be reached on foot.

A pedestrian buffalo hunt could be undertaken without a bluff. It required careful organization and planning by the people of several villages, and tended to encourage a culture of clans organized in a hierarchical manner. A leader was chosen and given absolute obedience during the hunt. Individual hunting that might incite an unplanned stampede was strictly forbidden and punished. "The leader organized all members of the village(s) to form a large circle around the herd," wrote Andrew C. Isenberg, Hall Distinguished Professor of American History at the University of Kansas. "On cue, the hunters slowly closed the circle, careful not to alarm the animals. Once they had closed the circle they fired the prairie grass, enclosing the herd, and proceeded to shoot the trapped animals with arrows" (2000, 38).

Native acquisition of the horse had an immense impact both on the hunting of buffalo and on the economic behavior and social structure of native societies. A large number of native societies transformed themselves into roving buffalo hunting bands. Elite societies of young men skilled at buffalo hunting emerged, forming the basis of the Plains warrior societies, who pursued the animals. A male buffalo can weigh a ton and can charge at 30 miles an hour.

When the men of a village realized that a buffalo herd was within a few hours' journey, they met to decide whether to organize a hunt. Unless other affairs intervened, the ready presence of sustenance was enough to get people moving. A crier was sent through the village or camp, announcing plans for the hunt, urging all able-bodied men to assemble with their horses, arrows at the ready, knives sharpened. Women also sometimes accompanied men on the hunt, to dress meat and hides, or just to ride along. Sarah Olden wrote (1999, 113): "The whole band . . . in feathers and war paint, bearing knives, clubs, bows, and arrows then mounted their lively, knowing, little horses and rushed out of camp to the beating of drums and the singing of songs for the buffalo chase."

The group usually appointed two leaders to enforce discipline. Guns were forbidden on buffalo hunts, and anyone using one could be beaten on the spot. Back in camp, an offender's tipi might be destroyed as well. The sound of gunfire could cause a stampede and wreck a hunt. Reaching the herd's range, the hunting party stopped to plan a strategy. The hunt was a team effort, and anyone who showed off by running ahead of the group was whipped and forced back into line—again, too much agitation could startle the animals and ruin the hunt.

At the leaders' signal, the hunters advanced on the buffalo, which at first usually stood their ground, as if dazed. After a prearranged sharp shout, the buffalo took off, with the mounted Indians following, isolating as many animals as needed and killing them. Occasionally, a bull might reverse field and charge into the hunting party. Some men died this way. After the hunt women dressed the meat and hides, which were loaded onto extra horses set aside for that purpose. Some of the meat was cooked and eaten as part of a celebratory feast before everyone returned home. Some of the dried meat and carcasses might be wrapped in hides and buried in the cool earth for future use (Olden, 1999, 114).

The tanning of hides was hard work, as described by a contemporary observer: "First the thick fat was scraped from the inside with a horn, and a mush or paste made of the brain, liver, and gall was rubbed over it again and again. The hide was turned toward the sun for a day or two and then soaked for some time in an infusion of sage brush. It was dried thoroughly and rubbed all over with a large stone . . . [to] make it soft and pliable" (Olden, 1999, 121).

How Native Cultures Changed

European immigration fundamentally altered many Native American cultures' relationship with the buffalo in two ways. First, the arrival of and adaptation to horses imported from Europe changed semi-sedentary cultures that had mixed agriculture with occasional buffalo hunting into mainly nomadic peoples adapted to following buffalo herds and using them as their major source of sustenance. Second, the arrival of capitalist mercantilism drafted many Native Americans into industrial roles, making buffalo robes for Europeans and European Americans—and thereby into the cash economy. During the 1870s and the early 1880s, the Society for the Prevention of Cruelty to Animals (SPCA) made opposition to the buffalo hide trade one of its early campaigns (Isenberg, 2000, 5).

The Native peoples were very sensitive to changes in their environments that preceded larger changes in their cultures wrought by the tide of immigrants. One such change was the arrival of European honeybees. By 1810, if not before, the bees, which had arrived in Virginia during the 1620s, had reached the Missouri River Valley. Naturalist John Bradbury wrote in 1810 that the honeybee had reached the Missouri River homeland of the U'ma'hos (Omahas), whom he called "Mahas": "Bees have spread over this continent to a degree, and with a celebrity so nearly corresponding with that of the Anglo-Americans that it has given rise to a belief, both among the Indians and the Whites, that bees are their precursors" (Bradbury, 1810, 58). Washington Irving, writing in a travel book dated 1835 (*A Tour on the Prairie*), noted swarms of honeybees and said, "The Indians consider them harbingers of the white man, as the buffalo is of the red man; and say that, in proportion as the bee advances, the Indian and the buffalo retire" (Irving, 1956, 50). The Indians also feared the honeybee as a sign that smallpox would soon devastate them.

The phrase "Indian summer" came into English as a signifier of cultural change during the nineteenth century. It refers to a period of mild weather, usually in early October, which followed the first frost (this cycle is often later today because of global warming). Native peoples were accustomed to moving between summer and winter camps. Following the incursion of European Americans, migrating Native peoples often found their way impeded by farms, livestock, railroads, and fences, so conflicts broke out. The nomadic lifestyle was supported by a trading culture with the whites that created demand for skins not only of buffalo, but also other animals, such as beaver, which also became fashionable on the East Coast and Europe during the nineteenth century.

Many Native peoples also knowingly adapted to a nomadic culture to avoid imported diseases, the most dangerous of which was smallpox. Sedentary peoples were much more likely to fall prey to contagions. Population estimates between 1780 and 1877 indicated that while sedentary peoples lost as many as 80 to 90 percent of their people (mainly to disease), nomads often lost 10 to 20 percent (Isenberg, 2000, 59).

The nomadic way of life could be risky, with periods of abundance alternating with hunger. One captive of the Oglalas, Fanny Kelly, described a diet of bison leavened with locusts: "The Indians seemed refreshed by feasting on such small game" (Isenberg, 200, 73). Andrew H. Long wrote in 1821 that the Plains Indians' "means of subsistence are precarious and uncertain . . . a state of constant alarm and apprehension" (Long, 1904, 166). The chancy nature of life is also reflected in the folk tales of the Lakota and Cheyenne, which may cast the buffalo as "both a mythic source of social and environmental stability and a wily, elusive antagonist" (Isenberg, 2000, 75).

Taboos Against Waste

Isenberg speculated that the risky nature of life contributed to a communal culture that valued cooperation and relatively equitable distribution of food and other resources, although it did not eradicate class differences (2000, 64–66, 80). Conflict sometimes also broke out among various parts of the same group, especially among Sioux bands such as the Hunkpapa, who were known for being cantankerous. The customs of many civic societies among Plains peoples such as the Sioux and Cheyenne also stressed the virtues of charity for the poor. Scarcity also lay at the root of strong cultural taboos against waste.

Several eyewitness accounts indicated that the taboo against waste was frequently broken, especially during large summer hunts that might kill 200 to 300 bison in one afternoon, leaving a tribe with much more meat than anyone could process. A large hunt turned into a feast at which everyone ate as much as he or she could. Custom called for putting every part of an animal to good use, but in practice, the boom-and-bust cycle sometimes left the cleaning up to packs of wolves. Charles McKenzie observed that most of the 250 carcasses were left to rot after a successful summer hunt, "on the field where they fell, excepting the Tongues which they dried for a general feast" (Charles, 1985, 282).

The robe trade changed many Plains Native cultures quickly and fundamentally. The size of buffalo hunts exploded to as many as about 1,500 animals in one day. Any remaining taboo on waste vanished, as nothing often was taken from the dead buffalo except their hides and their tongues. The size of wolf packs following the hunting parties grew apace. "The White Wolves," wrote George Catlin, "followed the herds of buffaloes . . . glutting themselves on the carcasses of those that fall by the deadly shafts of their enemies" (Townsend, 1839, 21, 170).

Men of prestige in Northern Plains tribes had long taken more than one wife, but with the coming of the robe trade, families with two or three wives became families with five, six, and seven. Each woman represented a source of income when she dressed buffalo robes. The average age of weddings among the Blackfeet declined from the late teens to as young as twelve years of age. Anglo-American female captives sometimes were pressed into service as robe dressers (Branch, 1997, 2–73).

Buffalo Slaughter

The number of bison (or buffalo) in North America, principally on the Great Plains, declined from between 25 and 30 million in 1800 to a tiny fraction of that by about 1900, after which their extinction was averted narrowly by carefully managed conservation efforts. There exists no way to know exactly how close the buffalo came to extinction during this holocaust. Estimates of the population remaining in 1900 range from a few hundred to about 100,000. The American Bison Society, a private group, cooperated with the tribes and government agencies to restore some of the herds. By 1995, a concerted effort to replenish buffalo herds had raised the population to an estimated 200,000. By 2010, buffalo were being raised commercially. Buffalo burgers went on sale in Omaha, and grocery stores stocked buffalo jerky.

The slaughter of the vast buffalo herds that had once roamed the Great Plains and prairies began in the 1840s. During most years of the 1870s, a million buffalo a year were killed by non-Indian hunters on the northern Plains. The railroads ran special excursions along their newly opened tracks from which self-styled sportsmen shot buffalo from the comfort of their seats.

The near-extermination of the buffalo was mainly a result of the European American incursion into the Plains, which seized their range for cattle that overgrazed buffalo habitats and spread diseases fatal to them, just as the Indians who had hunted them also were dying for the same reasons. Part of the population decline came about because of hunting for their skins, which became fashionable as coats among Europeans and their offspring in America. Part of the killing also was purposeful, without a trade stimulus, to deprive the Plains peoples of an animal vital to their cultures and economies. In this event, huge piles of buffalo carcasses were often left to rot, with only the tongues (a dietary delicacy) removed.

By the 1830s, steamboats were plying the Missouri and Mississippi rivers, hauling dressed buffalo robes to New Orleans *en masse*. In 1801, the annual exports could be counted on one's fingers; by 1825 to 1830, an average of 130,000 buffalo robes per year arrived from upriver at New Orleans (Isenberg, 2000, 105). Among the Lakota, Nakota, Dakota, Cheyenne, and other peoples, buffalo robes became the backbone of trade culture. All of this lasted a few decades, until the buffalo were nearly gone and robes went out of fashion. The many Plains peoples who had become suddenly prosperous suddenly descended into destitution. The winter count of a Blackfoot band that called itself the Buffalo Followers said 1854 was "the year we ate dogs" (Isenberg, 2000, 112).

The buffalo herds of the central plains were finished off during the 1860s with a technological boost from a new line of high-powered hunting rifles. The large buffalo herds that had roamed the southern plains, sustaining thousands of Native people (who still lived as they preferred, with the buffalo at the root of their economies), were largely destroyed by the 1870s. Hunters of the dwindling herds were followed by skinners, who (depending on market conditions) might strip the hides, or just remove the slain buffaloes' tongues. No one ever counted the number of buffalo that fell.

The Speed of Extermination

The extermination of the buffalo on the Great Plains of North America occurred so quickly during the last half of the nineteenth century that an unknown number of Native Americans starved to death, unable to adapt to a new way of life based on an economic system in which the animal was not the most basic food. Treaty commissioners warned of the impending extermination beginning in the 1850s, "but," wrote historian John C. Ewers, "as long as there were buffalo to be hunted, their efforts to induce nomadic hunters to become sedentary farmers met with very little success. The Indians were too thoroughly committed by both experience and inclination . . . to a hunting-trading economy to abandon [it] as long as they had any choice in the matter" (Ewers, 1997, 58).

In many cases, the U.S. and Canadian governments also were unable to establish alternative food sources quickly enough to prevent profound human suffering and death. Hunger provoked wars—one example being the Great Sioux Uprising, which began during 1862 in Minnesota when U.S. officials refused to release food stockpiles to starving Indians from warehouses. That uprising ended with the largest mass hanging in U.S. history (38 people) at Mankato, Minnesota. Locals wanted to hang more than 300, but President Abraham Lincoln pardoned most of them for lack of evidence.

By the 1870s, the West was being knitted together by the railroads, and most of the Native peoples were confined to reservations. The bison hunt for the most part was being taken over by whites, who stepped up the slaughter. By this time, European Americans were killing more buffalo than Native Americans. Of 1.2 million buffalo skins shipped east on the railroads in 1872 and 1873, about 350,000 (28 percent) were supplied by Indians. The hides of the buffalo were being used for more than robes; they became the leather belts that ran industrial machinery. Buffalo bones by the ton were being ground into black pigment and fertilizer. During the 1860s and 1870s, the number of non-Indians in Arapaho country exploded, and buffalo herds declined markedly, largely at the hands of white sharpshooters who destroyed much of the Arapahos' traditional culture and economy, as it had been modified by the fur trade.

During one winter (1872–1873) hide dealers in Dodge City, Kansas, shipped out about 400,000 hides on the newly arrived Santa Fe Railroad.

Unifying Themes

While the area around Dodge City had been thickly populated with bison in 1872, a year later, "where there were myriads of buffalo . . . there were myriads of carcasses. The air was foul with sickening stench, and the vast plain which only a short twelve months before had teemed with animal life was a dead, solitary, putrid desert" (Dodge, 1989, 150–151). By one estimate, the Santa Fe, Kansas Pacific, and Union Pacific Railroads shipped 1.4 million buffalo hides between 1872 and 1874. Many hides were ruined in processing and never were shipped, perhaps three to five to one (Isenberg, 2000, 136). By the late 1870s, buffalo on the Southern Plains had been nearly exterminated; a railroad spur opened to Miles City, Montana, and the process continued in that area. A *New York Times* reporter in Miles City wrote in 1880, "The prairies . . . are covered with the carcasses of bison" ("Montana's," 1880, 2).

The Plains were swarming with unemployed railroad workers, would-be farmers whose homesteads could not sustain their families, and hopeful miners caught between gold rushes. Buffalo populations were reduced to levels that would no longer sustain the trade; during the 1880s, there were an estimated 5,000 non-Indian hunters chasing them. By the early 1880s, the U.S. Army's version of total war against the Plains Indians had reached its goal: the buffalo were nearly extinct. Ten years earlier, some of the Plains Indians still had an ample supply of food; by the early 1880s, they were reduced, as General Sheridan had intended, to the condition of paupers, without food, shelter, clothing, or any of those necessities of life that came from the buffalo. The Great Plains buffalo culture was dead.

Buffalo Today

By 2012, buffalo in the United States numbered more than 500,000, many of them being raised as a lean alternative to beef. Ted Turner, who made a fortune in cable television and invested part of it in a large swath of the Nebraska Sand Hills, raised a large bison herd there. Upscale grocery stores sell bison steaks as a lean alternative to beef. The National Bison Legacy Act, introduced in the U.S. Senate in 2012, would designate bison as the "National Mammal of the United States," a new designation. A white bison in Texas was slaughtered during 2011 in what may have been a racial hate crime because of the animal's sacred nature.

Buffalo are still closely identified with Native American culture, so much so that when a rare white buffalo (one in 10 million) was born on a farm near Goshen, Connecticut during June 2012, many American Indians traveled there for four days of festivities and a naming ceremony on July 28. A white bison was believed by many Oglala Lakota to be a spiritual manifestation of the White Buffalo Calf Maiden, or *ptesan wi*, a prophet, who taught the Lakota sacred rituals and provided their sacred pipe (Applebome, 2012). The 30-pound calf was born on Peter Fay's farm in Litchfield County, Connecticut, an event that, according to an account in the *New York Times*, "made the Fay farm below Mohawk Mountain, for the moment at least, the unlikely epicenter of the bison universe" (Applebome, 2012).

People traveled to the Fay farm from across North America to see the white buffalo calf. "They're awesome animals, wild, not domesticated," Fay said. "You think of them in South Dakota, where it's a desert and hot in the summer and bitterly cold in the winter. They don't mind either one. And they don't get sick. They're not like a cow. They're very hardy. They can deal with anything" (Applebome, 2012). Fay said he carefully researched the bloodlines of the calf's mother and father, and he is confident the animal is all bison without any intermingling with cattle. But to be certain, he ascertained the bison's purity with a DNA test. Keith Aune, senior conservation scientist with the Wildlife Conservation Society, said some white bison are albinos and have difficulty thriving in the wild because they lack the black skin that absorbs sunlight during harsh winters.

Marian White Mouse brought her family from Wanblee, South Dakota, on the Pine Ridge Oglala Lakota reservation, to see what they regarded as a major spiritual event. "They are very rare, and when a white bison is born there is a reason for each one to be here," White Mouse said. "It's such a blessing for someone to take care of a bison like Peter Fay will. I told him when it was born, 'You don't even know what you have on your hands here'" (Applebome, 2012).

Further Reading

Applebome, Peter. "A Bison So Rare It's Sacred." *New York Times*, July 12, 2012. http://www.nytimes.com/2012/07/13/nyregion/sacred-white-bison-is-born-in-rural-connecticut.html

Bradbury, John. *Travels in the Interior of America in the Years 1809, 1810, and 1811*. London: Sheerwood, Neely, and Jones, 1810. In Reuben Golf Thwaites, ed., *Early Western Travels: 1748–1846*, Vol. 5. Cleveland: Clark, 1904.

Branch, E. Douglas. *The Hunting of the Buffalo*. Lincoln: University of Nebraska Press, 1997.

"Charles McKenzie's Narratives." In W. Raymond Wood and Thomas D. Thiessen, eds., *Early Fur Trade on the Northern Plains: Canadian Traders Among the Hidatsa and Indians, 1738–1818*. Norman: University of Oklahoma Press, 1985.

Dodge, Richard I. *The Plains of North America and Their Inhabitants*. Newark: University of Delaware Press, 1989.

Ewers, John C. *Plains Indian History and Culture: Essays in Continuity and Change.* Norman: University of Oklahoma Press, 1997.
Garretson, Martin S. *The American Bison: The Story of Its Extermination as a Wild Species and Its Restoration Under Federal Protection.* New York: New York Zoological Society, 1938.
Hedren, Paul L. *After Custer: Loss and Transformation in Sioux Country.* Norman: University of Oklahoma Press, 2011.
Hodgson, Bryan. "Buffalo: Back Home on the Range." *National Geographic* 186, no. 5 (November 1994): 64–89.
Hornaday, William T. "The Extermination of the American Bison with a Sketch of Its Discovery and Life History." *Annual Report of the Smithsonian Institution.* 1887, Vol. II. Washington, D.C.: Government Printing Office, 1889, 367–548.
Irving, Washington. *A Tour on the Prairie.* [1835] Ed. John Francis McDermott. Norman: University of Oklahoma Press, 1956.
Isenberg, Andrew C. *The Destruction of the Bison: An Environmental History, 1750–1920.* Cambridge: Cambridge University Press, 2000.
Johnson, Lowell, ed. *The First Voices.* Lincoln: University of Nebraska Press, 1984.
Klein, Alan M. "The Political Economy of the Buffalo Hide Trade: Race and Class on the Plains." In John H. Moore, ed., *Political Economy of North American Indians.* Norman: University of Oklahoma Press, 1993.
Long, Stephen H. "A General Description of the Country Traversed by the Exploring Expedition." In Reuben Golf Thwaites, ed., *Early Western Travels: 1748–1846*, Vol. 5. Reuben Golf Thwaites. Cleveland: Clark, 1904.
"Montana's Indian Puzzle." *New York Times*, April 4, 1880, 2.
Morris, Roy, Jr. *Sheridan: The Life and Wars of General Phil Sheridan.* New York: Crown Publishers, 1992.
National Bison Legacy Act website. [votebison.org]. Accessed July 25, 2012.
Olden, Sarah. "Part II: The People of Tipi Sapa." In Vine Deloria, Jr., *Singing for a Spirit: A Portrait of the Oglala Sioux.* Santa Fe, NM: Clear Light Publishers, 1999.
Townsend, John K. *Narratives of a Journey Across the Rocky Mountains to the Columbia River.* Boston: Perkins and Marvin, 1839.
Walker, James R. *Lakota Society*, ed. Raymond J. DeMallie. Lincoln: University of Nebraska Press, 1982.

Environmental Racism and the Demise of an Ice World

The native peoples of Alaska and the Canadian Arctic are experiencing global warming at a much more rapid rate than any other populated area on Earth. Their world, heretofore based on and adapted to ice and snow most of the year, is melting away because of fossil fuels that are being burned at lower latitudes—a graphic example of environmental racism on a huge geographic scale.

A dramatic example of the climatic vise in which Arctic peoples find themselves is provided by the several coastal Alaskan Native villages that have been declared disaster areas, as severe storms erode them into the sea. In a colder time, ice formed along the shore in early autumn and contained the sea during its annual period of roiling storminess. By the 1990s, however, the deep freeze of Arctic winter often was arriving too late. By 2015, more than 30 Alaska Native villages were experiencing substantial damage as severe storms lashed them. "Alaska is seeing all these things the rest of the country hasn't seen yet," said Jerome Montague, Native Affairs and Natural Resources adviser for the Alaskan Command Joint Task Force (Jessepe, 2012).

"Climate-induced displacement not only severs the physical ties and rights indigenous peoples have to their land and resources, but also the spiritual relationship they have with their traditionally occupied places," wrote Julie K. Maldonado of the Department of Environmental Studies at the University of California Santa Barbara (2013, 601). The damage was copiously documented in U.S. federal government reports, which also confessed that while the Army Corps of Engineers could attempt to contain the damage with barriers, agencies had no legal authority or funding to move entire villages to new sites at an estimated $100 million to $200 million each.

If the U.S. federal government was as good at arranging relocations as issuing reports about them, new sites would have been found for these villages long ago. A growing stack of government reports has described flooding and erosion threatening four villages (Kivalina, Koyukuk, Newtok, and Shishmaref), residents of which all agree that they must move. The Newtok Traditional Council issued the first report, completed in 1984. Government often lacks legal authority and funding that may support relocation of villages as whole units, so indigenous people scatter individually or in family groups as flooding and erosion destroys villages, ruining culture and community and often intensifying impoverishment.

Alaska's Great Thaw

During the fall of 1998, sea ice formed in northern Alaska more than a month later than usual, postponing the annual seal and walrus hunt. Average temperatures at the mouth of the Mackenzie River were 9° F above long-term averages during 1998. Making matters worse, several decades ago miners in the area deposited toxic wastes in ponds that were expected to remain frozen (and the toxic materials sealed by the permafrost). With warmer temperatures, some of these toxic dumps may thaw and leak. Like other coastal Native communities, Nelson Lagoon in the Aleutian Islands has been battling the effects of winter storms for several years, building break walls to impede increasingly violent storm surges. One structure that residents had hoped would provide protection for several decades was "reduced to kindling within just a few seasons" (McLean, 2010).

The Indian Country Media Network reported, "The Yup'ik village of Kotlik, Alaska, along with Unalakleet and other predominantly Native communities, were ravaged beginning November 9, 2013, by a series of four storms that battered hundreds of miles of Alaska's west coast with near hurricane-force winds, a sea surge as high as nine feet, freezing rain, and snow," Alaska governor Sean Parnell said. The storm surge wrecked food supplies ("Yup'ik," 2013). For a time, the entire town was flooded with seawater and chunks of ice. Rising seas and coastal erosion also destroyed several buildings in Tuktoyaktuk, a Dene and Inuit community near the mouth of the Mackenzie River. Ice that once protected the coast had receded out to sea. Extensive erosion washed away Tuktoyaktuk's school, and forced the village to relocate many other structures.

Alaska's great thaw has also been washing human remains out to sea in a Yup'ik village 400 miles west of Anchorage that was occupied between about 1300 and 1650 CE. The village, known today as Nunalleq, heretofore frozen into the permafrost, is being washed into the Bering Sea. Archaeologists in 2009 removed about 20,000 artifacts, including large ceremonial masks, caribou antler harpoon points, dolls carved out of driftwood, jewelry fashioned from the ivory tusks of walrus (scrimshaw), and slate arrowheads. The archaeologists are racing against the advancing ocean, which had eroded about 30 feet of shore in five years by 2014, as they fear that one intense winter storm could carry away what remains.

Yup'ik elders in the small coastal Alaskan village of Kipnuk believe the village is sinking, due to warming permafrost. Buildings in the village show signs of an unstable ground surface, signs that are consistent with those of an area that sits above thawing land. In Kotzebue, Alaska, the hospital has been relocated because it was sinking into the ground.

Kivalina Surrenders to the Sea

Kivalina, a village of about 400 primarily Inupiat people on Alaska's northwest coast about 100 miles north of the Arctic Circle, spreads across a thin, barrier reef island that was first used as a hunting ground by peoples who have lived in the area for thousands of years. In 1905, Native parents were required by the federal government to enroll their children in school there or face imprisonment. The parents moved in with the children and began a settlement around the school.

The people of Kivalina began to notice changes in their weather that destabilized the earth under their feet in the 1950s and 1960s. For many years, sea ice had routinely formed on the beaches fronting Kivalina early each autumn. The hard freeze provided a hard surface and the ice protected the settlement against storm-tossed seas. As temperatures have risen in recent decades, ice forms in late November or even December, exposing the village to rough seas and erosion during fall. The strip of land under Kivalina shrank from 55 acres of livable space in 1953 to 27 acres in 2003, as the Chukchi Sea eroded the shoreline from the west and Kivalina Lagoon at the mouth of the Wulik and Kivalina Rivers undercut it from the east (Shearer, 2011, 13, 14, 50). The people of Kivalina decided that their location was unsustainable by 1990, and voted to move first in 1992, but found that no aid was available.

In Kivalina and elsewhere in the Arctic, life has been rapidly changing. Ice is becoming thinner at all seasons. Animal migration patterns have changed, forcing hunters to adapt. "Permafrost," no longer frozen in summer, has softened. People have adapted as best they are able—no one survives the rigors of the Arctic without learning to adapt. "At first, people were able to adapt to such small changes, in order . . . to subsist on the wild foods that the land, sea, and air had provided for hundreds of years," said Colleen Swan, the village's tribal administrator. "But the changes have been increasing, making adaptation difficult" (Shearer, 2011, 76).

In Kivalina by 2004, what was once a bearable cycle of fall storms became an annual life-threatening endurance contest. The island "was falling apart into the Chukchi Sea before the very eyes of its inhabitants," who struggled to buttress the crumbling shoreline. "Every object placed along the edges," said Swan, "was being sucked into the angry sea." The violence of the storms during that and following years made evacuation by sea impossible. "There was nowhere to go, and nothing the volunteers did worked to keep the island together—the people were trapped!" (Shearer, 2011, 100).

As the government pile of reports grew, in 2004 and 2005, storms of unusual ferocity struck Kivalina anew, eroding between 70 and 80 feet of coastline, exposing the permafrost, and endangering several houses. Following a declaration of emergency, the Federal Emergency Management Agency (FEMA) provided sandbags. In 2005, the U.S. Congress passed Section 117 of the 2005 Consolidated Appropriations Act, which sanctioned Army Corps of Engineers' actions "to carry out storm damage protection projects for Alaska Native Villages at full federal expense" (Maldonado et al., 2013, 601).

By now, nearly everyone in Kivalina realized that they could "only . . . get out of the way and let the impacts of climate change take their toll," according to Swan (Shearer, 2011, 12). Instead, the U.S. government brought in contractors who built what turned out to be temporary barriers, some of them *very* temporary. One infamous barrier brought in during October 2006, without community advice, was sand stacked in baskets. The people of Kivalina said it wouldn't last, and it didn't, not even until its official dedication on October 12. A storm blew up, the ocean roiled in, in what had by then become a routine fall event, and the undertow sucked most of the sand out to sea. The official celebration was canceled (Shearer, 2011, 135). The next year, a series of storms in October wiped out as much as 70 feet of beach. Homes that had been assumed safe were dangling over cliffs more or less above the ocean.

In 2007, another major storm forced evacuation of Kivalina. By this time, erosion and flooding was pouring sediment into the community water system, requiring filtration to prevent ingestion of unsanitary water. People in Kivalina could take only sponge baths and had limited access to laundry for the entire winter. "As hand-washing and bathing decreased, respiratory and skin diseases increased," health aides said ("Climate Change Puts," 2011). Kivalina, hanging precariously onto its slender, eroding peninsula, was described by the U.S. Army Corps of Engineers as living on borrowed time. The Corps forecast that the sea would wipe it off the map by 2025.

The Army Corps of Engineers in 2008 and 2009 built a rock revetment that it said would buy the village 10 to 15 years—at most, barring further episodic flooding. Also during 2008, with assistance from several environmental groups, Kivalina filed suit in U.S. federal court against 24 fossil-fuel companies, seeking reimbursement for its relocation expenses (variously estimated at $100 million to $400 million), based on the argument that the companies' business led to greenhouse-gas emissions that have been provoking erosion of their village. The suit, *Kivalina v. Exxon-Mobil, et al.,* was dismissed, as was their argument for climatic justice: "aiming to help Kivalina residents draw attention to their situation and call for action from government and corporate officials [who] had so far largely ignored them" (Shearer, 2011, 7). Dismissal by Judge Saundra Armstrong was based on the ubiquitous nature of global warming, which Armstrong ruled could not be traced to emissions of specific companies, making liability impossible to assign. The inability to assign blame and assess damage was being used at the same time to dismiss climate justice lawsuits all over North America. If everyone does it, no one can be blamed: the tragedy of the commons.

Many of Kivalina's residents maintained that moving the entire village inland was the only real solution. However, with no authority to move an entire village, the U.S. government continued to respond piece by piece, as it compiled reports, procured sandbags, and loaded large rocks onto the shoreline. According to one independent observer: "No agency has complete responsibility for relocation, and there are few policies and protocols in existence to legally move the process forward. Instead, there are multiple agencies with different authorities, norms, and responsibilities, which Kivalina residents must try to bring together through their own efforts. In addition, there have been disagreements over the new relocation site and tribal knowledge between Kivalina residents and government agencies and contractors, which has further slowed the relocation" (Maldonado et al., 2013, 601).

As of 2018, Kivalina was hanging onto its eroding shore in bits and pieces, waiting for nature to finish it off.

A Legal Strategy to Battle "Climigration"

While the U.S. government maintains an intricate bureaucracy that issues reports describing the need to relocate villages, Alaska Native peoples quickly found out that no government body exists that can actually implement a remedy for a disaster of this type. Disaster programs and funds are allocated only *after* a specific disastrous event occurs.

Robin Bronen, a human rights attorney and director of the Alaska Immigration Justice Project, who began research about community relocations in Alaska since 2006, has published extensively in legal venues on the need to reform the entire legal structure to recognize a new kind of migration spawned not by random disasters, but by the slow-motion, enduring destruction of global warming. Adapting legal doctrines to accommodate "Climigration"—migration made necessary by climate change—has become Bronen's rallying cry, and Alaska's coastal villages, most notably Newtok, have become her primary examples.

In the short term, Bronen argued that U.S. law governing disaster relief (primarily the Robert T. Stafford Disaster Relief and Emergency Assistance [Stafford] Act, 42 U.S.C. §§5121–5208 [2006]), must be amended to cover long-range habitat destruction due to climate change. Longer-term, on a worldwide basis, she suggested that the United Nations should convene an expert working group to develop "Guiding Principles on Climigration":

Unifying Themes 119

"Climigration should be covered by an adaptive governance framework based in human rights doctrine" (Bronen, 2011, 357–408). According to Bronen, "The statutory framework that governs post-disaster recovery and hazard mitigation encourages rigid responses to specifically defined random weather events" (2011, 365–366). Seeking to provide temporary relief that does not require a lot of resources, existing law does not provide relief for "environmental disasters that occur gradually and require relocation" (Bronen, 2011, 366). Existing laws also have cost-effectiveness rules that all but disqualify small settlements in rural areas where spending per person is very high, such as Alaska's Native villages.

Bronen (2011, 407) asserted that migration related to climate change presents its own challenges:

> Hazardous waste cleanup is a critical component of the relocation process. Climate-induced ecological changes may create unique challenges to securing hazards. In Alaska, thawing permafrost and erosion are creating unstable ground that will prevent the traditional methods of abandonment, such as capping a landfill, from protecting the environment. Fuel tank farms and sewage facilities may collapse into the rivers or lakes as more erosion occurs. In addition, exposure to contaminants that were previously frozen and buried are a concern with erosion and melting permafrost because of the possibility that they can enter the soil and water sources. Determining the appropriate method to secure these facilities will require planning, money, and expert technical assistance.

Newtok's Life Runs Out to Sea

The Yup'ik Eskimos who live in the village of Newtok on the Ninglick River adjacent to the Bering Sea in far western Alaska, and whose ancestors have lived along the Bering Sea coast for 2,000 years or more, are known as Qaluyaarmiut ("dip net people"), one of about 230 federally recognized indigenous tribes in Alaska. Newtok was home, until recent years, of about 400 people in 63 houses, only a few of which are well insulated and some of which have been sinking into thawing permafrost. No roads connect Newtok to the outside; the only access is by small airplane (seating nine or fewer people and some food or other basic supplies) or by barge (before the town's loading dock was destroyed by the rampaging sea).

Arrivals by air are often delayed by fog and strong winds that drive ground blizzards. By 2014, Newtok had lost much of its infrastructure and housing to thawing permafrost, erosion, and violent weather, as its people were dispersing. Newtok shared a fate similar to Native communities on the coast of Louisiana that were experiencing climate change provoked by subsiding land, rising seas, and saltwater intrusion. As at Kivalina, several storms have muscled ashore (six of them major, historic-scale tempests between 1989 and 2006), speeding the demise of Newtok. The U.S. Federal Emergency Management Agency (FEMA) declared disasters after five of those six storms.

It would be difficult to imagine a place less suitable for repair than Newtok. The village's site is caught in a vise of problems, none of which can be addressed long-term by reconstructing the community in its present location. The village's public infrastructure (dumpsite, barge ramp, sewage treatment facility, and fuel storage facilities) has been destroyed by climate change.

Like Kivalina, Newtok formed around a government school. In 1950, Newtok's school site was chosen in large part because barges carrying construction supplies could land there. The families whose members moved in around the new school built sod houses. The Ninglick River now is steadily eroding closer to the village, as thawing permafrost, waves, and the river's current accelerates its approach. The river, a mile away in 1950s, is now undermining people's houses. According to the U.S. Army Corps of Engineers at the beginning of the century, anticipated erosion of the Ninglick River would reach the school, still the largest building in the village, by about 2017 (Bronen, 2011, 377). By May 2006, erosion was severing 70 feet of Newtok's land per year.

None of Newtok's houses have complete plumbing. Water is supplied from a shallow pond in the tundra to a pumping station on top of storage tanks. The last filling of any given tank must last through the winter, when the system freezes. Saltwater also has been seeping into Newtok's potable water supply. By 2016, the Corps of Engineers estimates that erosion will contaminate the pond that supplies Newtok's water.

Furthermore, Newtok lacks an adequate sewage disposal system, according to an on-the-scene report:

> As a result, "honey buckets"—five-gallon buckets with plastic bag liners—are used in most homes in place of plumbing and sewage disposal. Newtok residents dump raw sewage from the honey buckets into the Newtok River, located just adjacent to the community. Because this section of the river has become a slough, the river is not able to flush the waste away from the village. Raw sewage from the school is dumped into a sewage lagoon, an open-air pond between the school and the Newtok River. Due to the lagoon's close proximity to the Newtok River, it is subject to flooding and leaks into an area residents use to dry subsistence fish. (Bronen, 2011, 379)

Newtok lacks a sanitary landfill and sewage treatment. Garbage collected in the village must be transported across the Newtok River by boat at high tide. From 1994 to 2004, 29 percent of Newtok's infants were hospitalized with lower respiratory tract infections due to unhealthy levels of contamination and lack of potable water, which has become very scarce due to increasing saltwater intrusion.

Storm tides flooded the village water supply, causing raw sewage to spread through the community, displacing residents from homes, destroying food storage, and shutting down essential utilities. Public infrastructure has been significantly damaged or destroyed due to the combination of extreme weather events and ongoing erosion. A major storm in 2005 took out the Ninglick River barge landing, so fuel and other supplies could no longer be delivered by sea during the annual thaw.

Who would want to live in such a place? By 2003, Newtok residents had voted three times on a proposal to move to Nelson Island, nine miles away. Newtok even obtained a title to the site and named it Mertarvik in a land-exchange agreement with the U.S. Fish and Wildlife Service. As with Kivalina, Newtok's proposed move has been described in a thick file of federal government reports. The Newtok Traditional Council began a formal planning process for a "strategic relocation planning process" in 2006.

The beginnings of infrastructure have been built at the new site: a barge landing, six houses, and a foundation for what might become an emergency evacuation center. However, no sewage, water, or electric utilities were available as of 2017. Every step has encountered a governmental gauntlet. In the meantime, angry seas and melting permafrost slowly turn old Newtok into a climate-change memorial.

Shishmaref's Demise

Six hundred people in the Inuit village of Shishmaref, on a barrier island just north of the Bering Strait (called Kigiktaq by the Inupiaq in the village), on the Chukchi Sea, about 60 miles north of Nome, have been watching their village erode into the sea. The site had been occupied for almost 400 years when increasing storm surges began to erode more than 23 feet a year off its shoreline late in the twentieth century. Within a few years, the new climate regime in which ice no longer held back the increasingly turbulent sea was threatening the old village with destruction (Cordalis and Suagee, 2008, 47).

The permafrost that once reinforced Shishmaref's coast has been thawing. "We stand on the island's edge and see the remains of houses fallen into the sea," wrote Anton Antonowicz of the London *Daily Mirror.* "They are the homes of poor people. Half-torn rooms with few luxuries. A few photographs, some abandoned cooking pots. Some battered suitcases" (Antonowicz, 2000, 8). Percy Nayokpuk, a village elder, runs the local store, which now perches dangerously close to the edge of the advancing sea. "When I was a teenager, the beach stretched at least 50 yards further out," said Percy. "As each year passes, the sea's approach seems faster" (Antonowicz, 2000, 8). Several houses have washed into the sea; the U.S. Army Corps of Engineers has moved or jacked up others. The villagers have been told they will soon have to move.

Year by year, the hunting season, which depends on the arrival of the ice, starts later and ends earlier. "Instead of dog mushing, we have dog slushing," said Clifford Weyiouanna, 58, a reindeer herder near Shishmaref in 2000 (Antonowicz, 2000, 8). Villagers have been catching fish such as flounder, which are usually found in warmer water.

By the summer of 2001, the encroaching sea was threatening a rusty fuel-tank farm holding 80,000 gallons of gasoline and stove oil. "Several years ago," observed Kim Murphy of the *Los Angeles Times,* "the tanks were more than 300 feet from the edge of a seaside bluff. But years of retreating sea ice have sent storm waters pounding. . . . just 35 feet of fine sandy bluff stands between the tanks and disaster" (Murphy, 2001: A-1). Seawater is lapping near the town's airport runway, its only long-distance connection to the outside. At last count, three houses had been washed into the sea. Several more are threatened. The town's drinking-water supply also has been inundated by the sea.

Shishmaref hunters are being forced to search up to 200 miles from town for walrus, because of retreating ice. They now have to use boats to hunt seals that they used to track over ice. "This year the ice was thinner, and most of the year at least part of the sea was open. We don't normally see open water in December," said Edwin Weyiouanna, an artist who has lived most of his life on the Chukchi Sea (Murphy, 2001, A-1). In earlier years, the sea was more likely to be frozen during much of the stormy winter season. With warming, the erosive, wind-whipped ocean corrodes Shishmaref's waterfront. The town's residents have come to fear the full moon, with its unusually high tides.

Old photos recall a time when Shishmaref fronted on wide, sandy beaches. Today, each major storm carves off chunks of the island. Then, as now, most of Shishmaref's houses have no running water or plumbing, so the town's residents capture rain and snow for reuse, as most residents shower and wash their clothes at a public facility. As its island sinks and houses crumble into the sea, people crowd into what remains. Several plans to move have come and gone, and, by 2014, many people in the village had given up on moving because of its price tag of $179 million, according to a study by the Army Corps of Engineers.

Elders remember when "fourteen houses on Shishmaref's north side had to be put on skids and dragged down to the opposite end of the island after a major storm in October 1997. Another big storm in October 2001 sloughed off huge chunks of the northern shoreline" (Sheppard, 2014). In the meantime, money from the U.S. federal government dried up after Senator Ted Stevens was defeated. Sea walls have been built, and the sea has swallowed them. Talk of relocation, which included a popular vote in favor, did little except stymie life on the present site. "It stopped all investment in this community," said Percy Nayokpuk, owner of the island's general store. "There's been a lot of projects lost because of the vote to move. Voting was the easy part. Raising the money required to move the entire village proved much more difficult. That's about all that's resulted from that vote" (Sheppard, 2014). Dozens of reporters and television crews came and went, as the island continued to shrink over years and then decades. By 2014, Kate Sheppard wrote in the *Huffington Post*, "City and tribal leaders say the relocation effort is largely dormant, for now. Residents who had been involved in the relocation plan said they just got busy with other things. One woman was diagnosed with cancer and had to take a break. Others said they became wrapped up with family or work, or just got frustrated with the insurmountable nature of the task" (Sheppard, 2014).

Point Hope: Don't Drink the Water, or Eat the Meat

Point Hope, an Inupiaq community on a spit of land that juts into the Chukchi Sea, has been losing its battle against the sea. Almost $2 million was spent to shore up its runway (the only connection with the outside, except for an evacuation road restored by the Army Corps of Engineers). Potable water also has been falling prey to increasing algal blooms in the Point Hope community. In several areas, melting permafrost has drained rivers and lakes used to supply water to Native villages. Paradoxically, according to one scientific analysis, "Extreme precipitation events can lead to flood-related contamination and high turbidity levels that can overwhelm water treatment systems. Subsidence due to permafrost thawing and erosion are causing widespread physical damage to water infrastructure, sometimes interrupting services for months," according to one account (Cozzetto et al., 2013, 569).

"We used to have frozen whale meat and *muktuk* [a frozen meal of whale skin and blubber] all winter and summertime, too," said Joe

Towksjhea, a Point Hope resident, in the consortium's report. "It is not frozen anymore" ("Climate Change Puts," 2011). According to Sylvester Ayek, who hunts on King Island in the Bering Sea, the greater problem is the dwindling number of animals due to late freeze and early thaw. "What we hunt is usually around ice. And when the ice goes earlier, like these past few years, the game is gone," Ayek told Indian Country Today Media Network. If a hunter has no game, storage is a moot point. This issue appears to drastically affect villagers, and especially elders, in Point Hope, leading to more reports of malnutrition and anemia. Adding to the lack of available food, the period for rack-drying fish, seal, and caribou has shortened, increasing the likelihood of food-borne illnesses caused by bacteria—not to mention the lingering scent of raw meat in milder temperatures that attracts hungry polar bears ("Climate Change Puts," 2011).

Warming temperatures in the Arctic have wreaked havoc with traditional food-storage cellars used for thousands of years to store whale meat and other products of the hunt—so much so that many of the 700 residents in Point Hope contested their safety with Alaska health investigators. Before intensifying storms and rising seas provoked by climate change began to wash many of Point Hope's homes into the Chukchi Sea, it was an ideal location from which to hunt bowhead whales, a major food source for the people that defines traditions and identity, framing culture.

A thawed food cellar can be very dangerous as an incubator of botulism and gastroenteritis. A. J. Parkinson and B. Evengård wrote in *Global Health Action* (2009) that:

> Loss of the permafrost may result in spoilage of food stored below ground. Outbreaks of food-borne botulism occur sporadically in communities in the Arctic and are caused by ingestion of improperly prepared fermented traditional foods. Because germination of *Clostridium botulinum* spores and toxin production occurs at temperatures above 4 degrees C, it is possible that warmer ambient temperatures in these regions associated with climate change may result in an increase [in] the rates of food-borne botulism. Outbreaks of *Vibrio parahemolyticus* gastroenteritis are commonly associated with seawater temperatures above 15 degrees C. An outbreak of gastroenteritis caused by *V. parahemolyticus* was documented among cruise ship passengers consuming raw oysters in Prince William Sound, Alaska and provides direct evidence of an association between rising sea water temperature and onset of illness. In order to prevent further oyster farm outbreaks, a water temperature monitoring and shell-fish testing programme has been recommended. No additional outbreaks have been reported.

Unifying Themes

A warming climate brings other health problems to the North Country, in addition to toxic water and rotten meat. Parkinson and Evengård also found evidence that mosquitoes had spread West Nile virus into northern Manitoba, and that "in the Russian Federation infected birds and humans have been detected as far north as the region of Novosibirsk. In Sweden the incidence of tick-borne encephalitis (TBE) has substantially increased since the mid-1980s. This increase corresponds to a trend of milder winters and an earlier onset of spring resulting in an increase in the tick population (*Ixodes ricinus*) that carries the virus responsible for TBE and other potential pathogens. Similarly, in Northeastern Canada, climate change is projected to result in a northward shift in the range of *Ixodes scapularis*, a tick that carries *Borrelia burgdorferi*, the etiologic agent of Lyme disease" (Ogden et al., 2005).

Everyone was concerned: "the Mayor, the Tribal Council, President, other representatives of the city and tribal council, as well as the school, health clinic, fire department, police department, and public works. Elders were interviewed, including retired whaling captains, and there were discussions with students and presentations at Tikigaq School" (Brubaker et al., 2009).

Before climate change ruined it all, nature provided what the Inupiaq needed: whale bone and driftwood for a frame, sod for the roof, and frozen ground for refrigeration, at no charge. Today, the "permafrost" is no longer permanent, and whale meat spoils during the warmer months in mushy and sometimes flooded cellars, increasing illness and risk as the odor attracts animals, including hungry polar bears.

The traditional diet of Alaskan Natives, protective against several forms of cancer, heart disease, diabetes, and other metabolic disorders, is being ravaged by norovirus and by bacteria such as *Campylobacter*, *Salmonella*, and *E. coli*, as temperatures rise in the cellars. The ideal temperature to prevent growth of such things is zero to minus 10° F. Above zero, and especially above 32° F, bacteria, mold, and yeast proliferate. Food now must be preserved with high levels of salt, sugar, or acid to kill pathogens. Heat above 160° F may also work. All of this illustrates once more how difficult it has been for people whose lives were based on ice to adjust to a quick and damaging thaw

Rough Sledding for the Iditarod

The Iditarod, Alaska's annual celebration of the state's original form of indigenous transportation (now known as the Super Bowl of dogsled racing), has been running into some tough sledding in a globally warmed world. During January and February of 2001 snow was in short supply across much of Alaska. For several weeks, unusual rain soaked areas around Anchorage. The tundra along Norton Sound, near the end of the 1,850-kilometer (1,150-mile) Iditarod race trail was so bare in December that it caught fire. During training for the race in the Matanuska-Susitna Valley, 40 miles north of Anchorage, much of the ground was bare. The trails were so icy that dogs risked injury. Sufficient snow fell before the race's scheduled start in March, however.

In 2003, for the first time, the Iditarod was postponed for lack of snow. Snow was shipped in for the race's start March 1, 2003, and the race route was revised to avoid areas short on snow. As in 2002, unusual rain soaked parts of the race route. The route was finally changed as Alaska experienced its mildest winter in more than a century of record-keeping. At the same time, the eastern United States was experiencing intense cold and much above-average snowfall. Vermont was having its coldest winter in 25 years, and many of the big cities on the U.S. Eastern Seaboard experienced repeated heavy snow and ice storms. During 2004, however, the news in Alaska was that snow was available in abundance at race time—not something that used to be cause for comment there.

These days, conditions can vary from brutal to balmy, but no Iditarod in today's world matches the minus 100° F wind chills of the first race, in 1972. In 2012, it snowed so hard that transport was difficult, even for Alaskans, but in 2013 and 2014 snow was scarce and the winter too warm for proper racing. Sometimes dirt and boulders jutted through the snow and ice, beating up mushers and dogs.

Weather during the Iditarod (the first half of March) seems to be getting more variable, and irregularly warmer, ranging from record snows during 2012 to a paucity of snow and drizzly mildness in 2013 that forced race organizers to import snow for a largely ceremonial start of the race. After the faux start in Anchorage, dogs, sleds, and mushers were loaded onto trucks and driven north to the village of Willow for the "true" start of the race. By the time racers reached McGrath, on their way to Nome, the temperature had broken 50° F. One veteran onlooker quipped: "I've never sunbathed on the Iditarod Trail before!" (McGrath, 2013, 94).

In 2013, mushers "trudged over dirt patches and bramble, surrounded by tree branches that once held fluffy snow. Instead of subzero conditions, which are ideal for the sport, temperatures have been in the 30s and 40s. 'It's raining and not snowing' [said racer Luan Marques] during a recent training ride, maneuvering the dogs to avoid puddles on the trail. 'That's not good'" (Pilon, 2013). Lack of snow caused several qualifying events to be rerouted, postponed, or canceled. Annual snowfall in Anchorage and Fairbanks was 20 to 30 percent of average that year.

Sled dogs run best at zero to minus 20° F. The dogs risk overheating when it's too warm. They may also be injured by stepping on brambles that are usually covered by snow. Rough terrain also breaks bridles and wears out costly sled runners. Dogs with thinner coats are being bred, and some wear booties during races.

Mike Williams, a Yupiaq from the small village of Akiak on western Alaska's lower Kuskokwim River, has run the Iditarod for fifteen years, and described how snow cover has declined in an irregular fashion year by year. In recent years, a large number of mushers and dogs have been injured by rough terrain. Several mushers had to quit the race due to "broken sleds and broken spirits" ("Where's the Snow?" 2014). Unusually warm weather in 2014 also made training for the race very difficult. "We trained in ice and it rained most of the time and we only had half a day of good snow." Mike recounted. "All winter long back in Southwest Alaska, in our home, it was the worst training conditions we have seen. The ice was thin and we could not set our fish traps underneath the ice as was usual" ("Where's the Snow?" 2014).

The sloppy Iditarod was prescient. By early May, the ice was the thinnest Williams had ever seen, making hunting dangerous. "Our people are suffering for it," Williams said. "We are anticipating some erosion due to lack of permafrost and its continuously thawing. If we don't have normal winters anymore . . . " The lack of snow and cold upsets the natural cycle.

And so it went—one more year of improvised dog-sled racing in a climate no longer suited for what used to be a tradition only a few short decades ago.

Further Reading

Antonowicz, Anton. "Baking Alaska: As World Leaders Bicker, Global Warming is Killing a Way of Life." London *Mirror*, November 28, 2000, 8–9.

Bender, S., E. D. Burke, L. Chahim, L. L. Eshbach, F. Gordon, K. Kaplan, H. McCusker, M. Palevsky, D. Rowell, J. Battisti, J. Barcelos, J. Marlow, and S. Stzein. *Initial Assessment of Lead Agency Candidates to Support Alaska Native Villages Requiring Relocation to Survive Climate Harms.* Seattle: University of Washington Climate Justice Seminar Spring, Three Degrees Project, 2011.

Bronen, Robin. "Climate-Induced Community Relocations: Creating an Adaptive Governance Framework Based in Human Rights Doctrine." *New York University Review Law & Social Change*, 35 (2011): 357–408.

Brubaker, M., J. Bell, and A. Rolin. "Climate Change Effects on Traditional Inupiaq Food Cellars." CCH Bulletin No. 1. Alaska Native Tribal Health Consortium, Center for Climate and Health. 2009. http://www4.nau.edu/tribalclimatechange/tribes/docs/tribes_InupiaqFoodCellars.pdf

"Climate Change Puts Health of Arctic Villagers on Thin Ice." Indian Country Today Media Network, March 07, 2011. http://indiancountrytodaymedianetwork.com/article/climate-change-puts-health-of-arctic-villagers-on-thin-ice-21391

Cordalis, D., and D. B. Suagee. "The Effects of Climate Change on American Indian and Alaska Native Tribes." *Natural Resources and Environment* 22, no. 3 (Winter 2008): 45–49.

Cozetto, K., et al. "Climate Change Impacts on the Water Resources of American Indians and Alaska Natives in the United States." *Climate Change* 120 (2013): 83.

Jessepe, Lorraine. "Alaskan Native Communities Facing Climate-Induced Relocation." Indian Country Today Media Network, June 21, 2012. http://indiancountrytodaymedianetwork.com/article/alaskan-native-communities-facing-climate-induced-relocation-119615

Maldonado, J. K., J. Koppel, C. Shearer, R. Bronen, K. Peterson, and H. Lazrus. "The Impact of Climate Change on Tribal Communities in the U.S.: Displacement, Relocation, and Human Rights." *Climatic Change* 120 (2013): 601–614.

McGrath, Ben. "The White Wall: In the Iditarod, Alaska's Mushing Dynasties Confront the Elements—and a Generational Divide." *The New Yorker,* April 22, 2013, 81–95.

McLean, Kirsty Galloway. *Advance Guard: Climate Change Impacts, Adaptation, Mitigation and Indigenous Peoples: A Compendium of Case Studies.* United Nations University Institute of Advanced Studies. Traditional Knowledge Initiative. Darwin, Australia, 2010. http://archive.ias.unu.edu/resource_centre/UNU_Advance_Guard_Compendium_2010_final_web.pdf

Murphy, Kim. "Front-Row Exposure to Global Warming." *Los Angeles Times,* July 8, 2001. https://www.latimes.com/archives/la-xpm-2001-jul-08-mn-19961-story.html

Ogden, N. H., A. Maarouf, I. K. Barker, M. Bigras-Poulin, L. R. Lindsay, M. G.Morshed, et al. "Climate Change and the Potential for Range Expansion of the Lyme Disease Vector *Ixodes Scapularis* in Canada." *International Journal of Parasitology* 36 (2005): 63–70.

Parkinson, A. J., and B. Evengård. "Climate Change, Its Impact on Human Health in the Arctic and the Public Health Response to Threats of Emerging Infectious Diseases." *Global Health Action* 2 (2009). https://doi.org/10.3402/gha.v2i0.2075

Pilon, Mary. "Warm Weather Forces Changes Ahead of Iditarod Race." *New York Times,* February 5, 2013. http://www.nytimes.com/2013/02/06/sports/warm-weather-forces-changes-ahead-of-iditarod-race.html

Shearer, Christine. *Kivalina: A Climate Change Story.* Chicago: Haymarket Books, 2011.

Shearer, C. "The Social Construction of Alaska Native Vulnerability to Climate Change." *Race, Gender, Class* 19, no. 3–4 (2012): 61–79.

Sheppard, Kate. "Climate Change Takes a Village: As the Planet Warms, A Remote Alaskan Town Shows Just How Unprepared We Are." *Huffington Post*, December 14, 2014. http://www.huffingtonpost.com/2014/12/14/shishmaref-alaska-climate-change-relocation_n_6296516.html

"Where's the Snow? Mike Williams, First Stewards Board Member, Talks about Climate Change and Its Culture-Changing Impacts to the Native Communities of Alaska." First Stewards. May 8, 2014. URL not available.

Williams, A. R. "Rescuing Alaska Artifacts." *National Geographic*, October, 2014, 16.

"Yup'ik Villages Ravaged by Fierce Alaska Storms." Indian Country Media Network, November 20, 2013. http://indiancountrytodaymedianetwork.com/2013/11/20/yupik-villages-ravaged-fierce-alaska-storms-152341

CHAPTER THREE

Cases: United States East

Introduction

One unifying theme stands out in a survey of environmental racism in the eastern half of the continental United States (for our purposes, areas within the Eastern and Central time zones): the amount and degree of damage left over from the chemical effluent of decaying infrastructure in rust-belt cities, from Bridgeport, Connecticut, to Omaha, Nebraska, including Chester, Pennsylvania, and South Chicago, which are home to all manner of fatal substances, from PCBs and dioxins to lead, all present in soil and water. Rural areas also suffer from a large number of toxic hot spots in minority communities, from black neighbors of giant hog farms in North Carolina, whose homes are routinely sprayed with pig manure mist, to other towns in the same state, where people have been protesting unwelcome toxic dumps.

Akwesasne Mohawks in upstate New York can no longer eat fish from the St. Lawrence River that have been indelibly laced with PCBs from now-closed General Motors waste dumps. Within roughly half a century, this land of natural wonders has become a place where the flesh of animal life is laced at toxic levels with man-made carcinogens such as PCBs. In parts of Akwesasne, residents have been told to plow under their gardens and to have mothers' breast milk tested for contamination. In place of sustaining rivers and a land to which the Mohawks still offer thanksgiving prayers, capitalism has offered incinerators and dumps for medical and industrial waste.

Love Canal (near Niagara Falls, New York) has become a synonym for environmental toxicity. In 1978, a seeping toxic dump containing more than 20,000 tons of chemical waste (including about 200 different chemicals) was discovered under an elementary school downstream from Niagara Falls. So much hazardous waste was found there that residents were forced to move out, and their houses were destroyed.

Many such sites live, seared in local memory. In Anniston, Alabama, for example, more than $700 million in damage was done to human health by PCB contamination. A local coalition won multimillion-dollar settlements for damage done by toxic chemicals there. In Alabama, Triana, which is within the Huntsville-Decatur statistical area for Census purposes, rallied against a DDT dump in the late 1970s and early 1980s. By 2011, the town was rallying against pollution again.

Dickson County, Tennessee, is not a large place, and its black community is tiny. However, Robert D. Bullard (founding director of the Environmental Justice Resource Center at Clark Atlanta University, after which he became dean of the Barbara Jordan–Mickey Leland School of Public Affairs at Texas Southern University), who is probably the United States' foremost chronicler of environmental racism and justice, has called Dickson County the "poster child" of environmental racism. Dickson County has earned this distinction, according to Bullard, largely because the powers that be have channeled nearly every ounce of garbage in the county toward its small black community. They also have escaped prosecution for discrimination under the 1964 Civil Rights Act by denying that the dump was sited near the black community with "intent."

In Louisiana, between Baton Rouge and New Orleans where the population is heavily African American, there are so many dangerous plants operating that local residents and environmentalists call it "Cancer Alley," according to a report in Al Jazeera America. A total of 150 petrochemical companies and 17 refineries in the area release dangerous levels of toxic chemicals into the air and water. In a predominantly black community in southern Louisiana called Mossville, 91 percent of residents said they were experiencing health complications they believed to be related to the 14 facilities that manufacture, process, store, or discharge toxic or hazardous substances in that one small area (Chiles, 2015).

The eastern and Gulf of Mexico coasts of the United States are vulnerable to hurricanes, which have been intensifying as climate warms. Anywhere a hurricane strikes, it hits minority and poor people hardest, because they generally live in the lowest areas that flood first, dry out last, and are the least likely to receive emergency assistance. We include here the people of Puerto Rico, after their island was raked by Hurricane Maria in 2017, forcing them to endure several months without electricity and safe water.

Minority and poor neighborhoods also suffered the worst damage in epic flooding in and near New Orleans and Houston from Hurricane Katrina (2005) and Hurricane Harvey (2017). As enhancers of environmental racism, hurricanes sometimes also provoke accidents as well as fires at chemical plants that fill the surging floodwaters with carcinogens. This was especially true in Houston during five days of flooding rains from a stalled Hurricane Harvey. Even when the weather is tranquil, Houston, where dumps are clustered in minority and poor communities, is a stellar example of just how unequal environmental protection can get.

Further Reading

Chiles, Nick. "8 Horrifying Examples of Corporations Mistreating Black Communities with Environmental Racism." *Atlanta Black Star*, February 12, 2015. http://atlantablackstar.com/2015/02/12/8-horrifying-examples-of-corporations-mistreating-black-communities-with-environmental-racism/

Houston, Texas: Segregation, Sewage, and Environmental Racism

Houston, Texas, which deems itself "the energy capital of the world," is also a major center of environmental racism and justice activity. It is also the longtime home of Robert D. Bullard, who, after more than 40 years of publishing in the area, has become known as the "father" of environmental justice.

The Racial Politics of Garbage Dumps

The Orwellian nomenclature of garbage dumping only rarely reaches the refinement displayed in Houston, Texas, where dumps have names such as "Whispering Pines." Nor does the degree of environmental racism, where dumps have been clustered in the quarter of Houston's living areas that are predominantly black. Bullard, a leading academic expert in environmental racism, began work at Texas Southern University in 1978 and quickly zeroed in on the racial politics of garbage disposal and incineration in Houston. Of ten city-owned landfills and incinerators in the Houston area that had been used since the 1920s (all were not in continuous operation), he found that eight had been sited in mainly black areas and one in a Latino neighborhood. One had mainly white neighbors. Four other privately owned landfills in Houston as well as four more used by Houston residents but located outside the city were located in areas that were between 46 and 93 percent minority in 2014 (Bullard, 2014).

In 1978, according to Bullard's research, U.S. Census figures indicated that Houston, as a whole, was 52.3 percent white, 27.4 percent black, 17.6 percent Hispanic, and 2.7 percent Asian or other (Bullard, 2014). (By 2014, Harris County, which contains Houston, was 41 percent Hispanic, 33 percent white, 18.4 percent black, 8 percent Asian.) The Houston city government in 1978 was wholly white and male, a circumstance that has since markedly changed. "In place of NIMBY [not in my back yard]," remarked Bullard, Houston practiced "PIBBY" [place in black people's back yards] (Bullard, 2014). Houston's black community protested, but little changed.

On May 16, 1967, protests followed the drowning of an eight-year-old black male from the Sunnyside neighborhood in the Holmes Road dump, as Bullard, then a young sociologist who was just beginning to document environmental racism, was drawn into collecting information for a class-action lawsuit (*Bean v. Southwest Management*), seeking to block a new solid-waste disposal facility (Whispering Pines) in yet another black-majority neighborhood, Northwood Manor, a quiet area predominantly filled with schools and single-family homes that was 82 percent black. The suit did not block the siting of the facility, but it did become the first legal action to charge racial discrimination on environmental grounds (solid waste facility siting) under the 1964 U.S. Civil Rights Act. It also marked Bullard's first foray into environmental racism advocacy.

Bullard said of the lawsuit:

> We actually showed that the pattern was irrefutable. But we couldn't prove intentional discrimination. It's hard to prove intentional discrimination when people are not saying, "Well, we did it to the black people because that's where the landfills go." But unofficially, we were able to document, even without zoning, African Americans, basically from the '30s up 'til 1978, basically were the dumping grounds, unofficially. And as the population has changed and shifted, you know, black and brown communities bear the brunt of environmental pollution. (Goodman, 2017)

The case languished in court for seven years until 1985, when it was dismissed. The landfill was installed, and several other industrial plants also opened nearby. "Today, as a result of this downgrading intrusion," wrote Bullard (2014), "the original bucolic character of the neighborhood has been forever lost as the sprawling landfill looms near soccer fields, homes, and places of worship."

"Sacrifice Zones"

Houston is one of very few large cities in the United States with no garbage fees, which encourages generation of waste—420,000 tons of solid waste and 71,000 tons of yard waste per year as of 2014, thus an increasing demand for yard waste space. Nearly all of this ends up in landfills (Bullard, 2014). Houston households also recycle at a very low rate—ninth out of the United States' 10 largest cities. As of 2009, Houston recycled 16.7 percent of its refuse, compared to Los Angeles (65 percent), San Jose, California (60 percent), New York City (55 percent), and Chicago (52.4 percent) (Bullard, 2014). Another Texas city, San Antonio, recycled only 4 percent. Houston's low recycling rate creates demand for landfill space, most of it near majority black neighborhoods.

"Houston's growth in recent decades has made it the country's fourth-largest city," wrote Alexander Kaufman in the *Huffington Post*. "But its urban planning regulations are still rooted in the Wild West days." This lack of planning was evident in the lack of recycling and continuing expansion of garbage dumps within city limits, then around the urban core. The growing landfills were nearly always sited in or near black residential areas, where land costs and political influence were low. "No one has ever really seemed to care very much because those people don't have much political clout or voice," Paul Hart, a historian at Texas State University who grew up in Houston, told the *Huffington Post* (Kaufman, 2017). Bullard called these areas "sacrifice zones" (Kaufman, 2017).

Often, risks are not limited to garbage dumps in Houston's "sacrifice zones." "The petrochemical plants, oil refineries and shipping lanes that run adjacent to neighborhoods of color on Houston's east side spread toxic waste each time the city floods, adding to the woes of those communities," Bullard added (Kaufman, 2017). Residents in what are called industrial "fence-line" communities reported "unbearable" petrochemical smells in the air during Hurricane Harvey's heavy rains in 2017. A chemical leak forced officials in the Houston-area cities of La Porte and Shoreacres to tell people to stay indoors ("shelter in place"), close windows and doors, and turn off air conditioning and ventilation in the musty heat. According to Air Alliance Houston, a nonprofit environmental advocacy group, petrochemical plants released more than 1 million pounds of air pollution during the five days that Hurricane Harvey stalled over Houston.

"They not only have to deal with flooding in their homes, but pollution in water that's contaminated when water floods refineries and plants," Bullard said. "You're talking about a perfect storm of pollution, environmental racism, and health risks that are probably not going to be measured and assessed until decades later. The fact is that laissez-faire, unrestrained capitalism and lack of zoning means people with money can put protections up, and people without can't" (Kaufman, 2017).

The Manchester neighborhood of Houston is 97 percent black, with a third of the people living in poverty. The air pollution exceeds Environmental Protection Agency safety standards half the days of an average year. Taryn Fivek described it for Alternet (2016):

> The smell in the Manchester neighborhood of Houston is like hot Cuban coffee—nutty, bitter, and sweet. This isn't coffee, though. This is the smell of benzene spewing from the nearby Valero oil refinery at 1.5–4.7 ppm [parts per million], the threshold at which most humans can begin to smell the chemical and what the Centers for Disease Control calls a possible indication [of] "acutely hazardous exposure."

Neighbors share stories of their various cancers, and often attribute them to foul water and air produced by their industrial neighbors.

Organizing Against Environmental Racism

Juan Parras is a former labor organizer, and later director of T.e.j.a.s. (Texas Environmental Justice Advocacy Services), an environmental advocacy organization in Houston, formerly called UCER (Unidos Contra Environmental Racism). Parras has defined environmental racism for more than two decades by conducting a "toxic tour" through the energy-intensive neighborhoods of East Houston to educate people on environmental justice issues, including the fact that their neighborhoods are surrounded by large refineries and chemical plants, spewing toxins, where several thousand people work, live, and attend schools (T.e.j.a.s., 2017).

Parras decided to become involved in environmental activism after Houston officials decided to build César Chávez High School between an oil refinery, a toxic waste site, and a tire manufacturing plant, an action that exposed students, who were mainly Latino, to a wide variety of carcinogenic chemicals. Parras said that when Chavéz High School was planned, the same district was also building West Side High School, which was in a much more affluent area, without chemical exposure. Local activists pointed out this disparity in meetings with the city, including the mayor's office, the health department, school officials, and railroad representatives.

One city representative wanted to earmark the school in the toxic area as an "environmental magnet school," a double insult to nearby residents and students, pointing out toxic exposure under cover of environmental bureaucracy. They even built an air monitoring station, which didn't work (Fivek, 2016).

Parras's son Bryan, 40 years of age in 2017, who is Latino, has also been known for organizing publicity runs for economic justice, notably on hot, humid summer days, as described by the Natural Resources Defense Council (NRDC): "One day earlier this summer [2016], as the temperature climbed into the mid-90s and the humidity rose to match it, Bryan Parras decided to go for a run—a run between Houston and New Orleans. He's not crazy—he had a good reason. Participating in one leg of the Peace & Dignity Journeys run, Parras and a dozen or so others passed the baton to one another, relay-style, collectively covering between 50 and 100 miles a day. . . . For Parras . . . the experience also represented another opportunity to do what he's been doing his entire adult life: drawing attention to issues of environmental justice, specifically how communities of color are adversely affected by their proximity to some of our nation's most toxic oil-refining and chemical-processing facilities" (Turrentine, 2016).

"Outdoor Apartheid"

Houston, especially its industrial East Side, is notorious for its lack of zoning, wrote Taryn Fivek on Alternet (2016). To business people, this is advertised as a laissez-faire business environment, but it is also a slow death sentence for anyone who isn't rich enough. The families in Manchester sleep just meters away from tankers of explosive chemicals on nearby train tracks.

The siting of dumps, incinerators, and petrochemical plants can cause pollution levels to vary widely in the same urban area, with Houston as a prime example. A *Texas Monthly* article quoted a report by the Union of Concerned Scientists that indicated that the airborne concentration of 1,3-butadiene, which causes cancer and several neurological problems, is more than 150 times greater in Manchester and Harrisburg in East Houston than in affluent neighborhoods such as West Oaks on Houston's west side (Goodman, 2017). "What you're seeing in that kind of analysis is basically certain neighborhoods are unofficially zoned for it, what I call 'outdoor apartheid,'" said Bullard (Goodman, 2017).

Further Reading

Bullard, Robert D. "The Mountains of Houston: Environmental Justice and the Politics of Garbage." Offsite.org. 2014. https://www.ricedesignalliance

.org/cite-article/mountains-houston-environmental-justice-and-politics-garbage

Bullard, Robert D. *Invisible Houston: The Black Experience in Boom and Bust.* College Station, TX: Texas A&M University Press, 2000.

Fivek, Taryn. "Environmental Racism Is Poisoning Houston." Alternet, August 8, 2016. https://www.alternet.org/environment/environmental-racism-poisoning-houston

Goodman, Amy. "Invisible Houston: Full Interview with Dr. Robert Bullard, Father of the Environmental Justice Movement." Democracy Now! September 7, 2017. https://www.democracynow.org/2017/9/7/invisible_houston_full_interview_with_dr

Kaufman, Alexander C. "Houston Flooding Always Hits Poor, Non-White Neighborhoods Hardest." *Huffington Post*, August 29, 2017. https://www.huffingtonpost.com/entry/houston-harvey-environmental-justice_us_59a41c90e4b06d67e3390993

T.e.j.a.s. (Texas Environmental Justice Advocacy Services). Home page. 2017. http://tejasbarrios.org/toxic-tours/

Turrentine, Jeff. "Environmental Justice: One Texas Man's Refinery Fight: For Activist Bryan Parras, a Native of Houston's Refinery-Filled East Side, the Personal Is Very Much the Political." NRDC [Natural Resoures Defense Council]. August 26, 2016. https://www.nrdc.org/stories/environmental-justice-one-texas-mans-refinery-fight

Anniston, Alabama: A Plague of PCBs

Monsanto, the agricultural conglomerate, tried to sneak into Anniston, Alabama (about 60 miles east of Birmingham and 90 miles west of Atlanta), bearing toxic polychlorinated biphenyls (PCBs), a once-common electrical insulator that was banned during the 1970s amid intensifying health concerns. As early as 1938, scientists hired by Monsanto had reported that PCBs caused liver damage in rats (Kroft, 2002). In the 1950s, plant workers were told to wear protective clothing, but no one told the citizens of Anniston that they were living with poison that would degrade their health and that of their children for generations.

The people of Anniston knew such things from decades of experience, As CBS News' *Sixty Minutes* reported in 2002: "Imagine a place so saturated with toxic, cancer-causing chemicals that it's in the dirt people walk on, the air they breathe—even the blood that pumps through their veins. The 24,000 people living in Anniston, Alabama, don't have to imagine this. Many of them are living it. In fact, they have been living it for decades—they just didn't know it. The company responsible didn't tell them, and neither did the Environmental Protection Agency. . . . 'We have to wear masks if we cut our grass. Where else in the United States of America are people doing that?' said resident David Baker" (Kroft, 2002).

Chemicals, including PCBs, had been produced in Anniston since World War I; the Theodore Swann Company in 1929 became one of the first two Monsanto units to produce PCBs in the United States. "PCBs, which were used as insulating materials in various types of electrical appliances, gained in popularity and became a big business. Monsanto approached the Swann Company with an offer to purchase their Anniston PCB facility. In 1935 the deal was finalized and Monsanto took over ownership of the Anniston plant. PCBs were manufactured at this plant for some 41 years until Monsanto suspended Anniston's PCB production in 1971," wrote Robert G. Kaley II, director of environmental affairs for Solutia, a subsidiary of Monsanto at the time it became an independent company in 1997 (Kaley, 2000).

Once the people of Anniston learned that Monsanto had saddled impoverished, mainly black neighborhoods with a lifetime chemical curse that included PCBs as well as other chemical wastes, residents erupted in rage. The company suffered a stinging legal rebuke when, on April 25, 2001, residents who had united in the Anniston, Alabama, Sweet Valley/Cobb Town Environmental Task Force won a $42.8 million settlement against the chemical company, whose effluent had forced an entire community out of their homes. The case of Anniston vs. Monsanto became one of the landmarks in the environmental justice movement.

PCBs were outlawed in 1977 in the United States, and production ceased in 1979. As with so many tales involving persistent organic pollutants, however, problems didn't end with a cessation of production and a legal settlement. After a dozen years on remediation as a Superfund site, in 2016 and 2017, newly discovered "hot spots" of toxicity were still coming to light in areas that had once been declared clean. The PCBs and other hazardous chemicals, as is so often the case, are very tough to dislodge from the food chain, as they easily ignore lines drawn on corporate and bureaucratic maps.

It's in the Dirt and the Air

Residents of Anniston did not become aware of PCBs' perils until after their production stopped. Subsequently, more than 3,000 citizens of Anniston filed claims "for damages allegedly caused by releases of these PCBs into the area's air, lakes, rivers, and soil." That number later grew to 20,000. These citizens alleged that the company knew it was releasing

PCBs into the atmosphere, knew the hazards that accompanied exposure to PCBs, and consequently, did nothing to stop the discharges and did not take the appropriate measures to protect people living in Anniston (Anniston, 2000).

Given the nature of PCBs as persistent organic pollutants (POPs), damage only became evident over a number of decades as residents began to suffer a large number of cancers and other long-term ailments. The cause of such ailments over a long period is difficult to prove legally. Like other persistent organic pollutants, effects of PCBs also may be passed down from generation to generation. The affected area was overwhelmingly poor and black, so a case was made invoking environmental racism. Over several years, along with several forms of cancer, learning disabilities, increased asthma rates, and many grotesque reproductive deformities were reported by people living closest to the Monsanto plant. At first, the presence of PCBs was not associated with the presence of PCB residues in the air, soil, and water. Only after 1993, with rates of many maladies rising, was the connection established.

Largemouth bass with blistered scales and toxic levels of PCBs in their bodies were caught in Choccolocco Creek. Shortly thereafter, according to a government report, "The Alabama Power Company was preparing to break ground on a piece of land obtained years earlier from Monsanto. When the ground-breaking took place, a PCB landfill was mistakenly opened, spilling black tar onto the earth. This landfill was actually one of two unlined landfills used to dispose of hazardous waste that were located adjacent to the plant" (ATSDR Report, 2000). As a result of these two unexpected events, citizens rose up in anger. Anger intensified in 1995 after officials from Monsanto approached the congregation of Mars Hill Missionary Baptist Church and offered to buy its building, without first telling them that it would have to be destroyed because of PCB exposure. In 1999, Monsanto settled with the church for $2.5 million and a new church van. The church also became a key conduit in organizing against Monsanto's presence in Anniston.

The drive against Monsanto's presence in Anniston was coordinated by Citizens Against Pollution (CAP), which was also known as the West Anniston Environmental Justice Task Force. CAP's members coordinated the suit joined by more than 3,000 Anniston residents, while also aiding collection of soil samples and pressuring the Environmental Protection Agency (EPA) and state officials to take action.

After initial denial that its factory was causing the pollution, Monsanto, facing rising public anger, "conceded that much of the PCB contamination in Anniston was caused by their facility" (Kaley, 2000). The Alabama

Department of Environmental Management (ADEM) then ordered Monsanto to begin a major cleanup effort. Widespread knowledge of PCBs' persisting effects provoked Monsanto to demolish buildings on the contaminated land, as it laid plastic tarps and covered them with clean soil. According to Monsanto, the company contributed more than $30 million toward the cleanup in Anniston.

The Legal Context as Environmental Racism

Once Anniston's residents learned just how toxified their town had become, they sued with a vengeance, and met with success, which is uncommon in the environmental justice movement. The bill for Monsanto rose from $145 million to $700 million in two years, as the number of Anniston residents seeking relief from exposure to PCBs rose to 20,000. The Associated Press reported that as a result of the $700 million settlement, "The two companies said the settlement called for $600 million in cash. Monsanto will pay $390 million, Solutia will pay $50 million and the rest will be covered by insurance, according to a statement from Monsanto. Costs for clean-up, prescription drug and other programs detailed in the agreement will push the total amount to more than $700 million, said Stacy Smith, a spokeswoman for the plaintiffs' lawyers. Another plaintiff's lawyer, Jere Beasley, said the total would surpass $800 million" ("$700 Million," 2003).

The PCBs were enough of a hazard that money was set aside to provide homeowners with relocation funds "equaling approximately twice the appraised value of their property" (Kaley, 2000); even at that level, many refused to leave their homes that they had occupied for generations. A study of the sequence of events by Steven C. Washington, L. Dillon Burgess, and Glenn Johnson (2014) concluded that what occurred in Anniston was a classic case of environmental racism. They asserted that the Monsanto Company produced polychlorinated biphenyls (PCBs) for about 40 years, and the company discharged toxic waste into West Anniston Creek as it dumped several million pounds of PCBs into a number of open-pit landfills. Anniston became saturated with toxic, cancer-causing chemicals that laced the dirt, water, air, and food, permeating the blood of the people who lived there. In addition to Monsanto, the federal government also failed the residents of Anniston, Alabama. Governmental officials and Monsanto/Solutia deceived the residents, the study argued, forcing the Sweet Valley/Cobbtown Communities of West Anniston, as well as other communities of color to share an unfair burden of exposure to environmental contamination.

Long after the controversies and legal awards, Anniston's toxic nightmare continues. The PCBs remain lodged in Anniston residents' bodies in present and future generations. As the *Anniston Star* editorialized on September 22, 2017:

> Of the innumerable lessons from Anniston's unwanted marriage with PCB pollution is this truth: the pollution itself, like the legacy it creates, never fully dissipates. The last decade has seen Anniston claim serious victories over its polluted past. Many PCBs- and lead-contaminated properties have been remediated. Wide swaths of the former Fort McClellan have been cleared of unexploded ordnance. Even the Cold War–era chemical weapons are gone from their storage igloos at Anniston Army Depot. But Anniston still suffers from PCBs pollution. Our community mustn't forget that. In 2017, the toxicity of Anniston soil and water around the former Monsanto plant remains a real and viable concern. For years, we have championed the cleaning of Anniston's soil and the rehabilitation of its image as a contaminated community. . . . But this struggle isn't over. Work remains. Anniston can't consider this job complete. ("The PCBs Story," 2017)

Further Reading

Anniston, Alabama. *The People of Anniston, Alabama vs. Monsanto.* 2001. Environmental Justice Case Studies: http://umich.edu/~snre492/Jones/anniston.htm

(ATSDR Report). United State. Centers for Disease Control. Agency for Toxic Substances and Disease Registry. *Exposure Investigation Report: Solutia Incorporated/Monsanto Company, Anniston, Calhoun County, Alabama.* 2000. https://www.atsdr.cdc.gov/HAC/pha/PHA.asp?docid=843&pg=0

Kaley, Robert, II. "PCBs Fell on Alabama." *Ohio Citizen Online.* July 3, 2000. http://umich.edu/~snre492/Jones/anniston.htm

Kroft, Steve. "Toxic Secret. Alabama Town Was Never Warned of Contamination." CBS News *Sixty Minutes*, November 2, 2002. https://www.cbsnews.com/news/toxic-secret-07-11-2002/

"The PCBs Story Isn't Over." [Editorial]. *Anniston Star*, September 22, 2017. https://www.annistonstar.com/opinion/editorials/the-pcbs-story-isn-t-over/article_18d936ea-9fa5-11e7-89ff-3784ede6e409.html

"$700 Million Settlement in Alabama PCB Lawsuit." *New York Times*, August 21, 2003. http://www.nytimes.com/2003/08/21/business/700-million-settlement-in-alabama-pcb-lawsuit.html

Washington, Steven C., L. Dillon Burgess, and Glenn Johnson. "An African American community and the PCB Contamination in Anniston, Alabama: An Environmental Justice Case Study." *Race, Gender, and Class* 21, no. 1–2 (2014). https://www.researchgate.net/publication/288833019

_An_African_American_community_and_the_PCB_contamination
_in_Anniston_Alabama_An_environmental_justice_case_study

Dickson, Tennessee: Environmental Racism's "Poster Child"

Dickson, Tennessee, a town with a population of about 12,000, roughly 35 miles west of Nashville; is not a large place, and its black community is tiny. However, Robert D. Bullard, who is one of the United States' foremost chroniclers of environmental racism and justice, has called it the "poster child" of environmental racism (Bullard et al., 2007, 135), largely because the powers that be in Dickson County (which is only 4.5 percent black) have channeled nearly every ounce of garbage under their aegis toward Dickson's small black community. The county has also escaped prosecution for discrimination under the 1964 Civil Rights Act by denying that its convocation of dumps was sited near the black community with "intent." Thus, legally, for more than 40 years, Dickson's Eno Road community, which is overwhelmingly black, has been used as a regional center for garbage and toxic waste, a collection of several dumps that is something of a political accident (so claim county officials) (Bullard et al., 2007, 135).

The treatment of Dickson's black community is a potent illustration of Bullard's thesis: "Many dirty industries have followed the 'path of least resistance' allowing communities of color to become environmental 'sacrifice zones' and the 'dumping grounds' for all kinds of health threatening operations." "This," wrote Bullard, "provides a real-life example of the deadly mix of 'wastes and race' in the early years of the twentyfirst century—the Dickson County (Tennessee) Landfill and the contamination of an African American family's wells and their 150acre homestead. The goal of our analysis is to illustrate how sluggish and inept government response to an environmental emergency is endangering the health and safety of African Americans" (Bullard et al., 2007, 134). Bullard recommended that the Dickson County Commissioners immediately close all solid-waste facilities, including the garbage transfer station, recycling center, and construction and demolition landfill on Eno Road, and that the federal EPA and the state of Tennessee be required to clean up contamination caused by the landfill.

Dickson has a town water system, but many residents of the Eno Road community have no access to that system, so they rely on wells, drawing water that has become steadily more toxic as the area has become the county's only dump site. About 1,400 neighbors within a four-mile radius of the landfills (which are not lined) use wells for drinking water and have been, in effect, consuming poison as the collection of dumps leaked into the water table. As early as 1968, drums of industrial waste solvents were being buried there. Black residents thus have been forced to bear the toxic burden of their more affluent white neighbors, including several corporations that produce toxic wastes.

One such company is the Ebbtide Corporation (Winner Boats), which transferred wastes into the Dickson County Landfill in drums roughly every month for three to four years. The Scovill-Shrader Automotive manufacturing plant also delivered several drums of industrial waste solvents containing paint thinner and acetone. A 1991 Environmental Protection Agency report from 1991 said that soil testing indicated the presence of petroleum hydrocarbons, xylenes, benzene, toluene, and ethylbenzene (Braithwaite, et al., 2009, 190).

The Travails of the Holt Family

The Eno Road community originated more than a century ago, when families of freed slaves acquired several hundred acres of land on which they lived a largely peaceful life until the parade of dumps (some of them toxic) moved in and ruined their well water.

The Holt family, one of the founding families, and especially Harry Holt, has been particularly hard hit because their well was only about 50 feet from the seeping dumps. Various government agencies denied for several years that the well had been fouled, until many in the family fell ill of several ailments. After about a dozen years, the Holts' home was finally hooked into Dickson's town water system.

The Holt family reported several illnesses:

- Harry Holt—Prostate cancer, bone cancer, Type 1 diabetes, hypertension, kidney disease (he died on January 9, 2007)
- Beatrice Holt—Rheumatoid arthritis, diabetes, cervical polyps
- Sheila Holt-Orsted—Breast cancer, diabetes, arthritis, gastrointestinal disorder
- Bonita Holt—Arthritis, colon polyps, hypertension, gastrointestinal disorder
- Demetrius Holt—Diabetes, gastrointestinal disorder
- Patrick Holt—Immune disorder, arthritis (Edwards, 2003, n.p.)

Even though Dickson County stretches across roughly 500 square miles, its sole solid waste dump is located only 50 feet away from a farm of 150 acres owned by the Holts. "It is no accident or statistical fluke that all the permitted landfills in Dickson County are concentrated in this black community. Blacks make up less than five percent of the county's population and occupy less than one percent of the county's land mass," wrote Bullard (2007, 137). When *New York Times* columnist Bob Herbert queried Dickson County attorney Eric Thornton in an October 2006 article, "Poisoned on Eno Road," about why it was peculiar that the Eno Road community had been chosen to absorb so much of the county's garbage and hazardous waste, his reply was, "It has to be at some location" (Herbert, 2006).

The Holt family was told that their well water was safe even as the EPA reported toxicity in the area, and as the city bureaucracy served the landfill with five violation notices between July 18, 1988, and April 12, 1999, "including inadequate daily cover, violation of Groundwater Protection Standards, cadmium detected in ground water and springs at concentrations exceeding [federal standards], and violation of inadequate depth cover and pooling of water on landfill cover" (Braithwaite, et al., 2009, 190). As early as November 18, 1988, tests by the Tennessee Department of Health and Environment on the well water at the Holt farm showed TCE contamination, but a letter to them dated December 8, 1988, glossed over that fact, stating: "Your water is of good quality for the parameters tested. It is felt that the low levels of methylene or trichloroethene may be due to either lab or sampling error" (McWhorter, 1988). According to the U.S. Public Health Service: "Some of the health effects associated with ingestion of TEC include liver disease, hypertension, speech impediment, hearing impairment, stroke, anemia and other blood disorders, diabetes, kidney disease, urinary tract disorders and skin rashes" (Agency, 2003). On January 28, 1990, government tests found 26 ppb (parts per billion) TCE in the Holt well—five times above the established maximum contaminant level (MCL) of 5 ppb set by the federal EPA. A decade later, on October 20, 2000, Dickson hooked their home into the town water system.

Having surveyed copious evidence, Bullard concluded (2007, 140): "In the final analysis, the state handed the Holt family a 'death sentence.'" The Holt family filed a lawsuit against the City of Dickson, County of Dickson, and Scovill Inc., owner of the former Dickson Scovill-Shrader Automotive manufacturing plant—all to no avail. As in other cases of this type, courts held that there was no "intent" to discriminate under the 1964 U.S. Civil Rights Act. The Holts' lawsuit, filed in 2003, was pending when Harry died on January 9, 2007, at the age of 66.

These problems were summarized in detail by a report in the *Dickson Herald*:

> The county has a long history of noncompliance related to groundwater and leachate violations since at least 1983. These violations have resulted in fines, Commissioner's Orders, and NOV [Notice of Violation]. These

violations were related to such issues as major and minor leachate seeps and flows, failure to provide immediate cover, failure to provide erosion control, exceedance of groundwater standards for cadmium and TCE, discharge of leachate from the property without a permit, failure to maintain a storm-water pollution prevention plan, and implementation of required corrective actions. (Edwards, 2003)

Despite repeated violations at the Dickson County Landfill, state environmental authorities continued to grant site permits for at least four landfills between 1988 and February 2007, including a recycling center, a garbage transfer station, and a construction disposal landfill. An average of 20 to 25 heavy-duty diesel trucks per day rumbled along local roads, "leaving behind noxious fumes, dangerous particulates, household garbage, recyclables and demolition debris from around Middle Tennessee. The garbage transfer station alone handles approximately 35,000 tons annually" (Bullard, 2007, 137).

Compared to the Holts, white families whose wells were tested as possibly contaminated received accurate assessments, prompt remediation, and, in some cases, bottled water while they waited for new wells to be dug, along with speedy connection to the Dickson town water supply (Bullard et al., 2007, 141–142).

Further Reading

Agency for Toxic Substances and Disease Registry (ATSDR). Managing Hazardous Materials Incidents. Volume III—Medical Management Guidelines for Acute Chemical Exposures: Trichloroethylene (TCE). Atlanta, GA: U.S. Department of Health and Human Services, Public Health Service, 2003.

Braithwaite, Ronald L., Sandra E. Taylor, and Henrie M. Treadwell. *Health Issues in the Black Community*. New York: Wiley, 2009, 190.

Bullard, Robert D., Paul Mohai, Robin Saha, and Beverly Wright. "The 'Poster Child' for Environmental Racism in 2007: Dickson County, Tennessee." In *Toxic Wastes and Race at Twenty: 1987–2007*: A Report Prepared for the United Church of Christ Justice & Witness Ministries. 2007, 134–150. http://www.ucc.org/environmental-ministries_toxic-waste-20

Edwards, Holly. "Family Blames Health Woes on Dickson's Landfill." *Dickson Herald,* September 2, 2003, n.p.

Herbert, Bob. "Poisoned on Eno Road." *New York Times*, October 2, 2006. http://www.nytimes.com/2006/10/02/opinion/02herbert.html

McWhorter, Mark. Division of Solid Waste, Tennessee Department of Health and Environment to Harry Holt and Lavenia Holt, December 8, 1988. In files of Robert D. Bullard.

A 100 Percent Chance of Pig-manure Showers in North Carolina

The pig population in North Carolina rose more than 300 percent between 1990 and 2000, from 2.8 million to 9.3 million. Nationally, with about 9 million pigs in 2017, North Carolina was second only to Iowa. Duplin County alone houses 2.3 million hogs (Hellerstein and Fine, 2017). Massive pig farms on an industrial scale produce lakes of swine waste and imperil the air and water of disproportionally black and poor people in North Carolina who endure frequent dousings of pig manure sprayed around their homes to fertilize nearby fields. As Lily Kuo wrote in *Quartz* (2015), "a fine mist of liquefied feces collects on their houses and cars, attracting swarms of flies." "The poor people, they literally get shit on," said Kemp Burdette, who advocates for better water quality in North Carolina's Cape Fear River Watch (Kuo, 2015).

In the language of agricultural bureaucracy, these gigantic pig farms are known as swine CAFOs (confined animal feeding operations). The School of Public Health at the University of North Carolina–Chapel Hill reported that "these pig farms are responsible for both air and water pollution, mostly due to the vast manure lagoons they create to hold the enormous amount of waste from the thousands of pigs being raised for food" (Chiles, 2015). North Carolina is one of several states in which the number of pigs exceeds the human population, and they produce several times more waste per pig than human beings. No one seems to know exactly how much more (estimates range from two to 14 times).

Pig farming earns its proprietors a billion dollars a year in North Carolina, and money oinks at the state capitol, where legislators in April 2017 passed a law limiting the damages that local residents might collect as a result of lawsuits, resounding with themes of environmental racism—telling them, in effect, that pigs and profits come before poor, mainly black rural people. "Hog farms collect billions of gallons of untreated pig feces and urine in what are essentially cesspools, then dispose of the waste by spraying it into the air. Residents living in the area of the spray complain of adverse health effects and odor so bad that it limits their ability to be outdoors" (Goodman, 2017).

"Heaven for Hogs, Hell for Humans"

Kuo (2015) described the creation of the waste lagoons: "The technology behind the lagoons is rudimentary at best. The hogs defecate in their indoor stalls, their waste falling through slatted floors into slurries where it is flushed or pumped into a nearby lagoon. Solid waste forms sludge at the bottom of the basin, creating a semi-permeable barrier that helps prevent leakage into the ground. Liquid from the top of the pond is used as manure, and applied to crops with high-pressure spray guns. Unlike human waste, which is processed in municipal wastewater plants, the only treatment the pig manure receives is through exposure to naturally occurring bacteria in the lake."

Steve Wing, associate professor of epidemiology at the University of North Carolina's Gillings School of Public Health, told Amy Goodman of the Public Broadcasting Service (PBS): "It's easy for a big hog operation to have as much waste as a medium-sized city. Of course, the pit will fill up, so it has to be emptied. And they're emptied by spraying the liquid waste. . . . And that can drift downwind into the neighboring communities" (Goodman, 2017).

Wearing the Stench

Wing, who died in November 2016, described his research in a 2013 TED Talk: "In 1995, I began to meet neighbors of industrial hog operations," he said. "I saw how close some neighborhoods are to hog operations. People told me about contaminated wells, the stench from hog operations that woke them at night, and children who were mocked at school for smelling like hog waste. I studied the medical literature and learned about the allergens, gases, bacteria, and viruses released by these facilities—all of them capable of making people sick" (Hellerstein and Fine, 2017).

Shane Rogers collected evidence as an Environmental Protection Agency and U.S. Department of Agriculture environmental engineer, and found that the manure spraying was literally bathing people's homes in pig feces. He collected DNA swab samples from randomly selected houses, and "at every visit and every home, I experienced offensive and sustained swine manure odors to varying intensity, from moderate to very strong." Dust samples "contained tens of thousands to hundreds of thousands of hog feces DNA particles," Rogers wrote, "demonstrating exposure to hog feces bio-aerosols for clients who breathe in the air at their homes. Considering the facts, it is far more likely than not that hog feces also gets inside clients' homes where they live and where they eat" (Hellerstein and Fine, 2017).

Elsie Herring, one local resident, said: "You'd think it's raining. We don't open the doors up or the windows, but the odor still comes in. It takes your breath away. Then you start gagging. You get headaches"

(Goodman, 2017). Don Webb, who shut down his own hog operation, told Amy Goodman of Democracy Now! on PBS: "I got out of it. And I couldn't—I just couldn't do another person that way, to make them smell that. It is a cesspool that you put feces and urine in, a hole in the ground that you dump toxic waste in. And I've seen dead hogs in them and stuff like that. I've seen it. I've talked to the people. I've seen the little children that say, 'Mom and daddy, why do we got to smell this stuff?' You get stories like 'I can't hang my clothes out. Feces and urine odor comes by and attaches itself to your clothes.'" The stench and the way it was ruining the lives of decent people turned Webb into an activist. "These are human beings," Webb said. "They've worked their whole lives and are trying to have a clean home and a decent place to live, and they can't go on their front porch and take a deep breath" (Hellerstein and Fine, 2017).

The stench combines the odors of methane, ammonia, rotten eggs, and spoiled collard greens. Some residents find themselves vomiting. Rene Miller, who lives nearby, described the stench as "an odor so noxious that it makes your eyes burn and your nose run, [like] being surrounded by spoiled meat," which grows worse on hot, humid summer afternoons, "when the stink hovering in the stagnant, humid air can nearly 'knock you off your feet'" (Hellerstein and Fine, 2017). "I want to sit out on the front porch today but I can't because of the spray," Miller said, adding how it's "disgusting" that she sometimes walks inside her home covered with a layer of moisture from the spray (Strassmann, 2016).

Twelve miles from Miller's home, Jeff Spedding, who works at the world's largest pork producer and supplier, Smithfield Foods, said that farmers want to be good neighbors, but he sees no better way to get rid of the waste. "I've never had a complaint from any of my neighbors. We try to do what is right," he said. "It gets into what's cost-effective also. It also gets into what's reasonable. There isn't any technology that's more efficient than what we're doing" (Strassmann, 2016).

Health Problems and Hog Waste

Remnants of hog cesspool waste have been rising into some residents' water wells. "It can, I think, very correctly be called environmental racism or environmental injustice that people of color, low-income people bear the brunt of these practices," said Wing (Goodman, 2017). "These lagoons and spray fields cannot be allowed to continue in North Carolina; they are causing too many problems to our waters, our air, our people, our health. They have got to go," said Rick Dove, a local activist with the

Waterkeeper Alliance in New Bern, North Carolina and longtime campaigner against the lagoons (Kuo, 2015).

The contamination from North Carolina pig farms has yielded dangerous levels of groundwater nitrates, a leading cause of births with heart defects (blue-baby syndrome). Occasionally, massive amounts of hog waste break out of containment ponds and flood nearby waterways. During 1995, six major hog farm–related spills totaling about 30 million gallons were mixed with water that is used for other purposes, killing more than 15 million fish.

The situation in North Carolina is not unique. Witness Uniontown in northern Alabama, 90 percent black and overwhelmingly poor, which provides a final resting place for the refuse of 33 states. "Landfill is too clean a word for what they do there," wrote Imani Perry in *Harper's*. "As part of Uniontown's sewage system, liquid waste is spewed into the air to land on the hard Alabama clay earth. The town is showered in shit" (2018, 61–62).

It's not just the manure showers that bother locals in North Carolina. It's also the "dead boxes" filled with rotting hogs that attract gnats, swarms of large black flies, and buzzards. People loathe the destruction of their lives. Bumper stickers appeared, reading: "Welcome to North Carolina: Heaven 4 Hogs, Hell 4 Humans" (Hellerstein and Fine, 2017). Among neighbors of these pork factories, hydrogen sulfide has provoked noticeable increases in respiratory ailments. During the summer of 1995, seven major spills erupted from waste lagoons in North Carolina, six of which were hog-related. As a result of these spills, more than 30 million gallons of hog waste poured into the waterways, resulting in over 15 million fish killed in the state's rivers that year.

Steve Wing's work indicated that air pollution from nearby hog farms was related to higher than usual rates of nausea, high blood pressure, wheezing, and asthma, especially for children. Wing also coauthored a study that indicated contamination of nearby streams with fecal bacteria levels higher than state and federal water quality standards. Many of the same samples also showed excessive levels of *E. coli* and *Enterococcus*. Hog waste can also carry viruses, parasites, and even the "super-bug" MRSA.

C. D. Hearney and colleagues found: "Testing of 187 samples showed high fecal indicator bacteria concentrations at both up- and downstream sites. Overall, 40 percent, 23 percent, and 61 percent of samples exceeded state and federal recreational water quality guidelines for fecal coliforms, *E. coli*, and *Enterococcus*, respectively. . . . Results suggest diffuse and overall poor sanitary quality of surface waters where swine CAFO density is high" (Hearney et al., 2015, 676).

Kate Jenkins wrote (2015): "Fishermen have reported that after exposure to the water, their skin will sometimes develop the same sores that tend to show up on dead fish. These are all compelling reasons to avoid swimming and fishing in contaminated streams. 'When I used to go fishing, it used to be nothing to wade in that water . . . in tennis shoes, or barefoot! Would I do that now? No way!' [she was told by one resident]. 'If I catch a fish, you rest assured, it will be a catch and release.'"

Jenkins continued (2015): "The life of each community member I meet seems in some way defined by serious illness. Stories of late-term miscarriage, brain tumors, and unexplained childhood disease and death punctuate my two-day stay in hog country. These stories are not offered as evidence of anything—they are told offhand, in response to casual inquiries as to the speaker's well-being."

Pig Manure, Race, Class, and Corporate Control

Wing and fellow UNC researcher Jill Johnston said, "The state's industrial hog operations disproportionately affect African Americans, Hispanics and Native Americans." That pattern, they concluded, "is generally recognized as environmental racism" (Hellerstein and Fine, 2017). U.S. senator Cory Booker, a New Jersey Democrat, denounced the North Carolina hog industry, which he called "evil" for exploiting its African American neighbors. "They fill massive lagoons with [waste] and they take that lagoon stuff and spray it over fields," he said. "I watched it mist off of the property of these massive pig farms into black communities. And these African American communities are like, 'We're prisoners in our own home.' The biggest company down there [Smithfield] is a Chinese-owned company, and so they've poisoned black communities, land value is down, abhorrent. . . . This corporation is outsourcing its pain, its costs, onto poor black people in North Carolina" (Hellerstein and Fine, 2017).

Rather than stop the manure showers, Republican state representative Jimmy Dixon, a farmer whose campaign had received about $100,000 from the hog industry over five years, introduced the Agriculture and Forestry Nuisance Remedies bill to block a class action suit by nearly 500 mainly black residents seeking compensation from Murphy-Brown, North Carolina's largest pork producer. The class action suit was filed by the North Carolina Environmental Justice Network, Waterkeeper Alliance, and REACH (Rural Empowerment Association for Community Help) under the Civil Rights Act of 1964, which prohibits governmental agencies from doing business in a way that has a disproportionate impact on low-income communities.

"These claims are at best enormous exaggerations and at worst outright lies. Is there some odor? Yes. But I would like you to close your eyes and imagine how ham and sausage and eggs and fried chicken smell," Dixon told a statehouse hearing on the bill, which was passed by both houses of the legislature and forwarded to Governor Roy Cooper for signature. Cooper vetoed the bill, saying that he opposed "special protection for one industry" (Hellerstein and Fine, 2017). The General Assembly then overrode the veto during July 2017 by a vote of 74 to 40, mostly along party lines (Goodman, 2017). Under HB 467, homeowners may be compensated only for future reduction in their property's fair-market value, which already has been substantially reduced by the presence of the hog farms. The law also negated existing and prohibits future lawsuits.

Corporate control of state politics is an important reason why North Carolina has become a magnet for the corporate pork industry. *The Guardian* reported:

> Nobody was more influential in reshaping the industry than Wendell Murphy, a powerful Democratic state legislator and the subject of the *Charlotte News & Observer's* Pulitzer Prize-winning "Boss Hog" series. Murphy, a high school agriculture teacher turned farmer from Rose Hill, grew to become the nation's top hog producer during his tenure in the general assembly, from 1982–1993. While in office, he backed legislation to provide poultry and hog farmers with tax breaks and exemptions from environmental regulation, helping "pass laws worth millions of dollars to his company and his industry," the *News & Observer* reported. This included the 1991 "Murphy Amendment," which exempted poultry and animal operations from stricter regulations on air and water pollution, and a 1991 bill that barred counties from imposing zoning restrictions on hog farms. In 1986, he voted in favor of a bill that eliminated sales taxes on hog and poultry operations. (Hellerstein and Fine, 2017)

The industry, on the other hand, "argues that few studies show a direct link between hog CAFOs and harm to people's health or the environment. Pollutants can also come from other sources like fertilizer, municipal human waste, or wildlife, they point out. They say that the lagoons, if maintained properly, can last forever and pose little threat to the environment or nearby residents" (Kuo, 2015).

In 2013 a Chinese firm, WH Group, acquired Smithfield Farms because their industrial model is 50 percent less expensive than Chinese hog production, which uses thousands of small farms. It's one area in which the United States easily undersells the rest of the world—and that worries many of their neighbors, who are tired of the stench and manure showers.

"Even Smithfield's corporate owner in China uses what lagoon skeptics would call more advanced technology that North Carolina lawmakers deemed too expensive to force farms to use. WH Group's seven pork farms in China—which produced just 311,000 sows last year, compared to Smithfield's 14.7 million—use a dry manure removal process that separates the solids from the liquids and stores them in oxidized lagoons. Two of the farms use a digester system where the lagoons are covered and used to generate electricity" (Kuo, 2015).

Problems provoked by daily life amid the pig farms paled beside the destruction caused during September 2018 by Hurricane Florence, the first Category 4 storm to hit North Carolina after nearly all of the huge-scale farms had been built. The remains of the hurricane stalled for several days over pig-farming regions, unleashing as much as 40 inches of rain that flooded animal waste lagoons and industrial manufacturing plants on a scale never before seen.

Further Reading

Chiles, Nick. "8 Horrifying Examples of Corporations Mistreating Black Communities with Environmental Racism." *Atlanta Black Star*, February 12, 2015. http://atlantablackstar.com/2015/02/12/8-horrifying-examples-of-corporations-mistreating-black-communities-with-environmental-racism/

Goodman, Amy. "North Carolina Hog Farms Spray Manure Around Black Communities; Residents Fight Back." Democracy Now! May 3, 2017. https://www.democracynow.org/2017/5/3/nc_lawmakers_side_with_factory_farms

Hearney, C. D., K. Myers, S. Wing, D. Hall, D. Baron, and J. R. Stewart. "Source Tracking Swine Fecal Waste in Surface Water Proximal to Swine Concentrated Animal Feeding Operations." *Science of the Total Environment* (April 1, 2015): 676–683. https://www.ncbi.nlm.nih.gov/pubmed/25600418

Hellerstein, Erica, and Ken Fine. "A Million Tons of Feces and an Unbearable Stench: Life Near Industrial Pig Farms." *The Guardian* (London, UK), September 20, 2017. https://www.theguardian.com/us-news/2017/sep/20/north-carolina-hog-industry-pig-farms

Jenkins, Kate. "Industrial Hog Farming and Environmental Racism." STIR. December 20, 2015. http://www.stirjournal.com/2015/12/20/industrial-hog-farming-and-environmental-racism/

Kuo, Lily. "The World Eats Cheap Bacon at the Expense of North Carolina's Rural Poor." *Quartz*, July 14, 2015. https://qz.com/433750/the-world-eats-cheap-bacon-at-the-expense-of-north-carolinas-rural-poor/

Perry, Imani. "As the South Goes, So Goes the Nation." *Harper's*, July 2018, 60–66.

Strassmann, Mark. "North Carolina Hog Farms Accused of Putrid Pollution." CBS News, July 4, 2016. https://www.cbsnews.com/news/north-carolina-hog-farms-accused-of-putrid-pollution/

Bridgeport, Connecticut: A Spreading Web of Toxins

Bridgeport, Connecticut's brownfields are overwhelmingly located in black and brown neighborhoods. They are ringed by barbed wire and surrounded by wastelands and toxin-spouting heavy industry. Glenda Noblin, a high school teacher who lives in one of these neighborhoods, said: "I feel like we're caught in a vise." Noblin lives, amid polluted air, shrouded in dust as the foundation-cracking vibrations of heavy trucks rumble near her front yard (Motavalli and McFadyen, 1998). Jim Motavalli and Deidre McFadyen described the scenery from Noblin's front yard in *E—The Environmental Magazine*: "A forest of oil barge platforms, warehouse storage yards, stacks of sewer pipes and spent fuel tanks." John Percell, who lives near Noblin and shares her view, "says he remembers when this part of the city's East End was a beautiful coastal community. Now 43, he looks out on the giant tanks of Advanced Liquid Recycling—a 'full-service waste treatment' business serving the auto industry. Percell may soon have an even closer neighbor—an asphalt plant."

Plans for two asphalt plants in one Latino and black neighborhood drew about 600 people, most of whom bitterly opposed the plans, to a public hearing in Bridgeport, Connecticut's aging inner city. Many of them were in no mood to accept the industries' assertions that their new neighbors would be quiet, clean, and environmentally correct. Their streets already were choked with fumes from trucks servicing existing plants. "Citing grassroots health initiatives that kept out asphalt plants in Massachusetts and in North Carolina, state representative Chris Caruso noted Bridgeport's elevated levels of bronchitis, asthma and emphysema." Indeed, a recent Bridgeport Community Health Profile found that 21 percent of the households surveyed had kids with asthma, three times the U.S. average" (Motavalli and McFadyen, 1998).

"It's ridiculous, an insult," said Hispanic community activist Willie Matos, who added that the Strategic Plan for the city, which he had helped to write, calls for an emphasis on clean industries. Shirley Bean, a city councilwoman known for her fancy hats who is also a longtime resident of Seaview Avenue, lectured the members of the Planning and Zoning Commission: "We do not need an asphalt plant next to residential housing, where children are playing and going to school" (Motavalli and McFadyen, 1998).

Nothing New about Dumping in Bridgeport

Residents of Bridgeport have a long relationship with other people's industrial waste, according to one graphic report from the scene:

> There's nothing new about dumping on Bridgeport. The existence of a 100-foot-tall "Mount Trashmore" on the city's East Side brought Jesse Jackson to town in the early 1990s for a march against pollution. Illegal dumps are common, as are brownfield sites, the closed and contaminated plants that are the legacy of a once-vibrant manufacturing city. Now the Resco "garbage-to-energy" incinerator dominates the city skyline from its position in the city's African-American and Hispanic west side, and residents are fighting a huge expansion of the local utility's mostly coal-fired electric plants. "They call Bridgeport 'the armpit of the East,'" Percell told a weekend rally in front of his home. "They keep bringing in dirtier and dirtier proposals, and Mayor Joe Ganim [the recipient of both asphalt developers' campaign largesse] keeps giving them what they want." (Motavalli and McFadyen, 1998)

Acknowledging overwhelming opposition to the asphalt plants, Connecticut's State Senate passed a two-year statewide moratorium. As for the asphalt developers, both of whom lived out of town, Jaree Noblin (Glenda's daughter) said, "Maybe they'd feel differently about it if they had to live here" (Motavalli and McFadyen, 1998). This small victory over the Bridgeport asphalt plant was an exception to the general rule in the area. More typical is the slow-motion collapse of contaminated old factories.

Hugh Baily described the scene in the *Atlantic* (2015): "In the East Side neighborhood of Bridgeport, Connecticut, sits a decaying hulk of a factory that would look right at home in any of dozens of postindustrial cities nationwide. The series of buildings was once home to a huge Remington Arms plant, but the company has been gone for almost 30 years. Once a center of jobs and prosperity, the site is now a sinkhole, and the surrounding neighborhoods are among the poorest in the state. The predominantly black and Latino residents suffer from high crime rates and low job prospects, and a major reason is the continual neglect at the former factories, contaminated with all manner of pollutants, around which the city was built."

The East Side of Bridgeport is only one of many neighborhoods studded by "brownfields," scarred, toxified earth laced with industrial toxins. The Remington site, with its broken windows and trash-strewn empty lots, is surrounded by homes. Between 2002 and 2016, the U.S. government allocated close to $2 billion to aid in the cleanup of high-poverty, mainly black and Latino urban neighborhoods. The funding was advertised as seed money for future private redevelopment. It was a rare program that united environmentalists and business interests. In Bridgeport, where unemployment is chronically high, the lure of new businesses appealed to nearly everyone. The money was spent, and some areas were cleaned up, but fundamental problems remained the same, as little new industry moved in. Per capita household income in the East Side of Bridgeport is less than half of Connecticut's average; by 2010, more buildings were vacant than occupied.

Arsenic, Lead, and Petroleum-Based Pollutants

Remington's arms trade dwindled late in the nineteenth century. For half a century after that, General Electric manufactured various electrical devices, including small motors, on the 77-acre site. Linda Conner Lambeck described the contamination at the site in the *Connecticut Post* (2013): "Now, all that remains of the city's manufacturing past on the site are industrial contaminants, including arsenic, lead, and petroleum-based pollutants." By 2013, a proposal was being made to clean up the site and build Harding High School there. State environmental officials expressed approval, but required remediation after community pressure.

The *Post* reported that David Kooris, director of the city's office of planning and economic development, "said the GE parcel represents the best opportunity to build a quality school campus that will include a football field, track and other athletic fields. The East Side neighborhood is pockmarked with brownfields and there are few other available sites on which to build a new school, according to city officials" (Lambeck, 2013).

The Greenwich High School nearby had been built on reclaimed soil that had been laced with polychlorinated-biphenyls, or PCBs, as well as other toxins. After an uproar among parents that followed discovery of the contaminants, state health officials assured them the site was now safe. A list of schools that had been built on once-toxic soil was compiled, which also indicated to everyone who was paying attention just how widespread contamination of southwestern Connecticut had become.

Not everyone was convinced. "All of us are wary," said City Council member Lydia Martinez. "We know what was going on [at] that site." General Electric said it was prepared to donate as many as 17 acres for the school. The remediators had their work cut out. The *Connecticut Post* described the composition of the soil:

> Arsenic and lead were found at concentrations above those recommended for residential or school uses—16.3 percent of the samples tested for arsenic

and 5.9 percent for lead. Exposure to arsenic, for a long enough time and in sufficient quantities, is carcinogenic, while lead has been linked to developmental delays in children. The highest concentration of arsenic at the site was 122 milligrams per kilogram, found some 13 feet below ground. The state considers 10 milligrams per kilogram a safe level for homes and schools. Lead was found at levels up to 2½ times the recommended safe level of 400 milligrams per kilogram in the top four feet of soil. The metals antimony, beryllium, copper, mercury and silver also exceeded the exposure criteria, as did polynuclear aromatic hydrocarbons—heavy organic substances found in petroleum products—like asphalt, coal and combustion products. In addition, extractable total petroleum hydrocarbons and vinyl chloride were found to exceed standards.

The groundwater contained arsenic, cadmium, copper, zinc and perchloroethylene (a solvent used in dry cleaning) at levels above the safe standard. (Lambeck, 2013)

General Electric offered to pay for bulldozers to remove the toxic soil. Randolph Brown, an East End resident, urged GE to cleanse the entire 77 acres that would comprise the school's campus and athletic fields. "The rest of it [the site of the former GE factory] is still going to be contaminated," he said. Brown's remark was prescient. A year and a half after the Greenwich High School was offered as proof that a local site could be clean and clear, the *Connecticut Post* reported: "The discovery of PCBs and other contaminants at Greenwich High School two years ago is only part of a mosaic of cancer-causing toxics that have cropped up at various sites around one of the nation's wealthiest, most exclusive communities. Pollutants have now been confirmed at three other locations in Greenwich, providing new and expanding evidence of a decades-old trail of ash stretching from the high school to the west, down along both sides of the Interstate 95 corridor and directly into Long Island Sound" (Cummings, 2014).

Nine months after this report appeared, ground was broken for construction of Harding High School. It opened in 2018.

Further Reading

Baily, Hugh. "Where 'Brownfield' Is a Pretty Word for 'Toxic Dump'." *The Atlantic*, September 2015. https://www.theatlantic.com/politics/archive/2015/09/where-brownfield-is-a-pretty-word-for-toxic-dump/432843/

Cummings, Bill. "More Toxins Found in Greenwich Soil." *Connecticut Post*, December 17, 2014. http://www.ctpost.com/local/article/More-toxins-found-in-Greenwich-soil-5981761.php

Lambeck, Linda Conner. "Toxins Aside, Former GE Site Slated for New High School." *Connecticut Post*, June 22, 2013. http://www.ctpost.com/local/article/Toxins-aside-former-GE-site-slated-for-new-high-4615224.php

Motavalli, Jim, and Deidre McFadyen. "Toxic Targets: Polluters That Dump on Communities of Color Are Finally Being Brought to Justice." 1998. *E—The Environmental Magazine on Internet*. http://www.ejnet.org/ej/Estory.html

Chester, Pennsylvania: Unwilling Capital of Hazmat

Chester, southwest of Philadelphia on the Delaware River, contains about 44,000 people, of whom about 75 percent are black. Having lost many of its shipyards and auto plants, Chester was being relegated to a status of urban collateral damage, suffering high unemployment, as it became a center for unwelcomed hazardous-waste disposal. Pulmonary diseases spiked, as well as lung cancer and incidence of low-birth-weight infants. Local residents organized and forced some of the plants to close. Chester, located in Delaware County, with roughly 500,000 people, 90 percent of whom are white, and provides a striking example of how environmental toxicity has been concentrated in a relatively small enclave of minority inhabitants. In addition to its majority black population, Chester is also the poorest community in Delaware County.

As of 2019, Chester was the unwilling host to four hazardous and municipal waste treatment facilities, one of which is the United States' largest infectious medical waste treatment facility (named, rather innocuously, Thermal Pure Systems), which processes material from Virginia, Ohio, Maryland, New York, Delaware, and New Jersey. Chester is home as well to the nation's fourth largest trash-to-steam incinerator, "a wastewater treatment plant which in turn, incinerates the hazardous resulting sludge" (Mayfield, n.d.). An incinerator that will treat toxic soil was constructed in 2017 as well. Chester handles more than 98 percent of Delaware County's garbage, as well as some from neighboring states. The Westinghouse incinerator is especially notable as an importer of garbage from a wide hinterland. The waste dumps kept expanding 20 years after the initial protests, as, by 2014, Keystone Sanitary Landfill in Dunmore and Throop sought to expand.

"Chester City has suffered incredible disproportionate environmental impacts over the years," said Mark Wallace, a professor of religion and environmental sciences at Swarthmore College. "Chester as we know, suffers from disproportionate impacts particularly in regards to children" (Kauffman, 2017). Cancer rates in Chester are between two and three times the general occurrence in the rest of Pennsylvania; mortality rates and child mortality are also much higher. In other words, the people of Chester pay for other people's effluvia with their lives. This is part of everyday life, not a Superfund site, and there exist no plans to change anything. Environmental racism is very clearly defined.

During the early 1990s, several Chester residents were interviewed for a documentary film about living among an overload of out-of-state waste. Local residents' comments were revealing:

"It's a stench you've never smelled before. It is horrible."

"We have a high rate of cancer here . . . we have high rates of a lot of things we don't have answers to."

"Trash finds its way from Maryland. Trash finds its way from Virginia. Trash finds its way from Jersey" (Gibbons, 2014).

Organizing Against Toxic Dumps

Residents who had formed Chester Residents Concerned for Quality Living recalled that during the 1990s they had sued under the 1964 U.S. Civil Rights Act, asserting discrimination. The U.S. Supreme Court dismissed the case in 1998. The state formed a committee in 2001 to consider how to use principles of environmental justice in its decision-making when application was made for landfills, industrial wastewater plants, or coal mines. State environmental officials established an Office of Environmental Advocate and published criteria for "environmental justice areas," which included parts of the area near Chester. To be defined as an environmental justice area, a community must be within a half mile of a landfill, wastewater plant, or coal mine and have more than 20 percent of residents in poverty, or more than 30 percent minorities. Public meetings are required before permits may be issued. The entire process permits officials to disregard public opinion with a disclaimer, by which they are allowed to "exercise . . . administrative discretion in the future. DEP reserves the discretion to deviate from this policy statement if circumstances warrant" (Gibbons, 2014).

Still, the waste rolled into Chester. Researchers have studied the fact that while the wealthy get most of the goods produced by an affluent society, minority and poor communities receive most of their waste and shoulder many of the associated environmental risks. This is a worldwide pattern. "Without a doubt, the majority of people recognize that the reason this problem of environmental justice happens is because the groups we're talking about don't have a lot of political power," said Drexel University law professor Alex Geisinger, who has studied the subject for more than 20 years (Gibbons, 2014). Geisinger said, regarding the state's amended permitting process, "Notice what it doesn't do. It doesn't say you can't create more environmental harm here" (Gibbons, 2014).

Geisinger began teaching environmental law at the Thomas R. Kline School of Law at Drexel in 1996 after having practiced in the field since 1992. His students worked with Chester residents on legal issues. Both Geisinger and staff at DEP agreed that the purpose of the amended process was less about impeding construction or expansion of waste sites than about explaining bureaucratic prose to affected residents. In other words, the state was engaged in a bureaucratic song and dance. On the ground in Chester, the toxic waste continued to flow in.

A Phalanx of Hazardous-Waste Treatment Plants

Beginning in 1985, Russell, Rea & Zappala (now Gomulka), an investment company based in Pittsburgh, without consulting residents, financed and constructed a phalanx of hazardous-waste treatment plants in Chester. While residents asserted that the toxicity is connected to a rash of health problems, the state and the company contended that no cause-and-effect relationship had been proved. The courts also have rejected assertions by citizens of Chester that they have been targeted by environmental racism because they are mainly black.

Residents assert that chronic asthma, sore throats, headaches, and skin disorders are connected to the plants' emissions. In addition, property values have fallen sharply as garbage trucks loaded with tons of trash rumble along nearby streets, shaking and damaging their homes. Starting in 1994, studies by the U.S. Environmental Protection Agency (EPA) found that Chester's percentage of low-weight births is the highest in the state. Mortality from lung cancer averages more than 60 percent above the rest of Delaware County. Children in Chester also experience the highest concentration of lead in their bloodstreams compared to the rest of Pennsylvania, as well as the highest infant mortality rate in the state.

Citizen Resistance

Having informed citizens of Chester of their ailments, the EPA also said it had no power to shut down any of the plants. The state, by authority of its Department of Environmental Protection (DEP), continued to grant permits for expansion of existing plants and construction of new ones. Citizens were left more or less alone to organize resistance on their own and sue in generally unsupportive courts that find no existing legal basis for crime that attributes environmental harm to racial discrimination, the cornerstone of the environmental justice movement.

Meanwhile courts have tied private citizens' hands to deal with the problem through legal channels. Mike Ewall, director of the Energy Justice Network, pointed to a legal precedent set in 2001 that prohibits private lawsuits alleging a violation of Title VI civil rights without proof of intent. "If you can't prove that the disproportionate environmental impact is intentional, you're out of luck," he said (NAACP, 2012).

Left to their own devices, Chester residents organized Chester Residents Concerned for Quality Living (CRCQL) in 1992, with Zulene Mayfield as chairperson. CRCQL's federal lawsuit raised environmental racism as a defense, claiming discrimination under the Civil Rights Act of 1964, making a case that as home to only 8 percent of the county's population, Chester processes more than two-thirds of its waste. The lawsuit also accused the DEP of discrimination because a disproportionate number of Chester's hazardous waste facilities are located in black neighborhoods, a pattern that has been maintained across the state. In Delaware County alone, black neighborhoods host eight commercial-waste sites, while predominately white neighborhoods contain only three (Mayfield, n.d.).

Elsewhere in the Philadelphia area, other black communities find themselves in a similar situation. A report from the National Association for the Advancement of Colored People (NAACP) described another community colonized by polluting industry:

> If you need proof [of environmental racism], take a ride across the Passyunk Avenue Bridge, past the sprawling oil refinery owned by the recently formed Philadelphia Energy Group, and spend a few moments wandering the streets of Schuylkill Southwest—where residents have spent decades dealing with the mysterious odors that periodically emanate from the glowing stacks less than a mile away. Nearly three quarters of the neighborhood's population is African American—more than half earn less than $25,000 a year—and while their story is not unique, they share something . . . with similar populations of Americans scattered across the nation's post-industrial landscape: They are being disproportionately deprived of quality air. (NAACP, 2012)

Further Reading

"The Case for Environmental Justice in Chester, Pennsylvania" (PDF). Movement Technology Institute. 2017. https://ejatlas.org/conflict/clustering-of-waste-facilities-in-chester-usa

Chiles, Nick. "8 Horrifying Examples of Corporations Mistreating Black Communities with Environmental Racism." *Atlanta Black Star*, February 12, 2015. http://atlantablackstar.com/2015/02/12/8-horrifying-examples-of-corporations-mistreating-black-communities-with-environmental-racism/

Gibbons, Brendan. "20 Years After Waste Battle, Environmental Justice Still in Short Supply." *Scranton* [Pennsylvania] *Times-Tribune*, December 7, 2014. http://thetimes-tribune.com/news/20-years-after-waste-battle-environmental-justice-still-in-short-supply-1.1799159

Kauffman, Rick. "Chester Residents Air Environmental Concerns to Pa [Pennsylvania]." *Delaware County Daily Times News*, May 23, 2017. https://www.delcotimes.com/news/chester-residents-air-environmental-concerns-to-pa/article_b9a1aa56-4197-55fd-8480-4f2e5ec3defb.html

Mayfield, Zulene."Environmental Justice Case Study: Toxic Waste in Chester, Pennsylvania." Chester Residents Concerned for Quality Living, n.d. Accessed October 21, 2017. http://www.umich.edu/~snre492/polk.html

"NAACP Report Condemns Environmental Racism." *Philadelphia Tribune*, December 25, 2012. http://www.phillytrib.com/news/naacp-report-condemns-environmental-racism/article_ed34835d-4f6a-50b0-a936-bd96de2fa4b2.html

Nussbaum, Paul. "On the Bus for Eco-Tour of Chester. The Aim: See If the City Has Suffered from 'Environmental Racism,' Then Advise the EPA." *Philadelphia Inquirer*, June 28, 1998.

South Chicago: Life and Death in the "Toxic Doughnut"

Much of the environmental devastation described in this book concerns exceptional cases, such as the effects of Agent Orange. More typical, however, is grinding, everyday toxicity, as illustrated in South Chicago, Illinois's "Toxic Doughnut" at the Altgeld Gardens, a large apartment complex that is 97 percent black. Altgeld Gardens is an island in a sea of toxics-spewing industries and garbage disposal facilities.

Built on an abandoned landfill in 1945, the complex was meant to house 10,000 African American veterans returning from World War II. Today, Altgeld Gardens is surrounded by 53 toxic facilities and 90 percent of South Chicago's landfills, and two-thirds of the complex's residents live below the federal poverty level, yielding yet another textbook example of environmental racism. The people who live here are subject to elevated levels of ammonia, lead, DDT, polycyclic aromatic hydrocarbons, PCBs, heavy metals, and xylene.

Jim Motavalli and Deidre McFadyen wrote in *E-Magazine* (1998) that these conditions affect the health of the entire community. In 1984, a study by the Illinois Public Health Sector revealed excessive rates of prostate, bladder, and lung cancer. Additionally, medical records have indicated (1) high rates of children born with brain tumors, (2) high rates of fetuses that had to be aborted after tests revealed brains developing outside their skulls, and (3) much higher than usual rates of asthma, ringworm, and other ailments. Despite evidence of health problems, the residents of Altgeld Gardens have not been relocated to another public housing project.

Residents are subjected to an assortment of nauseating odors from a nearby water-treatment plant, as well as landfills, steel mills, and chemical and paint factories. "One night last summer, I woke up smelling butane gas," recalled resident Hazel Johnson, founder of People for Community Recovery, the nation's only environmental justice organization based in a public housing project. "I asked my daughter to go to the kitchen to check the stove, but the smell was coming from Waste Management's landfill" (Motavalli and McFadyen, 1998).

Motavalli and McFadyen wrote from the scene:

> On the right side of the road, mountains of garbage hid the view of beautiful Lake Calumet. Just a few blocks further east, Consolidated Edison's coal-fired power plant was coughing up puffs of smoke full of soot and mercury. "How can the people who live here stand it?" I wondered. The answer to my question was easy. There is no way the people can stand it. And the people of Southeast Chicago are rising up to stop the dumps. The waste dumps leak toxic chemicals into the groundwater as well as local lakes and rivers. On a sunny April afternoon, fishermen set up their poles on the banks of the debris-strewn Little Calumet River, ignoring the oily tincture of the water. For years, poor black families at Maryland Manors, abutting the southern edge of Altgeld Gardens, drank well water that was laced with cyanide, benzene, and toluene.

"Mother of Environmental Justice"

Everything in the effluent society goes somewhere. Waste Management, a national garbage conglomerate, was seeking a license in Chicago to expand its existing dump, adding 6 million tons of waste to its existing cache of 100 million tons over five years. Southeast Chicago houses the largest array of dumps in the middle of the United States, and residents there were fed up. In addition to its own waste, Illinois imports more garbage than any other state in the United States. South Chicago is one of the country's garbage capitals, built on top of a century of pollution by now-defunct steel mills. "They made the companies and the city rich," wrote Beatrice Lumpkin (2005). "The companies were allowed to foul the rivers and lakes, and pollute the soil and air. The workers and their families paid the price with higher rates of cancer, asthma, and other illnesses." The company offered community protesters a park on top of the landfill. Residents refused.

In 1982, at about the same time that people in Warren County, North Carolina, and Love Canal, New York, were organizing against toxic waste dumps, residents of South Chicago came together in their own group, People for Community Recovery. One of the early leaders was Hazel Johnson, a mother of seven, whose husband, John, had died of lung cancer in 1969 at the age of 41. She suspected foul air and other pollutants that had become endemic in South Chicago as a contributing cause of his death. Johnson and others soon discovered that cancer rates in their neighborhoods were twice those of other parts of Chicago. They began to link the afflictions of their everyday lives to environmental racism, which Johnson called "genocide" (Lumpkin, 2005).

Altgeld Gardens residents converged on South Chicago's city hall to protest. In 2005, 17,000 petition signatures gave Tenth Ward alderman John Pope an incentive to sponsor a two-year moratorium on dumping that unanimously passed the City Council, with a pledge to seek a permanent dumping ban in Southeast Chicago. Gathering 17,000 signatures required a very broad coalition, including more than 100 people from high school students to retirees. They went to schools and churches, businesses and parks, among other places.

Among her neighbors, Johnson quickly acquired the title "Mother of Environmental Justice." Johnson said her belief is, "The world should not be disintegrating around us because of our neglect. We should be able to pass on to our children the same blue sky and fresh air we grew up with" (Lumpkin, 2005). They drew inspiration from the activism of African Americans and their white allies in Warren County, who were protesting (and being arrested) fighting local installation of a dump for PCB-laced soil.

People for Community Recovery won some local victories, including water and sewer service for the senior housing annex of Altgeld Gardens. Their movement also spread south and eastward across the Illinois border with Indiana into Gary, where effluvia from steel mills and oil refineries had become an issue. They protested water quality in the Indiana Harbor Ship Canal, working with the Army Corps of Engineers.

"They are not worried about the signs that say, 'Don't eat the fish or swim in these waters.' (As though anyone would want to eat those fish!),'" reported Lumpkin (2005). "According to a 1996 U.S. Fish and Wildlife Service report, many of the fish have 'eroded fins, swollen eyes, deformed lower jaws, and evidence of internal hemorrhaging'" (Lumpkin, 2005).

The Army Corps of Engineers was on the scene to dredge the canal to enable continued delivery by ore boats to the steel mills. The local residents were more concerned with what was in that sludge—4.7 million cubic yards containing PCBs, lead, mercury, arsenic, zinc, chromium, benzene, and naphthalene, all dumped by unregulated oil refineries, steel mills, and city sewage plants.

Organizing Against a Pyramid of Garbage

Opposition flared after industries received permission from the city of East Chicago, Indiana to dump the poisoned mud near two schools, Central High and West Side Junior High. They planned to construct a "confined disposal facility," or CDF (Lumpkin, 2005). Over three decades, according to the proposal, the CDF, engorged with toxic waste, was projected to grow into a pyramid covering 134 acres, 28 feet high at its peak. Plans called for a "cap" of clay and soil on top of this mini-mountain to be installed only after the dump had reached maximum capacity. The entire plan took shape with no publicity or consultation with the proposed dump's neighbors, who were an ethnic mix. Soon the people united across ethnic boundaries to fight the dump proposal as Citizens for a Clean Environment. Roughly 88 percent of the people in East Chicago were people of color, including 52 percent Latino and 35 percent black (Lumpkin, 2005).

This was an impromptu civic group that organized in people's living rooms, formed at first to win safeguards for the health of students at schools adjacent to the proposed dump site. The residents also received technical information from scientists at nearby universities. Hundreds of people marched on city hall during April 2003, drawing attention from national media with clearly defined and scientifically supported charges of environmental racism. People held organizing rallies, sent letters, and signed petitions. Betty Balanoff, a coordinator for Citizens for a Clean Environment, said: "We do want the canal cleaned up because it is evaporating and polluting our air. But we do not want toxic wastes dumped in a CDF that is poorly built and will further pollute our air and soil" (Lumpkin, 2005). Initially, officials said no money was available to clean up the canal and dispose of wastes in a manner that would respect the health of community people. The response of Citizens for a Clean Environment was: "Find it! . . . The community cannot be expected to pay the difference in human life and damaged children" (Lumpkin, 2005).

They also won support from the United Steelworkers of America, AFL-CIO because the pollution was affecting their families as much as anyone else. The Steelworkers issued a remarkable statement that is worth quoting at length because it places South Chicago's local pollution in a global context, and does so from the vantage point of the factory floor:

> The problems of acid rain, global warming, ozone depletion, oceanic pollution and world poverty remind us that we can no longer think of ourselves solely as citizens of the U.S. or Canada, or even as North Americans. The potential catastrophe is global. Environment must be a global issue. But is it a union issue? Should we work to protect the environment merely as good citizens, or is there a special role for our union to play? We believe the answers are clear. Environment is an essential union issue. Environmental work must be part of our mission at every level of the union. We must continue to work for progressive legislation. This includes improving air and water quality, requiring reductions in toxic waste and restricting the use of toxic chemicals, promoting recycling in ways that protect union jobs, protecting "whistleblowers" who report suspected environmental violations, and workers who refuse to carry out an order that violates environmental laws or endangers the public. ("Steelworkers," 2005)

As a result of the protests (including mass meetings at city hall), the Army Corps was ordered to change its plans and add safeguards. And as a bonus, in an upset that nearly no one had suspected, East Chicago's mayor and the entire city council were defeated at the polls.

Further Reading

"Environmental Racism." Revolvy, n.d. Accessed October 21, 2017. https://www.revolvy.com/main/index.php?s=Environmental%20racism

Lumpkin, Beatrice. "Grassroots Environmental Victory in Chicago: No Dumps, No Deals, Again!" *People's World*, April 29, 2005. http://www.peoplesworld.org/article/grassroots-environmental-victory-in-chicago-no-dumps-no-deals-again/

Motavalli, Jim, and Deidre McFadyen. "Toxic Targets: Polluters That Dump on Communities of Color Are Finally Being Brought to Justice." 1998. E-magazine. http://www.ejnet.org/ej/Estory.html

"Steelworkers Union Supports Clean Environment." Chicago Independent Media Center. April 15, 2005. http://chicago.indymedia.org/archive/newswire/display/55954/index.php

Race, Class, and Toxicity at Love Canal

Love Canal, downstream from Niagara Falls, New York, became a synonym for environmental toxicity in 1978 when so much hazardous waste was found there that residents were forced to move out and their houses were destroyed, after a seeping toxic dump containing more than 20,000 tons of chemical waste (including about 200 different chemicals) was discovered under an elementary school. At the same time, disclosure of pervasive, life-threatening pollution at Love Canal also helped spur research and activism about environmental racism nationwide.

After discovery of its toxic trove, Love Canal became a household catch-phrase through copious media coverage, which helped to incite political action and frame the stakes in a growing national environmental movement. More than any other single event, the tragedy at Love Canal created the political context that secured creation of the Environmental Protection Agency's Superfund program in 1980 that allocated money to clean up hundreds of other toxic sites. This series of events also provided a window on just how closely bound pollution has become with race and class, as well as gender. It's also a story of multiethnic cooperation, since the victims were a combination of blacks and whites, and some of the major activism was organized by African American women cooperating with white church groups.

Alice Mah, assistant professor in the Department of Sociology, University of Warwick, United Kingdom (and author of *Industrial Ruination, Community, and Place*, University of Toronto Press, 2012), wrote:

> The health effects for the residents were staggering, with high incidences of cancer, miscarriages, rare diseases, and birth defects. It was the first U.S. state of emergency to be declared over a human-made disaster, and it was a sobering lesson about the effects of toxic pollution. Love Canal received international media attention and stands out as a significant turning point in the history of the global environmental justice movement. Yet the memory and lessons of Love Canal seem to be fading with passing generations. The Bhopal and Chernobyl disasters of the 1980s will be remembered for generations to come. They are widely considered to be the worst industrial and nuclear accidents in history, with enduring health and environmental impacts to this day. (Mah, 2013)

An Abandoned Canal and the Birth of a Toxic Waste Dump

The canal was named for William Love, an entrepreneur who started building it when canals (including the better-known Erie Canal that connected New York City's hinterland with the industrial U.S. heartland bordering the Great Lakes) provided major avenues of commerce. During the early 20th century, the Niagara Falls area prospered as tourists came to see its spectacular wonders, but it also became a hub for industry running on its hydroelectric power. Mah wrote (2016): "Belying its popular image as a tourist destination, Niagara Falls became a hub for heavy industry in the first half of the 20th century. Chemical factories lined the banks of the river, attracted by the extraordinary natural resource of the falls and the proximity to integrated Rust Belt industries. The industrial city expanded rapidly, attracting new workers in search of factory jobs."

Love sought to connect the upper and lower Niagara Rivers and power a company town he was planning, "Model City." A thousand yards into the project, Love ran out of money. By 1910, when Love abandoned his canal and took a substantial loss, it was clear that the new railroads had made them obsolete. The proposed canal languished incomplete and, between 1942 and 1953, became a toxic waste dump for Hooker Electrochemical Company, which later was acquired by Occidental Chemical Corporation. Approximately 20,000 tons of toxic industrial waste was poured into the abandoned canal. The waste was sealed with a clay cap on top, but the bottom contained no lining, and thus became subject to serious leakage. In 1953, its commercial use exhausted, the company filled the canal and sold it for $1 to the Niagara School Board, which built a school there. A hundred houses also were built nearby. Most new residents had no idea they were living on top of a chemical waste dump, even though Hooker had covered this possibility when it transferred the land to the school district with a contract clause that said it would not be held responsible for the harmful effects of its waste.

After the first hints that the school site was leaching toxic waste, authorities denied that a problem existed. Residents became suspicious as chemicals began to erupt into their basements and backyards after a harsh winter in 1977. Residents conducted their own research and forced testing by the government, as they provided reports of "numerous testimonies, reports and surveys of miscarriages, birth defects, deaths, cancers, and other illnesses of residents" (Mah, 2013). Mah herself found evidence of similar situations nearby, including the Highland Avenue African American community in Niagara Falls, New York, and the working-class community of Glenview-Silvertown, Niagara Falls, Ontario. Both were adjacent to chemical brownfields with unknown or disputed levels of contamination. Suddenly, concern over the declining values of their homes seemed to be the least of the Love Canal residents' worries. Chemical waste that they had not suspected had condemned them to a life sentence of misery.

Following pressure from residents, Love Canal became an officially recognized crisis. Mah (2013) summarized the events that followed:

In August 1978, the New York health commissioner declared a state of emergency in Love Canal and 239 families were evacuated. United States President Jimmy Carter subsequently announced a state of emergency, the first ever declared over a technological disaster, and funded the evacuation and relocation of 780 further families in March 1980, the same year that the federal EPA established the Superfund, which is a $1.6 billion trust fund raised by a levy on petroleum and chemical companies which was used to clean up ("remediate") several hundred toxic waste sites. (Even so, several hundred other such sites remain.)

Toxic Disaster as Racial Bridge

"As I started doing research into Lois Gibbs [a working-class white woman who was a major activist at Love Canal] I found out that there were significant parts of the Love Canal story that no one had really talked about—the activities of a group of African American women, for example, as well as a middle-class religious group. No one really talked about the men active at Love Canal—most studies just talk about Lois Gibbs and leave the rest out," said Elizabeth Blum, Troy University associate professor of history and author of *Love Canal Revisited: Race, Class and Gender in Environmental Activism* (2008), which was published on the 30th anniversary of the first toxic event there.

"When this neighborhood of Niagara Falls, New York, burst upon the nation's consciousness, the media focused on a working-class white woman named Lois Gibbs, who gained prominence as an activist fighting to save families from the poison buried beneath their homes. Gibbs' organization, the Love Canal Homeowners Association, challenged big government and big business—and ultimately won relocation. But as Elizabeth Blum now shows, the activists at Love Canal were a very diverse lot" ("Love Canal," 2008).

Blum explored how poor black women at Love Canal struggled to be heard, as their environmental activism was defined in the context of the civil rights struggle. She also examines how progressive whites (especially through the Ecumenical Task Force) helped to secure compensation for black families who were displaced by the pollution at Love Canal.

"A person's race, class, and gender played a pivotal role in how people experienced, talked about and became active at Love Canal," Blum said. "The black women saw the event as an opportunity to expose and press against racism, the white women as a way to enforce their value and worth as mothers and housewives, the religious groups as a way to link to wider environmental values, and the elite politicians and bureaucrats as a way to reinvigorate the economy of a dying city," she said. "In this case, however, the working-class women at Love Canal were specifically reacting against what they thought feminism was—they wanted to show that housewives and mothers had value in society, and could accomplish something positive," she said ("Troy," 2009).

New Housing, Same Old Toxicity

Sales agents at Black Creek Village, near Love Canal, insisted that the area was clean, but it wasn't. By 2011, a fresh wave of environmental illnesses were reported on the same site, and substantial toxicity remained, just as lawsuits over the first crisis were finally being resolved, and even as many of Love Canal's original residents had departed.

The Love Canal incident and its aftermath have spawned a sizable literature, which includes memoirs and organizing manuals (Gibbs, 1998, 2010), as well as scholarly analyses (Blum, 2008; Newman, 2016). Lois Gibbs argues in *Love Canal: The Story Continues* (1998): "People believe that no one has the right to make their family sick or their environment unsafe for any reason, certainly not because they are farmers, working class, poor, or live in communities of color. Nor is it fair that ordinary citizens are left with the burden of having to prove that they are sick from chemical exposures, while chemical corporations are presumed innocent of harming human health unless proven guilty" (Gibbs, 1998). Gibbs also established a Center for Environment, Health, and Justice following the Love Canal crisis, which provides technical assistance and training for people who need to confront environmental problems in their own communities and do not possess enough money to hire experts and lawyers.

Love Canal has become a worldwide example. In 2016, a toxic waste scandal at Changzhou Foreign Languages School in eastern China sickened several hundred students after they were transferred to a new site that had been used as a dump by several chemical companies. The poisoning came to be called "China's Love Canal." The discovery generated a public outcry, according to Alice Mah, writing in *China Dialogue* (2016). Soil and groundwater tests indicated serious toxicity, according to China Central Television reports. Students came down with headaches, rashes, nosebleeds, coughs, and several types of cancers, including lymphoma and leukemia.

As with Love Canal, the Changzhou School incident provoked vigorous citizen grassroots activity against toxic waste sites. China has had more than one toxic exposure that was compared to Love Canal, wrote Alice Mah in *China Dialogue*: "In February 2013, the furious online reaction to a blog post about dumping and groundwater contamination in Shangdong Province was described as China's Love Canal moment and heralded a plea in China for further action" (Mah, 2016). "Over the past thirty-five years," wrote Mah, "the environmental justice movement has grown internationally, with a number of significant advances in legislation, legal cases, scholarship, activism, and organizing. Activists and researchers have identified and challenged stark spatial patterns of environmental injustice and 'environmental racism,' where chemical factories, toxic waste sites, and other environmental hazards have been deliberately situated amongst poor, marginalized and vulnerable populations" (Mah, 2013).

Returning to Love Canal, Mah provided a description of its still-abandoned site in 2013:

> A tall wire fence encloses the vast evacuated site, and the periphery remains eerily abandoned, with weeds sprouting through uneven concrete sidewalks, crumbling skeletons of houses, overgrown lawns, and roads that end abruptly in open fields. You would have to look carefully to find the monument. The Love Canal evacuated site was declared "safe" by the Environmental Protection Agency in 2004 and officially removed from the list of Superfund waste sites. A new "bargain" housing development soon emerged beside it, named Black Creek Village. (Mah, 2013)

Further Reading

Blum, Elizabeth. *Love Canal Revisited: Race, Class, and Gender in Environmental Activism.* Lawrence: University Press of Kansas, 2008.

Gibbs, Lois. *Love Canal: and the Birth of the Environmental Health Movement.* Washington, D.C.: Island Press, 2010.

Gibbs, Lois. *Love Canal: The Story Continues.* Gabriola Island, British Columbia: New Society Publishers, 1998.

Johansen, Bruce E. *Resource Exploitation in Native North America: A Plague upon the Peoples.* Santa Barbara, CA: Praeger, 2016.

"Love Canal Revisited." University Press of Kansas, 2008. https://kansaspress.ku.edu/978-0-7006-1820-0.html

Mah, Alice. "Lessons from Love Canal: Toxic Expertise and Environmental Justice." August 7, 2013. https://www.opendemocracy.net/alice-mah/lessons-from-love-canal-toxic-expertise-and-environmental-justice

Mah, Alice. "The U.S. Love Canal Disaster and Its Legacy." *China Dialogue*, April 27, 2016. https://www.chinadialogue.net/article/show/single/en/8878-The-US-Love-Canal-disaster-and-its-legacy

Newman, Richard S. *Love Canal: A Toxic History from Colonial Times to the Present.* New York: Oxford University Press, 2016.

"Troy University Professor's Book Looks at Race, Class and Gender at Love Canal." Researchgate, May, 2009. https://www.researchgate.net/publication/2732 52393_Love_Canal_Revisited_Race_Class_and_Gender_in_Environ mental_Activism

North Carolina: Protesting Unwelcome Toxic Dumps

Environmentalists and civil rights activists came together to oppose a polychlorinated biphenyls (PCB)–laced landfill in Warren County, North Carolina, after state approval of a toxic dump in Afton, a small town that had been founded by former black slaves during Reconstruction, after the Civil War. In addition to being largely black, most people in this area are also poor. Average incomes in the area are roughly 75 percent of the state's average. In 1980, according to the U.S. Census, Warren County's 16,232 people were 60 percent black and had a median household income of $10,121 a year (about $35,000 in 2017 dollars).

The dump had been proposed to house 30,000 gallons of PCB-laden oil that previously had been sprayed illegally along 210 miles of North Carolina roads in 14 counties during June, July, and August of 1978. The citizens of Afton, 60 miles north of Chapel Hill, knew very little about PCBs when they were confronted with the dump in their home town. Soon, by deadly necessity, they learned that the PCBs were so toxic that the federal government outlawed them one year after the dump was built. Plans for this dump spurred national attention, large protests, and an unsuccessful lawsuit, and are now remembered as one birthplace of an organized environmental justice movement in the United States.

PCBs include 209 artificial chemical compounds that are resistant to fire and heat, and have been used to insulate and cool electrical equipment, as well as to manufacture plastics, paints, copy paper, and tape. They spread easily though air and water, and once lodged in the food chain are very difficult to remove. They are insidious as well as persistent because they biomagnify up the food chain (damage increases with each step). Thus, human beings who eat PCB-laced fish or meat receive a higher and more damaging dose than was contained in the animal's flesh. PCB exposure also has been associated with liver damage, impaired reproduction, suppression of immunity, reduction of mental acuity, and reduced intelligence. The PCBs also are known to cause liver and skin ailments, as well as birth defects, and are suspected of playing a role in several types of cancer.

Robert Burns and his sons Randall and Timothy, from Jamestown, New York, used a truck to spray the 210 miles of rural roadsides with the PCB-laden oil. Burns wanted to circumvent Environmental Protection Agency rules that would have made disposal of the PCBs more expensive. After the PCB-laced oil had been spread along North Carolina highways, the state erected yellow signs reading "Caution, PCB Chemicals on Highway Shoulders" (Katz, 2012). Burns and his sons later pleaded guilty to state and federal criminal charges and were sentenced to three to five years in prison.

Colluding to Create a PCB Dump

The PCB dumping on North Carolina roadsides was declared a threat to public health by the EPA, and the state was required to dispose of it. A year later, the North Carolina Department of Environment and Natural Resources and EPA Region 4 colluded to select Warren County, one of six counties that comprise the state's "black belt," as a deposit site for what turned out to be something of a toxic waste shell game.

What made the toxic dirt less a threat to public health near Afton than along 210 miles of North Carolina highways? The answer to that question (if it was even asked) may still be lodged in the warrens of state and federal bureaucracy. Scientific studies said that the new site was unfeasible due to a shallow water table that required drinking water to be siphoned only five to 10 feet below the surface, posing the danger that, should the disposal site leak, the people of Afton would be drinking water that could kill them.

As soon as North Carolina governor James B. Hunt Jr. proposed burial of the toxic soil in Warren County, his plan spurred furious opposition from residents. "Nobody wants to be known as a dump site," said Walter J. Harris, chairman of the County Commission ("Carolinians," 1982). Residents Fannie and Edgar Limer, who were being forced to become neighbors of the new toxic dump, reflected in a *New York Times* report: "We still like to believe that we've got what we've always had—safety and purity. . . . We just can't bring ourselves to believe the handwriting is really on the wall." Edgar Limer, a 62-year-old accountant, "said he did not believe assurances by the government that the landfill would not leak PCBs. There is also widespread concern that after the burial of the PCBs, property values will plummet, industry will be scared away, and a larger facility for disposal of other hazardous wastes will inevitably follow" ("Carolinians," 1982).

A Lawsuit, a Loss, and Protests

By one account (Katz, 2012): "The Rev. Willie T. Ramey III found the greasy PCB-laden residue near his church in Inez. Deborah Ferruccio encountered the same greasy substance as she drove home to Afton from a camping trip. Both were part of a small group of Warren County residents who began meeting shortly afterward, organizing a historic battle for their community's right to a clean and healthy environment."

According to Vann Newkirk's account (2016):

> Four years of litigation, independent scientific examination, and criticism in the local media could not dissuade [the state] and the E.P.A. from disposing of the PCBs in Afton. In 1982, as construction moved along on the landfill, organizations such as the United Church of Christ and the Southern Christian Leadership Conference sent in organizers to assist the protesters there. One of those organizers was Benjamin Chavis, a longtime activist in the civil rights movement. "Warren County made headlines," he said. "And because it made headlines in the media, we began to get calls from other communities. But you know that in the eighties you couldn't just say there was discrimination. You had to prove it."

So they proved it, with a report, issued in 1987, by the United Church of Christ's Commission for Racial Justice. Called "Toxic Wastes and Race in the United States," the report provided evidence that "race was more strongly correlated with the placement of a hazardous-waste facility than any other single factor, and remained so even when they controlled for income and geographic area" (Newkirk, 2016). According to the same report, three of the United States' largest commercial hazardous-waste landfills, containing 40 percent of the country's capacity, were in or near black or Latino population centers.

In 2012, Deborah Ferruccio told *Environmental Health News,* "What really ignited the community was that they said they were going to put [the landfill] in regardless of public sentiment. And that really does not sit well with people who don't even have zoning because they don't want anybody to tell them how to build their chicken coops. We found out about it just in time to put a notice in the paper, call a meeting, and in the few weeks that we had, a few of us in Afton literally ripped up the phone book and we each took X number of pages. I went door-to-door to all of the people who lived along the landfill road. [The response] was phenomenal" (Katz, 2012).

Within a few weeks, during January 1979, an angry crowd of more than 700 Warren County people compelled the County Commission to sue to ban the dump and the PCB disposal. The county dropped the suit for unspecified reasons. The county residents then sued privately with assistance from the church and the NAACP. "These folks believe that they're fighting for their lives, more so now than ever," said Ken Ferruccio, president of Warren County Citizens Concerned About PCBs, an organization with about 400 members. "People believe that PCB's are just the beginning. That's what frightens them" ("Carolinians," 1982).

From the beginning there was no racial conflict, said Ferrucio. "We all knew that PCBs are color-blind and they were going to affect us all. . . . But historically, the people had still never had an issue that brought them together. This brought them together in a way where black and white people were in the churches singing and holding hands, they were in front of the capitol singing and holding hands. . . . White people that were like the Daughters of the Confederacy with NAACP people. It was this new melding of people. . . . White people who had never stepped foot in a black church were there every night" (Katz, 2012).

The Limers became plaintiffs in a lawsuit, filed in federal district court, to halt the dump filed by the county chapter of the NAACP, along with a black Baptist church and 26 people who lived near the waste dump's proposed site. The suit was based on charges of racial discrimination by the state of North Carolina and the federal EPA under the 1964 U.S. Civil Rights Act. The suit also contended violation of state and federal environmental laws prohibiting burial of PCBs.

The Afton residents lost the case, due to a rationale that would become familiar in coming years to anyone who sued for environmental discrimination under the Civil Rights Act: lack of "intent," as legally defined. Judge W. Earl Britt ruled against the residents, saying, "There is not one shred of evidence that race has at any time been a motivating factor for any decision taken by any official—state, federal or local" ("Carolinians," 1982). The EPA then prepared to spend $2.54 million on the PCB disposal site.

Voicing Outrage

The first truckloads of toxic soil rolled into the site during September 1982 as several thousand environmentalists, civil rights advocates, and local residents loudly voiced their outrage. More than 500 people were arrested and spent some time in very well-packed local jails. The loading of the new landfill then continued as scientists, activists, and local residents continued to tell officials that it would poison their drinking water. (Two decades of suspected leaks later, the federal and state governments paid $18 million to detoxify the site that they had said wouldn't leak and cause problems for Afton residents.)

Word of the protests in Warren County spread among national civil rights, environmental, and religious opinion leaders, and soon became a signature conflict with polluting industry in collusion with government agencies. People came to town willing to block highways against a phalanx of toxic refuse–bearing dump trucks. The media, and police, quickly followed. Six weeks of demonstrations and several hundred arrests announced a new fusion of civil rights and assertion of "environmental justice," a new term at that time.

Despite the lawsuits, demonstrations, and publicity, the campaign to prevent the Warren County PCB dump failed, as more than 6,000 truckloads of PCB-laced soil were deposited on the site. Rev. Willie T. Ramey III, who was 32 and a new pastor at the all-black St. Stephen Baptist Church, recalled at age 67, in 2012: "Whatever the original intent was, we only ended up with *our* PCB that was put on the roadside in *our* county. It has not been the PCB that was trucked in from throughout the state, but it was only the PCB that was saturated in our county. And we didn't even want that. We wanted it to be taken away. But if we hadn't stood up, if we hadn't fought, then we would have been made a county where they would bring contaminated waste from other places as well" ("Environmental Racism," n.d.).

The *Duke University Chronicle* described the protests in Warren County as "the largest civil disobedience in the South since Dr. Martin Luther King, Jr. marched through Alabama" ("Environmental Racism," n.d.). For the first time in American history, citizens went to jail attempting to stop a toxic landfill. In an editorial titled "Dumping on the Poor," the *Washington Post* described the protests as "the marriage of environmentalism with civil rights" ("Environmental Racism," n.d.).

Further Reading

"Carolinians Angry over PCB Landfill." *New York Times*, August 11, 1982. http://www.nytimes.com/1982/08/11/us/carolinians-angry-over-pcb-landfill.html

"Environmental Racism." Revolvy, n.d. Accessed October 17, 2017. https://www.revolvy.com/main/index.php?s=Environmental%20racism

Katz, Cheryl. "Birth of the Movement: 'People Have to Stand Up for What Is Right.' A Q&A with Two Environmental Justice Pioneers." *Environment Health News*, June 20, 2012. https://www.climatecentral.org/news/birth-of-the-movement-a-qa-with-two-environmental-justice-pioneers

Newkirk, Vann R. "Fighting Environmental Racism in North Carolina." *The New Yorker*, January 16. 2016. https://www.newyorker.com/news/news-desk/fighting-environmental-racism-in-north-carolina

Donald Trump, Hurricane Maria, and Puerto Rico

After Hurricane Maria wracked Puerto Rico during September 2017, U.S. president Donald Trump employed tactics that were common in the 19th century by European colonialists all over the world. He at once claimed to be "very proud" of the people of the island while also saying that Puerto Ricans "want everything to be done for them" (Landler, 2017). The shifting tone and content of Trump's rhetoric defied analysis, consistency, or reason. This mixed response came after the island, with its 3.4 million U.S. citizens, was raked by the category 5 hurricane, which left most of its people entirely without electric power and drinking water for an extended period of time. Two months after Maria struck, in early December 2017, slightly less than half of Puerto Ricans still had no power.

One thing seemed evident: Trump talked to nonvoting Latino residents of Puerto Rico much differently than to those in Houston, Texas, and southern Florida, which also had suffered extensive damage from hurricanes Harvey and Irma just weeks before Maria bulldozed Puerto Rico. His rhetoric seemed to be political pantomime with plentiful racial subtext to his "base," the third of the U.S. electorate who supported him avidly even as more than half the electorate opposed him. In this way, his response to Hurricane Maria supported his near-constant run for office, playing to his supporters and building his brand without providing essential support to Puerto Rico.

The Atmospheric Context

Global warming does not *create* hurricanes, but it does *enhance* them. Hurricanes are heat engines, and they intensify rapidly over very warm water, strengthening wind speeds and raising rainfall totals. Harvey, Irma, and Maria all received boosts from ocean temperatures that were 4° to 7° F above long-term averages.

Only part of these disastrous hurricanes was due to human generation of greenhouse gases. Warmer air holds more moisture, which provokes more intense precipitation. Melting ice raises sea levels as warmth also expands seawater volume through thermal expansion, aggravating coastal flooding. The land under Houston, as well as much of the Gulf and Atlantic coasts (including Houston and New Orleans) is slowly sinking in part due to human withdrawal of underground water, but also because of geophysical factors. Urban expansion increases the amount of space devoted to parking lots, sidewalks, roads, and roofs, and reduces the area capable of absorbing torrential rains, just as warming causes storms to intensify. All of this makes flooding worse.

More than five weeks after Maria struck, with power restored to only 30 percent of Puerto Rico's residents, a team of 11 experts under the signature of the United Nations faulted the United States' slow and awkward response. "We can't fail to note the dissimilar urgency and priority given to the emergency response in Puerto Rico, compared to the U.S. states affected by hurricanes in recent months," said Leilani Farha, the United Nations special rapporteur on housing (Bruce and Robles, 2017).

Trump: "How Low" Can He Go?

"Americans have gotten into the uneasy habit of wondering how low President Trump might go each day in his multiple tirades against those he imagines as enemies, critics and easy targets," the *New York Times* editorialized October 12, 2017, three weeks after Maria struck Puerto Rico. "But did he really have to pick on the storm-ravaged American citizens of Puerto Rico, of all defenseless people, and reveal such a cold-hearted lack of empathy for their plight?" ("A Disaster," 2017).

President Trump had suggested the day before that Puerto Ricans were ingrates responsible for much of their suffering because of a debt crisis and crumbling power and water infrastructures, even as he said that federal aid would not be available "forever." The next day, he reversed his position, complaining that Puerto Rico's problems were stressing the federal budget. The *Times* pointed out that "the president displayed no hard-hearted budget alert in his previous tributes and vows to persevere in behalf of earlier hurricane victims in mainland Texas and Florida. He promised to be with them 'EVERY SINGLE DAY AFTER' to recover and rebuild. He pledged a personal donation of $1 million for the Houston area's recovery. The contrast with Puerto Rico, a United States territory with deep financial troubles before the storm and no vote in the presidential election, became painfully clear in Mr. Trump's tweets" ("A Disaster," 2017).

Trump displayed these contradictions at a time when more than 85 percent of Puerto Ricans lacked power and more than half had no access to potable water. Less than 10 percent of roads had been restored to service at that time. A month after Maria stuck, 80 percent of Puerto Ricans still had no power and raw sewage was still contaminating scarce water, as 15 sewage treatment plants remained closed. President Trump, meanwhile, gave the federal recovery effort a "ten" on a scale of ten.

On a visit to San Juan, Trump belittled the storm damage, comparing it to what he called "a real catastrophe like Katrina," which had devastated New Orleans a dozen years earlier. He ended up tossing paper towels to San Juan residents in a manner that led *New York Times* columnist Paul Krugman (2017) to headline his column "Let Them Eat Paper Towels," an allusion to a famous quote attributed to Marie-Antoinette, the queen of France during the French Revolution, who is reputed to have told the poor, "Let them eat cake."

As part of its claim that federal response to Puerto Rico's storm damage had been effective, Trump stressed what he said was a low official death toll of 62, compared to more than 1,000 from Hurricane Katrina. The *New York Times* conducted a detailed study of death records a month and a half after the storm's landfall and found that "a review of daily mortality data from Puerto Rico's vital statistics bureau indicates that . . . 1,052 more people than usual died across the island" (Robles et al., 2017). After that, death rates continued above statistical averages for several more weeks, at least, hastened by lack of medical treatment after electricity went out.

By August 2018, Puerto Rico's government had raised its official death toll for Hurricane Maria to 2,975 following a report supporting that figure from George Washington University. "Even though it is an estimate, we are officially changing, or we are putting an official number to the death toll," Governor Ricardo Rosselló said. "We will take the 2,975 number as the official estimate for the excess deaths as a product of Maria" (Santiago et al., 2018). The figure is not a list of names tied directly to the storm. The estimate was more than the death toll for Hurricane Katrina, making Maria the deadliest natural disaster on U.S. soil in more than 100 years.

The gap between the early official death toll and those compiled by medical experts widened over time. According to a study published in the *New England Journal of Medicine* on May 29, 2018, the number of deaths resulting from Hurricane Maria in Puerto Rico between September 20 and December 31, 2018, was at least 4,600 and possibly as high as 5,800, more than 70 times the 64 listed by the island's government (Kishore et al, 2018). Even that number may be low, the study said. "However, this number is likely to be an underestimate because of survivor bias. The mortality rate remained high through the end of December 2017, and one third of the deaths were attributed to delayed or interrupted health care" (Kishore et al., 2018). These numbers include people who died in the hurricane, as well as those who were indirectly killed afterward from injury or illness.

Chris Riotta of *Newsweek* in 2017 compared Trump's reactions to storm damage and human suffering in Puerto Rico, Texas, and Florida. While he often emphasized the self-reliant spirit of Texans and Floridians in the face of disaster, Trump, in his many tweets on the subject, seemed to present Puerto Ricans in a negative light.

> **Trump's response to Harvey in Texas:** "TEXAS: We are with you today, we are with you tomorrow, and we will be with you EVERY SINGLE DAY AFTER, to restore, recover, and REBUILD!"
> **Trump's response to Irma in Florida:** "With Irma and Harvey devastation, Tax Cuts and Tax Reform is needed more than ever before. Go Congress, go!"
> **Trump's response to Maria in Puerto Rico:** "Electric and all infrastructure was disaster before hurricanes. Congress to decide how much to spend . . . We cannot keep FEMA, the Military & the First Responders, who have been amazing (under the most difficult circumstances) in P.R. forever! . . . Now, I hate to tell you, Puerto Rico, but you've thrown our budget a little out of whack, because we've spent a lot of money on Puerto Rico." (Trump, October 12, 2017)

Puerto Rico's Infrastructure Problems

Puerto Ricans living on the island have no right to vote, although they may do so if they take up residence in the United States. "Indeed, the crisis in Puerto Rico is a case study of what happens when people with little political capital need the help of their government. Aid was slow in arriving, compared with the help extended to Florida and Texas after Hurricanes Harvey and Irma," commented Amy Davidson Sorkin in *The New Yorker* (2018). Aid began to arrive only after massive media coverage displayed the dimensions of the disaster.

At the time that Maria devastated Puerto Rico, the island was dealing with $74 billion in public debt and had filed for a status resembling bankruptcy protection in federal court to stave off creditors. Tax receipts had long fallen massively below expenses. Congress also had phased out preferences that granted tax advantages to companies establishing businesses in Puerto Rico, helping to intensify the financial crisis. Puerto Rico's poverty rates had risen to 45 percent after a decade of recession, as increasing numbers of people moved to the United States seeking jobs.

Instead of realizing the magnitude of a historic disaster, Trump accused Puerto Rico's political leadership of mismanagement and incompetence. Puerto Rico's governor, Ricardo A. Rosselló, anxiously called John F. Kelly, White House chief of staff, seeking assurance of aid. "Our country will stand with those American citizens in Puerto Rico until the job is done," Kelly said. The next day, Trump reversed himself (Baker and Dickerson, 2017). The Army Corps of Engineers, which was helping to rebuild Puerto

Rico's electrical grid, said that the task would require several years of sustained effort. The federal government retained a military presence in New Orleans for almost a year after Hurricane Katrina hit that area in 2005; the government maintained assistance there for more than five years.

"Blaming the Victims"

The *New York Times* reported from the scene that Trump's tone-deafness to massive human suffering had "provoked another wave of criticism from the island and its supporters. They expressed astonishment that Mr. Trump would assail the very people he was supposed to be assisting, in contrast to the tone he has taken with Florida and Texas, where National Guard troops and Federal Emergency Management Agency workers are also still helping with hurricane recovery" (Baker and Dickerson, 2017). Mayor Carmen Yulín Cruz of San Juan said that Trump once again was adding "insult to injury," as she called upon aid from international organizations to prevent "the genocide that will result from" Trump's inaction. "Tweet away your hate to mask your administration's mishandling of this humanitarian crisis," she said, addressing Trump. "While you are amusing yourself throwing paper towels at us, your compatriots and the world are sending love and help our way. Condemn us to a slow death of non-drinkable water, lack of food, lack of medicine while you keep others eager to help from reaching us" (Baker and Dickerson, 2017).

While Trump took little action, Puerto Rico was suffering one of the worst hurricane-wrought disasters in human history. The *New York Times* reported: "On a helicopter trip on Thursday morning to Cidra, a small city an hour south of San Juan, the devastated landscape was speckled with homes that were without roofs and covered with tarps. Almost every street was lined with huge piles of tree branches and other debris beginning to rot and stink" (Baker and Dickerson, 2017).

The daily struggle to survive in Puerto Rico was described by Caitlin Dickerson in the *Times* (2017):

> After a day spent working in an office in the dark, without air-conditioning, Iris Díaz arrived at her neighborhood CVS drugstore [in San Juan] desperate for what has quickly become one of the most sought-after items in Puerto Rico: bottled water. A sales clerk standing behind the checkout counter explained that the store had been out of stock for three days. "Ni una sola botellita?" Ms. Díaz pleaded in Spanish. "Not even one little bottle?" The employee shook her head and apologized. . . . Her home was still without electricity or water. She, her husband and their 12-year-old son

were growing impatient with having to drink a kind of storm tea—boiled tap water, which she said had turned a yellowish hue after the storm.

Dickerson continued: "People are so desperate . . . [that] the Environmental Protection Agency cited reports of residents trying to obtain drinking water from wells at hazardous Superfund sites. 'EPA advises against tampering with sealed and locked wells or drinking from these wells, as it may be dangerous to people's health,' the agency said. Waterborne diseases were reported to be spreading rapidly in many rural areas where people were subsisting on unfiltered water from rivers and ponds. 'What happened in Texas and Florida were disasters,' said W. Craig Fugate, who was FEMA administrator under President Barack Obama. 'What happened in Puerto Rico was a catastrophe'" (Dickerson, 2017).

For several months after Maria struck, Puerto Rico's problems were being compounded by factors other than the government's slow response, its fragile infrastructure, and its financial problems that had preceded the hurricane. As it was an island far from the mainland, electrical repair crews and road-clearing equipment could not easily converge from surrounding states. Aid had to be sent by air, with space and weight restrictions, or by ship, which took considerable time. As a result, commented Paul Krugman in the *New York Times* (2017), "Recovery has been painfully slow, [with] life actually getting worse for many residents as the cumulative effects of shortages of power, water, and food take their toll. And the Trump administration seems to increasingly see this tragedy as a public relations issue, something to be spun—partly by blaming the victims—rather than as an urgent problem to be solved. From the beginning, Donald Trump—who literally seems to think that he deserves praise for throwing a few rolls of paper towels into a crowd—has suggested that Puerto Rico is responsible for its own disaster, and he has systematically denigrated the efforts of its people to take care of one another. . . . How can we be abandoning them in their time of need?" asked Krugman. "Much of the answer, no doubt, is the usual four-letter word: race. Puerto Ricans would doubtless be getting better treatment if they were all of, say, Norwegian descent" (Krugman, 2017).

Backlash against Trump's tweets and public statements seemed to reach the White House as, after having demeaned Puerto Rico's people several times in earlier tweets, Trump read what seemed to be rehearsed lines on October 13th: "The wonderful people of Puerto Rico, with their unmatched spirit, know how bad things were before the H's [hurricanes]. I will always be with them! We're going to be there as Americans and we love those people and what they've gone through" (Baker, 2017). Another day had produced yet another confusing contradiction from the president of the United States.

Further Reading

Baker, Peter. "Trump: 'We'll Be There' for Puerto Rico, a Day After Critical Messages." *New York Times*, October 13, 2017. https://www.nytimes.com/2017/10/13/us/politics/reversing-course-trump-seeks-to-reassure-puerto-rico.html

Baker, Peter, and Caitlin Dickerson. "Trump Warns Storm-Ravaged Puerto Rico That Aid Won't Last 'Forever.'" *New York Times*, October 12, 2017. https://www.nytimes.com/2017/10/12/us/politics/trump-warns-puerto-rico-weeks-after-storms-federal-help-cannot-stay-forever.html

Cumming-Bruce, Nick, and Frances Robles. "U.S. Response to Storm-Hit Puerto Rico Is Criticized by U.N. Experts." *New York Times*, October 31, 2017. https://www.nytimes.com/2017/10/30/us/puerto-rico-whitefish-fbi-power-.html

Dickerson, Caitlin. "Finding Water in Puerto Rico: An Endless Game of Cat and Mouse." *New York Times*, October 12, 2017. https://www.nytimes.com/2017/10/12/us/puerto-rico-water-fema-.html

"A Disaster in the White House for Puerto Rico." [Editorial] *New York Times*, October 12, 2017. https://www.nytimes.com/2017/10/12/opinion/editorials/puerto-rico-trump-tweets.html

Kishore, Nishant, Domingo Marqués, Ayesha Mahmud, Mathew V. Kiang, Irmary Rodriguez, Arlan Fuller, Peggy Ebner, Cecilia Sorensen, Fabio Racy, Jay Lemery, Leslie Maas, and Jennifer Leaning. "Mortality in Puerto Rico after Hurricane Maria." *New England Journal of Medicine*, May 29, 2018. https://www.nejm.org/doi/full/10.1056/NEJMsa1803972

Krugman, Paul. "Let Them Eat Paper Towels." *New York Times*, October 13, 2017. https://www.nytimes.com/2017/10/12/opinion/trump-tweets-puerto-rico.html

Landler, Mark. "Trump Lobs Praise, and Paper Towels, to Puerto Rico Storm Victims." *New York Times*, October 3, 2017. https://www.nytimes.com/2017/10/03/us/puerto-rico-trump-hurricane.html

Riotta, Chris. "Trump Donated His Own Money to Texas, but He's Threatening to Cut Off Aid to Puerto Rico." *Newsweek*, October 12, 2017. http://www.newsweek.com/donald-trump-hurricane-response-puerto-rico-texas-florida-harvey-maria-irma-683534

Robles, Frances, Kenan Davis, Sheri Fink, and Sarah Almukhtar. "Official Death Toll in Puerto Rico: 62; Actual Deaths May Be 1,052." *New York Times*, December 9, 2017, A-1.

Santiago, Leyla, Catherine Shoichet, and Jason Kravarick. "Puerto Rico Revises Hurricane Maria Death Toll to 2,975 after Study." Cable News Network,

August 28, 2018. https://www.cnn.com/2018/08/28/health/puerto-rico-gw-report-excess-deaths/index.html

Sorkin, Amy Davidson. "Disasters Will Happen." *The New Yorker*, October 16, 2017, 21–22.

Trump, Donald. Twitter post, September 2, 2017, 9:56 a.m. https://twitter.com/realdonaldtrump/status/904025340049285121?lang=en

Trump, Donald. Twitter post, September 13, 2017, 5:36 a.m. https://twitter.com/realdonaldtrump/status/907946177022369792?lang=en

Trump, Donald. Twitter post, October 12, 2017, 3:58 a.m. https://twitter.com/realdonaldtrump/status/918430769776914432?lang=en

Triana, Alabama: Dumped On, Ceaselessly

Several toxic waste sites have not received the level of publicity that Love Canal did, especially those in small, rural communities with mainly black populations, which were sometimes called "black Love Canals." Two examples are PCB contamination in a landfill in Warren County, North Carolina (1973–1982), described earlier, and DDT contamination in Triana, Alabama (1977–1982). Triana, which is within the Huntsville-Decatur statistical area for Census purposes, rallied against a DDT dump in the late 1970s and early 1980s. By 2011, the town was rallying against pollution again.

Triana was incorporated in 1819, one of the older towns in Madison County, and named for Rodrigo de Triana, a member of the crew on Christopher Columbus's first voyage. It thrived early as a port on the Tennessee River, but, by late in the 19th century, railroads made its main livelihood obsolete. The town largely dissolved into the countryside, but was reincorporated in 1964, the only majority black town in the county, with about 500 residents in the late 1970s, when it became a focus for activism against DDT contamination. In 2016, Triana had a population of 529. Racial composition in 2000 was 86.5 percent black and 11.5 percent white. Median family income in 2000 was $30,750.

DDT in the River, the Fish, and the People

The Army Corps of Engineers' Redstone Arsenal worked with the Olin Corporation from 1947 to 1970, when it was sold, using the plant to manufacture DDT for sale to several companies, as well as to the army as a pesticide. Olin discharged DDT-laced wastewater containing as much as 4,000 tons of the chemical over a 2.3-mile watercourse. It flowed through Triana, where poor, black residents caught fish, a major part of their diet.

Local residents were tested. "The results showed that not only was DDT present in their blood, but that the levels were three times the normal levels of DDT found in other case studies. The compared case studies were of workers at DDT plants, yet none of the residents tested in Triana had ever worked at such a facility" (Rebitzke, 2017).

The chemical compound DDT was developed and first introduced during 1939 after a Swiss chemist, Paul Muller, found that it attacked the nervous systems of many species of insects. Jeffery Rebitzke wrote in *Environmental Justice Case Studies* that "it was widely used during World War II before Allied invasions to treat fields before invasions. DDT also came into use to kill insects that transmitted diseases such as typhus, yellow fever, elephantiasis, and other diseases spread by insects, especially mosquitoes. In India, DDT reduced malaria from 75 million cases to fewer than 5 million cases in a decade" (Rebitzke, 2017).

With publication of Rachel Carson's *Silent Spring* in 1962, which documented the dangers of DDT to humans and animals, especially birds, its use declined. In 1969, the U.S. government announced a ban, in large part because DDT did not break down naturally and biomagnified up the food chain. Biomagnification means that the effects of DDT (as well as other persistent organic pollutants (such as PCBs and dioxins) compound exponentially at each stage of the food chain. Thus, humans (or fish, bears, or eagles) eating anything with DDT in its flesh suffer a much higher level of contamination than was in the original source of food. Olin stopped making DDT at the Redstone Arsenal in 1970, but it remained in the local food chain. By the early 1970s, fish along the Huntsville Spring Branch were dying in large numbers.

Abnormally High Levels of DDT

In 1977, the Environmental Protection Agency warned that waterfowl and fish in the Huntsville Spring Branch contained abnormally high levels of DDT, which it said was being produced by the Olin Corporation plant at Redstone Arsenal. In 1979, the Tennessee Valley Authority (TVA) supported the EPA position, saying that fish caught in the area had 200 parts per million DDT in their flesh, 40 times the acceptable federal level. Between 1982 and 1997, an EPA-coordinated cleanup effort under the Superfund Act reduced DDT volume in the water by 97 percent, after citizen lawsuits supported by the U.S. Department of Justice compelled action by Olin.

In the meantime, the press was carrying reports of local residents with very high blood levels of DDT:

"We made our living off it, and that's been taken away from every commercial fisherman," said Felix Wynn, an 85-year-old resident of Triana, who has 3,300 parts per billion of DDT in his blood. That is more DDT than has ever been found in any human being. Along with DDT, polychlorinated biphenyls (PCBs) have also been detected in many of the residents. "These twin factors increase their risk of heart disease, strokes and kidney problems, although CDC has not tied any specific disease or illness in Triana to either chemical." Because of this, the mayor and the town of Triana decided to sue the Olin Corporation for one million dollars each. (Hollis, 1980, A-2)

The EPA then ordered the U.S. Army to conduct studies of DDT's effects on residents of Triana and clean up the residue. The army refused, contending that Olin was responsible. The EPA referred the matter to the Justice Department, which also refused to become involved because it said it had no power when one federal agency sues another. In the meantime, the lives of Triana's residents hung in the balance.

Finally, an "Interagency Group" was formed by the EPA, the Tennessee Valley Authority, the U.S. Fish and Wildlife Service, the Department of the Army, and the state of Alabama to oversee Olin Corporation's cleanup. In 1982, Olin reached an out-of-court settlement with the town of Triana and the Justice Department. For a decade, beginning in 1985, cleanup continued until DDT levels reached legally acceptable limits.

A group of four Triana residents (Mayor Clyde Foster, Marvelene Freeman, Robert Potts, and Max Turner) distributed the Triana Area Medical Fund, which applied to 1,178 people who had filed suit. In the suit, the community was said to be 75 percent African American, 866 of 1,158 area residents within and near the town of Triana. Annual median income of African Americans in the lawsuit was listed as $9,659 per year; the median for all Triana residents in the 1990 Census was $10,428 per year, well below poverty level.

According to one report, "What really sets the Triana lawsuit apart from the others was a plan proposed by Foster. He wanted to protect the people of Triana from any negative effects of DDT in the present and in the future, so he proposed that Olin establish a healthcare program for all residents that were exposed to DDT. In addition, the lawsuit would also require Olin to compensate the plaintiffs for their loss of income" (Rebitzke, 2017).

Under the agreement, the Olin Corporation agreed to pay the residents of the Triana area $24 million. Of that, $19 million would be dispersed to the plaintiffs over five years. The remaining $5 million was set aside for a health care program under the supervision of the Triana Area Medical Fund. The agreement also required Olin to pay cleanup costs of DDT in the contaminated area, estimated to be as much as $137 million (Rebitzke, 2017).

End of the story? Not quite. A report in the *Huntsville Times*, in a lengthy investigative story published in 2011, alleged that another illegal dump had set up shop near Triana in 2011.This story is worthy of quotation at length because it shows just how pervasive toxic pollution had become, along with the Orwellian nomenclature for a dump named Greenway Recycling Solutions, which is said to be "the only LEED-certified [e.g., environmentally correct] dump site in this area"—as if a toxic dump could ever be "green," or engaged in "recycling." The local situation was described in detail, with a sense of empathy, in a local newspaper, the *Huntsville Times*.

> Today, Triana residents feel they are once again being dumped on. But this time it's on land just east of the town where Greenway Recycling Solutions, owned by Wayne Ellis and his son, Todd Ellis, set up shop in 2008. "Nobody knew what it was at first," said local resident Caudle Jones. "They had a permit for recycling from [Madison] County. We just thought they were clearing the land." But residents, including Caudle and Karen Jones, both Triana natives, began noticing piles of leftover construction debris that grew bigger and bigger each week. Eventually, portable toilets were added and it gradually became such an "eyesore," Caudle said, she and Jones separately began documenting activity at the site. (Betowt, 2011)

Further Reading

Betowt, Yvonne. "Triana Residents Tired of Being Dumped On; Fighting to Remove Unauthorized Dump Site in Back Yard." *Huntsville Times*, October 24, 2011. http://blog.al.com/breaking/2011/10/triana_residents_fight_back_af.html

EPA. "National Priorities List Site Narrative for Triana/Tennessee River." U.S. Environmental Protection Agency, n.d. Retrieved October 17, 2017. https://www.epa.gov/superfund

Hollis, Mike. "The Persistence of a Poison; Effects of Chemical Plant Still Plague Alabama Town." *Washington Post*, June 15, 1980, A-2.

Rebitzke, Jeffery. "Triana Justice Page." *Environmental Justice Case Studies*, n.d. Retrieved October 17, 2017. http://www.umich.edu/~snre492/triana.html

Malathion and the Rosebud Sioux in Mission, South Dakota

The town of Mission, on the Rosebud Sioux reservation in South Dakota, was sprayed routinely with malathion until at least the middle

1990s. In 1995, the man who had sprayed the town died of cancer, according to Joe Allen, editor of *The Circle*, a Native American newspaper published in Minneapolis (Allen, 1995, 8–12).

The Circle published detailed accounts of Mission's spraying and the miseries it caused Native American residents there. The article began by comparing the massive press coverage provoked in the United States by the use of the nerve gas sarin in a Tokyo subway with widespread ignorance that a derivative of the same chemical, malathion, was being sprayed liberally on a South Dakota Indian reservation.

People living at Rosebud described the peculiar hissing sound of the spraying machine as it was driven on its rounds, spreading a dirty-gray fog along the reservation's dirt roads. When local residents confronted the sprayers, they were told the reservation was being treated for mosquitoes. Soon, everything in their homes smelled of the chemical—clothes, unwrapped food, furniture, curtains, and more.

Malathion was being sprayed in Mission despite the fact that the chemical itself posed a much larger human-health risk to people at Rosebud than the mosquitoes it was being used to eradicate. The area has no record of mosquito-borne disease, so the insects are more an irritant than a serious threat to human or animal health. Some Mission town officials were quoted in *The Circle* article saying that AIDS could be spread by mosquitoes (Allen, 1995, 8–12). No one knows who told them that, or whether they believed it. The city of Minneapolis decided in 1982 that malathion was little good against mosquitoes, because its effects on them largely vanished with the next substantial rainfall and egg-laying cycle. Salesmen of malathion-laced sprays were using mosquito-phobia to sell a dangerous product. The fact that most of Mission's residents are impoverished Native Americans made this act of salesmanship a rather abject case of environmental racism.

The malathion sprayed at Mission was probably given to the town by the U.S. Department of Agriculture, which, at various times, has had a policy of forwarding surplus pesticides to municipal governments. Malathion is especially dangerous to alcoholics, because the liver of most alcoholics has been damaged beyond ability to deal with the pesticide, which then overwhelms the body. It is also nearly as dangerous inhaled as absorbed through the skin. Roughly 75 percent of Rosebud's population suffers from alcoholism, according to Mission's Little Hoop Lodge Treatment Center (Allen, 1995, 10–12).

One Rosebud resident, Jane Kirby, was stricken with splitting headaches after spraying in her neighborhood. Within hours Kirby, who was pregnant at the time, developed head pains. She took no medication because of her pregnancy, but her husband, who also had headaches, took several doses of aspirin. They were no help. The same night, the Kirbys' daughter Gemma, two years of age, awoke at night breathing in raspy gasps.

The next morning, the Kirbys called Mission's mayor, Harvey Herman, and demanded an end to the spraying. Herman refused, and laughed in their faces. A physician's assistant provided the Kirbys with information on malathion; they were surprised to learn that it had been developed in Nazi Germany as a possible nerve-gas weapon. Four days after Mission's mayor had laughed in her face, Jane went into labor, as her husband became progressively dizzier, weaker, and prone to muscle cramps. Within a few days, the Kirbys learned that 14 other people on their street were suffering similar symptoms.

On July 9, 1992, a city crew appeared at the Kirbys' door with a notice that spraying would resume the next day. The spray crew's members pledged to avoid the couple and their one-day-old infant. The Kirbys had asked that their area be spared the spraying because of the infant, but Mayor Herman again refused. He said the machine spraying the malathion could not be shut down easily for one home on a given street. Instead of enduring the spraying, the Kirbys spent the next night at a friend's mouse-infested cabin in the nearby countryside. Back in town, all during the summer spraying season, people complained of headaches, of waking in the night gasping for breath.

During the summer of 1992, people at Rosebud also began to trade accounts of illnesses associated with pesticide spraying, including an account of a man in his twenties and his dog who lived in the tiny community of White Horse, near Mission. Both were found dead in their home during the summer of 1992 after the house was sprayed for cockroaches by an exterminator hired through the reservation housing authority.

During the summer of 1993, Anna Carol Thin Elk, 51, of Mission, was caught in a malathion spraying. She thought little of it and wore the same clothes the next day, without having taken a shower. By noon that day, pain was spreading through Thin Elk's wrists as she experienced waves of chills. Severe pain spread through her entire body during the next three days, until she was wracked by fever and leg spasms. She also experienced acute difficulty breathing. Thin Elk was taken to Rosebud Hospital, where she noticed, while waiting, that three or four children in the room also were having trouble breathing. The first question the doctor asked each of their mothers was: Have you been near the area being sprayed for mosquitoes? By the time a doctor saw Thin Elk an hour and a half later, she was semiconscious and nearly asphyxiated. Thin Elk was then taken by ambulance to Rapid City General Hospital, three hours away, the closest medical facility possessing the proper antidote for malathion poisoning.

Thin Elk was discharged from the hospital the next day. She had no medical insurance, no spare clothes, and no way to get back to Mission other than a ride that was offered to her that day. For a week, Thin Elk struggled with severe fatigue and dizziness, as her employers told her she had no sick leave. When Thin Elk complained to Mission's mayor, Harvey Herman, about how the pesticides affected her, according to *The Circle's* account, "I was told I should move out of town if I didn't like it" (Allen, 1995, 10).

The Circle published several other similar accounts of Mission residents who became ill from the spraying, some of whom experienced periods of near-paralysis. In the meantime, Ed Einspar, who had sprayed most of the malathion on Mission, died. One day, shortly before he died, Einspar completed his spraying rounds without wearing a gas mask. Shortly thereafter, he suffered severe gastrointestinal illness that aggravated his chronic asthma and emphysema. Einspar's niece, six-year-old Fianna White Hawk, suffered a type of chronic pneumonia that has been attributed to malathion exposure (Allen, 1995, 10–12).

Further Reading

ABEX Corp. Portsmouth, VA. National Priority List. Superfund. Environmental Protection Agency, n.d. Accessed October 10, 2017. https://www.epa.gov/superfund/national-priorities-list-npl-sites-state#CA

Allen, Joe. "Malathion in Mission." *The Circle* (Minneapolis), April 1995, 8–12.

AMCO Chemical. Oakland, California. National Priority List. Superfund. Environmental Protection Agency, n.d. Accessed October 10, 2017. https://www.epa.gov/superfund/national-priorities-list-npl-sites-state#CA

Houston, Texas: Always Awaiting the Next Flood

Houston, Texas, and the rest of southeastern Texas is generally flat, low in elevation, built on reclaimed swamps near the warm, moisture-rich Gulf of Mexico. Part of the disaster-prone scenario is due to human generation of greenhouse gases. Warmer air holds more moisture, which provokes more intense precipitation. Global warming does not *cause* hurricanes, but (given the co-incidence of favorable conditions in the atmosphere), it does *amplify* them. It raises their wind speeds, moisture level, and physical size, multiplying human and material peril. Thus, in 2017, the U.S. Weather Service ran out of superlatives to describe Harvey's record rainfall.

Hurricane Harvey was not an anomaly in Houston, but the soggy crown jewel of a new reality. By the end of 2018, Houston had endured four 200-year floods in three years (Harper's Index, 2018, 9).

Studies indicate that rain totals that do major damage in Texas are not restricted to a single hurricane. Chances of a 20-inch rainfall have risen sixfold in 25 years (and may triple again by the year 2100) because of human-provoked climate change. That study appeared in the *Proceedings of the National Academy of Sciences* (Emanuel, 2017). In the 1980s and 1990s, there was a 1 percent chance of a 20-inch rainfall somewhere in Texas in a given year. Now it's up to 6 percent, and by the end of the century, it will rise to 18 percent, said meteorologist Kerry Emanuel of the Massachusetts Institute of Technology, who led the study. "That's a huge increase in the probability of that event," and the change is the result of global warming, he said (Rice, 2017). "When you take a very, very rare, extreme rainfall event like Hurricane Harvey, and you shift the distribution of rain toward heavier amounts because of climate change, you get really big changes in the probability of those rare events," Emanuel said. "People have to understand that damage is usually caused by extreme events" (Rice, 2017).

Melting ice raises sea levels as warmth also increases seawater volume through thermal expansion. Even the weight of floods in Houston compressed the land by 2 centimeters. The temperature of the Gulf of Mexico was 7° F above average when Harvey rolled through. In addition, the land under Houston, as well as much of the Gulf and Atlantic coasts (including Miami, Houston, New Orleans, and nearby areas), is slowly sinking, in part due to human withdrawal of underground water, but also because of geophysical factors. Urban expansion increases the amount of space devoted to parking lots, sidewalks, roads, and roofs, and reduces the area capable of absorbing torrential rains, just as warming causes storms to intensify. All of this makes flooding worse.

Elevation and Environmental Racism

Low-lying areas of Houston that are prone to flooding received the brunt of the damage when Hurricane Harvey stalled over the area, delivering rainfalls of 30 to 50 inches. Homes and businesses built on floodplains, which usually are owned or rented by minority and poor people, tend to get the worst of it. Because of hurricane risk, elevation in Houston carries a price premium, as it does in New Orleans. Poor and minority people are most likely to live in areas where housing prices and rents are also depressed by proximity to the Houston urban area's large array of petrochemical plants, called the "Chemical Coast," many of which contain Environmental Protection Agency Superfund sites. When Hurricane Harvey submerged the Houston area in as much as four feet of rain during late August 2017, some of the area's 13 Superfund sites flooded, mixing toxic waste with floodwater. *The* Associated Press surveyed seven Superfund sites and found that each had been "inundated with water, in some cases many feet deep" (Liptak, 2017).

A local resident's experience with toxifying floodwaters was described in the *Washington Post*:

> As rain poured and floodwaters inched toward his house in south Houston, Wes Highfield set out on a risky mission in his Jeep Cherokee. He drove in several directions to reach a nearby creek to collect water samples, but each time he was turned back when water washed against his floorboard. "Yesterday as these large retention ponds filled up, eight feet deep in places, kids were swimming in them, and that's not good," said Highfield, a scientist at Texas A&M University's Galveston campus. The Brio Refining toxic Superfund site, where ethylbenzene, chlorinated hydrocarbons and other chemical compounds were once pooled in pits before the Environmental Protection Agency removed them, sits "just up the road, and it drains into our watershed," he said. (Dennis and Fears, 2017)

Alexander Kaufman wrote in the *Huffington Post*: "The city expanded outward, turning lands that once absorbed rainwater into parking lots, roads, and developments. There are no environmental zoning laws, only deeds that allow property owners to dictate how the land is used. In wealthier—which, in a city where Jim Crow once reigned, usually translates to whiter—areas, residents invited flood safeguards, such as dikes and berms, and spurned hazards such as chemical plants and refineries. Over the last 15 years or so, as the city has exploded in growth and they paved the wetlands, those middle-class white and upper middle-class areas, like Meyerland and Bellaire, those are even beginning to flood" (Kaufman, 2017).

Robert D. Bullard, who has studied environmental racism since the 1970s, said blacks and Latinos tend to benefit less from recovery programs, such as FEMA grants, small-business loans, and insurance payouts. "The people who are generally going to get left out are individuals on the margin, who may own a house, but may not have flood insurance or may not have a cushion or savings account to weather the storm until they get their insurance," Bullard said (Kaufman, 2017).

Toxic Flooding

At the height of Hurricane Harvey's deluge, almost a third of the area was inundated by floodwater. Some dams flooded over for the first time. Two Exxon-Mobil oil refineries east of Houston were also flooded, releasing pollutants. Flooding on such a scale "presents a huge challenge," said Mathy Stanislaus, who oversaw the federal Superfund program throughout the Obama administration (Dennis and Fears, 2017). Nancy Loeb, director of the Environmental Advocacy Center at Northwestern University's Pritzker School of Law, said that risks of contamination at Superfund sites where the contamination hasn't been completely resolved "are of the flooding picking up contaminants as it goes," Loeb said. "If the water picks up contaminated sediment from sites, that may get deposited in areas where people congregate—residential properties, parks, ballfields—that were never contaminated before. We can't say for sure it will happen, but it's certainly a possibility" (Dennis and Fears, 2017). Residents who use water from wells are especially vulnerable, Loeb said: "There's no testing of their water to know whether it's been contaminated" (Dennis and Fears, 2017).

At the Baytown Chevron Phillips chemical plant near Houston, 34,000 pounds of sodium hydroxide and 300 pounds of benzene, both of which are highly toxic, escaped through a damaged valve during Harvey's torrential rains. The plant, a joint venture between Chevron and Phillips 66, was only one of many that filled the Houston area with a toxic stew of waste, debris, and chemicals during the floods (Tabuchi et al., 2018).

In some cases, storm surges pushed onshore by hurricanes can also spill into toxic areas and spread contamination from seaside chemical plants that use contaminants too dangerous to inhale or touch, such as perchloroethylene, trichloroethylene, and chlorinated hydrocarbons, among others. Some businesses, such as dry cleaners, also use toxic chemicals that may mix with water during flooding. The denser an urban area, the higher the risk of contamination to larger numbers of people. Some chemicals, such as PCBs and dioxins, become part of the food chain and can become very difficult to eradicate. Alexander Kaufman wrote in the *Huffington Post* (2017) that in some areas floodwaters "ran thick with petrochemicals . . . the result of unbridled industry, Wild West regulations and environmental racism."

Harvey's rains caused a polluted site along the San Jacinto Waste Pits, on the river by the same name east of Houston, to flood, according to the

EPA. The floods damaged a cap on waste from a paper mill and exposed carcinogenic waste underneath. According to *The Verge*, "Some of the highly toxic chemicals found include dioxins . . . known to cause reproductive and developmental problems, damage the immune system, and cause cancer, according to the World Health Organization" (Potenza, 2017).

According to the same report, "A sediment sample at the site showed dioxins at 70,000 ng/kg [1 nanogram per kilogram = 1 part per billion]—orders of magnitude higher than the recommended level at the site, which is 30 ng/kg. That's already trouble, but it gets worse: Certain types of dioxins can be very hard to dispose of, increasing the risks of contamination. The dioxin in the Superfund site waste doesn't dissolve easily in water, but it can seep into the surrounding sediments, the EPA says" (Potenza, 2017). This was only one of several Superfund sites in and near Houston that suffered leaks and even explosions during nearly a week of flooding rains provoked when the remnants of Hurricane Harvey stalled there. The San Jacinto site was capped in 2011, but had required repairs at least six times after that during less severe rains. Environmentalists had warned for many years that the site would be vulnerable during heavy rainfall.

"Harvey caused me to look differently at the world we live in," said Judge Ed Emmett, the chief executive of Harris County, which encompasses Houston. "Three 500-year floods in three years means either we're free and clear for the next 1,500 years, or something has seriously changed" (Kimmelman, 2017). An estimate from Moody's Investors Service in November 2017 put Harvey's damage to infrastructure in the Houston area at an estimated $81 billion, a record for a natural disaster in the United States.

Prescriptions for the Future

"We need to get climatologists, politicians and policymakers talking to each other. They're not." said Jeff Lindner, meteorologist for the Harris County Flood Control District. "There's little question the earth is warming," he said. "Regardless of whether it's a natural cycle or human-induced, hotter air holds more moisture. And so for Harris County that means the potential for more extreme events" (Kimmelman, 2017). Jim Blackburn, a planner and environmental lawyer who for many years has been warning Houston that it is on "ground zero" for global warming's flooding potential, said: "The worst flood has not yet occurred." He warned, according to a *New York Times* report by Michael Kimmelman (2017), "A hurricane that pushes a massive storm surge from the Gulf of Mexico into Galveston Bay, up the ship channel, could overwhelm refineries and unleash a toxic tsunami, killing many and rattling the national economy."

Further Reading

Dennis, Brady, and Darryl Fears. "Houston's Polluted Superfund Sites Threaten to Contaminate Floodwaters." *Washington Post*, August 29, 2017. https://www.washingtonpost.com/news/energy-environment/wp/2017/08/29/houstons-flood-threatens-to-turn-polluted-superfund-sites-into-a-toxic-gumbo/?utm_term=.dcea7f506255

Emanuel, Kerry. "Assessing the Present and Future Probability of Hurricane Harvey's Rainfall." *Proceedings of the National Academy of Sciences*, November 13, 2017. http://www.pnas.org/content/early/2017/11/07/1716222114

Harper's Index, December 2018, 9.

Kaufman, Alexander C. "Houston Flooding Always Hits Poor, Non-White Neighborhoods Hardest." *Huffington Post*, August 29, 2017. https://www.huffingtonpost.com/entry/houston-harvey-environmental-justice_us_59a41c90e4b06d67e3390993

Kimmelman, Michael. "Lessons from Hurricane Harvey: Houston's Struggle Is America's Tale." *New York Times*, November 11, 2017. https://www.nytimes.com/interactive/2017/11/11/climate/houston-flooding-climate.html

Liptak, Andrew. "13 Houston Superfund Sites Remain Flooded after Hurricane Harvey; 28 Other Sites in the Area 'Show No Damage.'" *The Verge*, September 3, 2017. https://www.theverge.com/2017/9/3/16250146/houston-superfund-sites-flooded-after-hurricane-harvey-epa

Potenza, Alessandra. "Toxic Waste Seeps from a Houston Superfund Site after Harvey's Floods." *The Verge*, September 29, 2017. https://www.theverge.com/2017/9/29/16385568/hurricane-harvey-superfund-site-houston-dioxin-cancer-chemicals

Rice, Doyle. "Global Warming Makes 'Biblical' Rain Like That from Hurricane Harvey Much More Likely." *USA Today*, November 14, 2017. https://www.usatoday.com/story/weather/2017/11/14/global-warming-makes-biblical-rain-like-hurricane-harvey-much-more-likely/862270001/

Tabuchi, Hiroko, Nadja Popovich, Blacki Miglioozzi, and Andrew W. Lehren. "Floods Are Getting Worse, and 2,500 Chemical Sites Lie in the Water's Path." *New York Times*, February 6, 2018. https://www.nytimes.com/interactive/2018/02/06/climate/flood-toxic-chemicals.html

Akwesasne: Land of the Toxic Turtles

For several centuries of human occupancy, the site the Mohawks call Akwesasne was a natural wonderland: well watered; thickly forested with white pine, oak, hickory, and ash; home to deer, elk, and other game animals. The rich soil in the bottomlands of a valley into which several rivers flowed allowed farming to flourish. The very name that the Akwesasne Mohawks gave their territory about 1755 testifies to the bounty of the land. "Akwesasne" in the Mohawk language means "Land Where the Partridge Drums," after the distinct sound that a male ruffled grouse (partridge) makes during its courtship rituals. Lying at the confluence of the Saint Lawrence, Saint Regis, Racquette, Grass, and Salmon Rivers, Akwesasne, until recent times, also provided its human occupants with large runs of sturgeon, bass, and walleye pike.

Within roughly half a century, this land of natural wonders has become a place where one cannot eat local fish and game, because their flesh now is laced at toxic levels with PCBs and other carcinogens. In some places, one cannot drink the water, for the same reason. Akwesasne, which straddles New York State's border with Quebec and Ontario, has become the most polluted Native reserve in Canada, and a number-one toxic site in the U.S. Environmental Protection Agency's Superfund list of sites badly needing cleanup.

Within the living memory of many people at Akwesasne, the Land Where the Partridge Drums has inherited the toxicological consequences of General Motors waste lagoons in which animals have been found with levels of PCBs in their fat that qualifies them as toxic waste under U.S. Environmental Protection Agency guidelines. Akwesasne has become riskier to human health than most urban areas, a place where any partridge still living may be more concerned about its heartbeat rather than its drumbeat (Johansen, 1993, 1–3).

When Ward Stone, a wildlife pathologist for the New York State Department of Environmental Conservation, began examining animals at Akwesasne, he found that the PCBs, insecticides, and other toxins were not being contained in designated dumps. After years of use, the dumpsites had leaked, and the toxins had gotten into the food chain of human beings and nearly every other species of animal in the area. The Mohawks' traditional economy, based on hunting, fishing, and agriculture, was being poisoned out of existence.

The Mohawks started Stone's environmental tour of Akwesasne with a visit to one of the General Motors waste lagoons, a place called "unnamed tributary cove" on some maps. Stone gave it the name "Contaminant Cove" because of the amount of toxic pollution in it. One day in 1985, at the contaminant cove, the environmental crisis at Akwesasne assumed a whole new foreboding shape. The New York State Department of Conservation caught a female snapping turtle that contained 835 parts per million of PCBs. The turtle carries a special significance among the Iroquois, whose creation story describes how the world took shape on a turtle's back. To this day, many Iroquois call North America "Turtle Island."

Children's Playground to Toxic Dump

Soon after the St. Lawrence Seaway opened during the middle 1950s, General Motors, Reynolds Metals Company, and the Aluminum Company of America built plants directly upstream of Akwesasne. According to the state attorney general's office, General Motors never obtained a permit to operate its dumpsites (Johansen, 2003, 113–114; Thomas, 2001).

Paul Thompson of Akwesasne remembers his childhood in a more innocent time: in a cove off the St. Lawrence River, walleye pike leaped upstream to spawn every April. His family bought fresh catch from fishermen on the river's banks, as they "peer[ed] into their crates and pick[ed] out the evening supper: a perch, bass, or maybe a sturgeon head for soup" (Sengupta, 2001). Nearby sits a mound in which Thompson's brothers and sisters once had foraged. "They plucked scrap metal and sold it in town for extra cash. They burned the wood at home" (Sengupta, 2001). At the time, no one at Akwesasne realized that the nearby General Motors engine-parts factory, built during the 1950s, was turning the fish to toxic waste and the children's play mound into a toxic dump.

Nearby, Turtle Cove, an inlet leading into the St. Lawrence River, was a favorite swimming hole for children at Akwesasne. In the spring, boys, like generations of men before them, learned to spear bullhead pike making their way through the cove to spawn. The cove, which is a few feet from the General Motors foundry, is a swimming hole no longer. Instead, it is one of General Motors' toxic waste dumps.

Dana Leigh Thompson grew up with a 40-foot General Motors waste heap as a neighbor. The toxic hill slopes into "Containment Cove," a local swimming hole until tests revealed PCB levels many times toxic limits. "There were three big rocks out there," Thompson said. "When we taught kids how to swim, they could swim out to the middle and stand. It was an achievement" (Seely, 2001, n.p.).

Thompson and other local residents began to suspect toxicity in GM's waste dumps during the middle 1970s, but General Motors continued to dump PCBs in the area without a state permit until 1986. Cleanup efforts began about 1988, but have stalled over differing approaches to the problem. During 1988, according to residents of Akwesasne, "A crew of men, covered head to toe in white spaceman-like suits, covered it [the mound] with an impermeable sheath" (Sengupta, 2001). Meant to be temporary (in place until the dump was cleaned up), the capped mound remained in place 13 years later. The installation of the "temporary" cap, during 1983, initiated Thompson's former playground into the ranks of federal Superfund sites, as one of the most toxic (in this case, PCB-laced) patches of ground in North America.

Fish No Longer Safe to Eat

At first, "I didn't even know what PCBs were," said Jim Ransom, an Akwesasne resident and director of the Haudenosaunee Environmental Task Force, an environmental group that advocates on behalf of all Iroquois. "There was a high level of concern, but I think that there were also a lot of unknowns because people didn't know what this chemical was and what it could do to us." By the mid-1980s, preliminary testing showed that it was no longer safe to eat fish and wildlife caught in some areas of the reservation. Sheree Bonaparte, then a young mother with a farm near the GM landfill, laughed when GM first distributed bottled water to residents. At first, she said, "Everybody kind of thought it was ridiculous. The water comes from the earth and it seemed silly to go get it from a bottle" (Thomas, 2001).

The Mohawks, state agencies, and area universities soon began studying PCB levels in breast milk and in infants. "Those studies proved beyond any shadow of a doubt that at the beginning of the study, the Mohawks had significantly higher levels of PCBs," said David Carpenter, a professor of environmental health and toxicology at SUNY Albany (Thomas, 2001). Carpenter said that the Akwesasne Mohawks have higher-than-average rates of some diseases that are associated with PCB contamination. One such disease, hypothyroidism, is "strikingly elevated," Carpenter said (Thomas, 2001). This disease can lead to mental dullness, obesity, and learning disabilities in children. PCBs disrupt production of thyroid hormones, which leads to hypothyroidism.

For more than a decade, General Motors and the Akwesasne Mohawks have debated how best to clean up the company's waste lagoons. The company suggested sealing the dumps permanently in place, meanwhile also building a wall to prevent existing PCBs from migrating to other parts of Akwesasne. Federal officials have approved this plan, but General Motors requires access to the reservation to build the wall. The Mohawks have denied access because they believe GM is seeking a relatively inexpensive way out of a problem that requires removal, *en masse*, of all soil tainted by PCBs dumped there.

In the meantime, the U.S. Environmental Protection Agency commended General Motors for moving diligently to clean up its waste sites. General Motors found itself inching toward agreement with the Mohawks' solution. The company, for example, did remove 23,000 cubic yards of polluted sediment from the St. Lawrence River during 1995. During the year 2000, General Motors excavated contaminated sludge from inactive lagoons. By the end of 2001, the company was planning to have removed soil from the banks of the Racquette River.

Diseases Wrought by PCBs

"This is the only place we have, and we're going to be here forever," explained Ken Jock, director of the St. Regis Mohawk tribe's environmental division. "Our teachers have told us, when we make a decision we have to look at how it affects the next seven generations. It's a different sense of time" (Sengupta, 2001). Before the area was so widely contaminated, fishing, hunting and trapping "were something our parents had pride in handing down to our children," said Jock. Because Akwesasne residents have been advised by state officials not to eat local fish or game, fishing and hunting skills are being lost. "It's pretty important to our identity as a people" (Thomas, 2001).

Scientists have concluded that even low levels of PCB exposure here could have caused more serious illnesses than previously thought. "That small relationship we expect to see correlated with reduced I.Q., with poor performance in school, with some abnormality in growth, particularly sexual maturation, and increased susceptibility to certain chronic diseases such as thyroid disease and diabetes," said Carpenter. "This has adversely affected their health" (Sengupta, 2001).

Thompson's family has been wracked by illnesses that once were very rare at Akwesasne. Thompson himself has diabetes. Four of his five siblings have thyroid disorders of a type often aggravated by PCBs. Thompson's sister Marilyn had her thyroid gland removed when a tumor was discovered there. All six of her children have asthma; two of them also have learning disabilities; another suffers from a thyroid condition. A two-year-old granddaughter of Thompson was born with a muscle disorder that has affected her motor skills. Another family member has experienced 14 miscarriages (Sengupta, 2001).

Rowena General of Akwesasne said the contamination has led to a "health crisis" for the more than 10,000 people who live on the reservation. "Recent analysis of clinical and hospital records on the reservation shows an epidemic of thyroid problems and also the incidence of cancers, diabetes, and respiratory diseases is higher than average," General said (Johansen, 2003).

The distribution of certain chronic diseases at Akwesasne was determined using computerized medical records of the St. Regis Mohawk Health Services Clinic. Annual and five-year incidence rates were computed for the period January 1, 1992, to January 1, 1997, for asthma, diabetes mellitus type II, hypothyroidism, and osteoarthritis. The study indicated that hypothyroidism and diabetes "showed higher age-specific prevalence than in the general U.S. population. Osteoarthritis was extremely frequent among people 60 years of age and older, and it may also be elevated in prevalence in relation to the U.S. general population. The incidence and prevalence trends of diabetes type II and osteoarthritis were stationary, but those for asthma and hypothyroidism showed increases over the study period. Morbidity from asthma and acquired hypothyroidism should be monitored in the future and investigated through analytic epidemiologic methods for a possible association with lifestyle and environmental factors" (Negoita et al., 2001, 84).

A study conducted at Cornell University indicated that smokestack effluvia from the Massena Reynolds Metals factory also destroyed once-profitable cattle and dairy farms in Cornwall on the Ontario side of Akwesasne. The study linked fluorides to the demise of cattle as early as 1978. Many of the cattle, as well as fish, suffered from fluoride poisoning that weakened their bones and decayed their teeth. Ernest Benedict's Herefords died while giving birth, while Noah Point's cattle lost their teeth, and Mohawk fishermen landed perch and bass with deformed spines and large ulcers on their skins. The fluoride was a by-product of a large aluminum smelter in Massena, New York, that routinely fills the air with yellowish gray fumes smelling of acid and metal (Krook and Maylin, 1979, 1).

During late March 2001, New York attorney general Eliot Spitzer and the St. Regis Mohawk Nation gave notice to General Motors that they would sue the company in federal court unless it began cleaning up two PCB dumpsites at its Massena plant within 90 days. In a letter to GM, Spitzer said if the company does not make substantial progress within 90 days, he would ask a U.S. District Court judge in Albany to declare the site an "imminent and substantial endangerment" and order an immediate cleanup (Johansen, 2003, 116). "General Motors has been on notice since at least 1980 that PCBs were being released into the St. Lawrence River and onto the St. Regis Mohawk Reservation from its two hazardous waste dumps," Spitzer said. "The company also has known for the past 15 years that the landfills may endanger public health and the environment.

Despite this knowledge, General Motors has failed to control the release of these toxins from its property," he said (Johansen, 2003).

By June, barely within its 90-day deadline, the attorney general's office said that General Motors was taking PCB-removal talks with a new sense of seriousness. "If we have to, we are ready to file a lawsuit at a moment's notice, and GM knows that we are prepared to do so, if necessary," said Marc Violette of the New York Attorney General's office (Johansen, 2003).

Chris Amato, the assistant New York attorney general working on the case, said the injustice is clear. "This is another example of a Native American community being treated as second-class citizens," he said. "I guarantee you if this site was located next to a very middle-class, white neighborhood, this site would be well on its way to being remediated" (Thomas, 2001).

"General Motors' illegal industrial waste dump has been poisoning the Mohawk people for over 50 years," said Akwesasne Mohawk Loran Thompson. "Despite all of our efforts, the GM facility continues to discharge toxic contaminants into the Akwesasne environment. General Motors is guilty of environmental injustice and they have been completely negligent in overlooking the damages to the health, well-being, economy, and lifestyle of the Mohawk people" (Johansen, 2003).

A Tribute to Ward Stone

By 2012, Ward Stone, an environmental official for New York State, who had first detected near-lethal levels of PCBs at Akwesasne in the 1980s, had suffered several strokes, as the Mohawks at Akewesasne paid tribute to his research. Tom Sakokwenionkwas Porter shared Akwesasne people's appreciation of Stone and his work:

> We would like to take this opportunity to express our utmost gratitude to Ward Stone for all that he has done to help the Mohawk people. He has been a strong advocate for the health of Mohawks, especially at Akwesasne. In the 1980s, a midwife from Akwesasne. . .[Tekatsitsiakwa] Katsi Cook got in touch with Ward Stone and expressed concern about the effects of industrial pollution on the health of the people who reside there. Stone found extremely high levels of PCBs, insecticides, and other toxins in area fish and wildlife. His work led to irrefutable proof that the dumping of contaminants by nearby factories was responsible for the high level of P.C.B.s found in mother's milk at Akwesasne. As a result, the people at Akwesasne are benefitting from the awareness of what needs to be done to maintain a healthy environment for the generations to come. Ward Stone has worked tirelessly not only as a strong and dedicated spokesperson for the animals, insects, fish, birds, water, air and Mother Earth, but he has

also spoken up for the health and welfare of the people of the Northeast. *Niawenko:wa* (thank you), Ward Stone. ("Mohawks Express," 2012)

Decades after PCBs were banned, young people at Akwesasne still carry them in their bodies at levels double the national average. "Significantly higher levels of PCBs were found among individuals who were breastfed as infants, were first born, or had consumed local fish within the past year," the study found (Gallo et al., 2011, 1374).

The study "also revealed significantly higher levels in those who had eaten fish within the previous year, in those who were first-born, and in those who were breast-fed" (Hansen, 2011). "What this study is saying is that these chemicals are extremely persistent in people," said co-author Lawrence Schell, a professor at the State University of New York (SUNY at Albany). "Once you're exposed it's difficult to remove that exposure burden" (Hansen, 2011).

The Grasse River Alcoa site at Akwesasne continues to affect Mohawk life. "Though the river has been awaiting cleanup for 20-plus years," reported the Indian Country Today Media Network on January 21, 2013, "the only remediation recorded on the EPA website has been the 1995 removal of about 8,000 pounds of PCBs from the facility" ("Mohawks Say," 2013). Various cleanup options range from simply letting nature take its course, to a $1 billion cleanup to be billed to Alcoa. The U.S. Environmental Protection Agency in 2013 had opted for a $243 million plan to dredge some of the contaminated areas and cap others. The St. Regis Mohawk (Akwesasne) tribe favors a more expensive option that would dredge 7.2 miles of the Grasse River five feet deep. "Capping is not a permanent remedy, and ice scour is a constant threat to any cap in the Grasse River," Akwesasne Environment Division director Ken Jock said. "Therefore we do not support the capping of the highly contaminated sediments in the main channel. Nobody has any real-world evidence that a cap can withstand a major ice jam and ice scour" ("Mohawk Government," 2012).

The GM Landfill's Continuing Effects

Larry Thompson, 56 in 2011, having tired of waiting for General Motors to clean up a Superfund site next to his family's home at Akwesasne, was arrested in 2011 for taking a backhoe into a toxic landfill on August 11 of that year. He was charged with two misdemeanors and two felonies (second-degree criminal mischief, resisting arrest, and reckless endangerment) "after he drove onto the notoriously polluted mound, scooped up contaminated soil and loaded it into railroad cars that were waiting to cart away debris from the GM building that is being torn down in the wake of bankruptcy proceedings" ("Mohawk Man Arrested," 2011). Thompson's wife, Dana Leigh Thompson, told Indian Country Today Media Network: "She has since received numerous calls from people offering to donate time, backhoes and excavators to continue the protest ... Larry was given this order by the clan mother, Bear Clan Mother," Dana Thompson said ("Mohawk Man Arrested," 2011).

The landfill, known as the General Motors–Central Foundry Division Superfund Site at Massena, New York, is one of the country's most severely contaminated toxic sites. It had been capped with plastic, clay, and soil, and planted with grass and trees. Dana Thompson said, "It looks like any bucolic scene in rural New York State. But underneath lies a pile of chemicals and PCBs left over from the plant's heyday" ("Mohawk Man Arrested," 2011). "For 32 years we've been waiting for them to clean it up," Dana Thompson said. "Remove the pile, remove the Superfund site, take all their poison out of here and put it into a secure site," Thompson said. "They call it a cleanup but it's really a cover-up, because they're just covering it up" ("Mohawk Man Arrested," 2011).

Elizabeth Hoover brings the situation at Akwesasne up-to-date in *The River Is in Us: Fighting Toxics in a Mohawk Community* (2017), finding that while some of the pollution has been halted, the persistent nature of PCBs and other pollutants is making true cleanup very difficult. Many people still avoid tumor-ridden fish (traditional staples such as sturgeon, perch, walleye, and bullhead) because of contamination. Hoover's study is comprehensive, historically sound, richly detailed, and sensitive to the Mohawks' perception of the crisis as they wage a continuing struggle to rehabilitate their homeland, rallying to face an existential threat. Doug George-Kanentiio, editor, activist, and longtime resident of Akwesasne, confirmed as much during April 2018: "In the past two weeks there have been over a dozen deaths at Akwesasne, many of which are cancers and other illnesses related to the pollution there. Jake Swamp's son Andy, 55, was one of them as was my friend Ronnie Lazore, 64 and many others. Cancers, bone diseases, diabetes—all connected and we are dying in disturbing numbers. I believe parts of Akwesasne should be declared highly contaminated and perhaps vacated rather than, as some say, the entire community."

Further Reading

Gallo, Mia V., Lawrence M. Schell, Anthony P. DeCaprio, and Agnes Jacobs. *Chemosphere* 83, no. 10 (May 2011): 1374–1382. https://www.ncbi.nlm.nih.gov/pmc/articles/PMC3095889/

George-Kanentiio, Doug. Personal communication, April 14, 2018.

Hansen, Terri. "Akwesasne Mohawk Youth Are Still at Risk of Industrial Pollutants." Indian Country Today Media Network, June 20, 2011. http://indiancountrytodaymedianetwork.com/2011/06/20/akwesasne-mohawk-youth-are-still-risk-industrial-pollutants-39158

Hoover, Elizabeth. *The River Is in Us: Fighting Toxics in a Mohawk Community*. Minneapolis: University of Minnesota Press, 2017.

Johansen, Bruce E. *Life and Death in Mohawk Country*. Golden, CO: North American Press/Fulcrum, 1993.

Johansen, Bruce E. *The Dirty Dozen: Toxic Chemicals and the Earth's Future*. Westport, CT: Praeger, 2003.

Krook, L., and G. A. Maylin. "Industrial Fluoride Pollution: Chronic Fluoride Poisoning in Cornwall Island Cattle." *Cornell Veterinarian* 69 (Supplement 8) (1979): 1–70.

"Mohawk Government Opposes Grasse River Cleanup Plan." Watertown *Daily Times*, October 2, 2012. http://www.watertowndailytimes.com/article/20121002/NEWS09/710029710

"Mohawk Man Arrested for Taking Backhoe to Superfund Site." Indian Country Today Media Network, August 12, 2011. http://indiancountrytodaymedianetwork.com/article/mohawk-man-arrested-for-taking-backhoe-to-superfund-site-46891

"Mohawks Express Gratitude for Akwesasne Health Advocate." Indian Country Today Media Network, January 6. 2012. http://indiancountrytodaymedianetwork.com/article/mohawk-man-fights-to-remove-toxic-hazardous-waste-from-river-104947

"Mohawks Say EPA Alcoa-Superfund Cleanup Plan Falls Short." Indian Country Today Media Network, January 21, 2013. http://indiancountrytodaymedianetwork.com/2013/01/21/mohawks-say-epa-alcoa-superfund-cleanup-plan-falls-short-147131

Negoita, S., L. Swamp, B. Kelley, and D. O. Carpenter. "Chronic Diseases Surveillance of St. Regis Mohawk Health Service Patients." *Journal of Health Management Practice* 7, no. 1(2001): 84–91. https://www.ncbi.nlm.nih.gov/pubmed/11141627

Seely, Hart. "Toxins Remain 18 Years Later: Landfill Near Massena Polluting Water Where Mohawk Children Played." Syracuse *Post-Standard*, June 24, 2001, n.p.

Sengupta, Smini. "A Sick Tribe and a Dump as a Neighbor." *New York Times*, April 7, 2001. http://www.nytimes.com/2001/04/07/nyregion/07MOHA.html

Thomas, Katie. "Toxic Threats to Tribal Lands." *Newsday*, March 25, 2001.

The Toxics Plantation: Life and Death in Louisiana's "Cancer Alley"

Between Baton Rouge and New Orleans, a region that is heavily low-income and African American, so many dangerous plants operate that

Cases: United States East

local residents and environmentalists call it "Cancer Alley." A total of 150 petrochemical companies and 17 refineries in the area release dangerous levels of toxic chemicals into the air and water. In a predominantly black community in southern Louisiana called Mossville, 91 percent of residents said they were experiencing health complications they believed to be related to the 14 facilities that manufacture, process, store, or discharge toxic or hazardous substances in that one small area (Chiles, 2015). In two centuries, the area has been transformed from plantations worked by slaves to another kind of misery: ranks of pollution-spewing factories "where poor, rural African-Americans, descended from slaves, continue to live and work in conditions that are dehumanizing and that endanger their lives" (Mah, 2013).

Fourteen of 15 plants in the United States that produce vinyl chloride monomer (VCM) and ethylene dichloride (EDC), the basic building blocks used to make polyvinyl chloride (PVC), have been located in Louisiana and Texas. A large number of the incinerators that burn discarded PVC products are also located in low-income minority communities in the same area. Dioxin and dioxin-like pollutants, including PCBs, are produced and released into the air, water, and in hazardous waste during the manufacture of VCM, the incineration of vinyl products, and the burning of PVC in accidental fires.

Effects of Toxic Effluvia

The manufacture of polyvinyl chloride produces copious amounts of dioxins that "have been linked to immune-system suppression, reproductive disorders, a variety of cancers, and endometriosis," according to one observer, who continued: "Dioxins are an unavoidable consequence of making PVC. Dioxins created by PVC production are released by on-site incinerators, flares, boilers, wastewater treatment systems and even in trace quantities in vinyl resins" (Costner, 1995). Products manufactured with PVCs "create dioxins when burned, leach toxic additives during use . . . and are the least recyclable of all major plastics" (Johansen, 2003, 261–262). "The production of the carcinogenic monomer is what results in the highest levels of dioxin release," said Charlie Cray, a Greenpeace toxics campaigner ("Shintech: The Battle," 1999).

As early as November 1983, Versar, a U.S. Environmental Protection Agency contractor, learned that the production of vinyl feed stocks (ethylene dichloride and vinyl chloride monomer—EDC/VCM) was an inadvertent source of PCB production. Hinting that the entire life cycle of PVC should be examined more intensely for PCB contamination, Versar also concluded: "It would be necessary to consider input PCBs contaminating chlorinated feed stocks in further downstream processing" ("Dioxin Deception," 2001). In 1990, however, at the request of the Vinyl Institute and other VCM producers, the U.S. EPA deleted dioxin from the list of constituents of concern in a VCM waste stream, because of "the costs of analysis and the reluctance of waste-treatment facilities to take wastes designated as dioxin-contaminated" ("Dioxin Deception," 2001).

During 1987, 106 residents of Reveilletown, Louisiana, a small African American community about 10 miles south of Baton Rouge, filed a lawsuit against Georgia-Pacific and Georgia Gulf, arguing that they had suffered health problems and property damage. After settling out of court for an undisclosed amount, Georgia Gulf relocated the remaining families and then tore down every structure in town. Management at Dow Chemical's neighboring factory in Plaquemine followed suit soon afterward, buying out all of the residents of the small town of Morrisonville (Bowermaster, 1993).

The PVC plants incinerate dioxin-laced wastes. In so doing, according to Greenpeace, a portion of the originally discharged dioxins are emitted, undestroyed, and new dioxins are created as by-products of incineration. The presence of copper and other metals in PVC-industry wastes can act as a catalyst to further increase dioxin formation (Duchin, 1997). Under the usual operating conditions, several chemicals are burned in a constantly changing mixture, creating a variety of synergistic chemical-thermal reactions and emissions.

Greenpeace Resists Shintech's Expansion

Greenpeace has called on the U.S. Environmental Protection Agency to "impose a moratorium on permits for new vinyl facilities or expansion of existing facilities, and to modify permits at existing plants to require that dioxin releases to all media, including waste destined for disposal, be brought to zero within five years" (Duchin, 1997). Greenpeace advocates a ban on the use of PVC in many types of toys, as well as furniture, wallpaper, and medical devices such as intravenous bags. Moreover, Greenpeace has called for a ban of PVC in products that may be susceptible to fire, such as cabling and other construction materials, notably in appliances and vehicles; and "metals with PVC residues that are recycled in combustion-based processes (i.e., automobiles)" (Duchin, 1997).

During September 1998, Greenpeace activists joined the people of Covenant, Louisiana, three-quarters of whom are black, in celebration of the news that the Japanese chemical giant Shintech would not, after all, build an enormous, 3,000-acre polyvinyl chloride (PVC) factory in their town. Shintech had been trying since 1996 to locate three factories and an incinerator near homes and schools in Covenant. Local people argued against location of the plant in their town on civil rights grounds; they argued that Louisiana authorities would violate federal civil rights laws if they licensed the Shintech plant in a predominantly African American community where pollution was already making people sick (Johansen, 2003). This struggle was undertaken with the idea of providing other poor, minority communities with legal precedents that would be useful in fending off expansion of environmentally intrusive industries.

The proposed PVC plant would have been one of the largest of its type in the world. Local residents worried most about anticipated emissions of polyvinyl chloride (PVC), ethylene dichloride (EDC), and vinyl chloride monomer (VCM) that may reasonably be anticipated to result in an increase in mortality or an increase in serious, irreversible, or incapacitating reversible illness. In fact, vinyl chloride is a known human carcinogen that causes a rare cancer of the liver. According to the company, the proposed Shintech manufacturing plant would have released about 600,000 pounds of toxic chemicals into the air per year, and would have poured nearly 8 million gallons of toxic waste water each day into the Mississippi River, which provides drinking water for the city of New Orleans ("Public Notice," 1997).

Greenpeace's campaign against dioxins began during the 1980s. In 1988, the Greenpeace ship MC *Beluga* toured Cancer Alley; at the same time, Greenpeace also released a report, *We All Live Downstream*, documenting serious chemical pollution in the Mississippi River. During the middle and late 1990s, Greenpeace activists, often swimming at night in polluted water, sampled effluent from several U.S. vinyl producers and found dioxins at each of the 27 sites tested.

One sample, obtained at the Vulcan Chemicals facility in Geismar, Louisiana, contained 6 parts per million TEQ dioxin, a level as high as the historic levels in wastes left from Agent Orange production ("Dioxin Deception," 2001). "These data are important, since they add to the growing body of evidence pointing to the lifecycle of polyvinyl chloride (PVC) plastic as one of the largest single sources of the nation's total dioxin burden" (Duchin, 1997).

Concentrations of dioxins in some of the samples taken by Greenpeace were extraordinarily high, including:

Vulcan Chemicals, Geismar, Louisiana: 200,750 parts per billion (p.p.b.) dioxins in a sample of "heavy end" waste and Georgia Gulf at Plaquemine,

Louisiana: 1,248 p.p.b. dioxins in a waste sample from a tank labeled to contain "heavy ends," "tars" and other similar types of highly contaminated wastes. (Duchin, 1997)

On occasion, Greenpeace also blockaded trains transporting vinyl chloride at PPG Industries with two buses as it called for global elimination of dioxin and other persistent poisons. Of 28 residents whose blood was tested, 12 had elevated levels of dioxin or similar substances (Johansen, 2003, 274–275). A Greenpeace Web page asserted: "Cancers, respiratory problems, reproductive disorders are among those illnesses associated with dioxin contamination, and which are occurring with alarming frequency in Mossville" (Johansen, 2003, 287–288). By 1998 and 1999, Greenpeace was organizing "Toxics Patrols" with community activists to monitor chemical plants along the Mississippi and on the shores of Lake Charles.

Residents in Covenant turned their backs on arguments that the plant would provide them more jobs and economic prosperity. They argued that the town already hosts a bevy of high-technology industries that emit various toxins, yet 40 percent of the townspeople live below the poverty line. Most of the plants are highly automated with little need for workers possessing marginal skills. Instead, the plants tend to hire a few people (usually from the outside) with computer skills and a working knowledge of physics and chemistry. Shintech's controller, Dick Mason, said the new complex would bring with it 165 permanent jobs; the company also promised to spend $500,000 for local job training, even though Louisiana officials had agreed to give Shintech $130 million in tax breaks without setting any specific goals to commit the company to local hiring. One calculation from the Louisiana Department of Economic Development indicated that the state would be giving up $800,000 in tax breaks for each permanent job offered by Shintech in Covenant (March 24, 1997).

The state of Louisiana strongly supported Shintech's plans; its air, water, and coastal zone permits were granted, swiftly, "with the backing of nearly all the relevant state and local officials, and over the objections of over 18 groups and a large segment of the local population" (Johansen, 2003). In a precedent-setting decision during September 1997, the U.S. Environmental Protection Agency rejected the state air permit. The EPA found 49 deficiencies in the state's granting of the permit. The EPA also challenged state officials regarding questions of environmental racism in siting the plant. Represented by the Tulane Environmental Law Clinic, citizens' groups filed appeals to the air, water, and coastal-zone permits, citing official bias as well as technical and legal problems (Johansen, 2003, 131).

Local citizens also lodged a complaint under Title VI of the U.S. Civil Rights Act. In its own words, the 33-page complaint

> [A]sserts that statements and actions by Governor Foster, DED Secretary Kevin Reilly (the Governor's liaison on the Shintech matter), Secretary Givens and other DEQ officials and employees create bias, prejudice or interest toward Shintech and against the citizen groups and eliminate the legally-required appearance of complete fairness and impartiality. The pervasive evidence of bias or prejudice includes threats and investigations by the Governor and Mr. Reilly against plant supporters and the Tulane Environmental Law Clinic, and an extensive, taxpayer-financed effort by the DEQ Secretary's office to organize and assist a group in St. James to support Shintech and oppose the efforts of the community groups that object to the proposed facility. (Johansen, 2003)

Covenant's situation was grist for precedent; a review of 1990 census data "shows that communities living near the nation's existing 15 EDC/VCM facilities have a 55 percent higher percentage of people of color than the national average, and a 24 percent lower per capita income than the national average" (Johansen, 2003).

After the EPA rejected its air permit, the Louisiana Department of Environmental Quality was required, by law, to convene public hearings on Shintech's application. Nearly 300 citizens attended the hearings in Covenant on December 9, 1996. Testimony continued for more than eight hours, according to one account, with "at least 95 percent" against Shintech (Johansen, 2003). "Enough is enough," testified Patricia Melancon, president of the local group, St. James Citizens. "This is a low-income area, and less than half of the adults in this community have a high school diploma. We will get all of the pollution, but none of the jobs" (Cray, 1996).

To demonstrate public support at the hearing, Shintech flew in more than 40 employees from its Freeport, Texas, plant as well as its paid consultants whose testimony centered around potential employment and tax revenue from the company's proposal. "Why are they [Shintech] speaking of economic development at an air permit hearing?" asked Kishi Animashaun, a Greenpeace Toxics campaigner (Cray, 1996).

After withdrawing from Covenant, Shintech switched its building plans to Plaquemine, 30 miles north, where its executives hoped that local opinion would be more accommodating. Shintech said it planned to buy vinyl chloride monomer (feedstock finished PVC) from a Dow Chemical plant in Plaquemine. People in Plaquemine then organized People Reaching Out to Eliminate Shintech's Toxins (PROTEST). In their opposition to new PVC manufacturing there, the members of PROTEST cited already-high cancer rates in the town, falling property values, and a lack of emergency evacuation routes should an accident occur. Liz Avants, speaking for PROTEST, said, "Every day, we hear about more cases of cancer and other health effects" (Johansen, 2003, 117, 122).

The Greenpeace "Toxics Patrol"

A study released during 1999 by the Agency for Toxic Substances and Disease Control (ATSDR) indicated that dioxin levels in Mossville, one community in Cancer Alley (near Lake Charles), showed that the average concentration of dioxins and PCBs in the blood of its residents was three times the average background level of the general population.

On March 5, 1999, 60 Greenpeace activists from 22 different nations converged on the Louisiana State House to call attention to global health and environmental threats caused by numerous polluting PVC production facilities. Dressed in T-shirts with the slogan "Love Louisiana But Not PVC" in 16 languages, the Greenpeace Toxics Patrol called on Governor Mike Foster to clean up the state's Cancer Alley. The group then marched with local environmental activists from the capitol to the governor's mansion to deliver a "lunch" of contaminated fish and water from some of the state's most polluted waterways (Johansen, 2003, 130).

Greenpeace on June 22, 1999, launched a Toxics Patrol bus trip to more than a dozen of the state's chemical facilities whose emissions have made Louisiana a "global toxic hot spot." The bus tour began with stops at three controversial facilities: Rhodia, the nation's first napalm incinerator; Formosa, which makes components of vinyl; and Dow Chemical, another vinyl producer that planned to join with Shintech on a newly proposed vinyl plant in West Baton Rouge. With representatives of several state and local environmental groups, Greenpeace displayed posted signs at chemical facilities warning that toxic pollution "does not stop at the fence" ("With Public's," 1999).

"Louisiana ranks number one in the nation in per-capita toxic releases to the environment, and her citizens are bearing a terrible health burden for it," said Greenpeace Toxics campaigner Damu Smith. "Our Toxics Patrol is out to expose some of the state's worst toxic offenders. . . . Louisiana is at the center of the nation's growing problem of environmental racism and injustice" ("With Public's," 1999).

Acclaimed author Alice Walker, actress Alfre Woodard, actor Mike Farrell, Reverend Al Sharpton, and members of Congress Maxine Waters and John Conyers toured "Cancer Alley" on June 9, 2001 (Johansen, 2003, 129). After the walking tour, the delegation convened in New

Orleans for the first-ever National Town Meeting on Environmental Justice with residents, government officials, and representatives of the chemical industry. During the town meeting, the delegation heard personal testimonies of industrial-contamination victims who live in "Cancer Alley" communities along the Mississippi River between New Orleans and Baton Rouge and who are experiencing a variety of illnesses and social problems associated with toxic pollution. The town meeting was coordinated and sponsored by Greenpeace (Johansen, 2003).

Early Death in Cancer Alley

Bill Moyers's report "Trade Secrets," which aired on the Public Broadcasting System on March 26, 2001, described the lives and deaths of some "Cancer Alley" workers, such as Ray Reynolds, 43 years of age. Reynolds, who lived a few miles from the chemical plant where he had worked for 16 years, was dying of toxic neuropathy that had spread from his nerve cells to his brain. Another worker, Dan Ross, made his living for 23 years producing the raw vinyl chloride that is basic to the manufacture of PVC plastic. In 1989, Ross was told he had a rare form of brain cancer.

Corporate documents displayed by Moyers indicated that manufacturers of PVCs knew as early as 1959 that "500 parts per million is going to produce rather appreciable injury when inhaled seven hours a day, five days a week for an extended period" (Moyers, 2001). Moyers obtained this information from a 1959 memo to B. F. Goodrich, an archive of "secret" and "confidential" documents unearthed in a lawsuit by the widow of a Louisiana chemical worker (Kurtz, 2001, C-1).

As the years went by, the level at which exposure to PVC and other organochlorines were believed to cause injury to the human body was revised downward. In 1959, workers were regularly exposed to at least 500 ppm during their work shifts. Some workers described standing in clouds of the chemical at levels much above 500 ppm. Some x-rays showed workers' bones dissolving.

Further Reading

Bowermaster, J. "A Town Called Morrisonville." *Audubon*, July/August 1993, 42–51.

Chiles, Nick. "8 Horrifying Examples of Corporations Mistreating Black Communities with Environmental Racism." *Atlanta Black Star*, February 12, 2015. http://atlantablackstar.com/2015/02/12/8-horrifying-examples

-of-corporations-mistreating-black-communities-with-environmental-racism/

Costner, Pat. *PVC: A Primary Contributor to the U.S. Dioxin Burden: Comments Submitted to the U.S. EPA Dioxin Reassessment.* Washington, D.C.: Greenpeace U.S.A., 1995.

Cray, Charlie. "Hundreds Oppose Shintech Proposal in Louisiana." Greenpeace, December 9, 1996. http://lists.essential.org/1996/dioxin-1/msg00752.html

"Dioxin Deception: How the Vinyl Industry Concealed Evidence of Its Dioxin Pollution." March 27, 2001. http://www.greenpeaceusa.org/toxics/dioxin_deceptiontext.htm

Duchin, Lelanie. "Greenpeace's Secret Sampling at U.S. Vinyl Plants: Dioxin Factories Exposed." April 1997. http://pvcinformation.org/assets/pdf/DioxinFactoriesExposed.pdf

Johansen, Bruce E. *The Dirty Dozen: Toxic Chemicals and the Earth's Future.* Westport, CT: Praeger, 2003.

Kurtz, Howard. "Moyers's Exclusive Report: Chemical Industry Left Out." *Washington Post*, March 22, 2001, C-1.

Lerner, Steve. *Diamond: A Struggle for Environmental Justice in Louisiana's Chemical Corridor.* Cambridge, MA: MIT Press, 2005.

Mah, Alice. "Lessons from Love Canal: Toxic Expertise and Environmental Justice." Open Democracy, August 7, 2013. https://www.opendemocracy.net/alice-mah/lessons-from-love-canal-toxic-expertise-and-environmental-justice

Moyers, Bill. "Trade Secrets." Public Broadcasting System (PBS), March 26, 2001.

Shintech Corporation, Air Permit Application, "Public Notice and Shintech Application [to the Environmental Protection Agency] to Discharge Process Wastewater." December 1997.

"With Public's 'Right-to-Know' in Jeopardy, Greenpeace Kicks Off Bus Tour of Louisiana's Worst Chemical 'Hot Spots.'" Greenpeace, June 22, 1999. https://www.greenpeace.org/usa/news/greenpeace-posts-signs-in-calc/

The Demographics of Death in New Orleans: Race, Class, and Hurricane Katrina

As one might suspect in a city prone to occasional hurricanes that is slowly sinking, and much of which is already below sea level, New Orleans has an elevation premium. The highest priced housing is on its few higher perches, and most poor and nonwhite people live in the lower parishes. In a major hurricane, such as Katrina (2005), elevation can affect whose house is flooded and whose is not—and even who lives and who dies. The demographics of death in Hurricane Katrina were straightforward: most of those who passed away were nonwhite, usually elderly, and too poor to afford an automobile with which to escape drowning in the floods.

Who Died, and How Many?

The number of people who died during Hurricane Katrina and its aftermath was not precisely known even 12 years afterward—and this fact was related to race and class. One figure is 1,833 (Cook and Rosenberg, 2015), but several state, local, and federal government agencies added up the total differently, and some of the missing—most notably those who were poor and black—were never officially accounted for. Other death totals range from 971 to 1,400.

A Louisiana state report on 971 deaths directly caused by the storm found that the leading causes of death were drowning (40 percent), injury and trauma (25 percent), and complications from heart conditions (11 percent). Forty-nine percent of victims were people more than 75 years of age. Fifty-three percent of victims were men; 51 percent were black; and 42 percent were white. In Orleans Parish, the mortality rate among blacks was 1.7 to 4 times higher than that among whites for all people 18 years old and older. People 75 years old and older were significantly more likely to be storm victims (Brunkard et al., 2008).

"If an evacuee died after a heart attack two months following the storm, was that death attributable to Katrina?" asked John Ford of the Louisiana Department of Health and Hospitals (Cook and Rosenberg, 2015). Researchers have confirmed 986 victims whose deaths were definitely caused by the storm. "While the number of people who died in Hurricane Katrina is likely much higher, even the lower count shows the devastating impact of a huge storm that New Orleans was ill-equipped to handle," Cook and Rosenberg said (2015). "Many Hurricane Katrina victims faced difficult living conditions even before the storm arrived," wrote Isaac Shapiro and Arloc Sherman (2005) in a paper for the Center on Budget Priorities within a month after the hurricane. "Mississippi, Louisiana, and Alabama are, respectively, the first, second, and eighth poorest states in the nation. And of the 5.8 million individuals in these states who lived in the areas struck hardest by the hurricane, more than one million lived in poverty prior to the hurricane's onset" (Cook and Rosenberg, 2015).

According to Shapiro and Sherman (2005), shortly before Katrina made landfall in 2005, more than 19 percent of Louisianans were poor, far above the national poverty rate of about 13 percent, and higher than the poverty rate in all states except one—Mississippi, with a poverty rate of 21.6 percent. Alabama's poverty rate was 16.1 percent.

Shapiro and Sherman, using data from the 2000 U.S. Census, also cited poverty rates in areas most intensely impacted by Katrina, the counties the parishes and counties declared eligible for federal disaster assistance—roughly two-thirds of Louisiana and Mississippi, and one-sixth of Alabama. According to the Census, of 5.8 million people (2.1 million households) in these parishes and counties, more than 1 million, close to one-fifth of the population, lived in poverty. About 1.3 million of the 5.8 million people lived in the New Orleans metropolitan area, almost 500,000 million in New Orleans itself.

Census data indicate that 28 percent of New Orleans's residents were living in poverty at the time that Katrina hit, the sixth highest poverty rate among U.S. cities with 100,000 or more people. More than half of the poor households in New Orleans (54 percent) did not own a van, car, or truck. For elderly people, that proportion was nearly two-thirds (65 percent), which impeded their ability to escape the storm's most lethal effects from pervasive flooding (Shapiro and Sherman, 2005).

Census data also confirm that African Americans made up a disproportionate share of the hurricane's victims. African Americans living in New Orleans, especially the elderly and poor, were likely to be without a vehicle before the hurricane struck. "More than one in three black households in New Orleans (35 percent)—and nearly three in five *poor* black households (59 percent)—lacked a vehicle. Among white non-Hispanic households in New Orleans, 15 percent lacked a vehicle," wrote Shapiro and Sherman (2005).

New Orleans, Katrina, and Racism

According to its publisher, *After Katrina: Race, Neoliberalism, and the End of the American Century*, a book by Anna Hartnell, senior lecturer in Contemporary Literature at Birkbeck, University of London, contends that:

> the city of New Orleans emerges as a key site for exploring competing narratives of U.S. decline and renewal at the beginning of the twenty-first century. Deploying an interdisciplinary approach to explore cultural representations of the post-storm city, Hartnell suggests that New Orleans has been reimagined as a laboratory for a racialized neoliberalism, and as such might be seen as a terminus of the American dream. This U.S. disaster zone has unveiled a network of social and environmental crises that demonstrate that prospects of social mobility have dwindled as environmental degradation and coastal erosion emerge as major threats not just to the quality of life but to the possibility of life in coastal communities across America and the world. And yet *After Katrina* also suggests that New Orleans culture offers a way of thinking about the United States in terms that transcend the binary of national renewal or declension. The

post-Hurricane city thus emerges as a flashpoint for reflecting on the contemporary United States. (Hartnell, 2017).

Mainstream media were portraying the Houston area's response to Harvey's catastrophic flooding as painting "a picture of unity and resilience in the face of adversity," wrote Oliver McAteer in the London (UK) *Metro*. "It is race and social class which will determine the impact of the storm—just like they did during Hurricane Katrina in 2005," says Dr. Hartnell.

> A number of factors put black Americans at risk of suffering greater repercussions from Harvey. [Hartnell] told *Metro:* "Although Texas itself is more central to the American imagination than Louisiana—New Orleans in particular has been constructed as a kind of pariah—it is nonetheless home to pockets of extreme poverty. In Houston 30 percent of residents live below the poverty line. And like New Orleans and indeed most other urban centers in the United States, poverty in Houston is overwhelmingly and disproportionately racialized. Cheaper land tends to also be [on] floodplains. . . . Car and home ownership are measures of short-term and long-term resilience with respect to disasters like Hurricane Harvey, and just as with Hurricane Katrina, people of color in Texas are far less likely to own cars that might enable them to evacuate or homes on which they can claim insurance and rebuild later on."

Disasters Are Not Social Levelers

Hartnell said that the common belief that disasters are social levelers is a myth. Poor people usually live in areas that are prone to destruction by flooding from hurricanes' torrential rains, which ruin a greater number of homes more completely than any other type of disaster-related damage. Flooding is also only rarely covered by insurance, making recovery very difficult. "Resilience is not created equal but rather [is] something that is built into people and communities according to relative wealth and status," said Hartnell. "Beneath the narrative of resilience and unity that the mainstream media and the U.S. government and authorities have done their best to circulate, the reality is that race and class disparities will determine the impact of the storm [Harvey] just as unjustly, if not as dramatically, as they did in 2005 [Katrina]" (McAteer, 2017).

Hartnell also pointed out that both the Houston area (including coastal eastern Texas) and large parts of Louisiana house large concentrations of oil refineries and chemical plants that are surrounded by poor, mainly nonwhite residential neighborhoods. Some of these plants have been damaged in hurricanes (by wind and flooding), contributing to emissions of oil and toxic chemicals. "They are exposed to these pollutants on a daily basis," wrote McAteer, "an injustice that some commentators describe as 'environmental racism' . . . [as these] risks have been enormously exacerbated by the storm[s]" (McAteer, 2017).

"During disasters, poor people, people of color, and the elderly die in disproportionate numbers, and Katrina was no exception," wrote Caroline Heldman in *The Society Pages*, a journal of sociology. "Many decisions were made in the days leading up to and shortly after Katrina that amplified loss of life for these groups" (2011). In New Orleans, no effective evacuation plan existed for a large number of the "immobile poor," most of them black, who were essentially trapped in a flooding city below sea level. Most of these people live month to month, and the storm arrived during the last few days of August, when many had run out of money. Many had no money in the bank or usable credit cards. The storm terminated what employment they had, stopping cash flow. More than 30,000 people took shelter in the Superdome amid overflowing toilets, a leaky roof, lack of food, and a shortage of drinkable water. One man killed himself by leaping from a balcony.

Mayor Ray Nagin received nearly $20 million to establish a workable evacuation plan in plenty of time for Katrina, but it's questionable whether it was ever developed, and what plans the city may have had were not publicized. Two months before Katrina, wrote Caroline Heldman in *The Society Pages*, "[Mayor] Nagin spent money to produce and distribute DVDs in poorer neighborhoods to inform residents that they would be on their own if a storm hit because the city could not afford to evacuate them. In the days before the storm, Nagin sent empty Amtrak trains out of the city, failed to mobilize available school and other buses, and waited an entire day to call for a mandatory evacuation so he could determine whether the City would face lawsuits from local businesses. All of these decisions were deadly," Heldman wrote (2011).

On the federal level, President George W. Bush told the nation that New Orleans had "dodged a bullet." However, even as Bush spoke, three major levees were breaking, flooding the lowest and poorest parts of the city. Marc Cresswell, a medic from a private ambulance company, reported that "at one point I had 10 helicopters on the ground waiting to go, but FEMA kept stonewalling us with paperwork. Meanwhile, every 30 or 40 minutes someone was dying" (Heldman, 2011). "The day Katrina hit, [Bush] traveled to Arizona and California to promote his prescription drug plan, had birthday cake with John McCain, and attended a [San Diego]

Padres [major-league baseball] game," then went on vacation (Heldman, 2011). A week into the disaster, Bush did visit New Orleans and surrounding areas with a cadre of officials, and praised their work with his now-infamous statement, "Brownie [FEMA director Mike Brown], you're doing a heckuva job" (Heldman, 2011).

Mark Schleifstein reported in the *New Orleans Times-Picayune* (2009): "The dead were overwhelmingly old. Most lived near the levee breaches in the 9th Ward and Lakeview. About two-thirds either drowned or died from illness or injury brought on by being trapped in houses surrounded by water. The rest died from maladies or injuries suffered in or exacerbated by an arduous evacuation—or an inability to evacuate quickly enough, including many who died in local hospitals that lost power and other life-sustaining services."

Further Reading

Brunkard, Joan, Gonza Namulanda, and Raoult Ratard. "Hurricane Katrina Deaths, Louisiana Department of Health, 2005." *Disaster Medicine and Public Health Preparedness*. August 28, 2008. http://www.dhh.louisiana.gov/assets/docs/katrina/deceasedreports/KatrinaDeaths_082008.pdf

Cook, Lindsey, and Ethan Rosenberg. "No One Knows How Many People Died in Katrina." *U.S. News*, August 28, 2015. https://www.usnews.com/news/blogs/data-mine/2015/08/28/no-one-knows-how-many-people-died-in-katrina

Hartnell, Anna. *After Katrina: Race, Neoliberalism, and the End of the American Century*. Albany, NY: SUNY Press, 2017. http://www.sunypress.edu/p-6419-after-katrina.aspx

Heldman, Caroline. "Hurricane Katrina and the Demographics of Death." *The Society Pages*, August 29, 2011. https://thesocietypages.org/socimages/2011/08/29/hurricane-katrina-and-the-demographics-of-death/

McAteer, Oliver. "Just Like Katrina, Black Americans Will Be Hit Hardest by Hurricane Harvey." *The Metro* [United Kingdom], August 30, 2017. http://metro.co.uk/2017/08/30/just-like-katrina-black-americans-will-be-the-real-victims-of-hurricane-harvey-6890806/

Schleifstein, Mark. "Study of Hurricane Katrina's Dead Show Most Were Old, Lived Near Levee Breaches." *New Orleans Times-Picayune*, August 27, 2009. https://www.nola.com/news/weather/article_35741734-68e1-575e-86d0-29366eed38e5.html

Shapiro, Isaac, and Arloc Sherman. "Essential Facts About t\he Victims of Hurricane Katrina." Center on Budget and Policy Priorities. September 19, 2005. https://www.cbpp.org/research/essential-facts-about-the-victims-of-hurricane-katrina

CHAPTER FOUR

Cases: United States West

Introduction

The history of environmental racism includes a number of lawsuits based on the 1964 United States Civil Rights Act that have been thrown out of court because they lacked manifest "intent"—that is, the perpetrators did not declare that they meant to harm their victims. In our survey of cases in the United States' western half, which is dominated by damage done to Native American peoples and their homelands, attention should be paid to statements by officials, beginning in the 1970s, that Native lands were being regarded as "national sacrifice areas" for energy and natural resources. Most of these places are in rural areas, often out of sight and out of mind of the majority society. The toll of national sacrifice was evident by the early 21st century, as nearly 40 percent of U.S. Environmental Protection Agency Superfund sites were located on or near Indian reservations.

In the late 1970s, about the time that the environmental racism movement was acquiring social, political, and academic definition, I wrote the following in my first book (*Wasi'chu: The Continuing Indian Wars*, 1979), describing the degraded life of Emma Yazzie, a Navajo sheepherder who lived with suffocating air pollution near the Four Corners coal-fired power plant:

> For hundreds of years, Emma's forebears woke up to a turquoise sky. Now, she wakes to a brown sky smelling of burning dirty clothes and old tires. Some days the smoke funnels up the hill, over the poisoned lake and the chemical-coated grass, into her hogan. And then she becomes sleepy and ill. A few hundred yards in back of her home, a giant coal-mining dragline

scatters the bones of her ancestors, drawing from the earth coal which feeds the [Four Corners] plants' turbines and generators. In plush boardrooms in distant cities, Emma's home is called a "national sacrifice area." (Johansen and Maestas, 1979, 143)

From the Dine (whom the Spanish called Navajo) and the Laguna Pueblo (near Albuquerque, New Mexico), to their namesake Dene of Canada's Northwest Territories (described in the section on Canada, which follows), Native peoples were recruited beginning in the early 1950s to mine "yellow dust"—uranium—and then, over decades, died in large numbers of torturous cancers. Uranium-induced cancers have become the deadliest plague unleashed on Native peoples of North America. On Navajo land, its mining and milling are now illegal, as Native people heed their "original instructions" that some resources are better left in the ground.

Uranium mined from Native American lands supplied a substantial proportion of the fuel for early nuclear power plants as well as the U.S. nuclear arsenal. By the 1970s, many of the early miners were dying of lung cancer. In Washington State, nuclear waste from the Hanford plants afflicted the Yakamas. The Navajos succeeded in stopping uranium mining and milling only after several hundred people had died of its effects and many more had suffered the tortures of cancers that once were nearly unknown in their country.

By 2014, 350 to 400 former Navajo underground uranium miners, their bodies radioactive from the inside out, had died from maladies caused in large part by exposure to radiation, according to Chris Shuey, an environmental health researcher with the Southwest Research and Information Center (Knight, 2013). Many more Native people had also died of a wide variety of malignant cancers, not usually from mining uranium themselves but because they lived with the "yellow dirt" in windswept waste (tailings) piles that have now blown into every crack and crevice, indoors and outdoors, for decades.

In addition to the mining and milling of nuclear fuel, New Mexico also supplied for the United States its first test site for the atomic bomb, detonated on July 16, 1945, on a 100-foot tower. The Trinity Site, on today's U.S. Army's White Sands Missile Range, is surrounded by two Apache tribes, several Navajo communities, and 19 American Indian pueblos. Reports at the time by American Indians and government witnesses described a light ash fall for days after the explosion, the effects of which were not investigated until 2014, when the National Cancer Institute started a study of radiation levels in New Mexico from that first test blast. With no prior evidence of effects, no one has been eligible for compensation under the Radiation Exposure Compensation Act, which covers other nuclear and uranium workers as well as "down-winders" who were exposed to radiation from later atomic tests (Lee, 1997).

Our narrative includes a number of cases from Alaska, including plans to blast a harbor on Eskimo land on Alaska's North Slope with atomic bombs. This plan anticipated a prospective reality, not a Dr. Strangelove dystopian fantasy. The clerks of the atomic establishment had to be reminded that *people* live on the North Slope—the plan was shelved after strenuous protests.

In Alaska's Pebble Mine—again, on Native American lands—industrialists want to replace some of the world's richest salmon runs, which have sustained Native peoples for many centuries, with one of Earth's largest gold mines and attendant toxic mining waste. President Barack Obama stalled that plan, but Scott Pruitt, as Donald Trump's Environmental Protection Agency secretary, had revived it as of this writing. Elsewhere in Alaska, Natives' villages crumble into rising, stormy waters as seas and temperatures rise.

In one of many examples of "national sacrifice," the Little Rocky Mountains of Montana, which have long been regarded as sacred by the Assiniboine and Gros Ventre, are now laced by the effluent of open-pit gold mines, which have produced toxic acid-mine drainage. Andrew Schneider of the Seattle *Post-Intelligencer* described Gus Helgeson, the president of Island Mountain Protectors (a Native American environmental and cultural organization), standing atop Spirit Mountain as he scanned "the gashes, pits and piles of rock that once was his tribe's most sacred land" (Schneider, 2001).

Other stories in our narrative look to the future. For example, the Moapa Paiutes, a tiny American Indian tribe, live a few miles, as the toxic ash flies, north of Las Vegas, Nevada. After decades of suffering the suffocating ash clouds of an old coal-fired plant, they not only retired it with relentless protests, but also convinced the U.S. Department of the Interior to site two solar-powered arrays nearby, creating jobs.

Urban areas in the West yield stories of environmental racism and resistance as well. The Mothers of East Los Angeles, for example, have been uniting people of several ethnicities in their predominantly Latino barrio, rising up in readiness, and galvanizing their neighbors to stave off a hazardous waste incinerator.

For decades, a half-dozen smelters as well as the smokestacks of the gigantic Colorado Fuel & Iron (CF&I) steel mill dominated the skyline of Pueblo, Colorado, "the Pittsburgh of the West." Now rusting skeletons are all that remain in this city of about 100,000, like ghosts from another time. Legal marijuana is the new game in town. Pueblo has become increasingly Latino, about half the population. The city is cleaning up the toxic legacy of the steel mill and smelters—the lead and arsenic left behind from slag heaps of the rotting rust-belt infrastructure in Pueblo's barrio.

For more than 100 years, the black community of Richmond, California, has been neighbors of a huge Chevron refinery, originally built by Standard Oil, that can process 240,000 barrels of crude oil a day. The refinery includes a huge tank complex of 2,900 acres on a peninsula with a view of San Francisco Bay and the Pacific Ocean, producing gasoline, diesel, jet fuel, and several chemicals. Richmond's black, poor majority has organized against the oil complex's notorious pollution. In 2007, they elected Gayle McLaughlin of the Green Party mayor, as she pledged to bring the refineries to heel by forcing them to reduce pollution and pay higher taxes. Richmond thus became the largest city in the United States to be led by a Green Party mayor. The company also was forced to pay $10 million to partially defray the medical costs of residents affected by its pollution. It was largely a David vs. Goliath story, however, with Big Oil still very much in control.

Further Reading

Johansen, Bruce, and Roberto Maestas. *Wasi'chu: The Continuing Indian Wars.* New York: Monthly Review Press, 1979.

Knight, Danielle. "Native Americans Denounce Toxic Legacy." TWN: Third World Network, June 14, 2013. http://www.ipsnews.net/1999/06/environment-health-native-americans-denounce-toxic-legacy/

Lee, Susan. "Blockade of Nevada Test Site Highway." *Synthesis/Regeneration* 14 (Fall 1997). Green Party. http://www.greens.org/s-r/14/14-24.html

Schneider, Andrew. "'A Wounded Mountain Spewing Poison': The Mining of the West: Profit and Pollution on Public Lands." *Seattle Post-Intelligencer*, June 12, 2001. In Bruce E. Johansen, *Resource Exploitation in Native North America: A Plague upon the Peoples.* Santa Barbara, CA: ABC-CLIO, 2016, 109–210. https://books.google.com/books?id=bs-uDQAAQBAJ&pg=PA209&lpg=PA209&dq

Montana's Gros Ventre and Assiniboine: Gold Mining and Cyanide Poisoning

During 1855, the Assiniboine and Gros Ventre were moved to the Fort Belknap Reservation, which was named by the immigrants for a U.S. secretary of war. The Assiniboine and Gros Ventre gave up 40,000 acres of land in exchange for a government promise to feed, clothe, and care for them. At the time, federal Indian agents said nothing about the gold that was buried in Spirit Mountain, but they made it clear the tribes could either agree to their terms or starve. Spirit Mountain is part of the Little Rockies, an island of mountains in the nearly flat prairie. To Native Americans, the mountains were valued for their deer, bighorn sheep, herbs, natural medicines, and pure water. Gold mining has destroyed all of that.

In 1884, Pike Landusky and Pete Zortman discovered gold on the reservation. Facing starvation, in 1895, the Assiniboine and Gros Ventre signed an agreement negotiated by General George Bird Grinnell, selling portions of their gold-laced land to the federal government for $9 an acre worth of livestock and other goods, as miners besieged towns that had been named after the gold's discoverers. Under the terms of the General Mining Law of 1872, the government sold the land to individuals and private companies for $10 an acre.

A century and a half later, the land was exhausted and broken. Sammy Fretwell wrote in *The State* (Charleston, South Carolina, 2014): "Sheared off mountaintops, towering piles of rubble and deep pits make it hard to ignore Montana's recent history of gold mining. Dominant on the landscape, industrial-scale gold mines provided jobs and tax revenues for parts of three decades in small communities that came to depend on the economic support. But big open-pit gold mines had such an impact on the environment that Montana effectively banned new ones 16 years ago."

Some of the gold mines exposed sulfide-rich rocks. Once unearthed, where the sulfide interacted with air and water, sulfuric acid was created that, left by itself, could have leached into the water table for several centuries. A 2006 consulting report found that "60 percent of the hard rock mines researchers examined in the West had degraded the quality of groundwater and surface water nearby" (Fretwell, 2014). Leaching began during the 1980s and continued for about a decade and a half before environmental problems compelled the state to close the mine in 1998.

The Zortman-Landusky mine was only one of several heap leach mines near the Fort Belknap Indian Reservation. According to the *Environmental Justice Atlas* (2014): "This specific mining operation had over a dozen cyanide spills including one incident that resulted in over 50,000 gallons of cyanide being spilled. The mine was also found to be leaking acids, arsenic and lead. This large and frequent contamination led to extensive surface and groundwater contamination" (Zortman-Landusky, 2014).

"Like Watching Our Ancestors Die"

"The first time the mining company let me up here, let me see what they had done to our land, the pain surrounded me. It was like watching our ancestors die, raped of their honor," said Gus Helgeson. "They destroyed this place, took their gold off in armored trucks and left us a wounded mountain spewing poison on the people the mountain was stolen from," he said (Schneider, 2001).

Over several decades, according to Andrew Schneider's account, "scores of shafts were driven into the Little Rockies, and an estimated $1 billion in gold and silver was taken out of the ground—more than $300 million by the last owner of the mine, Pegasus Gold Corp. of Canada" (Schneider, 2001). Underground mining continued until the 1950s, after which open-pit strip mining was initiated. In 1979, as gold prices rose rapidly, the Pegasus Gold Corp. and a subsidiary, Zortman Mining Inc., built mines that extracted gold from heaps of low-grade ore with cyanide solutions.

The Pegasus Gold Corp., which owned several mines in the Little Rocky Mountains, went bankrupt when gold prices fell sharply after 1980, "leaving the state of Montana with a $100 million cleanup liability and the tribes with the prospect of perpetually polluted water" (Huff, 2000). Cyanide-assisted gold mining continued until 1990, during which time the mine was expanded nine times without any substantial environmental review, despite cyanide spills into the water table used by the Indians (Abel, 1997).

By 1990, the Assiniboine and Gros Ventre began to challenge the environmental side effects of cyanide-heap gold mining, forming a Native environmental advocacy group, Red Thunder, which joined with non-Indian environmental groups to resist federal permits for the Zortman-Landusky mine's next requested expansion. The groups' appeal was denied. By December 1992, Pegasus applied for another expansion of the mine, as Red Thunder joined with another Native environmental group, Island Mountain Protectors. Both prepared plans to challenge the expansion under the federal Clean Water Act, maintaining that the cyanide-leach method used in the mine was poisoning the reservation's water supply.

The Mine Leaks and Expands

During July 1993, a heavy thunderstorm brought a flood of acidified mine wastewater into the town of Zortman, after which the Bureau of Land Management required the mine's owners to develop a new reclamation plan. At about the same time, an Environmental Protection Agency study found that the mine had been "leaking acids, cyanide, arsenic and lead from each of its seven drainages" (Abel, 1997). The state of Montana soon joined the EPA in a suit based on the Clean Water Act, which was settled out of court in July 1996, with Pegasus and Zortman Mining pledging to pay $4.7 million in fines to the tribes, the federal government, and the state. The mine's owners also pledged to follow a detailed pollution-control plan in the future. Shortly thereafter, a request to triple the mine's size (from 400 to 1,192 acres) was approved by the Montana Department of Environmental Quality and the BLM (Abel, 1997). In January 1997, the Fort Belknap Community Council, National Wildlife Information Center sued the Montana Department of Environmental Quality, alleging that the agency's decision to allow an expanded mine violated state law.

Federal and state environmental agencies, during September 1997, fined Pegasus and Zortman Mining $25,300 for violating the clean water settlement by polluting a stream in the Little Rockies the previous summer. John Pearson, director of investor relations for Pegasus, asserted that discharges were the result of "acts of God" during "extraordinarily heavy rains" (Abel, 1997). By late 1997, with gold prices (and its share price) declining rapidly, Pegasus warned that its mine would close by January 1, 1998, if the expansion plan was not accepted. The state of Montana and local Native environmental activists wondered whether Pegasus would survive long enough as a corporate entity to complete the promised reclamation of existing mines. In January 1998, Pegasus filed for Chapter 11 bankruptcy protection.

In the meantime, Pegasus left behind open pits that were described by Schneider:

> Pegasus dug pits the size of football fields and lined them with plastic or clay. Crushed ore was dumped in mounds as high as 15 feet and soaked with a mist of cyanide. It was the largest cyanide heap–leach operation in the world. . . . The heavily contaminated water trickled and flowed through fissures in the mountain, into the surface streams and underground aquifers that supply drinking water for 1,000 people who live in and around Lodge Pole and Hays, reservation towns north of the mountains. (Schneider, 2001)

Streams Smell of Rotten Eggs

Streams flowing off the mountain smell of rotten eggs (the chemical signature of sulfide), cloudy and lifeless. "This is death," said John Allen, a tribal spiritual leader, as he filled his hands with putrid muck. "The mines take millions in gold from our land and leave us poisoned water. The miners and the government experts have argued for years about whether the water is bad. All they have to do is look, but they choose not to see" (Schneider, 2001). Allen, who was 60 years of age in 2015, has thyroid problems, as do three of his siblings. His father has lymphatic cancer. Doctors who specialize in environmental medicine have told the Assiniboine and Gros Ventre that the diseases they suffer stem from contaminated water. Environmental advocates among the two tribes also reported a high rate of stillbirths in 2016.

Health problems plagued people on the reservation long after the company had filed for bankruptcy and escaped its responsibilities by moving out of Montana, leaving "without proper reclamation of the land including leaving toxins like arsenic, hills of waste rock and exposed mountain sides" (Zortman-Landusky, 2014). In 1993, the EPA filed a Clean Water Act suit that required a $32 million cleanup, after leaching became obvious. According to one report (Fretwell, 2014), "By 1993, selenium, a metal associated with mine waste, began to show up in German Gulch, where an almost pure strain of native cutthroat trout lives."

Tests later revealed that the creek's fish and water bugs were contaminated with selenium, which can hurt the ability of cutthroat trout to reproduce. German Gulch Creek remains unsuitable for aquatic life and for drinking water. Acid drainage from the Zortman and Landusky mines turned some streams orange. Members of both tribes have generally refrained from drinking water from the area, said Ina Nez Perce, who manages environmental issues for both tribes at the Fort Belknap reservation (Fretwell, 2014).

The Gros Ventre and Assiniboine Tribes sued the U.S. Bureau of Land Management, citing lack of respect for their land from the heap leaching in the Zortman-Landusky mine. Pollutants cited in the suit included cyanide, arsenic, cadmium, aluminum, and iron. In 2005, Montana governor Brian Schweitzer signed legislation providing $1.5 million per year to cleanse contaminated water until 2018.

By 2014, state and federal taxpayers had spent at least $40 million to clean up environmental problems caused by four gold strip mines that shut down in the 1990s, according to the Montana Department of Environmental Quality and the U.S. Forest Service. The Zortman and Landusky mines had cost almost $24 million of that, with several million dollars yet to be expended (Fretwell, 2014).

Further Reading

Abel, Heather. "The Rise and Fall of a Gold Mining Company." *High Country News* 29, 24 (December 22, 1997). https://www.hcn.org/issues/121/3860

Fretwell, Sammy. "Toxic Legacy Haunts Montana; What Can SC [South Carolina] Learn?" *The State* (Charleston, South .Carolina.), October 11, 2014. http://www.thestate.com/news/local/article13897079.html

Huff, Andrew. "Gold Mining Threatens Communities." *The Progressive,* Media Project. July 11, 2000. In Bruce E. Johansen, *Resource Exploitation in Native North America: A Plague upon the Peoples.* Santa Barbara, CA: ABC-CLIO, 2016, 184. https://books.google.com/books?id=bs-uDQAAQBAJ&pg=PA209&lpg=PA209&dq

Schneider, Andrew. "'A Wounded Mountain Spewing Poison': The Mining of the West: Profit and Pollution on Public Lands." Seattle *Post-Intelligencer,* June 12, 2001. In Bruce E. Johansen, *Resource Exploitation in Native North America: A Plague upon the Peoples.* Santa Barbara, CA: ABC-CLIO, 2016, 209–210. https://books.google.com/books?id=bs-uDQAAQBAJ&pg=PA209&lpg=PA209&dq

Zortman-Landusky Gold Mine, Montana, United States. *Environmental Justice Atlas.* 2014. https://ejatlas.org/conflict/gold-mining-in-montana

The Mothers of East Los Angeles Stand Down a Toxic Incinerator—and More

In 1987, facing a classic case of environmental racism, a Latina grass-roots group calling itself Mothers of East Los Angeles (MELA) organized its neighborhood in opposition to the location of a very large toxic waste incinerator there—and drove its sponsors out. In the years since, the group has become a center of opposition to several other attempts to impose businesses (such as a gargantuan prison) in the barrio that more affluent neighborhoods did not want. By 2017, two groups with allied interests were operating: Mothers of East Los Angeles and Madres de Este Los Angeles, Santa Isabel. Both focus on environmental justice issues, with an emphasis on families and children.

Los Angeles Times staff writer Louis Sahagun captured the excitement of the group's emergence in a 1989 account:

> They emerged from nowhere three years ago, 100 mothers with two things in common: a white scarf tied around their heads and a deep-seated concern for the health and safety of their East Los Angeles neighborhoods. Galvanized by Father John Moretta of Resurrection Church to battle construction of a proposed $100-million state prison in East Los Angeles, the group of Latinas helped stall the project and have gone on to tackle issues ranging from environmental pollution to overcrowded classrooms. In the process, they have transformed themselves and their neighborhoods, say community leaders and activists, who have come to regard the grass-roots organization called Mothers of East Los Angeles as a leader in local environmental issues.

"In other times, similar groups tackled issues such as the Vietnam War, police brutality and media representation of minorities," said Rodolfo Acuna, professor of Chicano Studies at Cal State Northridge. "Right now, the Mothers are one of the few grass-roots groups in our community dealing with land use and quality-of-life issues." Los Angeles city councilwoman Gloria Molina characterized the Mothers, most of whom have lived in East Los Angeles most of their lives: "They've learned not to be frightened or intimidated by people in power" (Sahagun, 1989). The people in power had become accustomed to siting prisons, freeway interchanges, dumps, and other unpopular features of urban life in minority and poor neighborhoods until *las madres* came along.

Remembering Lucy Delgado

Lucy Delgado, founder of the Mothers of East Los Angeles, passed away April 11, 2012; she was 87. Delgado had joined Cesár Chavéz during his first fast against the use of pesticides on California grapes, recalled Del Pozo-Mora, noting that Boyle Heights–related causes were not the only issues Delgado cared about.

Delgado pioneered an alliance between East L.A. Latinas and Jewish women as well as other interethnic ties. She promoted the Jewish community's restoration of the Breed Street Shul and the establishment of the Japanese-American National Museum in Little Tokyo. She also was a founding member of the Boyle Heights Historical Society and the Breed Street Shul Preservation Committee. "Lucy was La Madre del Este Los Ángeles, the quintessential proud and loving mother of the East Side, and, in the words of the Jewish tradition, an exemplary *eyshet chayil*, woman of valor," said Stephen Sass, chairman of the board for the Breed Street Shul Project (Castillo, 2012).

Delgado was credited with helping to create a movement among regular people who were fed up with their neighborhood being the dumping ground for the public projects not wanted in other communities. "There were weekly Monday night demonstrations . . . hundreds of mothers along with their spouses and children would march up and down the Olympic Boulevard Bridge demanding that their voices be heard," states the MELA website, describing their protests. "The women would always wear scarves on their heads as a sign of peace, dignity and respect for their community" (Castillo, 2012).

Most of the Mothers were born and reared in East Los Angeles at a time when its low-income residents were afraid to fight government officials who railroaded disruptive projects—including freeways, prisons, and dumps—through their community. At first they shied away from politics and media confrontations, but within three years people who were organizing their own neighborhoods came to them for advice.

Many of the early members described themselves as shy housewives before they combined their efforts, easily unnerved by television cameras or government officials who berated their efforts to derail ostensibly economically beneficial projects. Wearing trademark red T-shirts showing a mother cradling a baby, they came to enjoy—and even relish—the surprise written on the faces of their affluent opponents. The Mothers of East Los Angeles soon were invited to advise white community organizers as guest speakers throughout California. By 1989, the Mothers had 400 active members, and they filed for incorporation, a move meant to allow more efficient fundraising and organizing for demonstrations, candlelight vigils, and letter-writing campaigns—tactics they used to pressure developers, politicians, and bureaucrats. "In the old days, if the government said, 'Move on,' people moved on," said Lucy Ramos, 40 years of age in 1989, and a mother of five who often served as spokeswoman. Her own taste in resistance was honed after the state told her family (and 10,000 other East L.A. residents) to "move on"—leave their East L.A. homes—to make way during the 1950s for several new freeways that would afflict the area with additional noise and automotive pollution. "There is a limit to how much junk they can dump on people, and this community has reached it" (Sahagun, 1989).

When the Mothers organized in 1986, they decided to concentrate on land-use, environmental, and basic quality-of-life issues. "If you witness their persistence, their doggedness, you would see something very natural, something wholesome," said Father Moretta. "They are mothers who have coalesced around something of immediate importance to them, the safety of their families and children" (Sahagun, 1989). Soon they had organized to stop the proposed $29 million hazardous waste incinerator in nearby Vernon that was planned to burn about 225,000 tons of solid waste in an average year. They also organized East L.A. to turn back an above-ground pipeline proposed by four oil companies. The residents, led by the Mothers, lobbied the Los Angeles City Council until its members voted against permits during 1987.

The prison proposal was announced in March 1985, following a directive by the state government to establish a new incarceration location in Southern California because the population and the number of people serving time were highest there. Plans were made with very little public attention to locate the prison in East Los Angeles, but once the proverbial cat escaped the bag, opposition organized. Father Moretta came up with the name "Mothers of East L.A." Soon, publicity was being generated by protests, which persisted for nearly five years, until the Los Angeles City Council refused a permit. The Mothers of East Los Angeles came out of this struggle with a core leadership and degree of organization that served it well when, in 1987, Thermal Treatment Systems announced plans for a hazardous waste incinerator to be called ChemClear (as is so often the case, a polluting company came under the cover of an Earth-friendly–sounding name). The waste incinerator was proposed within 7,500 feet of schools, businesses, and residences. Mothers of East L.A. quickly allied with Greenpeace to frequently and visibly oppose the facility.

Combating ChemClear

ChemClear had worked quietly for two years, acquiring all the permissions it needed except a final permit, before anyone was notified in Vernon, a poor Latino community adjacent to East Los Angeles, whose residents soon would be sharing their home with a factory burning 125,000 pounds of hazardous waste per day. The California Department of Health Services had declared that "new safety tests showed that the plant would hurt neither the environment nor the surrounding community, less than a week after a huge cloud of toxic chlorine gas from a plant in the East L.A. community of City of Commerce had forced the evacuation of about 27,000 people from their homes," Betsy Swart wrote in *On the Issues: A Magazine of Feminist, Progressive Thinking* (1992).

More than 200 people marched with signs and banners reading, "The People Will Stop the Incinerator," and "Don't Poison Me." Their first march brought out more than 200 people. Subsequent rallies attracted even greater numbers as well as the support of groups like Greenpeace and celebrities like Robert Blake. "They thought that if they picked a poor community," said Aurora Castillo, *la dona*—founding mother—of the group, "they wouldn't find any resistance. But we proved them wrong, very wrong" (Swart, 1992). Protests were conducted in English and Spanish, emphasizing the potential for health risks. The Mothers sued the Environmental Protection Agency for failure to follow legal procedures vis-à-vis required environmental impact statements. Hamstrung by dogged opposition, ChemClear in 1991 abandoned its plan for East Los Angeles and, instead, proposed a facility in Huntington Beach, which provoked considerable protest there.

Huntington Beach assemblywoman and Democrat Lucille Roybal-Allard spearheaded a petition drive with aid from the Los Angeles Unified School

District to stop the plant for safety reasons. Several groups protested to the state Department of Health Services and the EPA. According to a report in the *Los Angeles Times*: "Industrial wastes, including hexavalent chromium, acids and other hazardous materials from Los Angeles-area factories, would be hauled to the facility by tanker on freeways and city streets. Water would be separated from the materials and discharged into sewers. Sludge containing hazardous metals and other materials would be hauled by rail or truck to a Utah landfill that is owned by ChemClear, a subsidiary of Union Pacific Railroad" (Fernandes and Holguin, 1991).

The Mothers of East L.A. drew from the reputation of mothers as caregivers to extend private conceptions of the Latino home to the public sphere. They also worked with other groups to preserve quality of life in the area, groups including Watchdog, which rallies support on environmental issues, using public protest, science, and education. Their work has continued into the 21st century with a campaign to improve air quality in public schools. Their activities were described in a book, *Mexican American Women Activists: Identity and Resistance in Two Los Angeles Communities,* published in 1998 by Mary Pardo.

La Dona Wins a Prize

Aurora Castillo, 81 years of age in 1995, known as *La Dona* of East Los Angeles, won the world-renowned Goldman Prize for environmental activism, which *Time* magazine called "the Nobel Prize for environmental heroes." She never set out to be an ecological warrior. She told an international audience in San Francisco that all people, regardless of ethnicity, race, education, and income, "have a right to a clean environment." She fights for her beloved barrio, she said at the podium, because she is committed to the children who deserve "clean air, clean water and pure food." She fought back tears that later, at a private dinner attended by Mayor Frank Jordan and world-renowned environmentalists, she described as tears of struggle, of sacrifice, of survival. "With great joy, I accept this honor on behalf of the Mothers of East Los Angeles" (Quintanilla, 1995).

"My first impression of Aurora Castillo was one of quiet dignity," wrote Betsy Swart in *On the Issues* (1992). "As she welcomed me into a tidy office at the Church of the Resurrection in East Los Angeles, I wondered if this could be the same woman who over the past five years has gained a reputation as a tough fighter against toxic pollution in her community. But, as soon as she began to speak, I knew that this was, indeed, the woman whose passion for justice was helping to hold the line against the environmental destruction of her neighborhood. 'Did you see the children outside?' she asked me. 'It is for them—and all the others like them—that we fight.'" Swart continued:

> And nowhere is the risk more extreme than in minority communities. While wealthy and middle-class neighborhoods of Los Angeles are clustered where the air is cleanest, the city's poor are relegated to its most polluted areas. For example, according to one survey reported by Greenpeace, 70 percent of L.A.'s blacks and 50 percent of its Latinos live in the most polluted parts of the city. Blacks and Latinos also make up the largest percentage of employees in the city's polluting industries. And nearly half of California's lead-poisoning victims have Latino surnames. Recently, when Dr. Russell Sherwin began examining the lungs of inner-city L.A. kids who had died from accidents or street violence, he also found that eight out of 10 already had lung abnormalities caused by breathing the city's filthy air, and more than a quarter of them had severe lung lesions! (Swart, 1992)

Further Reading

Castillo, Gloria Angelina. "Mothers of East LA Founder Passes Away." EGP News, April 12, 2012. http://egpnews.com/2012/04/'mothers-of-east-la'-founder-passes-away/

Fernandes, Lorna, and Rick Holguin. "To Waste Plant Foes, It's David-and-Goliath Victory; Firm Says Recession Made It Drop Proposal, but Opponents Say, 'We Chased Them Out.'" *Los Angeles Times*, November 3, 1991. http://articles.latimes.com/1991-11-03/news/hd-1699_1_hazardous-waste

Holguin, Rick. "Group Launches Petition Drive Against Hazardous Waste Plant: Construction: The Opponents of the Facility Say a Full Environmental Impact Report Is Needed." *Los Angeles Times*, May 16, 1991. http://articles.latimes.com/1991-05-16/news/hl-2675_1_hazardous-waste

Pardo, Mary. "Mexican American Women Grassroots Community Activists: 'Mothers of East L.A.'" *Frontiers: A Journal of Women Studies* 11, no. 1 (March, 1990): 1–7.

Pardo, Mary S. *Mexican American Women Activists: Identity and Resistance in Two Los Angeles Communities.* Philadelphia: Temple University Press, 1998.

Quintanilla, Michael. "The Earth Mother: Aurora Castillo Has Long Protected Her East L.A. Now the Environmental Efforts of *la Dona* Are Being Rewarded." *Los Angeles Times*, April 24, 1995. http://articles.latimes.com/1995-04-24/news/ls-58227_1_aurora-castillo

Sahagun, Louis. "The Mothers of East L.A. Transform Themselves and Their Neighborhood." *Los Angeles Times*, August 13, 1989. http://articles.latimes.com/1989-08-13/local/me-816_1_east-los-angeles

Swart, Betsy. "The Passion of Aurora Castillo and the Militant Mothers of East L.A. Latina Women Demand a Safe Environment for Their Children." *On

> the Issues: A Magazine of Feminist, Progressive Thinking, Spring 1992. http://www.ontheissuesmagazine.com/1992spring/swart_spring1992.php

Pueblo, Colorado: The Toxic Legacy of the "Pittsburgh of the West"

Pueblo, Colorado was known during most of the twentieth century as the "Pittsburgh of the West," with its ranks of smelters and steel mills, their smokestacks belching ash-laced coal smoke. By 2019, only a few rusting skeletons of these now-closed industrial plants remained in Pueblo, a city of about 111,000 people south of Denver. The city is becoming a majority-Latino community where legal marijuana is a major industry, along with cleanup of arsenic and lead from the old factories' slag heaps.

By 2008, the Environmental Protection Agency and state authorities were testing and detecting toxicity in many Pueblo neighborhoods, focused, to begin, on the 50-acre site of the Colorado Smelter, located in what had become a light industrial and residential neighborhood near the Arkansas River and the central business district of Pueblo. The Colorado Smelter processed gold and silver in the Eilers and Bessemer neighborhoods of Pueblo between 1883 and 1908. One hundred and six years after it shut down, in December 2014, belated discovery of the smelter's toxic legacy prompted the EPA to list the site on its National Priorities List. The smelter bordered a ravine near a river, where its waste products accumulated in large slag heaps adjacent to residential properties as close as 200 feet.

Pueblo's Smelters at Peak Production

During their period of peak production, between the 1880s and 1920, Pueblo's smelters processed roughly 2,000 tons of metal per day. These included the Pueblo Smelting and Refining Company smelter (Pueblo Smelter), the New England & Colorado Smelting Company (also known as the Massachusetts Smelter), the Philadelphia Smelting and Refining Company, and the United States Zinc Company (aka Blende). (Colorado Department, 2008). The Pueblo Smelter, the largest, was operating eight blast furnaces at once by 1889. The smelters concentrated in that area to take advantage of nearby coal and lime deposits as well as railroad connections that brought in ore and shipped out finished metals. One of the smelters, the Rocky Mountain Steel Mill, was in operation as late as 1995. Ruins of the smelters and their waste heaps remained visible across Pueblo well into the 21st century.

The Colorado Coal & Iron Company (CC&I) steel works began operating in September 1881. In 1892, CC&I merged with the Colorado Fuel Company to form Colorado Fuel & Iron (CF&I). CF&I filed for Chapter 11 bankruptcy in 1990. In 1993 the mill was purchased by Oregon Steel Mills Inc. and renamed Rocky Mountain Steel Mills (Colorado Department, 2008). It continued to operate well into the new century.

During its heyday, CF&I Steel, owned by the Rockefeller family, was the largest corporate employer in Colorado, "an industrial conglomerate [that] spanned four states—an empire of iron mines, coal fields, limestone quarries, coking plants, smelters and blast furnaces." Samuel Gompers visited Pueblo in his drive to establish the American Federation of Labor. Strikes were so large and violent that state militia were called out in 1914 to quell one of them (among workers at a CF&I coal mine), and in the process killed 18 people. In 1959, a strike at CF&I continued four months and crippled Pueblo's economy. In 1997, a strike that barely caused a ripple in business sales. "Last time [1959], when nothing came out of those smokestacks, it affected the whole community," recalled Maggie Divelbiss, a longtime resident and executive director of a local arts center. "CF&I just doesn't loom as large as before" (Brooke, 1997).

A School Encased in Lead and Arsenic

The Colorado Smelter was combined with ASARCO (formerly American Smelting and Refining Company) in 1899, before it closed. After that, some of its arsenic-and-lead-laced slag was used as track ballast for railroad tracks between Florence and Cannon City. In 1923, several thousand bricks were removed from the blast furnace's smokestack and used to build Pueblo's St. Mary School. No one seemed sensitive at the time to the fact that everyone in the school had been studying encased in bricks laced with arsenic and lead.

Lead causes or contributes to many severe and sometimes fatal health problems, including profound effects on children's growth, behavior, and intelligence, inducing learning disabilities, problems with attention and fine motor coordination, and violent behavior. In the short run, exposure to arsenic can cause lesions and discoloration of skin as well as severe digestive problems, including nausea, abdominal pain, and diarrhea. In the long run, it contributes to cancers of the lungs, skin, liver, and bladder.

During 1989, the Pueblo County Health Department received reports that a waste pipe was dumping a red-orange "steady flow of a peculiar smelling polychromatic discharge through cracks in the eroded concrete" into the Arkansas River, a tributary of the Mississippi River that flows through Pueblo (Ramirez, 2013). Public health officials tested the discharge, detected several toxic materials (among them lead and arsenic), and traced it to the slag heap from which the bricks at the St. Mary School had been taken.

A Colorado state government report issued in 2008 said, "Emissions from smelting operations often contain inorganic constituents such as lead and arsenic. Soils contaminated with cadmium, arsenic, lead and zinc may be found in residential areas surrounding smelter plant sites. Ingestion of soil and inhalation of wind blown soil are potential human exposure pathways of concern and may occur due to the extent of off-site contamination in surface soils near the site" (Colorado Department, 2008). The former smelter's slag heap, 35 feet high at its peak, covers 25 acres, containing 50,000 cubic yards of arsenic and lead at levels that classify as toxic waste. In the case of arsenic, according to the 2008 report, the material in the slag heap routinely exceeds levels at which it is carcinogenic. Carcinogenic levels also were detected in the soil around several homes within a mile radius of the smelter site (Colorado Department, 2008).

Living with Lead

Residents of Pueblo's Latino barrio and other neighborhoods learned slowly, over several decades, just how contaminated their neighborhoods had become. By 2016, the EPA had tested 438 residential yards near the Colorado smelter site and found that "approximately 24 percent of [those] sampled exceed the current 400 ppm [parts per million] national screening level for lead in residential soil" (Colorado Smelter, 2017). Also in 2016, homeowners packed the Pueblo Public Library to be briefed on the language of remediation by the federal Environmental Protection Agency, which had declared parts of Pueblo Superfund sites.

As KOAA-TV in Pueblo reported from the scene:

Neighbors from Old Bojon Town packed into the Rawlings Library to learn just how unsafe levels of lead and arsenic in and around their homes will impact them. The EPA found high levels in the dust inside 19 of the 102 of the homes tested in December, in addition to the soil outside. That amounts to one in five homes, which is on par with similar sites around the country. "My dad bought a house a block away from the steel mill, and this was the surprise that we get," says Demetri Barton, whose home tested positive for unsafe lead and arsenic levels. The EPA will be putting him up in a hotel while they scrub the house clean. ("Pueblo Neighbors," 2016)

Barton said he knew of at least 10 people in his neighborhood who had been afflicted by several types of cancer, some of whom had died. He did not know whether the cancers had been induced directly by many years of exposure to lead and arsenic, but he said, "Something in this town that's been released is being a trigger to cancer to the people in this town." Toxicologists at the meeting said that high lead levels do put people at risk for brain and respiratory problems, but it is not a likely cause of cancer. "Lead isn't typically associated with cancer. However, some heavy metals that are also associated with smelter activities can indeed cause cancer," said toxicologist Deborah McKean ("Pueblo Neighbors," 2016).

Michael Wenstrom of the EPA's environmental justice program warned residents in the vicinity of the slag heap, "These are toxins that could cause serious health issues like brain damage or cancer, especially in children," as he advised residents living on 1,900 properties in the area to sign up for testing. Even after warnings, several hundred property owners had not requested tests. He told residents, "The overall EPA testing and analysis for the site is likely [to] take several years, a process that comes before any cleanup" (Lewis, 2015).

Carcinogenic or not, declaration of Superfund status depressed property values, so property owners who wished to escape the bad news by moving away were having a tough time finding buyers. "Once cleanups take place, then property values will definitely be able to rise again, but there are always a lot of factors that impact property values," said EPA remedial project manager Sabrina Forrest, who attended hearings in Pueblo with home-sales figures from such sites in other cities. The EPA also provided equipment to test arsenic and lead contamination of dust in the air and residue in the soil, as well as forms to reimburse people for blood tests and assessments of homes for lead in their paint.

The EPA also hosted a Community Involvement Workgroup for the Colorado Smelter Superfund site, which was locally nicknamed "The Lead Fair," coordinated by Barton. "For one thing, for 120 years the people haven't been told anything; they've been misled. They were told that there was one smelter but there were six smelters in Pueblo," Barton said. "What came from those stacks from the smelters and the steel mill went in the ground. It causes lead poisoning just from touching the dirt, plus learning disorders and the health issues that it causes" (Zillstrom, 2017).

According to an account in the *Pueblo Chieftain*, "The fair provided free food, games and giveaways for kids, but the fair's biggest draw was a small station near the park's entrance, where representatives from the Pueblo City-County Health Department provided free testing for lead contamination" (Zillstrom, 2017). Pueblo resident Heather Daniels told Zach

Zillstrom of the *Chieftain* (2017): "We needed to get the lead test done for the school and it sounded like fun." Daniels said, "Truthfully, lead poisoning does so much brain damage and so much damage to the children, and we're in the middle of [a lead-affected] area, so we need to be aware if it's damaging our children." "That's what it's about. The people, the kids," Barton said. "Our families have been left in the dark so long. It's just a blessing to be able to share some information to keep our families safe for a lead-free Pueblo" (Zillstrom, 2017).

While at first glance Pueblo may look like a casualty of Rust Belt malaise, it has moved on. Not only has marijuana growing flourished after the state approved its consumption for recreational uses, but Foundation Health Systems in 1997 delivered 1,200 new jobs paying an average of $42,000 a year, an event that was announced at Pueblo's new convention center. "'These are not hamburger-flipping or minimum wage jobs,' said Malik Hasan, the president of Foundation Health Systems, sporting a big red button with the . . . message: 'Happy New Jobs! '98'" (Brooke, 1997). During the next two decades, several medical centers also opened or expanded their facilities in Pueblo, including St. Mary Corwin, Parkview Medical Center, and the Colorado Institute of Mental Health. A list of Pueblo's largest employers, issued in 2019, listed only one heavy industry plant (Republic Steel), behind the Trane Company, two school districts, and several others.

"A century ago, the pride of Pueblo urbanism was a city park dominated by the Mineral Palace, a neo-classic extravaganza featuring statues of King Coal and Queen Silver," wrote James Brooke in the *New York Times* (1997).

However, wrote Brooke, "Today, it is Riverwalk, a $25 million environmentally sensitive pedestrian and entertainment district, which will bring greenery and water flowing through 1.5 miles of downtown. When completed, by the end of the decade, Riverwalk will feature bicycle paths, water taxis, an amphitheater and outdoor cafes. Riverwalk is part of a downtown renewal that will surround the $9 million convention center with a new $2 million children's museum and a new $4 million historical museum." By 2018, this park had expanded to 32 acres of water and walking trails and gondola boat rides, restaurants, and a regular schedule of festivals and other entertainment. The park received 500,000 visitors in 2018.

Further Reading

Brooke, James. "Pittsburgh of the West Is Made of More Than Steel." *New York Times*, December 29, 1997. http://www.nytimes.com/1997/12/29/us/pittsburgh-of-the-west-is-made-of-more-than-steel.html

Colorado Department of Public Health and Environment, Hazardous Materials and Waste Management Division. "Preliminary Assessment: Colorado Smelter, Pueblo, Colorado." April 28, 2008. https://environmentalrecords.colorado.gov

Colorado Smelter Superfund Site: Community Properties (OU1), Pueblo City, Pueblo County, Colorado. Denver: U.S. Environmental Protection Agency Region 8, June 5, 2017. https://semspub.epa.gov/work/08/1884221.pdf

Lewis, Shanna. "When the Superfund Site in Your Backyard Isn't Your First Priority." Colorado Public Radio, June 16, 2015. http://www.cpr.org/news/story/when-superfund-site-your-backyard-isn-t-your-first-priority

"Pueblo Neighbors Learn More about Smelter Contamination Impacts." KOAA (Pueblo: TV/NBC), June 7, 2016. https://www.koaa.com/soil-contamination-work-progresses-in-pueblo-superfund-neighborhood

Ramirez, Matt. "Guilty Knowledge—PULP's Three Month Investigation into Pollution at the Old Colorado Smelter Site." *Pueblo Pulp*, 2013. http://pueblopulp.com/131guilty-knowledge-pulps-three-month-investiation-into-pollution-at-the-old-colorado-smelter-site/

Zillstrom, Zach. "Lead Fair Shines Light on Contamination; Clean-up at the Homes That Tested for High Levels of Lead and Arsenic Is Set to Begin Before the End of June." *Pueblo Chieftain*, March 11, 2017. http://www.chieftain.com/news/pueblo/lead-fair-shines-light-on-contamination/article_1be3d23f-03e9-5576-9c69-aa07acf61940.html#disqus_thread

Richmond, California: The Greens vs. Big Oil

For more than 100 years, the black community of Richmond, California, has lived with an overbearing, nasty neighbor: a huge Chevron refinery that produces gasoline, diesel, jet fuel, and several chemicals. Originally built by Standard Oil, the refinery can process 240,000 barrels of crude oil a day. The refinery includes a huge tank complex of 2,900 acres on a peninsula with a view of San Francisco Bay and the Pacific Ocean. The relationship between the community and the refinery has been expensive in terms of lost health and early death, the very definition of environmental racism: According to one account, "Decades of toxic emissions from industries—as well as lung-penetrating diesel particles spewed by truck routes and rail lines running next door to neighborhoods—may be taking a toll on residents' health. The people of Richmond, particularly African Americans, are at significantly higher risk of dying from heart disease and strokes and more likely to go to hospitals for asthma than other county residents" (Chiles, 2015).

"Hell on Steroids"

About 80 percent of the people who live within one mile of the Chevron refinery are people of color. Kinshasa Curl, administrative chief of Richmond's environmental division, said, "People of color in Richmond live on average ten years less than white people living in other parts of [Contra Costa] County" (Kay and Katz, 2012). Some people in the Bay Area may have stunning views of the bay and the ocean, but in North Richmond the scenery is dominated by an otherworldly, toxic landscape that routinely erupts in fires and explosions. Some residents call it hell on steroids. While North Richmond's schools practice earthquake drills (as do most others in California), in Richmond they also have chemical-explosion drills.

The scenery in Richmond is stunning in an otherworldly way. As *Scientific American* described it: "From the house where he was born, Henry Clark can stand in his back yard and see plumes pouring out of one of the biggest oil refineries in the United States. As a child, he was fascinated by the factory on the hill, all lit up at night like the hellish twin of a fairy tale city. In the morning, he'd go out to play and find the leaves on the trees burned to a crisp. 'Sometimes I'd find the air so foul, I'd have to grab my nose and run back into the house until it cleared up'" (Kay and Katz, 2012).

A reporter does not have to travel very far, or dig very deep, to find a story about toxic explosions in North Richmond. Michael Okwu and Jason Motlagh described a toxic explosion in Richmond for Al Jazeera:

> On Aug. 6, 2012, Courtney Cummings and her family were in their front yard when a massive fire erupted just six blocks away. "There was a big boom," she said. "I got really scared. I saw this big fireball go in the air and we all took off running into the house." The fire was at the Chevron refinery, and the smoke and toxic fallout sent more than 15,000 Richmond residents to the hospital with respiratory problems. Many residents insist that the 2012 fire is emblematic of a willful negligence that dates back decades, at the expense of the low-income minorities who can't afford to leave. (Okwu and Motlagh, 2014)

Clark, who was 68 years of age in 2012, recalled that the Chevron refinery flared gases, accompanied by surges of "energy and heat waves that would rock our house like we were caught in an earthquake." Smokestacks spewed black smoke that smothered his neighborhood for several days in a row. Children streamed home from schools near the refinery, and, after each explosion or fire in the refinery complex, their parents wondered how many hours or days would pass until the next one. Sandy Saeteurn was raised in North Richmond, part of an immigrant family from Laos. She arrived with her five sisters, two brothers, and mother when she was three months old. She attended elementary school across a highway from the refinery's fence. A community activist at age 27 (in 2012), she recalled: "I remember once coming out and the playground was enveloped in smoke. The smell was really awful, a strong, sort of gassy smell, and you couldn't see a couple of feet in front of you. We were all coughing" (Kay and Katz, 2012).

The Reverend Kenneth Davis, who in 2012 was living in senior housing within eyeshot of the refinery, said of North Richmond: "It's like we're on an island." Davis said, "No grocery store to get fresh fruits and vegetables and meat. The only things you can buy are drink and dope. There's nothing but old nasty rotten food on the shelves and plenty of beer, wine and whiskey" (Kay and Katz, 2012).

History of a Contaminated Community

Some blacks began migrating to Richmond from the agrarian, segregated South about 1890, but the community near the refinery grew swiftly during World War II as people streamed in, looking for jobs in the shipyards. They were segregated out of everywhere else, and housing in North Richmond was affordable—the only place open to them. And so the city of Richmond grew to a population of more than 100,000, a world apart from the chic (and expensive) enclaves of San Francisco (25 miles south) and Silicon Valley, with their seven-figure starter homes. A place in Richmond could be had for much less, "within a ring of five major oil refineries, three chemical companies, eight Superfund sites, dozens of other toxic waste sites, highways, two rail yards, ports and marine terminals where tankers dock" (Kay and Katz, 2012). Within North Richmond, closest to the steel jungle of factories and Superfund sites, the population of 3,717 (as of the 2010 U.S. Census) was 97 percent black, Latino, and Asian; the figure for Richmond as a whole was 83 percent, compared to 60 percent for California as a whole.

North Richmond could be in the Third World, given the rarity of basic urban services, lighting, and paved streets. Median household income listed in the 2010 Census was $36,875, about half of Contra Costa County's ($78,385). African Americans in North Richmond suffer heart disease and asthma at much higher rates than others in the county, and it is no secret that a toxic environment is a primary cause. Jane Kay and Cheryl

Katz wrote in *Scientific American* (2012) that "people in north and central Richmond are exposed to a greater array of contaminants, many of them at higher concentrations. Included are benzene, mercury and other hazardous air pollutants that have been linked to cancer, reproductive problems and neurological effects."

Richmond's toxic load (in air and water) routinely includes several carcinogens, some of which also have neurological effects: benzene, 1,3-butadiene, toluene, hydrocyanide, ammonia, sulfuric acid, and ethylbenzene, which can have respiratory or neurological effects—and this was *after* Chevron cut its total toxic air emissions at the refinery stacks by 43 percent between 2004 and 2012. The company has made "significant investments in environmental controls and equipment over the past four decades," said Melissa Ritchie, a refinery spokeswoman. These include burners to cut nitrogen oxides (which contribute to smog) and a 90 percent cut in burning ("flaring") of waste products (Kay and Katz, 2012).

However, some toxics (among them lead, benzene, tetrachloroethylene, and sulfuric acid) have been slow to decline. One General Chemical fire, in 1993, flooded the air with sulfuric acid. Chevron, ConocoPhillips, and BP Richmond discharged 14 tons of benzene, a cause of leukemia, in 2010. Add to this catalogue: "General Chemicals West also is a major source of emissions, including more than a ton of sulfuric acid, a chemical that can trigger respiratory problems, in 2010. Airgas Dry Ice put 16,884 pounds of corrosive ammonia into the air. Chevron's research site, Chevron Technology Center, reported more than 6,000 pounds of N-hexane and toluene, solvents that can affect the nervous system" (Kay and Katz, 2012).

The toxic load also includes polycyclic aromatic hydrocarbons (PAHs), some of which are very potent carcinogens that also are associated with neurological effects, including lower IQs for children who were exposed in the womb. Add to this emissions from a tangle of freeways that crisscross Richmond and shipborne pollution from its port, as well as emissions from other factories, and the ingredients exist for a constant stream of health-eroding toxicity.

Richmond is also home to several Superfund sites, including one that is loaded with DDT and other chemicals that leak into Richmond's harbor through a canal, all of which is used by Asian immigrants and blacks for subsistence fishing. North Richmond resident Sylvia Hopkins said: "Why do we live here? Poor people live here. People don't move here if they have a lot of money. That's the way it is in industrial towns" (Kay and Katz, 2012).

Political Organizing in Richmond

Richmond's black, poor majority has organized from time to time. In 2007, for example, they elected a Green Party mayor, Gayle McLaughlin, who pledged to bring the refineries to heel, to force them to reduce pollution and pay higher taxes. McLaughlin, who was born in 1952 (and is Anglo-American), was first elected to Richmond's City Council in 2004, then elected mayor in 2006 and 2010. Richmond thus became the largest city in the United States to be led by a Green Party mayor. By law, McLaughlin, who also founded the Richmond Progressive Alliance, could serve only two terms as mayor, so she was reelected to the City Council in 2014.

The realignment of Richmond's city government hardly budged the refineries and chemical plants, but local activism did produce some victories. However, a major fire at Chevron in 2012 provoked a lawsuit that produced a $2 million fine. The company also was forced to pay $10 million to partially defray medical costs of residents affected by its pollution. It also installed an air-pollution monitoring station with readings displayed online.

"It's a case of environmental injustice. It's a case of environmental racism," McLaughlin said. "We see how Chevron operates in Nigeria. We see how Chevron operates in Ecuador. They disregard communities that they feel aren't organized enough or aren't empowered enough to fight back." In 2013, Richmond's City Council endorsed McLaughlin's proposal to sue Chevron for "years of neglect, lax oversight and corporate indifference to safety inspection and repairs." "When we push back, we're fighting for our lives," she said. "We are fighting for our dignity as a community that has a right to health and well-being" (Okwu and Motlagh, 2014). Chevron's management mocked the lawsuit as a waste of city resources and "yet another example of failed leadership" (Okwu and Motlagh, 2014).

However, when McLaughlin petitioned the U.S. Chemical Safety Board (a U.S. federal agency that investigates chemical accidents, it backed her and the City Council, finding that "In the case of the Chevron refinery fire [in 2012], the reactive system of regulation simply did not work to prevent what was ultimately a preventable accident" (Okwu and Motlagh, 2014). To most of North Richmond's weary residents, the ruling was a restatement of obvious, daily reality.

Further Reading

Chiles, Nick. "8 Horrifying Examples of Corporations Mistreating Black Communities with Environmental Racism." *Atlanta Black Star*, February 12, 2015. http://atlantablackstar.com/2015/02/12/8-horrifying-examples-of

-corporations-mistreating-black-communities-with-environmental-racism/

"Hazmat Team Controls Spill Near Chevron Refinery in Richmond." KRON-4 TV. San Francisco, June 9, 2017. https://www.kron4.com/news/hazmat-team-controls-spill-near-chevron-refinery-in-richmond/

Kay, Jane, and Cheryl Katz. "Pollution, Poverty and People of Color: Living with Industry: Low-Income Residents in North Richmond, Calif., Save Money on Shelter, but Pay the Price in Health." Special Report: Pollution, Poverty and People of Color; Communities across the United States Face Environmental Injustices." *Scientific American*, June, 2012. https://www.scientificamerican.com/article/pollution-poverty-people-color-living-industry

Okwu, Michael, and Jason Motlagh. "California City Wages War Against Environmental Racism." Al Jazeera, February 17, 2014. http://america.aljazeera.com/watch/shows/america-tonight/america-tonight-blog/2014/2/17/calif-city-leaderslockhornswithoilgiantoverhealthworries.html

Alaska's Pebble Mine: Corporate Gold vs. Natives' Salmon

The Pebble Partnership has proposed a 1,700-foot-deep, two-mile-wide open-pit mine 200 miles southwest of Anchorage. The mine, which would have underground mines as well, would dump mining wastes into some of the world's most fertile salmon spawning grounds and the home of Earth's largest wild sockeye run. Twenty-five federally recognized Alaskan Native tribes live in the Bristol Bay watershed, having maintained a culture and economy based on salmon for at least 4,000 years. On average, 37 million sockeye return each year to Bristol Bay, supporting more than 12,000 Eskimo and non-Native commercial fishing people. The Pebble Mine could turn part of this salmon spawning ground into a toxic dump. While the United States put brakes on the mine's development under President Barack Obama, the administration of Donald Trump by 2017 was eager to revive it.

A Seven-Square-Mile Strip Mine

Joby Warrick of the *Washington Post* (2015) described the region's "marshy lowlands [which] are dotted with kettle lakes and crisscrossed by countless streams. In the spawning season, icy rivers turn into roiling torrents of red fish as tens of millions of Pacific salmon make their way inland to spawn." The area has been known as a rich potential source of gold for 30 years, but the day is past when freelancers could pan chunks of gold from streams or dig them out of the earth. The Pebble Mine's riches are embedded in fine particles throughout the soil. "To extract the gold profitably," wrote Warrick, "requires excavating huge amounts of soil and rock from an open-pit mine that could, according to preliminary design plans, eventually cover a seven-square-mile area, making it one of the world's largest. The project would create mountains of rocky spoils, while the wastewater from extracting the ore would be kept in large containment ponds."

Anglo American, a mining conglomerate headquartered in London, proposed to join with British Columbia's Northern Dynasty Minerals in digging the mine near Bristol Bay. It would include facilities to crush and separate rock as well as tailings (waste) dumps that would eventually become far larger than the mine, which itself would be the largest open-pit mine in North America. Potential yield over the life of the mine has been estimated at 110 million ounces of gold and 80 billion pounds of copper. Even so, the mining companies insisted that salmon runs and wildlife habitat would not be harmed. An EPA assessment issued in March 2012 came to a different conclusion: "The project would entail the destruction of 55 to 87 miles worth of so-far-untouched streams and 2,500 acres of wetlands—and that doesn't even begin to address the potential for disaster if any of the tailings ponds were to leak their acidic water and heavy metals into salmon spawning grounds" ("Bristol Bay," 2013). The EPA assessment was a best case, assuming that earthen dams (some of them 700 feet high) holding tailings ponds intact would not break or leak.

In September 2013, Anglo American withdrew from an industrial consortium seeking to develop the Pebble Mine. "Our focus has been to prioritize capital to projects with the highest value and lowest risks within our portfolio, and reduce the capital required to sustain such projects during the pre-approval phases of development as part of a more effective, value-driven capital allocation model," said Mark Cutifani, chief executive of Anglo American ("Anglo American Withdraws," 2013). Given such language, the company seemed to have decided that the Pebble Mine was too risky and too expensive, given resistance, including probable legal action under several environmental laws, by the people living there.

Indigenous People's Reactions

Callan J. Chythlook-Sifsof, a Yupik/Inupiat Eskimo who was raised in Aleknagik, Alaska, an indigenous Yupik Eskimo village near the site of the proposed mine, recalled his youth in a community whose members fished for a living before he became a member of the U.S. snowboarding team in the 2010 Winter Olympics:

> I spent my summers on the back deck of family fishing boats working multiple fisheries. The boats and fish camps are maintained by generations of families harvesting salmon not only for income, but also for food. I remember long days of processing hundreds of pounds of salmon, setting nets, cleaning and filleting, filling tubs of salt brine, putting fresh water in clean white buckets and hanging neat rows to dry and smoke. . . . As a child, I had no idea what magic this life was—it was just the way we did things. It's the way many Alaska Natives live—through self-reliance and hard work to harvest the many gifts of the land and sea. (Chythlook-Sifsof, 2013)

The native peoples who had lived along this coast for many generations are no fools. They know environmental poison when they see it. Their way of life depends on the salmon runs, which are both the economic and spiritual center of their lives. Most Alaskans agreed with them.

In a survey by the Natural Resources Defense Council, 68 percent of Alaskans opposed the mine. More than 75 percent of 900,000 public comments on the project collected by the EPA opposed the project. "It's truly alarming," wrote Chythlook-Sifsof (2013), "when Pebble's chief executive officer, John Shively, blithely says that, sure, the mine will damage some salmon habitat, but the company will just build 'comparable' habitat nearby. His comments show a lack of understanding of salmon life cycles, habitat and ecosystems—not to mention the people of Bristol Bay" (Chythlook-Sifsof, 2013). Native peoples urged the EPA to reject the plans for the mine under the aegis of the federal Clean Water Act.

Mine Permit Refused by Army Corps of Engineers in 2014

A total of 360 scientists from the United States, Poland, Canada, Australia, and other countries signed a letter on February 3, 2014, urging the EPA to disapprove the Pebble Mine development. "Over three years, EPA compiled the best, most current science on the Bristol Bay watershed to understand how large-scale mining could impact salmon and water in this unique area of unparalleled natural resources," said Dennis McLerran, regional administrator for EPA Region 10. "Our report concludes that large-scale mining poses risks to salmon and the tribal communities that have depended on them for thousands of years. Based on the results of the assessment, we are very concerned about the prospect of large-scale mining in the unique and biologically rich watersheds of southwest

Alaska's Bristol Bay," the scientists wrote. "The preponderance of evidence presented in the watershed assessment indicates that large-scale hard rock mining in the Bristol Bay watershed threatens a world-class fishery and uniquely rich ecosystem, and we urge the Administration to act quickly to protect the area. Therefore, we urge EPA to use its authority under the Clean Water Act to take the necessary next steps to protect Bristol Bay" ("360 Scientists," 2014).

Following the appeal by the 360 scientists as well as a visit to Washington, D.C., by representatives of the 31 Native villages in the Bristol Bay watershed—all adamantly opposed to the Pebble Mine proposal—in late February 2014, the EPA refused to allow the U.S. Army Corps of Engineers to issue a permit to Northern Dynasty Minerals Ltd of Canada. "Extensive scientific study has given us ample reason to believe that the Pebble Mine would likely have significant and irreversible negative impacts on the Bristol Bay watershed and its abundant salmon fisheries," EPA administrator Gina McCarthy said.

"It's why EPA is taking this step forward in our effort to ensure protection for the world's most productive salmon fishery from the risks it faces from what could be one of the largest open pit mines on earth. This process is not something the Agency does very often, but Bristol Bay is an extraordinary and unique resource." The EPA statement pointed out that water quality is crucial to the area's average annual run of 37.5 million sockeye salmon as well as smaller runs of Chinook, coho, pink, and chum salmon. "In addition, it is home to more than 20 other fish species, 190 bird species, and more than 40 terrestrial mammal species, including bears, moose, and caribou," the EPA said. Digging an open-pit gold and copper mine a mile deep and 2.5 miles wide would require at least three earthen tailings dams as high as 650 feet that "would irreparably harm the ecosystem" ("Native Alaskans," 2014).

On December 16, 2014, President Obama signed a presidential memorandum that declared the Bristol Bay watershed, "these beautiful and pristine waters," off limits from all future oil and gas drilling ("Obama Declares," 2014). He invoked Native Alaskans' key role in preserving the watershed by shielding it. The order did not address the Pebble Mine proposal, which had already been denied. With so much at stake, however, the miners and drillers would not take "no" for an answer.

Forewarned: Tailings Spill at Mt. Polley Mine

Before dawn on August 4, 2014, three weeks after the Pebble Mine's rejection and as its sponsors were getting ready to resubmit the proposal, a tailings pond burst in British Columbia's Mount Polley Mine, sending 4 billion gallons of mining waste (2.6 billion gallons of water mixed into a slurry with 1.2 billion gallons of fine sediment laced with metals) into rivers and lakes awaiting the return of salmon. Knight Piesold Consulting, the firm that designed the burst dam, had also been hired as a contractor to design the tailings pond for the Pebble Mine, according to a report filed in 2006 by Northern Dynasty Mines Inc. with the Alaska Department of Natural Resources.

Critics of the Pebble Mine proposal saw the Mount Polley Mine tailings spill as a prelude and a warning. "We don't want this to happen in Bristol Bay," said Kim Williams of Dillingham, director of Nunamta Alukestai (which means "Caretakers of Our Land"), a conservation group of Alaska Native tribes and corporations, to the *Cordova Times*. "With all the similarities between Pebble and the Mount Polley copper mine, we're urging the EPA to take immediate action to finalize mine waste restrictions in Bristol Bay. Our hearts go out to those in British Columbia who live downstream from this devastating mine failure." "It's Bristol Bay's worst nightmare," said Carol Ann Woody, a fisheries scientist with the Center for Science in Public Participation ("Company," 2014).

"The Pebble project would be bigger—a lot bigger," wrote Joel Reynolds, western director and senior attorney for the National Resources Defense Council, in the *Huffington Post*. "While Imperial Metals has been mining about 20,000 tons per day at its Mount Polley mine, Northern Dynasty has anticipated about ten times that at Pebble, with a tailings pond many times larger in footprint and scale" ("Company," 2014).

Several First Nations people live in the area of the spill and depend on its salmon runs. "Our communities are filled with sorrow, frustration and anger as they are left wondering just what poisons are in the water, and what is being done to address this disaster," said Williams Lake chief Ann Louie and Xat'sull chief Bev Sellars. "Monday's devastating tailings pond breach is something that both our First Nations have lived in fear of for many years," the chiefs said. "We have raised repeated concerns about the safety and security of this mine, but they were ignored. Now we are being ignored again. Enough is enough" ("Horrific," 2014).

Pebble Bay Back in Play

Under the Obama administration, the EPA had committed three years to study of the mine proposal, gathering several million public comments, most of them opposed. Alaskans, living in a state where a sustainable fishery is written into the state constitution, were overwhelmingly opposed, backing up the commercial fishing people and Native Americans who have lived and fished in the area for 10,000 years. Someone added up the number of salmon that the Bristol Bay fishery had provided Alaskans, and came up with an estimate of 2 billion. "It took 95 years to catch the first billion, and just 38 years to catch the second," wrote Brendan Jones in the *New York Times* (2017). Alaska's U.S. senator Ted Stevens, a Republican who usually sided with miners, opposed the project. President Obama's EPA agreed, concluding that Pebble Mine would commit "irreversible" damage to the wetlands, resulting in "complete loss of fish habitat due to elimination, dewatering and fragmentation of streams, wetlands and other aquatic resources" (Jones, 2017).

Then Trump was elected and appointed Scott Pruitt to head the EPA. Jones, a commercial fisherman at Bristol Bay, wrote in the *New York Times*, "On May 1 [2017], Scott Pruitt, the new administrator of the EPA, met with Tom Collier, the head of the Pebble Mine project [of Northern Dynasty Minerals], for breakfast. Later that same morning, Mr. Pruitt ordered the EPA regulations scrapped, telling the company it could proceed with permitting. And like that, the mine was back in play" (Jones, 2017). The battle switched to the actual permitting process, with its complex system of environmental impact statements at the federal and state levels. For example, on June 26, 2019, the House of Representatives passed amendment 90 to the Energy and Water Appropriations Act (H.R. 2740) bill. If passed by both chambers of Congress and signed by President Donald Trump, an unlikely event, the amendment would prohibit the U.S. Army Corps of Engineers from using funds to issue a permit for the mine.

Thus, this story is not over. Northern Dynasty originally had proposed to blow the largest manufactured hole on Earth in one of the planet's last large salmon fisheries and call it "sustainable." The revised proposal calls for a smaller hole but, as Jones noted, "Once drilling begins, permits are easily amended. What mine in the history of the world has ever left gold in the ground? The company also proposes that the mine's toxic wastewater be kept in a reservoir protected by an earthen dam—in one of North America's most active earthquake zones" (Jones, 2017).

Further Reading

"Anglo American Withdraws from Pebble Mine." Environment News Service, September 2, 2013. http://ens-newswire.com/2013/09/20/anglo-american-withdraws-from-alaskas-pebble-mine

"Bristol Bay Tribes' Fight to Fend Off Pebble Mine Highlighted in *National Geographic*." Indian Country Today Media Network, November 19, 2013.

Cases: United States West

  http://indiancountrytodaymedianetwork.com/bristol-bay-tribes-fight-to-fend-off-pebble-mine-highlighted-in-national-geographic

Chythlook-Sifsof, Callan J. "Native Alaska, under Threat." *New York Times*, June 28, 2013. http://www.nytimes.com/2013/06/28/opinion/native-culture-under-threat.html

"Company That Designed Burst B.C. Tailings Pond Was Hired by Pebble Mine in Bristol Bay." Indian Country Today Media Network, August 8, 2014. http://indiancountrytodaymedianetwork.com/2014/08/08/company-designed-burst-bc-tailings-pond-was-hired-pebble-mine-bristol-bay-156315

"Horrific Toxic Spill in B.C. Called Another Exxon Valdez." Indian Country Today Media Network, August 7, 2014. http://www.nativenewstoday.com/2014/08/07/horrific-toxic-spill-in-b-c-called-another-exxon-valdez

Jones, Brendan. "A Gold Rush in Salmon Country." *New York Times*, November 24, 2017. https://www.nytimes.com/2017/11/24/opinion/sunday/gold-mine-salmon.html

"Native Alaskans Laud Environmental Protection Agency's Nixing of Pebble Mine in Bristol Bay." Indian Country Today Media Network, March 3, 2014. http://indiancountrytodaymedianetwork.com/2014/03/03/native-alaskans-laud-environmental-protection-agencys-nixing-pebble-mine-bristol-bay

"Obama Declares Bristol Bay Off Limits to New Oil and Gas Drilling Leases." Indian Country Today Media Network, December 17, 2014. http://indiancountrytodaymedianetwork.com/2014/12/17/obama-declares-bristol-bay-limits-new-oil-and-gas-drilling-leases-158329

"360 Scientists Urge Environmental Protection Agency to Quash Bristol Bay Pebble Mine." Indian Country Today Media Network, February 14, 2014. http://indiancountrytodaymedianetwork.com/2014/02/14/360-scientists-urge-environmental-protection-agency-quash-bristol-bay-pebble-mine-153559

Warrick, Joby. "Gold vs. Salmon: EPA Becomes Target by Employing Rare Preemptive 'Veto.'" *Washington Post*, February 15, 2015. http://www.washingtonpost.com/national/health-science/internal-memos-spur-accusations-of-bias-as-epa-moves-to-block-gold-mine/2015/02/15/3ff101c0-b2ba-11e4-854b-a38d13486ba1_story.html

Alaska Natives: Swamped by Warming

  Temperatures in Alaska, as elsewhere in the Arctic, have risen much more rapidly than global averages since the 1970s. Gunter Weller, director of the Center for Global Change and Arctic System Research at the University of Alaska in Fairbanks, said mean temperatures in the state have increased by 5° F in the summer and 10° F in the winter in 30 years.

Moreover, the Arctic ice field has shrunk by 40 percent to 50 percent over the last few decades and has lost 10 percent of its thickness, studies show. "These are pretty large signals, and they've had an effect on the entire physical environment," Weller said (Murphy, 2001, A-1).

Temperature increases are expected to continue. These changes pose serious problems for Alaska Native populations, including "malnutrition and food insecurity from lack of access to subsistence food; contamination of food and water; increasing economic, mental, and social problems from loss of culture and traditional livelihood; increases in infectious diseases; and the loss of buildings and infrastructure from permafrost erosion and thawing, resulting in the relocation of entire communities" ("Indigenous Peoples," 2014). Permafrost, subsoil that formerly remained frozen, now sometimes dissolves into a melting, muddy mess, no longer the "glue" that provides a base for building.

Evidence of rapid warming is everywhere. In the Eskimo village of Kaktovik, Alaska, on the Arctic Ocean roughly 250 miles north of the Arctic Circle, for example, a robin built a nest in town during 2003—not an unusual event in more temperate latitudes, but quite a departure from the usual in a place where, in the Inupiat Eskimo language, no name exists for robins. In the Okpilak River valley, which has heretofore been too cold and dry for willows, they are sprouting profusely. Never mind the fact that in the Inupiat language *Okpilak* means "river with no willows." Three kinds of salmon have been caught in nearby waters in places where they were once unknown.

Correspondent Jerry Bowen, on the CBS Morning News on August 29, 2002, from Barrow, Alaska, the northernmost town in Alaska, quoted residents who had just witnessed their first mosquitoes. Ice cellars carved out of permafrost were melting as well, forcing local Native people to borrow space in electric freezers for the first time to store whale meat. Average temperatures in Barrow have risen 4° F during the past 30 years (Bowen, 2002). The average date at which the last snow melts at Barrow in the spring or summer has receded about 40 days between 1940 and the years after 2000, from early July to, some years, as early as mid or late May (Wohlforth, 2004, 27).

Multiple Perils for Native Alaskans

Coastal erosion is provoking health problems, including "loss of clean water for drinking and hygiene, saltwater intrusion, and sewage contamination that could cause respiratory and gastrointestinal infections, pneumonia, and skin infections" ("Indigenous Peoples," 2014). Permafrost thaw also threatens Native food supplies as it destroys ice cellars or icehouses used to store meat acquired by hunters. Food may be spoiled with risk of contamination and consequent illness, forcing many Native people to rely on imported food that is less healthy and much more expensive than anything caught by hunters.

In the roughly 230 federally recognized Alaska Native communities and villages many residents obtain sustenance by hunting walrus, caribou, and other land animals, as well as fishing for salmon and other species. In Alaska, these climate-induced changes threaten village infrastructure, water supplies, health, and safety. Loss of sea ice as well as extensive wildfires, occurring with a frequency and ferocity unknown before, have altered the hunting landscape on both land and sea in Alaska. Lichens, which provide food for caribou in winter, do not recover from fire for 70 years.

In Alaska, where roughly 80 percent of glaciers are receding, forests of dead spruce surround Anchorage, a casualty of a spruce-beetle epidemic caused at least in part by rising temperatures, which accelerate the insect's reproduction cycle. Large patches of Alaskan forests have been described as drowning and turning gray as thawing ground sinks under them. Trees and roadside utility poles, destabilized by thawing, lean at crazy angles. The warming has contributed a new phrase to the English language in Alaska—"the drunken forest."

Warming temperatures in Alaska (and elsewhere) are melting glaciers. On one hand, warmer temperatures in rivers and streams are harming salmon and other cold-water fish. In addition, the release of meltwater from these melting glaciers also releases persistent organic pollutants (POPs) that were used in pesticides and herbicides in the middle latitudes beginning in the 1950s and then deposited on glaciers by atmospheric circulation. Now these chemicals have become part of the habitat, as they recycle through the food chain from generation to generation. According to one State of Alaska report, "First [country] foods in contaminated areas may no longer be safe to eat" (Verbrugge, 2010).

U.S. General Accountability Office studies in 2003 and 2009 described more than 200 Alaska Native villages that were being affected by flooding and erosion; 31 of them were facing enough of a threat to consider moving. Flooding threats in Alaska can come from several sources: early snowmelt, heavy rain and snowfall, melting permafrost, rising sea levels, and melting sea ice (Curry et al., 2011, 12). The situation at Newtok and Shishmaref, which are sliding into the sea, is shared by several other villages. At least 26 were in imminent danger by 2010, according to the U.S. Army Corps of Engineers, which also estimated the cost of moving one of them,

Newtok, at $130 million (McLean, 2010). A new sea wall was built during 2006 along the village of Kivalina, costing $3 million, to quell erosion. It has done little good. (For details on coastal erosion, see "Environmental Racism and the Demise of an Ice World" in chapter 2, "Unifying Themes.")

Changes Exceed Historical Experience

Rural indigenous Alaska (excluding the North Slope, with its oil) is the largest poverty-stricken area in the United States. Household incomes are low, while fuel and other goods acquired in the cash economy are more expensive than elsewhere, largely because of distance. Gasoline that may cost $2.50 per gallon in the "Lower 48" sold in 2015 for $5.00 to $8.00. The prices for food purchased commercially are 200 to 300 percent what most urban-dwelling people pay. Unemployment rates are high as well, as so few jobs are available that provide cash income. Given economic necessity as well as tradition and spiritual relationships, "country food" remains important. Because of this reliance, climate change affects many rural indigenous Alaskans (as it does other Arctic peoples) as a matter of daily survival.

Thinning sea and river ice is the talk of many indigenous coastal villages in Alaska. Changes affect hunters' lives, making harvest of wild foods more dangerous. Animals migrate differently than in the past. Changes to permafrost alter river runoff. Sea levels are rising, and tidal fluctuations have become more extreme. Some fish species have migrated northward in ways that traditional knowledge does not anticipate. Melting permafrost under lakes and streams contaminates some villages' water supplies, as "deteriorating water and sewage systems increase the risk of skin and respiratory infections. Warming may bring new diseases to the Arctic through diseases in harvested foods or through northward-moving insect and vertebrate vectors such as the northward movement of giardiasis in beaver that follow the climate-induced expansion of shrubs in western Alaska" (Cochran et al., 2013, 557).

Yup'ik Eskimo leader Caleb Pungowiyi, special adviser on Native affairs with NOAA's Marine Mammal Commission (who passed away in 2011), reported from Kotzebue, Alaska, that beginning in the late 1970s, Alaska Natives in communities along the coast of the northern Bering and Chukchi Seas noticed changes in the weather affecting the ocean and animals living there. They had been accustomed to changes year to year, but much of what they now see was outside of their historical experience.

> The winds are stronger, commonly 10 to 25 miles per hour, and there are fewer calm days. The wind may shift in direction, but remains strong for long periods. In spring, the winds change the distribution of the sea ice

and combine with warm temperatures to speed up the melting of ice and snow. When the ice melts or moves away early, many marine mammals go with it, taking them too far away to hunt. Near some villages (such as Savoonga, Diomede, and Shishmaref), depending on the geography of the coast, the wind may force the pack ice into shore, making it impossible to get boats to open water to go hunting or to move boats through if they are already out. The high winds also make it difficult to travel in boats for hunting (even winds of 10 to 12 mph from the wrong direction can create waves 2–3 feet high, stopping small boats), reducing the number of days that hunters can go out. For all these reasons, access to animals during the spring hunting period is lower now than it was before. (Pungowiyi, n.d.)

During the summer, winds blew more frequently from the south, bringing more rain than previously. Sea ice has been receding, and with more open water in the fall, winds and waves as high as 30 feet have battered the coast, eroding village land, eroding what used to be sandy beaches to rocky remnants (Pungowiyi, n.d.). Pungowiyi described ways in which changes in seasonal ice formation influences the flow of nutrients in the seawater: "The formation of sea ice in fall has been late in many recent years, due largely to warmer winters, though winds play a role as well. In such years, the ice, when it does form, is thinner than usual, which contributes to early break-up in spring. Another aspect of late freeze-up is the way in which sea ice forms. Under normal conditions, the water is cold in fall, and permafrost under the water and near the shoreline helps create ice crystals on the sea floor. When they are large enough, these crystals float to the top, bringing with them sediments" (Pungowiyi, n.d.).

Precipitation has become more variable as well, including long periods during the long, cold seasons with little or no snow, followed by other periods (notably in late winter and early spring) with heavy amounts. "The lack of snow makes it difficult for polar bears and ringed seals to make dens for giving birth or, in the case of male polar bears, to seek protection from the weather," Pungowiyi reported. "The lack of ringed seal dens may affect the numbers and condition of polar bears, which prey on ringed seals and often seek out the dens. Hungry polar bears may be more likely to approach villages and encounter people" (Pungowiyi, n.d.).

Life is changing on the tundra in other ways as well: "In spring, bird migrations are early. Geese and songbirds have been arriving in late April, earlier than ever before. Sudden cold snaps at this time of year can harm the birds. Snipe seem to be affected most, perhaps because they need unfrozen ground to feed, and many die in such cold spells. . . . In the warm summers, especially if they are also dry, many different kinds of insects appear on the tundra. These include lots of caterpillars on bushes, and then butterflies. Other bugs that haven't been seen before have appeared, though mosquitoes are still the same" (Pungowiyi, n.d.).

Further Reading

Bowen, Jerry. "Dramatic Climate Change in Alaska." CBS News Transcripts; CBS Morning News. August 29, 2002.

Cochran, P., O. H. C. Huntington, S. Pungowiyi, S. F. Tom, H. P. Chapin, III, N. G. Maynard, and S. F. Trainor. "Indigenous Frameworks for Observing and Responding to Climate Change in Alaska." *Climatic Change* 120 (2013): 557–567.

Curry, Renee, Charissa Eichman, Amanda Staudt, Garrit Voggesser, and Myra Wilensky. *Facing the Storm: Indian Tribes, Climate-Induced Weather Extremes, and the Future for Indian Country*. Washington, D.C.: National Wildlife Federation, March 2011. http://www.indiaenvironmentportal.org.in/content/336721/facing-the-storm-indian-tribes-climate-induced-weather-extremes-and-the-future-for-indian-country/

"Indigenous Peoples, Lands, and Resources." Chapter 12, *National Climate Assessment*, U.S. Global Change Research Program, 2014. http://nca2014.globalchange.gov/report/sectors/indigenous-peoples

McLean, Kirsty Galloway. *Advance Guard: Climate Change Impacts, Adaptation, Mitigation and Indigenous Peoples: A Compendium of Case Studies*. United Nations University Institute of Advanced Studies. Traditional Knowledge Initiative. Darwin, Australia, 2010. http://archive.ias.unu.edu/resource_centre/UNU_Advance_Guard_Compendium_2010_final_web.pdf

Murphy, Kim. "Front-Row Exposure to Global Warming; Climate: Engineers Say Alaskan Village Could Be Lost as Sea Encroaches." *Los Angeles Times*, July 8, 2001, A-1.

Pungowiyi, Caleb. Native Observations of Climate Change in the Marine Environment of the Bering Strait Region. NOAA, n.d. Accessed July 23, 2014. https://www.pmel.noaa.gov/arctic-zone/essay_pungowiyi.html

Verbrugge, L. "Traditional Foods in Alaska: Potential Threats from Contaminants and Climate Change. State of Alaska Division of Public Health." 2010. http://www.climatechange.alaska.gov/docs/afe10/3_Verbrugge.pdf

Wohlforth, Charles. *The Whale and the Supercomputer: On the Northern Front of Climate Change*. New York: North Point Press/Farrar, Straus and Giroux, 2004.

The Point Hope Eskimos: An Atomic Harbor and a Nuclear Dump as a Neighbor

At times, nuclear weapons have been proposed as construction devices in Indian Country. This is not a parody of *Dr. Strangelove*. During 1958, seeking "peaceful" uses for the weapons, the Atomic Energy Commission

(AEC) seriously, officially, proposed dropping five atomic bombs at Cape Thompson on the North Slope of Alaska to blast out a harbor. Project Chariot, as it was called, was part of the agrarian-sounding Operation Plowshare, named from the biblical concept of peacemaking, beating swords into ploughshares, a piece of bureaucratic poetry invoking civilian uses for nuclear bombs. Project Chariot's authors had forgotten, disregarded, or did not know that they were proposing bombing the homeland of the Point Hope Eskimos on the North Slope of Alaska. The plan called for underground explosions that would force land to sink into the sea.

The plans were precise—five bombs with 100 times the explosive power of the first atomic bomb that had obliterated and radiated Hiroshima and Nagasaki. The AEC and other agencies recruited Alaskan political leaders and newspaper publishers, but residents in the Inupait village of Point Hope, about 450 people living 30 miles from the intended target site, rallied against the harbor project as ecological insanity.

Nuclear Boosterism

When word reached people on Point Hope that their homeland was being suggested as a sacrifice for nuclear boosterism, they were outraged, especially after the Bureau of Land Management approved the AEC's request for a test site.

The plan to blast a harbor at Point Hope was championed by Edward Teller (1908–2003), who was popularly known as the "father" of the hydrogen bomb, although he disdained the moniker. Notwithstanding his preference in nicknames, Teller, who was also known for his explosive personality, was an advocate of using nuclear energy to address many technological problems, of which the idea of opening a harbor near Point Hope was one. Teller toured Alaska promoting the idea as the territory was preparing for statehood, and at one point rallied newspaper editors and civic boosters behind the idea. Given his recklessness with nuclear bombs, Teller has long been considered an inspiration for the main character in Stanley Kubrick's *Dr. Strangelove* (1964), a parody of atomic insanity. This proposal, however, was no Hollywood movie.

The Plowshare name was attributed to Isaiah 2:3–5, a passage focused on repurposing the weapons of war for the tools of peace:

> *They will beat their swords into plowshares*
> *and their spears into pruning hooks.*
> *Nation will not take up sword against nation,*
> *nor will they train for war anymore.*

Teller believed that nuclear blasts could be contained, and that a radiation-free bomb was on the way. He loved to imagine that nuclear explosions were so easily controlled that the Chariot team could "dig a harbor in the shape of a polar bear, if desired" (Mead, 2012). He called the use of atomic bombs as excavation devices "the nuclear shovel." "Among other things the Point Hope people were told that the fish in and around the Pacific Proving Grounds were not made radioactive by nuclear weapons tests and [there would not be] . . . any danger to anyone if the fish were utilized; that the effects of nuclear weapons testing never injured any people, anywhere" (Mead, 2012).

Operation Plowshare had plans for much more than Point Hope. According to one retrospective (Mead, 2012):

> Plowshare's vision was as enormous as its tools. One proposal, called Project Carryall, would have used nuclear bombs to cut a new 11,000 foot long railway pass through the Bristol Mountains in California. According to a 1964 feasibility study, Carryall would have required 22 bombs ranging between 20 and 200 kilotons to gouge out the deepest parts of the pass, which would have measured about 350 feet deep. Parts of the pass ranging around 100 feet deep would have been dug with conventional non-nuclear bombs. The nukes were to be saved, as with the Alaska project, for the heavy lifting.

The Plowshare project produced 27 nuclear test explosions, most of them at a federal government nuclear test site in Nevada, part of which was described as: "Project Sedan . . . the second Plowshare experiment to be carried out . . . basically was a test to see how big of a hole a nuclear bomb could make." It proved to be a *really big* hole. The 104-kiloton device moved 12 million tons of earth, producing the largest man-made crater in the country, which measured 1,280 feet wide and 320 feet deep. Shot in Nevada, Sedan spewed fallout over Iowa, Illinois, Nebraska, and South Dakota, and contaminated more Americans than any other nuclear test in the United States (Mead, 2012; Fay, 2018, 95).

Operation Plowshare also played a role in the development of natural-gas drilling technology. Having tried dynamite, machine guns, bazookas, and napalm to extract the gas from unforgiving (the oil industry jargon is "tight") underground rock formations, Operation Plowshare was called upon to pulverize it. "In 1967," wrote Lawrence Wright in *The New Yorker* (2018, 46), "the Atomic Energy Commission, working with Lawrence Livermore Laboratory and the El Paso Natural Gas Company, exploded a 29-kiloton nuclear bomb, dubbed Gasbuggy, 4,000 feet below the surface, near Farmington, New Mexico [at the northeastern edge of the Navajo Nation]." The explosions proved successful at liberating the gas from the pulverized rubble, but one side effect that the project's engineers should have anticipated made it unmarketable: The gas was radioactive.

An "Overture to the New Era"?

The proponents of Project Chariot seem to have forgotten that the Point Hope area was populated. An editorial in the July 24, 1960 *Fairbanks News-Miner* said, "We think the holding of a huge nuclear blast in Alaska would be a fitting overture to the new era which is opening for our state" (Mead, 2012). A few conservationists joined the Eskimos in opposition, which grew when news of the proposal reached a broader ecologically oriented community in the "Lower 48," including the Sierra Club, the Wilderness Society, and the Committee on Nuclear Information, led by Barry Commoner. The growing wave of popular revulsion against the idea provoked the AEC to suspend Project Chariot in 1962, although it was never fully canceled.

Aside from its potential ecological damage and radiation exposure to the Eskimos, the atomic harbor project had other problems, once the boosters' gloss wore off. One major obstacle was the fact that the harbor had absolutely no commercial potential. Nuclear researchers could not leave the site alone, however. They turned their Project Chariot into a study of how nuclear fallout could affect the indigenous communities of Point Hope, Noatak, and Kivalina, "to measure the size of bomb necessary to render a population dependent after local food sources have become too dangerous to eat due to extreme levels of radiation" (Davis, 1973, 143).

Radiation Tests' Effects on Eskimos

After the harbor project was suspended, the AEC conducted environmental studies, which suggested that radioactive contamination from the blasts it had proposed would have adversely affected local people as it rendered radioactive the animals they hunted. The AEC studies indicated that even without local atomic blasts, radiation from other blasts' fallout in distant locations, such as the U.S. Southwest, carried by prevailing winds, was moving with unexpected rapidity up the Eskimo food chain from lichen, which was consumed by caribou, which then were eaten by the native peoples. The Eskimos paid for these tests with abnormally high rates of cancer for at least 30 years afterward (Vandegraft, 1993).

The Point Hope site was also contaminated with radioactive materials in 1962 during an experiment, carried out by the U.S. Geological Survey under license from the AEC, that gauged the effects of radioactive bioaccumulation on caribou, lichen, and humans in the area. For the test, the AEC planted radioactive materials in 15,000 pounds of soil obtained from a Nevada nuclear test site (on Western Shoshone land mainly in Nevada) around Point Hope. This soil contained strontium-85 and cesium-137 (Badger, 1992, B-5). The strontium typically would have lost all its radioactivity years before its deposit at Point Hope, and the cesium would still have had about half its radioactivity after 30 years, according to government officials.

The Native people of the Point Hope area were never informed of the experiment. In fact, they didn't learn of the project until a University of Alaska researcher made a Freedom of Information Act request in 1992. After it became known, the residents demanded and won cleanup funds from the U.S. Department of Energy more than 30 years after they had unknowingly been used as test subjects with live radioactivity (LaDuke and Cruz, 2013, 43).

Cancer Rates Rise

For many years, the Inuit in the area had suffered cancer rates that far exceeded national averages. The government acknowledged that soil in the area contains "trace amounts" of radiation, but denied that its experimental nuclear dump had caused the Inuits' increased cancer rate. According to Dan O'Neill, the nuclear dump was clearly illegal and contained "a thousand times . . . the allowable standard for this kind of nuclear burial" (Grinde and Johansen, 1995, 238–239).

The nuclear waste that was buried near Point Hope had remained unmarked for 30 years, during which time hunters crossed it to pursue game and caribou migrated through it. Not until September 1992 did the U.S. government admit that it had buried 15,000 tons of radioactive soil at Cape Thompson, 25 miles from Point Hope, on the Chukchi Sea in northwestern Alaska. Until the dumps were disclosed during the late 1990s, the Inuit in Port Hope had no clue as to why the incidence of cancer in their village had jumped to 578 per 100,000 within two generations. Some doctors blamed the rise in cancer rates on smoking by the Inuit. In 1997, Dr. Robert Bowerman, chief medical officer of the borough of Barrow, Alaska, published findings linking the increase in cancer incidence to the burial of nuclear waste near Port Hope (Colomeda, 1998).

"I can't tell you how angry I am that they considered our home to be nothing but a big wasteland," said Jeslie Kaleak, mayor of the North Slope Borough, which governs eight Arctic villages, including Point Hope. "They didn't give a damn about the people who live up here." When Frank Murkowski, Republican senator from Alaska, visited the village, an elderly woman threw herself at him and shouted, "You have poisoned our land!" (Egan, 1992, A-26).

Energy Department spokesman Tom Gerusky acknowledged that the Geological Survey erred in burying the waste but said a person standing on the mound for a year would be exposed to only a small fraction of radiation, the same amount received on a single cross-country jet flight (Badger, 1992, B-5). A series of studies in the 1980s by the federal Centers for Disease Control and the Indian Health Service concluded that while radiation from Soviet tests was detected in a number of Alaska villages during the 1960s, the bulk of cancers in the region involve lung and cervical cancer, types that are not generally associated with exposure to radiation.

Further Reading

Badger, T. A. "Villagers Learning a Frightening Secret: U.S. Reveals That It Has Buried Radioactive Soil Near Alaska Town 30 Years Ago. Residents Fear That Atomic Testing May Have Damaged the Food Chain." *Los Angeles Times*, December 20, 1992, B-5.

Colomeda, Lori A. Salish Kootenai College, Pablo Montana. "Indigenous Health." Speech delivered in Brisbane, Australia, September 9, 1998. http://www.ldb.org/vl/ai/lori_b98.htm

Davis, Robert. *The Genocide Machine in Canada: The Pacification of the North*. Black Rose Books, 1973, 143–151.

Egan, Timothy. "Eskimos Learn They've Been Living Amid Secret Pits of Radioactive Soil." *New York Times*, December 6, 1992, A-26.

Fay, Jennifer. *Inhospitable World: Cinema in the Time of the Anthropocene*. Oxford: Oxford University Press, 2018.

Grinde, Donald A., Jr., and Bruce E. Johansen. *Ecocide of Native America: Environmental Destruction of Indian Lands and Peoples*. Santa Fe, NM: Clear Light, 1995.

LaDuke, Winona, and Sean Aaron Cruz. *The Militarization of Indian Country*. East Lansing: Michigan State University Press, 2013.

Mead, Derek. "The U.S.'s Insane Attempt to Build a Harbor with a Two Megaton Nuclear Bomb; The AEC Almost Destroyed an Alaska Town in Its Attempt to Build a Nuclear Shovel." *Motherboard*, August 9, 2012. https://motherboard.vice.com/en_us/article/d777ak/the-u-s-s-insane-attempt-to-build-a-harbor-with-a-two-megaton-nuclear-bomb

O'Neill, Dan. "Project Chariot: How Alaska Escaped Nuclear Evacuation." *Bulletin of the Atomic Scientists* 45 (December 1989). https://books.google.com/books?id=8wUAAAAAMBAJ&lpg=PA28&dq=Operation%20Chariot%20nuclear&pg=PA28#v=onepage&q&f=true

O'Neill, Dan. *The Firecracker Boys: H-Bombs, Inupiat Eskimos, and the Roots of the Environmental Movement.* New York: Basic Books, 1995 and 2007.

Vandegraft, Douglas L. "Project Chariot: Nuclear Legacy of Cape Thompson." Proceedings of the U.S. Interagency Arctic Research Policy Committee Workshop on Arctic Contamination, Session A: Native People's Concerns about Arctic Contamination II: Ecological Impacts. May 6, 1993, Anchorage, Alaska. http://arcticcircle.uconn.edu/VirtualClassroom/Chariot/vandegraft.html

Wright, Lawrence. "The Glut Economy." *The New Yorker*, January 1, 2018, 42–53.

"The Most Bombed Nation on Earth"

Since 1985, many Western Shoshone people have joined with environmentalists to resist nuclear weapons testing in Nevada, trespassing on the world's only remaining nuclear weapons proving ground, northwest of Las Vegas. The test site occupies land that President Harry Truman confiscated from the Western Shoshone for "national security" purposes during 1951, forcibly relocating 100 Native American families. The seizure of Western Shoshone land for nuclear weapons testing has never been fully tested in court.

Traditional Shoshone chief Corbin Harney "came out from behind the bush," as he said, in 1985, initiating protests of the U.S. government's nuclear weapons testing (Harney, 1996). He also has taken hundreds of people (Indians and non-Indians) into sweat lodges to pray against testing. Corbin and other Western Shoshone leaders repeatedly have crossed a gated cattle guard onto the 1,350-square-mile test site. On occasion, they have been joined by large groups of people marching in support of a ban on nuclear testing. The marches, which have included several thousand people, sometimes are held on Mother's Day (for Mother Earth). At some of these marches hundreds of people were arrested.

Underground Tests and Radiation

Harney cited evidence that the underground tests leak radiation above ground. "Down-winders," people who live downwind from nuclear weapons test sites, especially in southern Utah, have, according to Harney, "observed extremely high numbers of cancers, leukemia, and other physical deformities in their population" (Harney, 1996). Harney compared these reports to similar findings among citizens of Kazakhstan (in the former Soviet Union) who lived downwind from a nearby test site. They have reported similarly high levels of cancer, leukemia, illness, and birth deformities. Protests later closed the test site at Kazakhstan. During 1993, when Harney visited Kazakhstan, he learned that local water had been irreversibly contaminated with dangerous levels of radiation. "You can't drink a glass of water there anymore," he said. "All they had to drink was vodka, cartons of juice, and bottled water imported from Europe" (Harney, 1996).

About 700 nuclear tests for Great Britain and the United States have been conducted at the Nevada Test Site since 1951 on lands belonging to the Western Shoshone under the Treaty of Ruby Valley (1863). Until 1963, the tests were conducted above-ground. Atmospheric tests were banned by international treaties during the 1960s; in the 1970s tests also were limited to a 150-kiloton explosive yield.

The Environmental Protection Agency has documented cumulative deposits of plutonium in soil samples more than 100 miles north of the test area. "We are the most-bombed nation in the world," said William Rosse Sr., a Western Shoshone elder. "We've had more than our share of radiation, and now they want to dump more nuclear waste on our land at Yucca Mountain" ("Havasupai Fight," 1992). "We have always been a free tribe, never have we been conquered and never have we sold land to the U.S.," said John Wells of the Western Shoshone National Council. "My people are still suffering from the 828 underground nuclear weapons tests and 105 above-ground nuclear weapons tests at the Nevada Test Site" (Hodge, 2001).

Large-Scale Civil Disobedience at the Nuclear Test Site

During 1992, on Easter, several hundred people were arrested for crossing the Nevada test site's cattle guard. About 1,000 drum-pounding people protested that year, 761 of whom were arrested. They were packed into the Nye County Jail at Beatty, charged with misdemeanor trespassing, and released the same day (Rogers, 1992, n.p.). Keith Rogers, a reporter for the Las Vegas *Review-Journal*, described the scene at the 1992 Easter Sunday protest:

> Dressed in yellow coveralls with a plastic nose that served as a makeshift rabbit suit, Hugh Romney, the 1960s anti-war activist better known as Wavy Gravy, stood before the line of police at the cattle guard. "There's

nobody left to blow up but ourselves," he said about nuclear testing moments before his arrest. "It's an insult to our planet." Then in 1960s fashion, the throng chanted, "The whole world is watching," while some threw flowers in the air and [others] put some flowers on a barbed-wire fence. (Rogers, 1992, n.p.)

During the early morning of April 3, 1997, a cold, snowy day, two vans loaded with antinuclear activists tried to blockade Highway 95 five miles east of the test site. They had planned to lock a junked car into freshly poured concrete, along with "custom devices that would link seven humans, six men and seven women, aged 20 to 55, to the car, to concrete-filled, barrels and to each other" (Lee, 1997).

The protesters assembled their blockade under the eyes of a small audience that included several newspaper reporters, a Japanese public television crew, and official representatives of *hibakasha* (Japanese survivors of atomic bombings at Hiroshima and Nagasaki) who draped the participants with paper-crane necklaces and antinuclear protest buttons. Several peace activists and a representative of Nelson Mandela also looked on.

Blockade plans were disrupted when the protesters were routed by police. Some protesters lay down across the highway and locked themselves together to obstruct police buses. Five hours passed before the state highway patrol and the N.T.S. Wackenhuts (commercial security guards) cleared the four-lane-wide human blockade.

During those five hours, according to one participant, "We were photographed, fed, watered, massaged, glared at, and in the case of the north-side blockaders and the Greenpeace spokesman, threatened by an irate trucker with a gun he claimed to have in his cab. Luckily one of our peacekeepers and some of the officers . . . heard the threat and surrounded the trucker and calmed him down. . . . Traffic was backed up several miles on each side of the highway, mainly trucks (including one or two hauling low-level radioactive waste to be buried in shallow trenches at the test site)" (Lee, 1997).

The protesters were arrested and taken to the Clark County Jail in Las Vegas, charged with trespass and obstruction of an officer, held overnight, and then released without bail.

Once again, during May 2000, roughly 700 people gathered at the test site to celebrate Mother's Day and [to] demand an end to the radioactive poisoning of Mother Earth. Following a rally at the test site gates featuring music and speakers from around the world, 198 people crossed into the restricted area and submitted to arrest. As the arrests were taking place, Ian Zabarte, representing the Western Shoshone National Council, told test site officials that they were trespassing on Shoshone lands in violation of international law, as well as a treaty signed with the U.S. government in 1863. The rally drew a variety of Shoshone and non-Native people intent on stopping nuclear testing. About 175 activists also participated in a Western Shoshone "occupation" of the test site as they erected a tipi on restricted ground and joined in a sunrise prayer ceremony led by Harney. Another tipi was erected more than five miles inside the test site perimeter, high on a ridge top, where another sunrise ceremony was celebrated "by tired but inspired activists" (Lee, 1997). A third tipi was built well inside the front entrance of the test site, which was visible to workers at the test site as they arrived at dawn.

Further Reading

Harney, Corbin. *The Way It Is: One Air, One Mother.* Nevada City, CA: Blue Dolphin Publishing, 1996.

"Havasupai Fight to Save Grand Canyon from Uranium Mining." July 21, 1992. http://www.ratical.org/ratville/native/havasuEFN.txt

Hodge, Damon. 2001. "Dumpy Meeting: Final Vegas Hearing on Yucca Mountain Plagued by the D.O.E." *Las Vegas Weekly*, September 11. In Bruce E. Johansen, *Resource Exploitation in Native North America: A Plague upon the Peoples.* Santa Barbara, CA: ABC-CLIO, 2016, 199. https://books.google.com/books?id=bs-uDQAAQBAJ&pg=PA199&lpg=PA199&dq="Dumpy+Meeting:+Final+Vegas+Hearing+on+Yucca+Mountain+Plagued+by+the+D.O.E."&source=bl&ots

Lee, Susan. "Blockade of Nevada Test Site Highway." *Synthesis/Regeneration* 14 (Fall 1997). Green Party. http://www.greens.org/s-r/14/14-24.html

Rogers, Keith. "Nevada Anti-Nuclear Protest." *Las Vegas Review-Journal*, April 20, 1992, n.p.

Utah's Goshute Asked to House Waste Uranium—but Were Denied

The government of the tiny Goshute band of Indians in Utah, near Salt Lake City, is a rare example of a Native American tribe that has willingly submitted itself to energy colonization for a price. In this instance, the issue is nuclear waste storage, and the price may be as much as $300 million. The Goshutes' leadership wants to host one of the country's largest nuclear waste dumps, but federal officials are concerned that the group cannot even keep its own drinking water clean (Miniclier, 2001).

Only 25 people live on the 7-by-8-mile, 17,700-acre reservation in the desert about 70 miles southwest of Salt Lake City; only 15 of 121 enrolled tribal members live on the reservation. They live in a cluster of trailers and other homes on the western slope of the Stansbury Mountains. Pioneers named the place Skull Valley after finding some skulls near a spring (Miniclier, 2001).

The Goshutes' council wants to lease about one square mile of the reservation for a nuclear waste dump. Ultimately, the plan must be approved by the Nuclear Regulatory Commission. Several Utah groups have combined to oppose the Goshutes' invitation to become a major waste dump. These include the environmental justice foundation Ohngo Guadedah Devia (a grassroots group of residents from the Skull Valley Goshute reservation) and the Environmental Justice Foundation. Both joined with the state of Utah and a number of other environmental groups to wage a legal battle against the Bureau of Indian Affairs, which was supporting the Goshutes' desire to host the dump, seeking to declare a lease signed by Private Fuel Storage (a consortium of eight nuclear power utilities) with the Goshute Tribal Council "null and void," on grounds that the provisions of the lease were never put to a referendum vote nor disclosed to tribal members.

Serious Objections to Nuclear Storage Proposal

The Utah legislature, Utah governor Mike Leavitt, and the Southern Utah Wilderness Alliance all objected strenuously to the deal. Advocates of the arrangement assert that the dump will close after permanent waste storage on a national scale becomes available at Yucca Mountain, Nevada (which has not happened as of 2019). Private Fuel Storage (PFS) signed its deal in December 1996 with the three-member Skull Valley Tribal Council and local landowners for $300 million in exchange for their support of the dump. The deal committed the Goshutes to host a nuclear waste facility for 25 years with an option to extend the agreement for another quarter century.

The Goshutes' land, which is already surrounded by several industries that emit toxic effluents, has been chosen by Private Fuel Storage as the site for a temporary above-ground private storage area. "I will deploy every tool I can to fight the storage of high-level nuclear waste in our state," Governor Leavitt said. "We don't produce this waste; we shouldn't store it. We are engaging in serious legal warfare to keep this lethally hot waste out of Utah" (News Release, 2000).

The Goshute reservation sits in the middle of a bevy of activities that nearly no one else would want to host. Nearby are the Utah Test and Training Range, where the Air Force tests F-16 fighters and cruise missiles; the Dugway Proving Grounds, a test center for chemical and biological weapons; the Deseret Chemical Depot, with its stockpile of nerve and blistering agents; and the Tooele Chemical Demilitarization Facility, where military chemicals are destroyed (Miniclier, 2001).

According to the PFS contract with the Goshutes, an 840-acre site on the reservation will be designated to receive as much as 40,000 metric tons of spent uranium for temporary storage (20 or 40 years). Pending federal approval of the plan, PFS will remove spent uranium fuel rods from nuclear power plants coast to coast in the United States, place them on specially designed rail cars, and ship them to Skull Valley. Under the agreement, the Skull Valley reservation would house the first private, high-level radioactive storage site in the history of the United States. The government of Tooele County, which surrounds the Goshutes' reservation, has come out in support of the plan in exchange for promises of up to $200 million in "mitigation fees."

Problems with Drinking Water

Leon Bear, chairman of the Goshutes' tribal council (which signed the agreement with PFS), ignored three deadlines set by the Denver regional office of the Environmental Protection Agency to clean up the reservation's dangerously polluted drinking water, according to the *Denver Post*. Bear's unwillingness to clean up the reservation's water supply has raised concerns about the tribe's ability to safely store large amounts of nuclear waste. The EPA's tests indicated that the Goshutes' water system, which uses untreated surface water, contains coliform and *E. coli* bacteria "whose presence indicate the water may be contaminated with human or animal waste" and "is a threat to human health" (Miniclier, 2001). Most of the reservation's residents drink bottled water supplied by the EPA. Dianne Nielson, director of Utah's Department of Environmental Quality, asked, "If the tribe can't provide safe drinking water, how is it going to handle high-level nuclear waste?" (Miniclier, 2001). Bear replied that "tribal members have been drinking the surface water for years [and that] the [Goshute tribe] will have no management responsibilities for the nuclear storage facility, but will merely lease the site" (Miniclier, 2001).

Bear dismissed such concerns, saying: "Little minds have little thoughts. . . . I'm always fighting with the EPA about water" (Miniclier, 2001). "I'm more afraid of the nerve gas at Tooele Army Depot or the chemical/biological experiments at Dugway Proving Ground than I am of the storage facility," said Bear, who envisioned the waste dump as economic salvation for his shrinking tribe (Miniclier, 2001). When he signed a lease with Private Fuel Storage, Bear reasoned that the area was surrounded with toxic industries, so nuclear waste storage "would provide a lucrative, safe, nonpolluting source of income" (Miniclier, 2001).

Who Bears Responsibility for Nuclear Waste Leaks?

As a limited-liability company, Private Fuel Storage wrote the contract to excuse itself from any responsibility for damage caused by accidents or other unforeseen circumstances. Given the fact that Chairman Bear also has excused the Goshutes from any similar responsibilities, state officials have wondered out loud regarding who or what would be responsible should the stored nuclear waste cause pollution or any other type of accident. Environmentalists point out that the area is prone to earthquakes and is overflown regularly by roughly 4,000 F-16 fighter planes a year to and from nearby test-bombing ranges.

Plans to install a nuclear waste dump on the Goshutes' reservation provoked dissension within the tribe. Bear's opponents insist that he was ousted in a recall vote called by antinuclear activists on August 25, 2001, but Bear asserted he was still leader of the 112-member Goshute Tribe. The local Bureau of Indian Affairs superintendent, Allen Anspach, agreed with Bear. The leadership question is key to whether the Goshutes will honor the dump agreement (which the Bureau of Indian Affairs had conditionally approved) (Taliman, 2002, A-1).

The Skull Valley Band of Goshutes' offer to take 44,000 tons of nuclear waste on tribal land to substitute for a site at Nevada's Yucca Mountain (which was opposed by the Shoshones and many environmental activists) was denied by the U.S. Bureau of Indian Affairs (which had changed its position under new management during the Obama presidency) and the Bureau of Land Management. Utah then offered a private site—a Tooele County landfill 80 miles west of Salt Lake City. By 2015, an Energy Solutions disposal site on Goshute land was being prepared to receive 250,000 tons of nuclear waste and to store it "forever." Brian Maffly reported for the *Salt Lake City Tribune* (2015):

> The barrels look harmless enough. Tucked away in a sterile metal shed in the middle of Utah's West Desert, the 55-gallon plastic drums show no hint of what lies beneath the metal lids—radioactive waste that will only get hotter over time. Energy Solutions executives hope the 5,400 containers eventually will become a waste stream that could sustain the company for years—approximately 250,000 metric tons of depleted uranium in all. The waste-management company has prepared a burial ground for the

stuff—a vast pit, 10 feet deep, where tens of thousands of the drums would be lined up and covered in concrete, clay and rocks. Forever. Or at least as far into the future as humans can plan.

Depleted uranium, a low-level hazard when generated, becomes more radioactive over a long period of time, potentially outlasting the activities that created it. In 2015, 750,000 metric tons of such waste was being stored by U.S. Department of Energy sites in Kentucky, Ohio, and South Carolina. Pending acceptance of its bid, Energy Solutions may become the United States' largest radioactive-waste dump.

As of 2019, proposals for the dump remained frozen amid controversy within the tribe and opposition by environmental groups. In the meantime, several parts of Skull Valley are already used for toxic disposal of wastes that are not radioactive, including a hazardous waste landfill, a nerve gas storage facility, two hazmat incinerators, a magnesium plant that emits chlorine gas, and the Intermountain Power Plant that emits toxic chemicals. The U.S. government in the past has tested biological weapons near Skull Valley. The area is clearly no place for a picnic, even without nuclear waste.

Further Reading

Maffly, Brian. "Utah Stepping Closer to Taking 250,000 Tons of Radioactive Waste—Forever." *Salt Lake City Tribune,* April 12, 2015. http://archive.sltrib.com/article.php?id=2351660&itype=CMSID

Miniclier, Kit. "Nuclear-Storage Plan Targeted; E.P.A. Cites Indians' Inability to Keep Water Supply Clean." *Denver Post,* June 17, 2001. https://www.denverpost.com/2019/02/14/epa-plan-perflourinated-chemicals/

News Release: Office of the Governor, State of Utah, Salt Lake City. "Governor Leavitt Opens Office High-Level Nuclear Waste Opposition." December 7, 2000. http://www.state.nv.us/nucwaste/news2000/nn10935.htm

Taliman, Valerie. "N.R.C. Reviews Goshute Nuke Plan." *Indian Country Today,* April 10, 2002, A-1, A-2.

The Laguna Pueblo and Anaconda's Jackpile Uranium Mine

Until 1982, the Laguna Pueblo (50 miles east of the Navajo Nation in New Mexico, and 40 miles west of Albuquerque) was the site of the world's largest uranium strip mine. Anaconda Minerals Co., a subsidiary of Atlantic Richfield, mined uranium there from 1953 through 1982 from three open pits: Jackpile, North Paguate, and South Paguate. The mines closed in 1982, when uranium prices dropped below profitable levels, having ripped and run as the people of Laguna were left with a poisoned landscape and many debilitating and sometimes fatal health problems.

Until it closed, the mine made the people of Laguna Pueblo affluent by most reservations' standards. The price of this affluence, in many cases, was slow death by pervasive radiation. When it closed, Jackpile was employing about 800 people. When miners were diagnosed with lung cancer in unusually large numbers, the mine's supporters said what Navajo miners also heard: they had smoked too many cigarettes. John Redhouse of the Southwest Indigenous Uranium Forum disagreed. "The social costs and health impacts outweigh any jobs and money that goes to Laguna," he said. "Whatever apparent benefits accrue do not necessarily go to the communities but to the multinational energy companies" (Knight, 2013).

Toxicity Seeps into Water

The Jackpile and Paguate mines grew to 7,868 acres of arroyos and canyons. Hazardous substances leached into the Rio Paguate's and Rio Moquino's streambeds, as they flow together along and through open pits and waste dumps, merging into the Rio San José. The toxic load included not only uranium, but also barium, arsenic, cobalt, copper, chromium, manganese, vanadium, lead, selenium, and zinc.

Resident Gloria Lewis, who lives in Laguna, remembered that relatives and friends rallied to patriotism during the 1940s and 1950s, agreeing to locate the mines close to their homes because many veterans and military families believed that the United States "needed our help to fight the war," including the manufacture of atomic bombs. She despaired when the mines closed and unemployment shot up to 85 percent, but at the same time she resented that "the uranium belt was called the sacrifice zone. The human population wasn't even considered," she said.

Lewis's house was condemned after blasting and mining underneath Paguate Village caused walls of several traditional stone-and-mortar homes to crack, she said (Nauman, 2014). At the same time, Ronnda Ross, a neighbor of Lewis, recalled "a lot of women having miscarriages in the last 30 years" (Nauman, 2014). Radiation polluted the air, through radon mine dust, contaminating fruit trees, sheep and other meat animals, and just about everyone's homes, said resident June Lorenzo. "Decades later, people who worked in the uranium mines are finding all kinds of cancer," she said. "Everyone knows that it's connected [to the mining], but companies insist that it's not" (Nauman, 2014).

Living on Borrowed Time

Decades into the Jackpile mine's active life, some people at Laguna knew they were living on borrowed time. One of them was the internationally renowned writer Paula Gunn Allen. Barbara Alice Mann, an honors professor at the University of Toledo and a friend of Allen's, said, "Paula Gunn Allen was wiped out by the same cancer effects, and even before she was diagnosed, she told me that she knew she would die of cancer, simply because of where she grew up and where her family still lived" (Mann, 2013).

The agricultural valley that had sustained the Laguna Pueblo for centuries before the advent of the mine also was ruined. Before 1952, the Rio Paguate had provided water for a valley flush with farms and ranches. Winona LaDuke, writing in *Native Americas* (*Akwe:kon Journal*), described the postmine landscape: "Rio Paguate now runs through the remnants of the strip mine, emerging on the other side a fluorescent green in color" (LaDuke, 1992, 58). Since 1973, the EPA had known that the mine was leaching radiation into the Laguna Pueblo's water supply. By 1975, the U.S. Environmental Protection Agency (EPA) had issued reports describing large-scale groundwater contamination. The Laguna tribal center, the community center, and many reservation houses also were dangerously contaminated. The problem was compounded when Anaconda used low-grade uranium ore to surface many roads on the reservation.

By 2013, Jackpile was being cleaned up by the Laguna tribe at a cost of $48 million, paid by ARCO (Atlantic Richfield), a major oil company that as of the year 2000 became a subsidiary of British Petroleum (BP). Many Laguna said that although the "remediation" would restore the mine site to its former condition, uranium already had leached into soil and water, making total cleansing impossible. "Two tributaries near the mine and the Rio San Jose have already tested positive for radiation contamination," said Manual Pino of the Laguna-Acoma Coalition for a Safe Environment. "It's one of the best kept secrets of the United States" (Knight, 2013).

A Grim Radioactive Legacy

Realizing that "Native Americans in the United States and Canada have inherited a grim legacy of increased rates of cancer and a ruined environment because of uranium mining on tribal homelands" (Knight,

2013), representatives of several indigenous communities gathered on the Laguna Indian Reservation during June 2013 for the tenth annual conference of the Indigenous Environment Network. As they met, long-shuttered uranium mines in some parts of the United States were being opened again, in some cases to fuel nuclear power plants as an "environmentally friendly" alternative to fossil fuels.

New projects threaten scarce water supplies on Navajo land, said Kathleen Tsosie, secretary of the Eastern Navajo Diné Against Uranium Mining. In Tsosie's home town, Crownpoint, New Mexico, Hydro Resources Inc. has announced plans "to leach uranium from the groundwater in three places in the Northwestern part of the state. The underground leach mining process is different from traditional open-pit mines since it occurs in the groundwater itself when chemicals are injected into the aquifer to dissolve the ore and is then pumped out. 'How can this not possibly threaten our water supply?' said Tsosie. 'And many of our sacred sites are near these wells'" (Knight, 2013). Several Navajo groups petitioned the Nuclear Regulatory Commission (NRC) to revoke the company's mining permit.

"They said the mine would make us rich but I'm still poor and almost everyone around me is dying of cancer and strange diseases," said Dorothy Purley, a woman who was dying of lymphoma cancer in a home about 1,000 yards from the mine. She'd worked for Anaconda Jackpile for eight years (Knight, 2013), but she was never told that her life was at risk from radiation or what precautions were required to shield herself. In Paguate, a small town where Purley lived her entire life, about 50 miners died from cancers or related maladies. About 20 other people who were not miners and lived downwind of the mine also had died by 2013, she said. Purley said that in one instance,

> When the crusher got stuck we were down at the bottom using hammers to break the rocks down so the crusher could start going back up into processing, and I helped haul the ore from P9 where they were mining underground the richest ore that was coming out. We hauled back to the ore cars to have it transported. We came home, went to bed, never was a word said that there was contamination [because] of radiation. [I] just realized when I came to deal with this cancer, I found out. This cancer has really taught me a lot . . . and gotten me to a lot of places and I've realized what cancer really means. ("Uranium Mining," 1996)

The ore was loaded onto open cars by the Santa Fe Railroad as it blew over everything on its way out of town. No one tested the tracks for radioactive contamination. The mine's crusher was on the east side of town, and the prevailing east wind blew yellow powder all over the area.

Purley was one of few women hired at the mine. She worked in several capacities, from receptionist to security guard, to jobs near the mines. "They used to blast sometimes four times a day," she recalled. "When there was no wind, that sulfur that they put in the blasting powder would just kind of sit over the village and sometimes we had to cover our food. We Indians dried our meat and some of our vegetables out in the sun; we never realized how much contamination there was in the air 'til we realized cancer was the main thing killing our people here in Paguate" ("Uranium Mining," 1996).

Three times, she miscarried. The loss of children broke her heart. Once, she required surgery after nearly bleeding to death. She knew several women who did not miscarry, but their babies were deformed. Once, she watched a cat give birth to kittens with no tails. Many children grew up mentally impaired, and nearly everyone suffered allergies that had been rare or unknown before the strip mine unearthed the yellow powder. Purley herself had asthma and bronchitis before she was diagnosed with breast cancer. People didn't complain because the paychecks put bread and butter on the table. "Money," said Purley, "is the maker of all evil" ("Uranium Mining," 1996).

In 2013, three decades after the abandoned Jackpile Mine did most of its damage, it was listed as a "National Priority" Superfund site, after 17 years of halting, ineffectual cleanup had taken place. By then, the plague of cancer that mining had unleased was still spreading. People living in the Laguna Pueblo, like the Navajos, were considering a ban on mining. "A lot of our people have suffered," said Paguate resident Lawrence Encino. "We don't want more mining" (Nauman, 2014).

Further Reading

Knight, Danielle. "Native Americans Denounce Toxic Legacy." TWN: Third World Network, June 14, 2013. http://www.ipsnews.net/1999/06/environment-health-native-americans-denounce-toxic-legacy/

LaDuke, Winona. "Indigenous Environmental Perspectives: A North American Primer." *Akwe:kon Journal* 9, no. 2 (Summer 1992): 52–71.

Mann, Barbara A. Personal communication, July 25, 2013.

Nauman, Talli. "Laguna Pueblo Still Affected by Uranium Mine." Indianz.com. August 25, 2014. http://www.indianz.com/News/2014/014847.asp

"Uranium Mining and the Laguna People." Dorothy Purley, interviewed by Susan Lee, July 1995, in Paguate Village on the Laguna Pueblo Reservation. *Synthesis/Regeneration* 10 (Spring, 1996). http://www.greens.org/s-r/10/10-07.html

The Navajos' Nuclear Legacy

In 1950, Paddy Martinez, a Navajo sheepherder, brought a strange-looking yellow rock into Grants, New Mexico, from nearby Haystack Butte, initiating a mining boom. Navajo uranium miners at first hauled radioactive uranium ore out of the earth as if it were coal or any other mineral. Some ate their lunches in the mines and slaked their thirst with radioactive water. Their families' homes sometimes were built of radioactive earth, and their neighbors' sheep may have watered in small ponds that formed at the mouths of abandoned uranium mines. On dry, windy days, the gritty dust from uranium waste-tailings piles covered everything in sight.

About half the recoverable uranium in the United States lies in New Mexico—and about half of that is beneath the Navajo Nation. The Navajo language has no word for "radioactivity." Initially, no one told the miners that within two or three decades, many of them would die of radiation-induced cancers. In their rush to profit from uranium mining (and the lives of the miners), very few mining companies provided ventilation in the early years. Some miners worked as many as 20 hours a day, entering the mines just after the blasting of sandstone had filled the mines with silica dust. Many mine owners didn't even provide toilet paper. When miners relieved themselves, they wiped with fistfuls of radioactive "yellowcake"—uranium ore.

The Kerr-McGee Company, the first corporation to mine uranium on Navajo Nation lands (beginning in 1948), found the reservation location extremely lucrative. There were no taxes at the time; no health, safety, or pollution regulations; and few other jobs for the many Navajos who had recently arrived home from service in World War II. Labor was cheap, and uranium, in demand for stockpiles of nuclear armaments, was expensive.

The first uranium miners in the area, almost all of them Navajos, remember being sent into shallow tunnels within minutes after blasting. They loaded the radioactive ore into wheelbarrows and emerged from the mines spitting black mucus from the dust, coughing so hard that many of them experienced headaches. Such mining practices exposed the Navajos who worked for Kerr-McGee to between 100 and 1,000 times the level of radon gas later considered safe. Officials for the U.S. Public Health Service (PHS) estimated these levels of exposure after the fact; in the earliest days, no one was monitoring the Navajo miners' health.

Carrie Arnold (2014) wrote in *Environmental Health Perspectives*, published by the National Institutes of Health, that the miners and their families "were not told that the men who worked in the mines were breathing carcinogenic radon gas and showering in radioactive water, nor that the women washing their husbands' work clothes could spread radionuclides to the rest of the family's laundry" after they had worked in the 521 now-abandoned uranium mines on the reservation ranging in size from "dog holes" that could accommodate only a single man to large mines from which radioactive ore was extracted in carts on rails.

Arnold wrote that health workers were allowed to interview uranium miners only after they agreed not to inform the miners of the potential health hazards of their work. Seeing it as the only way to convince government regulators to improve safety in the mines, the researchers accepted. The PHS monitored the health of more than 4,000 miners between 1954 and 1960 without telling them of the threat to their health. By 1965, the investigators reported an association between cumulative exposure to uranium and lung cancer among white miners and had definitively identified the cause as radiation exposure. The effects had been no secret, even as early as 1950, when government workers monitored radiation levels in the mines that were as much as 750 times the limits deemed acceptable at that time.

"Radioactive from the Inside Out"

More than 99 percent of the rock that the uranium mines produced was waste, cast aside as tailings near mine sites after the usable uranium ore had been extracted. The massive tailings piles, radioactive enough to be dangerous, but not rich enough to be sold, were dumped on the reservation. One of the mesa-like waste piles grew to be a mile long and 70 feet high. On windy days, dust from the tailings blew into local communities, filling the air and settling into water supplies. At the time, beginning during the 1950s, the Atomic Energy Commission (AEC) assured worried local residents that the dust was harmless.

When mining was initiated, no one considered environmentally appropriate ways to deal with its tailings piles. Even if the tailings were to be buried—a staggering task—radioactive pollution could leak into the surrounding water table. A 1976 Environmental Protection Agency (EPA) report found radioactive contamination of drinking water on the Navajo Nation in the Grants, New Mexico, area near a uranium mining and milling facility (Eichstaedt 1994, 208).

Arnold (2014) described the mine tailings' legacy more than half a century after the first uranium was mined:

In a low, windswept rise at the southeastern edge of the Navajo Nation, Jackie Bell-Jefferson prepares to move her family from their home for a temporary stay that could last up to seven years. A mound of uranium-laden waste the size of several football fields, covered with a thin veneer of gravel, dominates the view from her front door. After many years of living next to the contamination and a litany of health problems she believes it caused, Bell-Jefferson and several other local families will have to vacate their homes for a third round of cleanup efforts by the U.S. Environmental Protection Agency.

Members of Bell-Jefferson's family had used radioactive water for years. The water, which had no distinctive taste or smell, was used for drinking, cleaning, and cooking. Gilbert Badoni of Shiprock, New Mexico, said that as a child, he played in the tailings with siblings and drank radioactive water during the decades his father worked in uranium mines in Colorado in the 1950s and 1960s. Badoni said that his father arrived at home after work covered in yellow uranium dust, which covered everything in their small home as their mother brushed it off his clothes. Badoni blamed his lung problems and his siblings' cancers on that exposure. "The U.S. government has abused innocent women and children. They have abused my family," Badoni said, choking back tears. "They have abused my Navajo people. That's not right" ("Uranium Miners," 2000).

Uranium mine dust produced silicosis in the miners' lungs in addition to lung cancer and other problems associated with exposure to radioactivity. By the 1960s, nearly 200 miners had already died of uranium-related causes. That number had doubled by 1990. Radioactivity also contaminated drinking water in parts of the Navajo reservation, producing birth defects and Down syndrome, both previously all but unknown among the Navajo. Of all infant deaths in areas served by the Navajo Indian Health Service area for the years 1990 through 1992, 35 percent were caused by congenital anomalies. Mortality attributed to malignant neoplasms (age-adjusted rate) was 78.5 percent in the years from 1990 through 1992 (Colomeda, 1998). A 1976 EPA report found radioactive contamination of drinking water on the Navajo reservation in the Grants area near a uranium mining and milling facility.

The government knew of the risk at least by 1978, however, when the Department of Energy released a Nuclear Waste Management Task Force report disclosing that people living near the tailings piles ran at least twice the risk of lung cancer as the general population. Even then, the Coalition for Navajo Liberation was aware that a number of miners were dying of lung cancer. As Navajo miners continued to die, children who played in water that had flowed over or through abandoned mines and tailings piles came home with burning sores. Downwind of uranium processing mills, the dust from yellowcake sometimes was so thick that it stained the landscape half a mile away.

Dry winds blew dust from tailings piles through the streets of many Navajo communities. "We used to play in it," said Terry Yazzie of an enormous tailings pile behind his house. "We would dig holes and bury ourselves in it" (Eichstaedt, 1994, 11). The neighbors of this particular tailings pile were not told it was dangerous until 1990, 22 years after the mill that produced the pile had closed and 12 years after Congress authorized the cleanup of uranium mill tailings in Navajo country. Abandoned mines also were used as shelter by animals that inhaled radon and drank contaminated water. Local people milked the animals and ate their contaminated meat.

Peter Eichstaedt wrote that miners watched members of their families die because of radiation poisoning that permeated their entire lives. Some miners were put to work packing thousand-pound barrels of yellowcake. Some of the miners ingested so much of the dust that it was "making the workers radioactive from the inside out" (Eichstaedt, 1994, 11).

Opposition to Uranium Mining

Through opposition to uranium mining among Indians and non-Indians alike runs a deep concern for the long-term poisoning of land, air, and water by low-level radiation. By the 1970s, these concerns had provoked demands from Indian and white groups for a moratorium on all uranium mining, exploration, and milling until the issues of untreated radioactive tailings and other waste-disposal problems were faced and solved. Doris Bunting of Citizens Against Nuclear Threats (a predominantly non-Native group that joined with efforts by the Coalition for Navajo Liberation [CNL] and the National Indian Youth Council in opposition to uranium mining) supplied data indicating that radium-bearing sediments had spread into the Colorado River basin, from which water is drawn for much of the Southwest.

The specter of death that haunted former Navajo uranium miners came at what company public relations specialists might have deemed an inappropriate time. By late 1978, more than 700,000 acres of Indian land were under lease for uranium exploration and development, in an area centering on Shiprock and Crownpoint, both in the Navajo Nation. Atlantic Richfield, Continental Oil, Exxon, Humble Oil, Homestake, Kerr-McGee, Mobil Oil, Pioneer Nuclear, and United Nuclear were among the companies exploring, planning to mine, or already extracting ore. During the 1980s, the mining frenzy subsided somewhat as recession and a slowing of the nuclear arms race reduced demand. Some ore was still being mined, but most of it lay in the ground, waiting for the next upward spike in the market.

Even as the boom ended, many of the miners who had been condemned to slow death by lung cancer did not yet know that the yellow ore they had mined was killing them. Peter Eichstaedt's painstakingly detailed study, *If You Poison Us* (1994), described how the miners learned what had been done to them and how they went about winning at least the possibility of compensation from the U.S. government. Using a combination of interviews and scientific data, Eichstaedt demonstrated that the U.S. government (particularly the Atomic Energy Commission (AEC)) knew that uranium mining was poisoning the Navajos almost from the beginning, a key point in the debate over compensation that has thus far resulted in a small proportion of miners collecting $100,000 each. The government and the mining companies kept medical knowledge from the miners themselves out of concern for national security and profits.

"Original Instructions," Uranium Mining, and Navajo Cultural Values

The mining of uranium became a major political and cultural issue among the Navajo during the 1970s as the cancer death toll mounted. Lung cancer became so widespread that it had major cultural implications, provoking many Navajo to reexamine traditional teachings about the need for harmony with regard to the Earth. Following debate centered on this examination, uranium mining and milling henceforth became illegal on the Navajo Nation.

Activists in the CNL sought to have uranium mining and milling outlawed on the reservation as soon as its human toll became evident, a position that eventually prevailed in the Navajo government after a quarter of a century of debate and industry lobbying. Esther Keeswood, a member of the CNL from Shiprock, a reservation town near several tailings piles, said in 1978 that the CNL had documented the deaths of at least 50 residents (including several uranium miners) from lung cancer and related diseases. The number of deaths increased steadily after that.

Uranium's yellow dirt is part of the natural order of things in Navajo Country, and a ban on its mining and milling was regarded by traditional people as a cultural victory, a return to the original instructions of creation. The yellow dirt in mythology is believed to be the antithesis of the life-giving yellow powder of corn pollen: "In one of the stories the Navajos tell about their origin, the *Dineh* (the people) emerged from the third world into the fourth and present world and were given a choice. They were told to choose between two yellow powders. One was yellow dust from the rocks, and the other was corn pollen. The Dineh chose corn pollen, and the gods nodded in assent. They also issued a warning. Having chosen the corn pollen, the Navajo were to leave the yellow dust in the ground. If it was ever removed, it would bring evil" (Eichstaedt, 1994, 47).

In this cultural interpretation, the commercial use of the yellow dirt turned it into *Leetso*, a powerful monster that inflicted punishment on the Navajo people in the form of disease and suffering. The only way to restore harmony with nature (a very important attribute in Navajo culture) is *hozho nashaadoo* ("to walk in harmony"). The only proper response was to restore harmony by banning the mining and milling of uranium. The yellow dirt is a poison that disrupts the gathering of sacred herbs in contaminated areas. The Navajo seek to balance elements of land, water, and sunlight (fire). Some of the elders blamed themselves for allowing disruption of *hozho nashaadoo*.

In 2018, encouraged by the Trump administration, uranium miners again were filing mining permits on the Navajo Nation, even as the people continued to struggle with the legacy of radioactive water that remains from past mining. "The Navajo town of Sanders, Ariz., a dusty outpost with a single stoplight, is a reminder of uranium's lasting environmental legacy," wrote Hiroko Tabuchi in the *New York Times* (2018). "In Sanders, hundreds of people were exposed to potentially dangerous levels of uranium in their drinking water for years, until testing by a doctoral researcher at Northern Arizona University named Tommy Rock exposed the contamination. 'I was shocked,' Mr. Rock said. 'I wasn't expecting that reading at all.'" At least some of the radiation was more than 40 years old, stemming from the 1977 Church Rock spill, described in the next essay. No one in Sanders was told their water was radioactive until 2015.

"The town's school district, whose wells were also contaminated with uranium, received little state or federal assistance. It shut off its water fountains and handed out bottled water to its 800 elementary and middle-school students," Tabuchi reported. "I still don't trust the water," said Shanon Sangster, who still sends her 10-year-old daughter, Shania, to school with bottled water. "It's like we are all scarred by it, by the uranium" (Tabuchi, 2018).

Further Reading

Arnold, Carrie. "Once upon a Mine: The Legacy of Uranium on the Navajo Nation." *Environmental Health Perspectives*. 2014. http://ehp.niehs.nih.gov/122-A44

Colomeda, Lori A. "Indigenous Health." Speech. Brisbane, Australia, September 9, 1998. http://www.ldb.org/vl/ai/lori_b98.htm

Eichstaedt, Peter. *If You Poison Us: Uranium and American Indians*. Santa Fe, NM: Red Crane Books, 1994.

Tabuchi, Hiroko. "Uranium Miners Pushed Hard for a Comeback. They Got Their Wish." *New York Times*, January 13, 2018. https://www.nytimes.com/2018/01/13/climate/trump-uranium-bears-ears.html

"Uranium Miners, Families Bring Tales of Pain to Washington." *Arizona Republic*, April 15, 2000. https://www.business-humanrights.org/sites/default/files/reports-and-materials/Mining-1991-2000.htm

---

The Largest Uranium Spill in the United States

The largest expulsion of radioactive material in U.S. history occurred at 5 a.m. on July 16, 1979, in New Mexico's Navajo Nation. On that morning, more than 1,100 tons of uranium mining wastes—tailings mixed with water—gushed through a breached packed-mud dam near Church Rock. With the tailings, 100 million gallons of radioactive water flowed through the dam before the crack was repaired.

By 8:00 a.m., radioactivity was monitored in Gallup, New Mexico, nearly 50 miles away. The contaminated Rio Puerco showed 7,000 times the allowable standard of radioactivity for drinking water below the broken dam shortly after the breach was repaired, according to the Nuclear Regulatory Commission (NRC). The few newspaper stories about the spill outside of the immediate area noted that the area was sparsely populated and that the spill posed no immediate health hazard. The New Mexico Environmental Improvement Division said that while the spill had been "potentially hazardous . . . its short-term and long-term impacts on people and the environment were quite limited" (Johansen, 1997, 11). With these soothing words, the same reports also recommended that ranchers in the area avoid watering their livestock in the Rio Puerco. After the Rio Puerco spill, however, several Navajos said that calves and lambs were born without limbs as well as other severe birth defects. Other livestock developed sores, became ill, and died after drinking from the river.

The same report noted that the river water was not being used for human consumption and that "the extent to which radioactive and chemical constituents of these waters are incorporated in livestock tissue and passed on to humans is unknown and requires critical evaluation" (Johansen, 1997, 12). The report also said that the accident's effect on groundwater should be studied more intensely. Tom Charley, a Navajo, told a public meeting at the Lupton Chapter House that "the old ladies are always to be seen running up and down both sides of the [Rio Puerco] wash, trying to keep the sheep out of it" (Johansen, 1997, 12). The Centers for Disease Control examined a dozen dead animals and called for a more complete study in 1983, then dropped the subject.

"Uranium Capital of the World"

Even as the Rio Puerco ran radioactive because of the 1979 spill, the town of Grants styled itself the "Uranium Capital of the World." New pickup trucks appeared on the streets and mobile home parks grew around town, filling with non-Indian workers in the uranium boom. For several years, before the boom abruptly ended in the early 1980s, many workers in the uranium industry earned $60,000 or more a year (about $180,000 in 2017 dollars). Following a collapse of demand for uranium in the early 1980s, Grants dropped the nickname "Uranium Capital of the World" and began promoting itself as a haven for retirees under the new slogan "Grants Enchants."

More problems began to appear. A waste pile at the United Nuclear mill that had produced the wastes that gushed down the Rio Puerco in 1979 was detected leaking radioactive thorium into local groundwater. On May 23, 1983, the state of New Mexico issued a cease-and-desist order to United Nuclear to halt the radioactive leakage. The company refused to act, stating that its leak did not violate state regulations. Allendale and Appalachian, two insurance companies that were liable for roughly $35 million in payments to United Nuclear because of losses related to the accident, sued the company on the belief that it knew the dam that burst was defective before the spill. The dam was only two years old at the time of the accident.

Along the Rio Puerco, several white and Navajo ranchers who doubted state assurances that the spill left no long-term effects reacted by selling their land, for millions of dollars, to the federal government. The ranchers sold out under the Relocation Act, which had been passed in 1974 and was meant to move Navajos from the former "joint-use area" claimed by the Hopis. The land was purportedly acquired to relocate Navajos who had lost their homes in the land dispute with the Hopis. The Navajos asked the EPA, the Bureau of Indian Affairs, and the Relocation Commission for assurance that the land was safe. All three declined to provide the requested written assurance to the Navajos. The Navajos raised several questions, including the extent of contamination in underground aquifers, the extent of remaining radioactivity in surface waters and soils, the effects of wind-blown dust from the contaminated area, and the long-term effects of the contamination on livestock and people in the area.

Uranium contamination of river water was one problem after the 1979 spill. Lack of groundwater for wells was another side effect of uranium and other mining. As a result of mining generally, the U.S. Geological Survey predicted that the water table at Crownpoint would drop 1,000 feet and that it would return to present levels only 30 to 50 years after the mining ceased. Much of what water remained could be polluted by uranium residue, the report indicated. The Indians owned the surface rights; the mineral rights in the area were owned by private companies, such as the Santa Fe Railroad. "If the water supply is depleted, then this [Crownpoint] will become a ghost town," said Joe Gmusea, a Navajo attorney. "The only people left will be the ones who come to work in the mines" (Johansen, 1997, 11).

John Redhouse, associate director of the Albuquerque-based National Indian Youth Council, said that the uranium boom is "an issue of spiritual and physical genocide. . . . We are not isolated in our struggle against uranium development. . . . Many Indian people are now supporting the [anti–uranium mining] struggles of the Australian aborigines and the Black indigenous peoples of Namibia [South West Africa] against similar uranium developments. We have recognized that we are facing the same international beast" (Johansen, 1997, 11).

Cleanup Planned at a Few Spill Sites after Three Decades

After almost three decades of appeals from the Navajo Nation, the Environmental Protection Agency approved plans in September 2011 to clean up the Northeast Church Rock Mine near Gallup, the largest abandoned uranium mine in Navajo territory. The mine was used between 1967 and 1982 by the United Nuclear Corporation, which left behind roughly 1.4 million tons of uranium and radium-contaminated soil near its 125-acre uranium mill site. This mill and mine was the site of the dam failure that released radioactive waste into the Rio Puerco. According to the Navajo Nation, the spill, "combined with more than 20 years of discharges of untreated and poorly treated uranium mine water, has contributed to long-term contamination of the Puerco River in New Mexico and Arizona" ("Cleanup," 2011).

The area has long been designated a Superfund site by the EPA, co-managed by the NRC. The site is near the border of the Navajo Nation, on trust territory, but the mill site is privately owned. A small number of people live near the site, downwind and downstream of mine tailings waste piles. The people in the area graze cattle, sheep, and horses. The cleanup was expected to require several years and, according to an Environment News Service report, "will place the contaminated soil in a lined, capped facility employing the most stringent standards in the country. When complete, the cleanup will allow unrestricted surface use of the mine site for grazing and housing, according to the EPA." People in the area have been at risk "from inhaling radium-contaminated dust particles and radon gas or utilizing contaminated rainwater and runoff that has pooled in the ponds. There is an elevated risk associated with livestock that may graze and [drink] water on the site." Radium exposure at high levels over several years, according to the EPA, "can result in anemia, cataracts, and cancer, especially bone cancer, and death" ("Cleanup," 2011).

"This is an important milestone in the effort to address the toxic legacy of historic uranium mining on the Navajo Nation," said Jared Blumenfeld, administrator for the Pacific Southwest Region. "This plan is the result of several years of collaboration between the EPA, the Navajo Nation, and the Red Water Pond Road community living near the mine." "On behalf of the Navajo Nation, I appreciate the efforts of the U.S. EPA and Navajo EPA, and the cooperation from the state of New Mexico to clean up contaminated Navajo trust lands," said Ben Shelly, president of the Navajo Nation ("Cleanup," 2011).

Some other abandoned uranium mines were also being slowly cleansed. One was the Skyline Mine. Jason Musante, an EPA coordinator for a cleanup costing $6 million, told Judy Fahys of the *Salt Lake Tribune*, "I've got to make this hazard go away as soon as possible. . . . It's already been too long." Radioactive debris was being packed into plastic bins (which Musante described as "giant Tupperware"), then buried underground (Fahys, 2011). Most of the mining companies that abandoned sites on Navajo land have gone out of business. General Electric, however, has been billed $44 million for its role in the Northeast Church Rock Mine near Gallup. The EPA itself has spent $60 million. Chevron paid an undisclosed amount to clean up the Mariano Lake Mine in New Mexico. "The government can't afford it; that's a big reason why it hasn't stepped in and done more," said Bob Darr, a spokesman for the Department of Energy. "The contamination problem is vast" (MacMillan, 2012). Cleaning all the mines would probably cost hundreds of millions of dollars, according to Clancy Tenley, a senior EPA official who oversees its "uranium legacy program."

Many "hot spots" remained. During the summer of 2010, a Navajo cattle rancher, Larry Gordy, found one such site in his grazing land near

Cameron, Arizona, 60 miles east of the Grand Canyon, and called the EPA, which found a radioactivity level that, in two days, would expose a human being (or sheep) to levels of toxicity considered unsafe for a year. Such exposure can lead to malignant tumors and other serious health problems, according to Lee Greer, a biologist at La Sierra University in Riverside, California (MacMillan, 2012). "If this level of radioactivity were found in a middle-class suburb, the response would be immediate and aggressive," said Doug Brugge, a public health professor at Tufts University Medical School and an expert on uranium. "The site is remote, but there are obviously people spending time on it. Don't they deserve some concern?" (MacMillan, 2012).

Radiation Remediation at a Personal Level

Elsie Mae Begay's family experienced levels of radiation more than 80 times the EPA limit, as described in the film *The Return of Navajo Boy* (2000). Begay was forced to leave her hogan during cleanup but expressed a strong desire to return home even as Musante admitted that the land "can never go back to what it was before" ("Cleaning Up Uranium," 2011). In 2011, according to the Indian Country Today Media Network, "the Navajo Nation is already dealing with contamination from previous uranium mines and its attendant high rates of cancer, heart disease and birth defects. Cleanup efforts are taking years, and the U.S. Environmental Protection Agency (EPA) is evaluating more than 500 sites in the western part of the Navajo Nation."

Uranium tailings cleanup has its own perils. Parts of the Navajo reservation have been so polluted by uranium mining that families whose members have lived there for hundreds of years are being forced to leave their homes and lands so that contaminated soil can be removed. The mines and mills have been closed, but the waste piles endure, polluting water when it rains and creating deadly dust during long, droughty periods. Federal environmental officials have been stunned at the extent of uranium contamination. Unrecorded mine sites continue to surface, in many cases after people have fallen into abandoned shafts. "It is shocking—it's all over the reservation," said Jared Blumenfeld. "I think everyone, even the Navajos themselves, have been shocked about the number of mines that were both active and abandoned" (Frosch, 2014, A-12).

In 2014, Bertha Nez, who lives near Church Rock, was facing the prospect of having to abandon her ancestral home at age 67. She had spent months in Gallup motel rooms as radioactive soil was removed from her community. "This is where we're used to being, traditionally, culturally," she said. "Nobody told us it was unsafe. Nobody warned us we would be living all this time with this risk." An enormous pile of uranium mine waste near Nez's home may require eight years of cleanup. Relocations are voluntary, but many Navajos are skeptical whether radioactivity can be restored to safe levels. "Our umbilical cords are buried here, our children's umbilical cords are buried here. It's like a homing device," said Tony Hood, 64, who worked in the mines. "This is our connection to Mother Earth. We were born here. We will come back here eventually" (Frosch, 2014, A-12).

Between 2008 and 2012, U.S. federal agencies spent $100 million on the cleanup, according to the EPA. An additional $17 million was spent by energy companies responsible for some of the tailings. Waste removal is encumbered by bureaucracy. An application to remove tailings requires filing paperwork with the NRC, which conducts environmental reviews. Required public hearings also can stall actual removal of toxic waste for several years. "That time frame seems unreasonably long for tribal members, who said that spending so long living away from the reservation has been difficult" (Frosch, 2014, A-12). By the end of 2013, the EPA had spent $1 million on temporary housing for residents of Nez's community, much of it billed to General Electric, which acquired the old Northeast Church Rock Mine site in 1997 and its subsidiary, United Nuclear Corporation, operator of the mine.

In a decision handed down on December 12, 2013, Allan L. Gropper, U.S. bankruptcy judge, said that Anadarko and Kerr-McGee are liable for damages between $4.1 billion and $5.1 billion to a large group of plaintiffs that include "the United States, 22 states, four environmental response trusts and a trust for the benefit of certain tort plaintiffs" ("Navajo Nation," 2013). The Navajo Nation was scheduled to receive about $1 billion of the settlement to clean up 49 mining and milling sites. As large as the settlement seemed, it left untouched about 90 percent of the more than 500 abandoned radioactive sites that affect the Navajo.

Navajo Nation president Ben Shelly said that "any funds resulting from this lawsuit are welcomed and long overdue." The Navajo Nation's abandoned uranium mines are part of roughly 2,000 sites across the United States that have been "contaminated with various toxic compounds, radioactive waste and other chemicals that are compromising health for numerous communities. The plaintiffs are joined under a litigation trust, which was seeking $25 billion to clean up the U.S. sites" ("Navajo Nation," 2013). Given the nature of the proceeding (bankruptcy) and the fact that it will be appealed, whether and when the Navajos and other parties will receive anything remains an open question.

The Navajos said that, even lacking payment, legal validation had some value: "While we recognize the uncertainties of the appeal process and the long road that may be ahead of us, this is still a day of celebration for the Navajo Nation. A federal judge has issued a ruling that could result in over a billion dollars being made available for cleaning up some of the uranium contamination from past uranium mining and processing on the Navajo Nation" ("Navajo Nation" 2013).

Further Reading

Brugge, Doug, Timothy Benally, and Esther Yazzie-Lewis, eds. *The Navajo People and Uranium Mining.* Albuquerque: University of New Mexico Press, 2006.

"Cleaning Up Uranium in the Navajo Nation." Indian Country Today Media Network, May 31, 2011. http://indiancountrytodaymedianetwork.com/article/cleaning-up-uranium-in-the-navajo-nation-36290

"Cleanup Planned for Largest Abandoned Uranium Mine on the Navajo Nation." Environment News Service, September 29, 2011. http://ens-newswire.com/2011/09/30/cleanup-planned-for-largest-abandoned-uranium-mine-on-the-navajo-nation/

Fahys, Judy. "Uranium Cleanup Under Way on Navajo Land." *Salt Lake Tribune*, May 25, 2011. http://www.sltrib.com/sltrib/politics/51833502-90/begay-cleanup-epa-helen.html.csp

Frosch, Dan. "Amid Toxic Waste, a Navajo Village Could Lose Its Land." *New York Times*, February 20, 2014, A-9, A-12. http://www.nytimes.com/2014/02/20/us/nestled-amid-toxic-waste-a-navajo-village-faces-losing-its-land-forever.html

Johansen, Bruce E. "Victims of Progress: Navajo Miners" [Review of Eichstaedt, *If You Poison Us*]. *Native Americas* 12, no. 3 (Fall 1995): 60–61.

Johansen, Bruce E. "The High Cost of Uranium in Navajoland." *Akwesasne Notes New Series* 2, no. 2 (Spring 1997): 10–12, 1997. http://ratical.com/radiation/UraniumInNavLand.html

MacMillan, Leslie. "Uranium Mines Dot Navajo Land, Neglected and Still Perilous." *New York Times*, March 31, 2012. http://www.nytimes.com/2012/04/01/us/uranium-mines-dot-navajo-land-neglected-and-still-perilous.html

"Navajo Nation Could Get $1 Billion in Damages for Uranium Mess." Indian Country Today Media Network, December 18, 2013. http://indiancountrytodaymedianetwork.com/2013/12/18/navajo-nation-could-get-1-billion-damages-uranium-mess-152782

Hunting Grounds to Dumping Grounds

A cruel irony for Native Americans turns on the fact that so many of their former hunting grounds have been turned to dumps for nuclear and other toxic wastes. In addition to being rooted in their homelands, Native Americans maintain historical, spiritual bonds to the land that foster attention to environmental threats. While they observed "Mother Earth," immigrant Europeans saw the same lands as a "mother lode" and, by and by, industrial garbage dumps.

Indigenous environmental activism (including visceral opposition to development of extractive industries) stems from long historical experience with resource colonization, which works in synthesis with a spiritual ethos that invests a living spirit in everything natural. While European religions often restrict their blessings to humanity, many Native Americans interpret "all my relations" to mean all of nature—animate and not—even the rocks upon which we walk. This respect for nature is fundamental and enduring, and at the root of traditional Native American responses to economic development. Definitions of "balance" are couched in this context.

A Village of Tents and Tipis Blocks a Nuclear Dump in California's Ward Valley

A village of tents and tipis grew in the desert 22 miles west of Needles, California, during the last half of February 1998 as several hundred Native American and non-Indian environmentalists put their bodies on the line in an attempt to stop construction of a dump for low-level nuclear waste on land they regard as sacred. By the third week of February, roughly 250 people were camped at "ground zero" of Ward Valley, 80 acres of federally owned land designated for the waste site. The encampment prevented soil testing necessary for planning of the dump, which had been proposed to receive waste from hospitals, nuclear plants, and other industries that cannot dispose of radioactive materials in other landfills.

By February 19, occupants of the encampment had defied two sets of federal orders to leave the site and had blocked roads leading to it. A 15-day order that had been issued in late January expired on February 14. A new five-day eviction order issued that day expired on February 19, with protesters still eyeball to eyeball with a circle of Bureau of Land Management (BLM) vehicles that had surrounded their camp. Protesters said that the BLM and other federal agents had been rumbling around the camp in large Land Rovers and flying over it in small aircraft and helicopters at odd hours of the night in an attempt to intimidate the campers and deprive them of sleep. Religious ceremonies continued in the camp amid the glare of headlamps and the drone of aircraft overhead. Some of the protesters had chained themselves together. After complaints (and the arrival of news media reporters), the vehicles were withdrawn from the perimeter of the camp.

Steve Lopez, a Fort Mojave native spokesman, said that the Ward Valley is central to the creation stories of many Native American peoples in the area as well as the habitat of endangered tortoise species. "Taking away the land is taking away part of ourselves. They used to use bullets to kill our people off. Now it's radioactive waste," Lopez said (Johansen, 1998, 7). Ward Valley is also sacred to many Native peoples in the area because of its proximity to Spirit Mountain, the birthplace of their ancestors.

The protesters included a number of elders affiliated with five Colorado River basin tribes (Fort Mojave, Chemehuevi, Cocopah, Quechan, and Colorado River Indians) who, along with the rest of the protesters, refused to move. Instead, people in the encampment sent out appeals for supplies and more visitors, asking, according to a Colorado American Indian Movement (AIM) posting on the Internet, for "the physical presence of anyone willing to travel to Ward Valley and participate in the protection of this sacred land and the people defending it." Donations of food, water, blankets, batteries, and rain gear were requested. Wally Antone of the Colorado River Native Nations Alliance said, "Our ceremonies will continue here and our elders will not move. You will have to drag us out, and I say those words with honor" (Johansen, 1998, 7).

On February 18, as the BLM's second deadline was set to expire, leaders of the camp invited five BLM officials to their central fire for a religious ceremony, after which the officials were told that the protesters would not move. Andy Mader of Arizona AIM said via the Internet that all the cellular phones in the camp were malfunctioning. Some suspected that the government had shut them down. Meanwhile, supporters of the protest outside the camp had received phone calls indicating that several other AIM chapters were sending people to Ward Valley.

Tom Goldtooth, national director of the Indigenous Environmental Network, reported from the camp via the Internet that the protest had become so vigorous not only because the land is regarded as sacred by Native peoples but also because many southern California and Arizona urban areas rely on the Colorado River for water that could be polluted by the proposed waste dump. The same water is used to irrigate crops in both the United States and Mexico.

A position paper circulated by Save Ward Valley, an environmental coalition, stated that the proposed dump lies above a major aquifer 18 miles from the Colorado River. Furthermore, the report asserted that all six of the presently active nuclear waste dumps in the United States are leaking. U.S. Ecology, the contractor selected for the Ward Valley site, presently operates four of those six dumps, the position paper said.

The coalition also asserted that all the waste buried at such sites is not low level. As much as 90 percent of the radioactivity proposed for burial would come from nuclear power plants, including cesium, strontium, and plutonium, the statement said. Speaking on behalf of the coalition, Goldtooth, who coordinated protests by non-Native supporters, evaluated the protest, which eventually caused plans for the dump to be shelved as a measure of environmental justice:

> Incorporating the importance of . . . traditional ways and the use of the sacred Fire as the foundation for guidance and resistance as we fight for environmental justice and Native rights has proven successful at Ward Valley. I applaud the many non-Natives from the peace movement to the anti-nuclear movement and the global human family that raised the consciousness of the world that the sacred tortoise and the ecology of a desert environment must not be sacrificed anymore by the whims of the nuclear waste industry. I witnessed the coming together of the non-Native supporters and the Colorado River tribal communities and Tribal Nations in an historical moment where everyone agreed to fight together with one mind and one spirit to defend the sacredness of the Mother Earth and to defend the sovereignty of the Fort Mojave Tribal Nation. (Goldtooth, 2001, in Johansen, 2016, 197)

Washington State's Yakamas and Hanford's Radioactive Legacy

The Hanford Nuclear Reservation in eastern Washington State (within the treaty boundary of the Yakama Nation) has become a storage site for roughly 53 million gallons of high-level chemical and radioactive wastes that released irradiated water 30 miles upstream from the Yakama Reservation between 1945 and 1989. The presence of this porous depository in their midst has exposed some people to levels of radiation similar to that of the Chernobyl nuclear accident.

Due to this decades-long bath of radiation dumped directly into the river system, oysters caught at the mouth of the Columbia River were so toxic by the early 1960s that when one Hanford employee ate them and returned to work the following day, he set off the plant's radiation alarm. An investigation revealed that the day before, he had eaten a can of oyster stew contaminated with radioactive zinc. The oysters had been harvested in Willapa Bay, along the Pacific Coast in Washington State, 25 miles north of Astoria, at the mouth of the Columbia.

The 560-square-mile Hanford Nuclear Reservation was established during 1943 on lands traditionally used for hunting, fishing, and gathering by the Yakama and Umatilla. The same area is adjacent to the homeland of the Nez Perce. The Hanford facility produced the plutonium used in the first atom bombs dropped on Hiroshima and Nagasaki. Thus, releases of radioactive materials have been contaminating these peoples, as well as the Coeur d'Alene, Spokane, Colville, Kootenai, and Warm Springs tribes, for many years. In 1986, after disclosure that radiation was secretly released into the air and water from 1944 until January 1971, when the last of Hanford's reactors was closed, Yakama leaders were among the first to call for a thorough study of the danger.

For nearly 30 years, ending in 1971, eight of the nine nuclear reactors at the Hanford complex were cooled by water from the Columbia River. Millions of gallons of water that had been pumped directly through the reactor cores picked up large amounts of nuclear material, making the Columbia downstream the most radioactive river in the world, according to state and federal authorities (Schneider, 1990, A-9). In July 1990, a federal panel said that some infants and children in the 1940s absorbed enough radioactive iodine to destroy their thyroid glands and to cause an array of thyroid-related diseases.

Although Hanford has stopped producing plutonium, recently released documents indicate that radioactive materials leaking from storage tanks there have continued to contaminate groundwater in the area. The Indigenous Environmental Network reported that "the Hanford site also has eight nuclear reactors that have . . . contaminated the Columbia River on which many of the Tribes depend for basic sustenance" (Johansen, 2016, 23). Unaware of the contamination, indigenous people collected berries near the Columbia, hunted for eels in its tributaries, and took salmon from its waters.

New York Times reporter Keith Schneider (1990, A-9) described the Colombia below the Hanford Reservation: "Dammed in the 1950s below Hanford and developed by industrial companies, the river's water is green and gray now. Salmon runs are much smaller than they were before World War II, and Johnny Jackson, a 59-year-old fisherman . . . said some fish he catches were marred by deep, infected welts and growths. . . . Documents declassified beginning in 1986 said that radiation spread to the river's bacteria, algae, mussels, fish, birds and the water used for both irrigation and drinking."

Radiation in the river has caused concern at Hanford for decades. In 1954, the situation was reviewed in secret meetings at the Washington, D.C., headquarters of the Atomic Energy Commission (AEC), which operated the plant. Lewis L. Strauss, the commission's chairman, flew to Hanford in the summer of 1954 and was told that "levels of radioactivity in some fish in the Columbia River, particularly whitefish, were so high that officials were considering closing sport fishing downstream" (Schneider, 1990, A-9). Ducks, geese, and crops irrigated with Columbia River water also were said to pose a potential health threat. The public never was alerted.

Further Reading

Goldtooth, Tom. "Indigenous Environmental Network Statement to Nora Helton, Chairwoman, Fort Mojave Indian Tribe, Other Lower Colorado River Indian Tribal Leaders, Tribal Community Members, Elders and Non-Native Groups and Individuals, in Reference to the Ward Valley Victory Gathering to Celebrate the Defeat of a Proposed Nuclear Waste Dump, Ward Valley, California." February 16, 2001. In Johansen, *Resource Exploitation*, 2016, 197.

Johansen, Bruce. 1998. "Ward Valley: A 'Win' for Native Elders." *Native Americas* 15, no. 2 (Summer 1998): 7–8.

Johansen, Bruce E. *Resource Exploitation in Native North America: A Plague upon the Peoples.* Santa Barbara, CA: ABC-CLIO, 2016.

"Prairie Island Indian Community Calls for Permanent Nuclear-Waste Solution." Indian Country Today Media Network, September 5, 2012. http://indiancountrytodaymedianetwork.com/article/prairie-island-indian-community-calls-for-permanent-nuclear-waste-solution-132820

Schneider, Keith. "Washington Nuclear Plant Poses Risk for Indians." *New York Times*, September 3, 1990, A-9.

The Moapa Paiute: Good-Bye Toxic Ash: Solar In, Coal Power Out

Quite a few people who would like to retire smoke-belching, sulfur-spewing, carbon-pumping, coal-fired power plants might consider taking lessons from the Moapa Paiutes, whose reservation north of Las Vegas, Nevada, was under the ash-laced emissions of an old, coal-fired power plant until they organized, and successfully closed it. Next, they acquired seed capital from the Department of the Interior for two large solar arrays, creating jobs and taking advantage of southern Nevada's plentiful sunshine.

On March 16, 2017, the first solar farm on Native American land began operation, with 250 megawatts generated by more than 3.2 million solar panels covering 2.2 square miles of shimmering desert, enough to power about 110,000 average homes. Most of the power is being sold to Los Angeles–area utilities, part of a plan to derive one-third of that city's power from renewable sources by 2020 and one-half by 2025 (Ritter, 2017).

Closing Down Dirty Coal

In 2013, the Reid Gardner Generating Station, a coal-fired power plant adjacent to the Moapa River reservation (about 50 miles north of Las Vegas), was slated for closure in 2017. The closure was good news, but the Moapa Band of Paiutes had a new problem: ramping up pressure on its owner, NV Energy, Inc., to clean up residual pollution. On August 8, 2013, the band and the Sierra Club filed suit in U.S. district court in Las Vegas to legally compel the cleanup. NV Energy was bought out in May 2013 by Warren Buffett's MidAmerican Energy Holdings, which has taken an active role in raising Iowa's use of wind power for electrical generation to about two-thirds of its production by 2017. Reid Gardner is the last coal-burning power plant in Nevada. The lawsuit claimed "that the federal Resource Conservation and Recovery Act and the Clean Water Act have both been violated over the years by dumping that has compromised the health of nearby residents and threatens the drinking water of millions" ("Moapa Paiute Sue," 2013). The lawsuit alleges that for several years, the power plant illegally dumped toxins into the Muddy River, flowing into the Lake Mead reservoir behind Hoover Dam, a source of drinking water for more than 2 million people.

Coal's Health Effects

"We are all looking forward to the retirement of the Reid Gardner coal-fired plant that has for decades polluted our reservation," said Vickie Simmons, a leader of the Moapa Band of Paiutes Committee for Health and the Environment. "And for the sake of our families' health, we must ensure that the toxic waste from the power plant is fully cleaned up. The safety of our community and the future of our children depend on it" ("Moapa Paiute Sue," 2013). "Now, we have to find out what kind of remediation they're going to do—a complete restoration, a conversion to gas or some other type of project," tribal chairman William Anderson told the Associated Press. "To us, the ultimate goal would be to remove everything and put the land back the way it was. We'll be able to come to closure after almost 50 years" ("Moapa Paiute Sue," 2013). On Earth Day 2012, the Moapa Paiute had protested the Reid Gardner Power Plant in Las Vegas with members of the Sierra Club on a 50-mile "Cultural Healing Walk" that took three days in 100-degree temperatures.

Reservation residents said that the plant has been a threat to their health for several years. William Anderson, Moapa Band chairman, said, "The high percentage of thyroid and respiratory problems is a big concern for the tribal members on the reservation. . . . We need a proper study from air monitoring equipment installed on the reservation to study the emissions we're breathing in. That would help determine what needs to be done for our people's health. We also need more stringent storage conditions for coal ash and a study to be conducted to show the health risks associated with breathing in coal ash" ("Moapa Paiute March," 2012).

"We asked the EPA to at least study the plant or give us a grant to do the study to see exactly what poisons were coming from there, but we were told we didn't qualify for the study or the grant," said Vernon Lee, a Moapa Paiute. "In order to get a federal study grant, there have to be 500 people affected. There are only about 300 members of the Moapa Band and not all of us live on the reservation." The Indian Country Today Media Network reported from the scene:

> Air pollution takes the form of toxic coal dust, which tribal members say arrives in giant clouds that send people scurrying indoors, but that's not the only problem they have observed. "There are also several settling ponds for coal ash residue, there are enormous piles of coal that are uncovered, and a huge coal ash landfill that is also uncovered," said Barb Boyle of the Sierra Club, in an article published on the *Huffington Post*'s website, written by Mary Ann Hitt, director of the Sierra Club's Beyond Coal campaign. Boyle said that the Tribe "has borne this burden for decades. It's time to stop." The plant was built in 1965, and the Moapa Paiute say they have witnessed their own standard of living plummet over time. "In my era, we were all healthy people," Aletha Tom, who runs the Moapa school house, [said]. "We didn't have the asthma, thyroid problems, cancer, diabetes, but we have that on our reservation. It's so major now." ("Moapa Paiute March," 2012)

Soon, due to the tribe's persistence, local television stations and newspapers brought the plague of ash-borne illness to a broader audience. A video, *An Ill Wind: The Secret Threat of Coal Ash*, reached people from the tribe's website, reporting that the power station "dumps toxin-laden coal ash, a byproduct of combustion, into landfills that lie just a few hundred yards from the reservation. On windy days, coal-ash dust from the plant billows over the reservation, with clouds so thick that you can see and taste them, tribal members say. At such times, residents don't dare let their children play outside. That apparently offers limited protection, though, as the dust seeps into homes, schools and cars" (Woodard, 2012). The Sierra Club, Earthjustice, and Greenpeace assisted the tribe's efforts.

Winning Allies

In their long campaign, the Moapa Paiutes won allies. Senator Harry Reid, Democrat of Nevada, called the Reid Gardner Power Station a "dirty relic" and supported its closure. In June, tribal chairman William Anderson told Indian Country Today Media Network that "the Interior Department gave the Moapa Paiutes fast-tracked approval to build the first-ever utility-scale solar-energy project on tribal lands—which seems especially suitable in this region, with its many months of scorching sun."

The 350-megawatt plant generates enough power for 100,000 homes, bringing lease income for the tribe, as well as new jobs. It also provided about 400 jobs at peak construction and 15 to 20 permanent jobs—real career jobs tribal members can look forward to, said Anderson. "Our energy customers will likely be in California, where people have an interest in renewable-energy sources." Construction, which was completed over several years, included a preserve for the endangered desert tortoise. "We're right by an energy corridor, with many above- and below-ground lines for electricity, natural gas, fiber optics, and more easily accessible," Anderson said. "Connecting is much less expensive than if we were farther away" (Woodard, 2012).

As bright as the future was in 2014, when the solar array was begun, the Moapa Paiute at that time were still suffering the coal plant's effects. "Every home has someone—or even everyone—using a breathing apparatus or inhaler," Anderson said. "We see frequent deaths, the most recent being someone in the home closest to the plant." All along, NV Energy said it was continuing its commitment "to operate the Reid Gardner Generating Station in an environmentally responsible manner, in compliance with all federal and state laws, and in the best interests of its customers" (Woodard, 2012).

In May 2014, the Moapa were awarded a second solar-energy array by the Department of the Interior just as construction began on the first. The second array, on 850 acres of Moapa land, is sited 20 miles northeast of Las Vegas. The second array, which will provide power for 60,000 homes, was being constructed to minimize water usage. Secretary of the Interior Sally Jewell said that the array "reflects the Obama administration's steadfast commitment to work with Indian Country leaders to promote strong, prosperous and resilient tribal economies and communities. . . . This solar project and these grants also deliver on the President's Climate Action Plan goals to spur important investments and jobs in tribal communities that can be leveraged to address some of the impacts from climate change that threaten tribal lands, waters and ways of life" ("Moapa Paiute to Host," 2014).

In August 2015, for $4.3 million, the Moapa settled a lawsuit against NV Energy filed in 2013 with the Sierra Club, alleging that the Reid Gardner Power Generation Station had harmed their health and water supply, thus violating the Resource Conservation and Recovery Act and the Clean Water Act. "For years the band has suffered the consequences of breathing dangerous dirty air from the Reid-Gardner coal plant and this settlement is a step forward," said Senator Reid. "While the settlement will provide relief and help make the tribe's home healthier and safer, no amount of money can pay for the sickness caused by a half-century of pollution from the coal plant. The Moapa Band of Paiutes and all Nevadans deserve a clean, healthy environment to raise their families in and pass on to their children" ("$4.3 Million," 2015).

Further Reading

"$4.3 Million Settlement over Reid-Gardner Coal Plant for Moapa Paiute." Indian Country Today Media Network, August 6, 2015. http://indiancountrytodaymedianetwork.com/2015/08/06/43-million-settlement-over-reid-gardner-coal-plant-moapa-paiute-161299

"Moapa Paiute to Host Second Solar Project on Its Lands." Indian Country Today Media Network, May 29, 2014. http://indiancountrytodaymedianetwork.com/2014/05/29/moapa-paiute-host-2nd-solar-project-its-lands-155071

"Moapa Paiute March 50 Miles in Anti-Coal Protest." Indian Country Today Media Network, April 27, 2012. http://indiancountrytodaymedianetwork.com/article/moapa-paiute-march-50-miles-in-anti-coal-protest-110450

"Moapa Paiute Sue over Coal Plant Contaminants." Indian Country Today Media Network, August 9, 2013. http://indiancountrytodaymedianetwork.com/2013/08/09/moapa-paiute-sue-over-coal-plant-contaminants-150806

Ritter, Ken. "Officials Mark Completion of First Tribal Solar Power Plant." *Santa Fe New Mexican*, May 17, 2017. http://www.santafenewmexican.com/news/officials-mark-completion-of-tribal-land-solar-power-plant/article_479f55f5-e849-5d05-b277-bfa1a2e19dad.html

Woodard, Stephanie. "Moapa Paiutes Find Solar Solution Amid Coal Ash Plague." Indian Country Today Media Network, August 17, 2012. http://indiancountrytodaymedianetwork.com/article/moapa-paiutes-find-solar-solution-amid-coal-ash-plague-129554

CHAPTER FIVE

Cases: Canada

Introduction

Canada contains a very large number of environmental racism case studies, many of them in Arctic regions that popular imagination stereotypes as clean, pristine, and snow-swept. Nothing could be further from the truth. Not only is the region experiencing the planet's highest rate of warming due to human combustion of fossil fuels (which is ruining traditional styles of life and subsistence), but prevailing winds have deposited huge amounts of persistent organic pollutants in the Arctic. Most of these (PCBs and dioxins being the most prominent) have been outlawed after substantial advocacy by the Inuit, but they are very difficult to remove from the food chain. As a result, the Inuit style of life has been changed, possibly forever, due not only to the continuing melting of a world where life has been wedded to ice and snow, but to the persistent afflictions of synthesized chemicals imposed on them by the industrialized world.

Canada, which often prides itself on an allegedly humane civil rights record regarding indigenous peoples (which usually are called First Nations there), has become a major source of indigenous environmental contamination and conflict. These conflicts span the country from the east to the west, and from north to south. The Innu of Labrador have been afflicted with sulfide mining, aluminum smelting, and noise pollution from squadrons of military aircraft. Along the Arctic Circle, the native Inuit suffer major problems ranging from contamination by the previously mentioned persistent organic pollutants such as dioxins and PCBs, among others. Few other peoples have had their lives so fundamentally changed over such a short time. Inuit mothers appealed to the world to stop the toxification of their homeland—and won, at least on paper negotiated through international diplomacy. The Inuit of Canada played a major role in convincing the world that most persistent organic pollutants should be banned worldwide in the Stockholm Convention.

It is, however, a long road back. These chemicals are still embedded in the Arctic food chain (as they are in many similarly polluted places further south) to a degree that diplomacy simply cannot remove. Similarly, with regard to the rapid warming of the Arctic, the laws of geophysics, most notably thermal inertia, guarantee that until the proportion of carbon dioxide and other greenhouse gases in the atmosphere starts to decline worldwide, rapidly warming temperatures will continue to heat the atmosphere for at least 50 years after our energy sources change from fossil fuels to renewables. The world has yet to confront a fundamental issue that some scientists now call the question of "unburnable carbon," which estimates how much oil, natural gas, and coal will have to remain in the ground to avoid catastrophic global warming.

In the meantime, the fossil-fuel economy itself, irrespective of its emissions' effect on the climate, rapes the lands of Native peoples across Canada, a graphic example being the Crees of Alberta, whose homelands have been scarred by the mining and processing of tar sands to the point that they resemble a "moonscape," pockmarked and mainly lifeless. The oil industry mines and refines sand-laced oil tar that requires more energy to manufacture than will be produced by its use, thereby increasing its impact on the climate of a warming Earth.

Some of the most intense resource exploitation in Canada takes place in remote locations, such as among the Lubicon Cree of northern Alberta, whose lands were so inaccessible in 1900 that treaty makers completely missed them. Today, roads have opened their lands to massive oil drilling and logging. The lands of the Cree in Quebec have been scarred by widespread dam building near James Bay that has contaminated large areas with toxic methyl mercury, as well as other pollutants. Uranium mining has decimated the Dene in Canada's Northwest Territories much as it has ravaged the Navajo in the southwestern United States. The catalogue of indigenous environmental issues in Canada spans the range of resources—from hydropower, to diamonds, uranium, gold, silver, and sulfide, aluminum, oil, and natural gas.

Some of Canada's toxification involves the kind of chemical plants that are more common in the United States. Between 1962 and 1970, before it ceased operations, a Dryden paper mill poured more than 10 tons of mercury into the Wabigoon-English River system, and into the fish and bloodstreams of people in the Grassy Narrows community in Ontario.

The plant was long gone by 2017, but the mercury and its debilitating effects remained.

"In Canada, as the environmental law group Ecojustice has argued," wrote Stephen Bede Scharper, who teaches religion and environment at the University of Toronto, in the *Toronto Star*, "examples of environmental racism can be found among black communities in Nova Scotia, and in the contaminated water that pockmarks dozens of indigenous communities across Canada." As a member of the Nova Scotia Legislative Assembly, Karla MacFarlane, has argued, "What we have to realize is that environmental racism remains a reality for all people, and has been for generations." Recognizing the connection "between race, socioeconomic status and environmental risk," MacFarlane continued, "We can't continue to keep the blinders on" (Scharper, 2016).

Kaitlyn Mitchell, Ecojustice national program director, wrote in the *Huffington Post*, "Environmental racism remains a reality in Canada." On a national scale, nothing illustrates Canada's startling environmental inequities more clearly than the lack of access to clean drinking water in First Nations communities. In the absence of a national water law, communities under federal jurisdiction, such as First Nations reservations, have virtually no legal protection of their drinking water. As of January 2015, drinking water advisories were in effect in 126 First Nation communities across Canada. In fact, according to a 2009 study by the United Nations, First Nations homes are 90 times more likely to be without safe drinking water than other Canadian homes (Mitchell, 2015).

Further Reading

Mitchell, Kaitlyn. "Environmental Racism Remains a Reality in Canada." *Huffington Post*, May 7, 2015. http://www.huffingtonpost.ca/ecojustice/environmental-racism-canadal_b_7224904.html

Scharper, Stephen Bede. "Grassy Narrows Mercury Disaster a Form of Environmental Racism." *The Star* [Toronto, Ontario], June 29, 2016. https://www.thestar.com/opinion/commentary/2016/06/29/grassy-narrows-mercury-disaster-a-form-of-environmental-racism.html

Grassy Narrows, Ontario: The Continuing Toxic Toll of Mercury

"No more fancy talk, no more studies. We just want it cleaned up," said Chief Simon Fobister of the Grassy Narrows First Nation during June 2016, expressing his resolve to combat more than half a century of life-threatening mercury levels in the water of his people's reserve in northwestern Ontario. Between 1962 and 1970, before it ceased operations, a Dryden paper mill poured more than 10 tons of mercury into the Wabigoon-English River system, and into the fish and bloodstreams of people in the Grassy Narrows community. The plant was long gone by 2017, but the mercury and its debilitating effects continued. "While Chief Fobister suggests his community's unaddressed mercury contamination is a result of 'willful neglect,' it might also be the result of something more insidious. It also smacks of racism, specifically, environmental racism," wrote Stephen Bede Scharper in the *Toronto Star* (2016).

Mercury, a persistent organic pollutant (POP), is very tough to remove from the food chain. It is especially toxic because it bioaccumulates in living things—that is, effects increase as it is consumed up the food chain, "inflicting increasing levels of harm on higher-order species," according to Environment and Climate Change Canada (Bruser and Poisson, 2017). Bacteria that multiply in liquid environments with low oxygen levels (including lake bottoms) cause mercury to change into methylmercury, an especially toxic form, which bioaccumulates in fish, then increases its potency in people who eat them.

Deformed babies continued to be born on the Grassy Narrows First Nation in Ontario decades after Dryden Chemical Co. dumped neurotoxins into the river. More than half of 160 people who were examined there had symptoms of mercury poisoning, 40 percent of whom had Minamata disease, a form of acute, long-term mercury contamination that causes seizures, tremors, tunnel vision, and loss of coordination. Mercury visible in the soil is "gross industrial pollution," said leading mercury scientist John Rudd, who has studied Grassy Narrows and has been involved in the remediation of other industrial facilities that used mercury in the production process. "When you see that, it's the worst possible situation. I've seen that at other plants. That mercury then dissolves into the groundwater and the groundwater could then move the mercury toward the river" (Bruser and Poisson, 2017).

Tests of well water pollution in the area, which reflect groundwater levels, have indicated astoundingly high toxic mercury levels, as high as 4,482 times the contemporary standard established by Ontario's government at 0.29 micrograms per liter. Many of the tested wells were old, poorly constructed, and rusty, which may have led to underreporting of contamination levels (Bruser and Poisson, 2017). Some of the wells were destroyed after initial testing, complicating record-keeping over time.

"Both the federal and provincial governments need to recognize and effectively address the lasting issue of mercury exposure in First Nation communities along the English Wabigoon River system," Assembly of First

Nations (AFN) national chief Shawn A-in-chut Atleo said. "The federal and provincial governments' callous disregard for the health and well-being of the Grassy Narrows community is appalling," said AFN regional chief Angus Toulouse, speaking for the chiefs of Ontario. "The poverty and ill health currently being experienced by Grassy Narrows' citizens are the direct consequences of unregulated development, and disregarding the community's right to free, prior and informed consent on activities that occur within their traditional territory" ("Mercury Poisoning," 2012).

Extent of Mercury Poisoning Revealed

Canadian authorities were slow to recognize the extent of the poisoning. Japanese scientists did the early work linking the Dryden Chemical Company's emissions with illnesses induced by mercury toxicity. By 1984, a panel of scientists appointed by provincial and federal authorities advised the government that remediation (e.g., cleanup) was overdue. The governmental bodies still did not allocate money. Decided against action, the provincial authorities decided to let nature "remediate itself," repudiating the scientists.

When the extent of mercury poisoning in Grassy Narrows' waters was revealed during the 1970s, its economy, which had been based on fishing, suffered major damage that has never been repaired. The fish contained levels of mercury that made them inedible. The tourist fishing industry also collapsed; subsistence fishing people went on welfare, along with tour guides. The mercury, which is a potent neurotoxin, also toxified the walleye that had been a staple of the indigenous diet for centuries, producing loss of muscle coordination and tunnel vision in people who ate them. Fetuses were most vulnerable to brain damage.

Absorbed through the digestive tract, methylmercury "readily enters the brain," where it can remain for a long time, according to Health Canada. In a pregnant woman, it can build up in the fetal brain and other tissues (Bruser and Poisson, 2017). The Japanese specialize in mercury toxicity because of their experience with it (methylmercury poisoning was discovered in 1956 in the town of Minamata, Japan). The disease in an extremely concentrated form provokes severe effects, including paralysis, coma, and death.

Decades Pass, Little Changes

Several decades of poisoning passed and little changed at Grassy Narrows. Canada had, in effect, turned its back on the Grassy Narrows First

Nation. "For Craig Benjamin, indigenous rights coordinator for Amnesty International," wrote Stephen Bede Scharper (2016), who teaches environmental studies at the University of Toronto, Grassy Narrows is "a clear example of environmental racism." He added, "The government's failure to acknowledge the nature of the harm inflicted on the community, to conduct ongoing health monitoring, to provide specialized health services for mercury poisoning, and to clean up the river spelled out something more than neglect. In light of these and other failings, Benjamin cannot but interpret the saga as one of 'racism and discrimination against indigenous peoples.'"

Tensions between the Grassy Narrows residents and Ontario's provincial government intensified in November 2017, after the *Toronto Star* published reports that mercury was continuing to leak from the old factory site, creating an ongoing source of toxicity. What was worse, in the eyes of indigenous peoples in the area, was that the officials had known that mercury had continued to leach into the soil, then into the water table, as well as the river for two decades after the government had told them it had stopped, and that the earth would repair itself naturally. The leaks were upstream from the Grassy Narrows First Nation's lands, so toxicity was continuing, even as officials classified their reports, which had been commissioned by Domtar (present owner of the mill site) and submitted to the provincial government during 2016.

"Further," reported the *Star*, "the report—which is based on a 'collection of historical sampling' from the mill's effluent—also reveals that groundwater samples taken from wells on the mill property over the years have come back with extremely high mercury levels. The province's Environment Ministry said it was unaware of this well data until it got the report in July 2016" (Bruser and Poisson, 2017). This assertion contradicted the report, which said that provincial officials had known of the continuing (and cumulative) contamination from two sites since some point in the 1990s, when the company disclosed the information (Bruser and Poisson, 2017).

The Ontario Environment Ministry met news that the report had been disclosed with its own public relations, saying that several million dollars was being spent to assess the situation to produce a plan to cleanse the river of mercury contamination that might require as much as $85 million Canadian. The ministry had said that the entire process would be transparent, and that all information would be shared. After decades of evasions, coverups, and lies, this news was greeted at Grassy Narrows with a degree of cynical resignation. Asked why the report describing continuing contamination had not been released, Ontario Environmental Ministry said that it could not release a third-party report that it did not own—a statement taken as a facile evasion by many people at Grassy Narrows.

Grassy Narrows grandmother and health advocate Judy Da Silva called news of the report "sickening." "It shows how lowly we are, the Anishinabeg, to the government and corporations. Like we are not worth it to be alive," said Da Silva. "They knew about this poison and they did nothing. They didn't even tell us. It is awful" (Bruser and Poisson, 2017). Grassy Narrows chief Simon Fobister said: "For decades I have been seeking justice for my people for mercury poisoning, searching for answers, searching for help. Never once was I told that mercury poison is still under the mill, right next to our river. I was told over and over that the mill site was cleaned up and that the problem ended in the '70s. I now see that was a deception and my people have paid the price with their health" (Bruser and Poisson, 2017).

Testing confirmed that mercury poisoning continued to be an acute problem. The *Toronto Star* reported, "The [Japanese] research team, which examined dozens of people of all ages in both communities during a 2014 trip, found that nearly all those tested had sensory disturbance—a telltale sign of mercury poisoning that includes a loss of sensation in the hands or feet and around the mouth. That rate is 'extremely high,' according to a report released by the researchers." Canadian officials showed little interest in the team's findings. The Japanese paid their own expenses (Bruser and Poisson, 2016). The Japanese who conducted the 2014 study were the same group that had been testing for mercury at Grassy Narrows and neighboring indigenous communities since 1975.

Rudd said that the delays in reporting the continuing mercury contamination is "very disappointing," because had it been known sooner, "the situation would have been very different now. It might be much better." He added: "What happens with pollution like this is it spreads and spreads, and until you turn off the source, the situation gets worse and worse. If this had been well understood in the 1990s and something was done, then there would be a lot smaller cleanup job than there is going to have to be now" (Bruser and Poisson, 2017).

Further Reading

Bruser, David, and Jayme Poisson. "Signs of Mercury Poisoning in Grassy Narrows Youth, Say Japanese Experts." *Toronto Star*, September 20, 2016. https://www.thestar.com/news/canada/2016/09/20/signs-of-mercury-poisoning-in-grassy-narrows-youth-say-japanese-experts.html

Bruser, David, and Jayme Poisson. "Ontario Knew about Grassy Narrows Mercury Site for Decades, but Kept It Secret." *Toronto Star*, November 11, 2017. https://www.thestar.com/news/canada/2017/11/11/ontario-knew-about-mercury-site-near-grassy-narrows-for-decades-but-kept-it-secret.html

"Mercury Poisoning Five Decades Later for Grassy Narrows and White Dog First Nation." Indian Country Today Media Network, June 12, 2012. http://indiancountrytodaymedianetwork.com/article/mercury-poisoning-five-decades-later-for-grassy-narrows-and-white-dog-first-nations-117843

Scharper, Stephen Bede. "Grassy Narrows Mercury Disaster a Form of Environmental Racism." *The Star* [Toronto, Ontario], June 29, 2016. https://www.thestar.com/opinion/commentary/2016/06/29/grassy-narrows-mercury-disaster-a-form-of-environmental-racism.html

The Aamjiwnaang of Ontario: Immersed in a Toxic Bath

The roughly 800 people who have lived in Ontario under the aegis of the Aamjiwnaang First Nation (previously known as the Sarnia Cree) for several centuries have found themselves with unwelcomed neighbors since the middle of the twentieth century: industrial plants representing about 40 percent of petrochemical manufacturing in Canada, a smaller analogue to "Cancer Alley" in Louisiana. "In 2011," according to Ecojustice of Canada, "the World Health Organization said that the people of Sarnia breathe some of the most polluted air in all of Canada. The Aamjiwnaang First Nation's homeland had heretofore been known as 'The place at the spawning stream—where the water flows spiritually like a braid'"— a cruel historic irony when this community of about 2,300 members, living on the St. Clair River, within the city of Sarnia, Ontario, found itself immersed in a toxic chemical bath.

Many people on the reserve live within eyesight of the chemical plants' smokestacks, and "sirens can blare at any time of the day to warn people to stay indoors when all-too-frequent pollution incidents occur. Sometimes, incidents happen and residents only learn about them after the fact. Seldom do they hear about government follow-up and enforcement measures" ("Changing Course," 2016).

A Wide Array of Health Maladies

For several decades, the mothers of Canada's Aamjiwnaang First Nations community have begun giving birth to a very low percentage of boys, and exposure to estrogen-blocking chemicals may be the reason. "While we're far from a conclusive statement, the kinds of health problems they experience—neurodevelopment, skewed sex ratios—are the health effects we would expect from such chemicals and metals," said Niladri Basu, an associate professor at Montreal's McGill University. A study in 2005 revealed that only about 35 percent of Aamjiwnaang infants were male (Bienkowski, 2013).

The Aamjiwnaang reserve lies about 15 miles from "Chemical Valley" (with more than 50 chemical factories, oil refineries, and other pollution sources) near the U.S.–Canadian border along Lake Huron, east of Michigan, across the St. Clair River. About 850 of 2,300 tribal members live on the reserve. Four types of PCBs have been measured in 42 children and mothers at Aamjiwnaang at levels two to seven times higher than average among Canadians. Most of the PCBs, which skew sex ratios, are common in fish in that area, but few of the people had eaten them. Basu suspected that the chemicals remained in the soil and air from decades ago, before they were banned in the 1970s. "Aamjiwnaang" means "at the spawning stream," describing their historical diet of fish, but anyone in the area has been warned since the 1970s not to eat fish from the lake and rivers.

"I'm struck by the elevated PCB levels," said Nancy Langston, a professor of environmental history at Michigan Technological University who was not involved in the study, "and the fact that all are anti-estrogenic." Some PCBs are anti-estrogenic, which means that they block the hormone, while others are estrogenic, which means that they mimic it (Bienkowski, 2013).

Other health problems also became common in the community. Brian Bienkowski, an expert in the field, described a wide variety of maladies in *Environmental Health News*:

> In addition to PCBs, the mothers and children had elevated levels of cadmium, some perfluorinated chemicals and the pesticides hexachlorocyclohexane and DDT compared with the Canadian average. . . . In addition to the skewed sex ratio, 23 percent of Aamjiwnaang children have learning or behavioral difficulties—a rate about six times higher than children in a neighboring county, according to a 2005 community study. . . . The asthma rate for children on the reservation is about 2.5 times higher than the rest of the county, according to a 2007 study by Ecojustice, a Canadian environmental organization. Birth complications also are commonplace. Of 132 women surveyed in the community in 2005, 39 percent had at least one stillbirth or miscarriage. The average for U.S. women is 15 percent, according to the National Institutes of Health. (Bienkowski, 2013)

Industrialization in the area increased as the Sarnia refinery owned by Suncor Energy expanded to handle tar-sands production from Alberta.

This also was true in other areas experiencing increases in petrochemical refining: "Men in Fort Saskatchewan—downwind of refineries and chemical manufacturers and tar sands processors—suffer from leukemia and non-Hodgkin lymphoma at higher rates than neighboring communities. . . . Two known carcinogens—butadiene and benzene—were found at higher levels in rural Fort Saskatchewan than in many of the world's most polluted cities," reported Isobel Simpson, lead author of the study and a chemist at the University of California, Irvine (Bienkowski, 2013).

Battling Ontario's Government

Despite protests, the Ontario provincial government continued to approve additional pollution "with no consideration of the environmental or health effects it could have when combined with existing pollution in the area. To make matters even worse, some of these government decisions—including those at issue in the lawsuit—are made in secret, without community input. Residents filed suit, asserting that these decisions violated their Charter (in the United States, constitutional) rights to equality and security of person.

Ecojustice lawyers representing two members of Aamjiwnaang First Nation, Ron Plain and Ada Lockridge, filed suit during 2011 "in their fight to ensure that the health of people living in one of Canada's most polluted communities—Sarnia's Chemical Valley—is protected."

According to Ecojustice, "Our clients asked the court to declare that an order issued by Ontario's Ministry of the Environment that allows Suncor Energy Products to increase production at part of its Sarnia refinery violated their Charter rights. Our clients believe that the government's failure to take into account the cumulative effects of pollution from all the industrial activity around their community violates Ada and Ron's basic human rights under sections 7 and 15 of the Canadian Charter of Rights and Freedoms—their rights to life, liberty and security of the person, and the right to equality" ("Defending," 2017).

The legal pressure produced extrajudicial negotiations and publicity. By 2017, the Ontario government had made enough progress for the suit to be withdrawn, according to Ecojustice. "To achieve our shared goal of reducing harmful pollution in Ontario communities, we're now focusing our energy on ensuring the government makes good on its new initiatives—starting with its efforts in Chemical Valley" ("Defending," 2017).

"We believe all Canadians have a right to breathe clean air and that governments have a responsibility to protect people and communities from unsafe levels of industrial pollution," wrote Ecojustice in a statement that accompanied the resolution of the lawsuit, adding that:

> The unjust distribution of the country's pollution burden, and the impact for Aboriginal communities like Aamjiwnaang, has both health and human rights implications. We are concerned by the Ontario government's practice of assessing each source of air pollution individually to determine whether emissions fall within safe limits. Instead, [the plaintiffs] believe Ontario should assess cumulative impacts in pollution "hot spots" like Chemical Valley by evaluating overall air quality to determine whether a new source of pollution would raise emissions from all sources to an unsafe level. ("Defending," 2017)

"When we first launched this case," Ecojustice said, "few people in Canada had an understanding of what 'environmental rights' were." Five years later, a groundswell of public support had led more than 130 municipalities, representing a third of Canada's population, to pass declarations in support of environmental rights. This was remarkable progress, Ecojustice said. "Recognizing the right to a healthy environment is the natural next step in the progression of human rights law in Canada" ("Defending," 2017).

Legal Pressure Produces Changes

Legal pressure through negotiations and lawsuits by Ecojustice has produced some changes: Companies involved in petrochemical production have committed to monitoring air quality regularly and posting readings online. "More than 110 countries around the world have already taken steps to enshrine their residents' right to a healthy environment in law," said an Ecojustice post addressing the situation in Sarnia and elsewhere in Canada. "When governments decide to stand up for environmental rights incredible things can happen. Now it's Canada's turn" ("Changing Course," 2016).

Kaitlyn Mitchell, national program director of Ecojustice, wrote in the *Huffington Post* (2015): "For several years I have been a part of the team of lawyers representing Ron Plain and Ada Lockridge, two members of Aamjiwnaang First Nation, in their fight to protect the health of one of Canada's most polluted communities. . . . The facilities in Chemical Valley collectively emit tens of millions of kilograms of air pollutants each year. Residents of Aamjiwnaang have expressed concerns about health risks posed by pollution and its impact on their ability to hunt, fish or plant food. Ecojustice lawyers got involved in this case because we are convinced that this is not just an environmental problem but a human rights issue as well."

Further Reading

Bienkowski, Brian. "Contaminated Tribe: Hormone-Blocking Chemicals Found in First Nation Families." Environmental Health News, November 11, 2013. https://www.tandfonline.com/doi/abs/10.1080/13621025.2015.1075470?scroll=top&needAccess=true&journalCode=ccst20

"Changing Course in Chemical Valley." Ecojustice, April 26, 2016. https://www.ecojustice.ca/changing-course-chemical-valley/

"Defending the Rights of Chemical Valley Residents." Ecojustice, 2017. http://www.ecojustice.ca/case/defending-the-rights-of-chemical-valley-residents-charter-challenge/

Mitchell, Kaitlyn. "Environmental Racism Remains a Reality in Canada." *Huffington Post*, May 7, 2015. http://www.huffingtonpost.ca/ecojustice/environmental-racism-canadal_b_7224904.html

Dumping on Blacks in Africville, Nova Scotia

"While the term 'environmental racism' remains unfamiliar to many Canadians, experiences in communities across the country demonstrate that it is a very real problem," wrote Kaitlyn Mitchell, national program director of Ecojustice, Canada's only national environmental law charity, in the *Huffington Post* (2015). "A prime example is Nova Scotia's Africville, a community on the northern edge of the Halifax peninsula that was home to hundreds of descendants of African slaves, black loyalists who had settled there after the American Revolution, part of the roughly 10 percent of the new United States' population who fled the country during the 1780s to avoid persecution for their British loyalties.

"Residents of the tight-knit community fished, planted crops and worked odd jobs in the area until Halifax's industrial boom led to a need for new dumping sites for waste from the growing city" (Mitchell, 2015). By that time, the *Earth Island Journal* (Klingbeil, 2016) reported that the investigators had found high rates of several illnesses, including cancers and diabetes, which they suspected were caused by contaminated water that was leaching into local soils. They could not draw direct causation, however, because research participants in North Preston, a mainly African Canadian community, and another Mi'kmaq community at Membertou, also reported relatively high rates of similar illnesses. They concluded that more research would be required to establish causation. Air quality also was poor, and open garbage pits were drawing raccoons, bears, skunks, and swarms of insects, all from a landfill opened in 1974 (a second landfill opened in 2006).

Africville Organizes

The city of Halifax in 1969 declared Africville a slum and an eyesore, and set out to evict residents and demolish their churches and homes as part of an "urban renewal" drive to make way for industrial development. Failing that, the city surrounded the community with garbage dumps and other waste-processing facilities, as well as an infectious disease hospital and a slaughterhouse with associated animal waste, which soon clustered in and near Africville. The whites seemed to sense no historic value in a community that was more than two centuries old. At one point, many residents' homes were bulldozed and they were told to migrate elsewhere. With very few options, many remained anyway.

By the 21st century, people in Africville were organizing and demanding compensation as victims of starkly racially motivated environmental discrimination. Residents of a reviving Africville were quoted as saying, "We are excited that Nova Scotia is leading by example and hope that this bill is the first step in a public conversation that is long overdue in this country. And, we want to remember that this problem is bigger than Nova Scotia" (Mitchell, 2015).

For four years, Ingrid Waldron, a sociologist and assistant professor of nursing at Dalhousie University in Halifax, Nova Scotia, directed the ENRICH Project (Environmental Noxiousness, Racial Inequities, and Community Health), leading a team that included several people from Nova Scotia, including seven academic researchers, three research staff (one of whom was Dave Ron, an activist who initiated the project), and 10 students, "all determined to investigate and address environmental racism in African Nova Scotia and Mi'kmaq communities" (Klingbeil, 2016).

An Attempt at Legislation

The situation in Halifax has assumed an important role in Canada as a reminder that environmental racism needs to be addressed. "Canada can't just import these measures from the U.S., given our unique demographics and history, but notions of environmental justice and racism must nonetheless be addressed in Canadian law" (Mitchell, 2015). Lenore Zann, a member of Nova Scotia's Legislative Assembly, was also drawn into the effort to deal with environmental racism in Halifax. Zann and Waldron combined efforts on Bill 111, the first effort to combat environmental racism by law in Canada. In 2011, Canada's National Household Survey said that 20,790 people in Nova Scotia had African roots, and 33,850 people were Aboriginal (Klingbeil, 2016).

In May 2015, the Nova Scotia legislature passed (on first reading) "An Act to Address Environmental Racism," introduced by Lenore Zann, to alleviate "a legacy of environmental racism in Nova Scotia." The bill would have directed the provincial government to create a committee on the issue with public hearings, then prepare recommended remedies to address "the interconnectedness of environmental health, socio-economic conditions, and racialized discrimination" (Mitchell, 2015).

The bill did not pass. "While that was disappointing, I'm very pleased it was debated," Waldron said, adding that the creation of the bill "attracted media attention and helped raise valuable awareness of the existence of environmental racism in Nova Scotia among both politicians and the general public" (Klingbeil, 2016).

Even though the environmental racism bill did not pass, people did organize and learn to monitor their environment: "Communities have been encouraged to address their situation collectively and to achieve objective documentation. A current ENRICH project . . . involves teaching residents how to test their own water for contaminants. If that project is successful . . . it could be brought to other communities, too. 'This is a real, tangible, community-capacity building aspect to the project that I think is important,' Waldron says. 'People can see something is actually happening'" (Klingbeil, 2016).

Maps of Environmental Racism

The pervasiveness of environmental racism in Nova Scotia was portrayed for the first time by a set of interactive digital maps, which led a Canadian Broadcasting Corporation (CBC) report to say, "For years, marginalized communities living close to foul-smelling toxic sites around Nova Scotia have been able to smell environmental racism" (Donovan, 2016). The maps were developed by the ENRICH Project, described at http://www.enrichproject.org/map/. As well as mapping environmental racism, the ENRICH Project also investigates effects of toxic emissions adjacent to African Canadian and Mi'kmaq communities. Lynn Jones, a Truro-based activist who has been involved with the ENRICH Project from the beginning, says the map makes visible what many communities have long suspected. "The whole province is on the map, it will actually show the disproportionate impact on African Nova Scotian and aboriginal communities. You'll be able to say, 'Oh, there's a waste disposal place here, and it's only two kilometers away from an African Nova Scotian or aboriginal community'" (Donovan, 2016).

An account in the *Canadian Geographic* provided a detailed description of the maps: "To visualize environmental racism in the province, ENRICH plotted the locations of industrial polluters such as landfills, coal plants and toxic waste facilities on a map of Nova Scotia. According to ENRICH's Lynn Jones, the map shows industrial pollution disproportionately affects African Nova Scotian and Aboriginal communities. The map is fully interactive, allowing users to zoom in on communities to see exactly how they are affected by nearby sources of pollution" (Hall, 2016).

In 2016, ENRICH published an "Africville Story Map," describing its history. Far from a slum or an eyesore, a half century after official policy called for the community to be eradicated, the *Canadian Geographic* called it "one of Nova Scotia's most storied neighbourhoods" (Hall, 2016).

In addition to the cluster of noxious industries around Africville, the maps display an effluent-treatment operation at Boat Harbour near the Pictou Landing First Nation. The maps are being used to explicitly illustrate how closely toxic effluent parses with nonwhite communities in the province, said Jones. "She hopes the map will do more than validate the experiences of affected communities; by making the phenomenon explicit, she wants the map to encourage those who are skeptical of environmental racism to recognize its existence," reported CBC News (Donovan, 2016).

By that time, 30 former Africville residents argued for reparations before the Nova Scotia Supreme Court. An account by the Ecology Action Center said: "This is happening at the same time that city officials are speaking out about the need to address 'root causes' when it comes to recent violence in African Nova Scotian communities. As former Poet Laureate El Jones has commented, 'If the city wants to stop the violence, begin with compensating the Africville survivors. If you're going to go to court to prevent paying reparations, then how dare you turn around and say you care about our communities?'" ("Halifax," n.d.).

The Ecology Action Center argued in favor of compensation, standing with Africville residents and descendants "[i]n their fight to have the City of Halifax acknowledge their complicity in the continued legacy of environmental racism facing African Nova Scotian communities." As EAC staff member Sadie Beaton described, "We've been working at EAC to reflect on our own complicity in the racist legacies of environmental organizations so that we can better act in solidarity with impacted communities. While it may be challenging, all parts of society have a responsibility to work towards environmental justice, including the City of Halifax" ("Halifax," n.d.).

"The proposed Act to Address Environmental Racism in Nova Scotia is a powerful step in that direction," Mitchell wrote in the *Huffington Post* (2015). Generalizing from Africville's experience, she asserted:

> We believe that Canada needs to go further and recognize that everyone in this country—regardless of who they are or where they live—has a Charter right to a healthy environment. An even more basic step would be to admit that we, as a country, have a problem. Turning a blind eye to the links between race, socio-economic status, and environmental risks doesn't make the issue any less real. The fact is, environmentally harmful activities take place in some communities more than others. We have to name that reality before we can begin to address it.

The ENRICH project's stated goal since it was founded in 2012 has been "to address the health and socio-economic impacts of environmental racism," which it defines as the disproportionate proximity of sources of industrial pollution to "communities of colour and the working poor" (Hall, 2016).

Further Reading

Donovan, Moira. "Nova Scotia Group Maps Environmental Racism: The ENRICH Project Looks at the Cause and Effects of Toxic Industries Near Marginalized Communities." CBC News, March 16, 2016. http://www.cbc.ca/news/canada/nova-scotia/ns-environmental-racism-map-1.3494081

"Halifax Should Own Up to Environmental Racism and Compensate Africville Community Members." Ecology Action Center, n.d. Accessed November 10, 2017. https://ecologyaction.ca/AfricvilleReparations

Hall, Thomas. "Mapping Environmental Racism in Nova Scotia." *Canadian Geographic*, March 16, 2016. https://www.canadiangeographic.ca/article/mapping-environmental-racism-nova-scotia

Klingbeil, Cailynn. "Taking On Environmental Racism in Nova Scotia." *Earth Island Journal*, November 10, 2016. http://www.earthisland.org/journal/index.php/elist/eListRead/taking_on_environmental_racism_in_nova_scotia/

Mitchell, Kaitlyn. "Environmental Racism Remains a Reality in Canada." *Huffington Post*, May 7, 2015. http://www.huffingtonpost.ca/ecojustice/environmental-racism-canadal_b_7224904.html

British Columbia: Native Canadians vs. Mining's "New Prosperity"

To the Taseko mining company, a massive strip mine for gold and copper meant "new prosperity," but to the Tsilhqot'in (Chilcotin) indigenous people of British Columbia it meant genocide. They united with environmentalists and other indigenous peoples across Canada and won a reprieve. "As a Nation, we've made a decision to focus our energies on the real battle of defeating this project, full-stop," said Chief Marilyn Baptiste of the Xeni Gwet'in, one of the communities comprising the Tsilhqot'in National Government (TNG) ("Tsilhqot'in," 2012).

"Our Land Is Not for Sale"

Over several years, the Tsilhqot'in and their allies forced the scaling down (and finally cancellation) of the mine. An early proposal would have severely damaged the trout fishery in Teztan Biny (Fish Lake). The new plan said it would spare that area, but still would have turned a smaller body of water, Little Fish Lake, into a tailings pond. To stop it, the Tsilhqot'in went to court and set up a blockade. "It's a simple No," said Baptiste, "Our land is not for sale. Our position has not changed and cannot change for the destruction of our lands, our waters and our way of life. Our wild rainbow trout has survived in that lake system for hundreds of years, as our people have. We will not, and cannot, agree to such destruction in the headwaters by Taseko" (Ball, 2012).

The company asserted that its plans were environmentally responsible, but opponents did not relent. In June 2012, Taseko delivered a revised proposal at its annual meeting in Vancouver, BC, which asserted that it would reduce environmental damage, according to President and Chief Executive Officer Russell Hallbauer. "This project . . . holds exciting potential for the company's stakeholders, including shareholders and local communities," Hallbauer wrote. "These revised plans address the environmental concerns identified in the original environmental assessment process, and importantly, includes the preservation of Fish Lake" (Ball, 2012).

Chief Joe Alphonse, tribal chairman of the Tsilhqot'in National Government, reiterated his nation's opposition to the mine. "We're not opposed to development," Alphonse said, "but this is not the way to do it. . . . This is the first time in Canada that a mine has been approved a second time [after being rejected]," he said. "They've reloaded and they're coming back with a Conservative majority federally" (Ball, 2012). Alphonse described Teztan Biny (Fish Lake) as a thriving ecosystem of vital importance. "You can see the fish jumping out of Fish Lake, and wolf tracks, moose tracks," he said. "We have the most consistent sockeye run in North America—the only run on the Fraser [River] that's still healthy" (Ball, 2012). The Union of B.C. Indian Chiefs (UBCIC), representing British Columbia's First Nations, also voiced opposition to the proposed mine. Its president, Grand Chief Stewart Phillip, accused Prime Minister Stephen Harper's Conservative government of colluding with mining companies. "We were shocked and appalled when we learned the Harper government and his cronies in the mining industry got a second kick at the can," Phillip said. "The second proposal . . . is far more destructive" (Ball, 2012).

Celebrating the Mine's Rejection

On February 26, 2014, the Canadian Ministry of the Environment issued a final rejection of the New Prosperity Mine, as the Tsilhquot'in and their allies celebrated across the country, following two decades of conflict. This was the government's third rejection, centered on the company's proposal to turn Fish Lake, which is sacred to the Tsilhqot'in, into a tailings pond. The third proposal made a case that the mine and area lakes could coexist. Neither the Native people, their non-Indian allies, nor the Ministry of the Environment was buying it. The government asserted that the mine, which the company said could be one of the largest new sources of gold and copper on Earth, was "likely to cause significant adverse environmental effects that cannot be mitigated" (Lazenby, 2014).

"We are celebrating this decision to reject once again this terrible project, which threatened our pristine waters, fish and aboriginal rights," said Chief Alphonse. "We commend the federal government for not bowing to industry lobbying and instead respecting the science and the independent process which came to the conclusion that this project would have devastating impacts on the environment and our Nation's ability to practice our rights in a sacred spiritual site. These impacts could not be mitigated" (Smitten, 2014).

Taseko may return, however, after having already committed Canadian $300 million to the mine. The government said that a new proposal was possible if environmental concerns were addressed. Taseko president and CEO Russell Hallbauer said that New Prosperity "could be built to a high standard of environmental integrity, including the full protection of Fish Lake" (Lazenby, 2014).

Shortly after the environmental ruling favoring the Tsilhqot'in's 3,000 people in six communities, the Supreme Court of Canada granted them aboriginal title to more than 1,750 square kilometers (about 675 square miles). In Canada, this was the first grant of aboriginal title by the federal Supreme Court, a watershed legal ruling. This ruling overturned a Court of Appeal decision from 2012 that Tsilhqot'in bands were "semi-nomadic" with few permanent encampments to allow for aboriginal title. "There is no suggestion in the jurisprudence or scholarship that Aboriginal title is confined to specific village sites or farms, as the court of appeal held," the Supreme Court ruling said. "Rather, a culturally sensitive approach suggests that regular use of territories for hunting, fishing, trapping and foraging is 'sufficient' use to ground Aboriginal title."

"Pour Him a Tall One!"

Before dawn on August 4, 2014, three weeks after the Pebble Mine's rejection in Alaska (see Cases: United States West: "Alaska's Pebble Mine: Corporate Gold vs. Natives' Salmon") and as the New Prosperity Mine was rejected in Canada, a mine waste deposit pond burst at British Columbia's nearby Mount Polley Mine, sending 4 billion gallons of mining waste (2.6 billion gallons of water mixed into a slurry with 1.2 billion gallons of fine sediment laced with metals) into rivers and lakes awaiting the return of salmon. The huge spill provided ammunition to critics of both projects. Knight Piesold Consulting, the firm that designed the burst dam, had also been hired as a contractor to design the tailings pond for the Pebble Mine, according to a report filed in 2006 by Northern Dynasty Mines Inc. with the Alaska Department of Natural Resources

Critics of the Pebble Mine proposal saw the Mount Polley Mine tailings spill as a prelude and a warning. "We don't want this to happen in Bristol Bay," said Kim Williams of Dillingham, director of Nunamta Alukestai, which means Caretakers of Our Land, a conservation group of Alaska Native tribes and corporations, to the *Cordova Times*. "With all the similarities between Pebble and the Mount Polley copper mine, we're urging the EPA to take immediate action to finalize mine waste restrictions in Bristol Bay. Our hearts go out to those in British Columbia who live downstream from this devastating mine failure." "It's Bristol Bay's worst nightmare," said Carol Ann Woody, a Center for Science in Public Participation fisheries scientist ("Company," 2014).

After Imperial Metals president Brian Kynoch bragged that he would drink the water downstream after the Mount Polley spill, the Indian Country Today Media Network headlined: "Pour Him a Tall One!" ("Pour,"

2014). "It's very close to drinking water quality, the water in our tailings," Kynoch said, according to the Canadian Broadcasting Corporation news. "There's almost everything in it but at low levels. . . . No mercury, very low arsenic and very low other metals. . . . I apologize for what happened. If you [had] asked me two weeks ago if this could have happened, I would have said it couldn't" ("Pour," 2014).

Several First Nations people live in the area of the spill and depend on its salmon runs. "Our communities are filled with sorrow, frustration and anger as they are left wondering just what poisons are in the water, and what is being done to address this disaster," said Williams Lake chief Ann Louie and Xat'sull chief Bev Sellars. "Monday's devastating tailings pond breach is something that both our First Nations have lived in fear of for many years," the chiefs said. "We have raised repeated concerns about the safety and security of this mine, but they were ignored. Now we are being ignored again. Enough is enough" ("Horrific," 2014).

NASA's Earth Observatory described the Polley Mine dam breach as viewed from satellites high above the Earth:

> On August 5, nearly all of the wastewater in the retention basin had drained, exposing the silty bottom. Hazeltine Creek, normally about 1 meter (3.3 feet) wide, swelled to a width of 150 meters (490 feet) as a result of the spill. In the aftermath of the flood, a layer of brown sediment coated forests and stream valleys affected by the spill. Notice how much forest immediately north of the retention basin was leveled. Debris, mainly downed trees, are visible floating on Quesnel Lake. (Note that some of the variations in colors between the two images are caused by different lighting conditions and viewing angles.) The breach released more than 10 million cubic meters (350 million cubic feet) of water and 4.5 million cubic meters (150 million cubic feet) of sand into Polley and Quesnel Lake, according to the British Columbia's Ministry of Environment. That is enough water to fill 4,000 Olympic-sized pools. (Dam Breach, 2014)

Native peoples were not persuaded by Imperial Metals' insistence that the mine waste behind their ruined dam was not harmful. "As of last night, Department of Fisheries and Oceans has banned salmon fishing in the Cariboo and Quesnel Rivers due to Mount Polley," said Chief Bob Chamberlin, vice president of the Union of B.C. Indian Chiefs, on August 6. "Mount Polley will have an immediate and devastating effect on First Nations like Lhtako Dene, Lhoosk'uz Dene, Nazko and Esdilagh who may not be able to fish for salmon at all this year. First Nations are anxiously awaiting the water-test results, the possible . . . closures afterwards

Cases: Canada

and the harmful impacts on future salmon runs of the Fraser" ("Horrific," 2014).

New Pressure for "New Prosperity"

On June 13, 2019, Taseko received permission from the Supreme Court of Canada to conduct geotechnical work at the company's New Prosperity Gold-Copper Project. The Supreme Court dismissed the Tsilhqot'in First Nation's appeal of earlier rulings by the B.C. Supreme Court and the Court of Appeal. "Getting permission to mine in British Columbia may be difficult, but it's not impossible. It just takes patience," said Russell Hallbauer, president and CEO of Taseko. "The SCC decision is clear. Provincial permits authorizing mineral exploration and development can, if done with care and consideration, withstand any possible legal challenge" ("Canada's," 2019).

The Supreme Court's decision vacated a Canadian federal government decision against the proposed mine that was based on a federal environmental review. Taseko continued to support partial draining of Fish Lake, near Williams Lake, B.C., to use the lake and its watershed for waste ponds that would contain cast-off rock from mining, "a slurry of toxic chemicals, rocks and waste water, created by the mine. Fish Lake drains into Fish Creek, the Taseko River, Chilko River, the Chilcotin River and finally into the Fraser River" (Defending, 2017).

Lawyers for Ecojustice, a Canadian environmental law advocacy group, have intervened, representing MiningWatch Canada in an environmental review. According to Ecojustice, "Mining companies used to have to build their own tailings ponds but an amendment to Canada's Fisheries Act in 2002 allowed natural lakes and creeks to be reclassified as 'tailings impoundment areas.'" Since then, the federal government has reclassified up to 20 lakes as dumps for mine waste. The company asked for the same reclassification for the Prosperity Mine at Fish Lake.

"In our view," said the Ecojustice case filing, "MiningWatch's participation in this case may help set an important environmental law precedent by supporting the panel's precautionary approach to uncertainty in environmental assessments—a principle we believe should inform all environmental decision-making in Canada. . . . Along with protecting the Fish Lake watershed and the river system, and once again affirming the Tsilhqot'in people's rights over their traditional lands, we believe that a decision that supports the Panel's careful approach to allowing public participation and dealing with uncertainty about potential environmental impacts would improve the quality of future environmental assessments in Canada" ("Defending," 2017).

Further Reading

Ball, David P. "Tsilhqot'in Vow to 'Stand Ground' against New Prosperity Mine at Taseko AGM." Indian Country Media Network, June 7, 2012. http://indiancountrymedianetwork.com/article/tsilhqotin-vow-to-stand-against-new-prosperity-mine-at-taseko-agm-116686.

"Canada's Highest Court Confirms Taseko's Right to Work at New Prosperity Gold-Copper Project." Taseko Press Release, June 13, 2019. https://www.tasekomines.com/investors/news-releases/canada-s-highest-court-confirms-taseko-s-right-to-work-at-new-prosperity-gold-copper-project

"Company That Designed Burst B.C. Tailings [Dam] Was Hired by Pebble Mine in Bristol Bay." Indian Country Today Media Network, August 8, 2014. http://indiancountrytodaymedianetwork.com/2014/08/08/compamy-designed-burst-bc-tailings-pond-was-hired-pebble-mine-bristol-bay-156315

"Dam Breach at Mount Polley Mine in British Columbia." NASA Earth Observatory. August 17, 2014. http://earthobservatory.nasa.gov/IOTD/view.php?id=84202&src=eoa-iotd

"Defending Fish Lake from the Prosperity Mine." Ecojustice. 2017. https://www.ecojustice.ca/case/defending-fish-lake-from-the-prosperity-mine/

"Horrific Toxic Spill in B.C. Called Another Exxon Valdez." Indian Country Today Media Network. August 7, 2014. http://www.nativenewstoday.com/2014/08/07/horrific-toxic-spill-in-b-c-called-another-exxon-valdez/

Lazenby, Henry. "Taseko Stocks Tumble as Fed Rejects New Prosperity B.C.—Again." *Mining Weekly*, February 27, 2014. http://miningweekly.com/article/taseko-stocks-down-as-fed-rejects-new-prosperity-bc-again-2014-02-27

"Major Victory: Canadian Supreme Court Hands Tsilhqot'in Aboriginal Title." Indian Country Today Media Network, June 216, 2014. https://indiancountrymedianetwork.com/news/first-nations/major-victory-canadian-supreme-court-hands-tsilhqotin-aboriginal-title/

"Pour Him a Tall One! Mining Exec Insists He'd Drink Water from Tailings Pond." Indian Country Today Media Network, August 7, 1014. http://indiancountrytodaymedianetwork.com/2014/08/07/pour-him-tall-one-mining-exec-insists-hed-drink-water-tailings-pond-156294

Smitten, Susan. "First Nations Exult as Canadian Government Rejects Taseko's New Prosperity Mine." Indian Country Today Media Network, February 27, 2014. http://www.indiancountrytodaymedianetwork.com/2014/02/27/first-nations-exult-canadian-governmnt-rejects-tasekos-new-prosperity-mine-153777

"Tsilhqot'in Acquiesce to Test Drilling. Still Determined to Stop New Prosperity Mine." Indian Country Media Network, March 2, 2012. http://indiancountrymedianetwork.com/article/tsilhqotin-acquiesce-to-test-drilling-still-determined-to-stop-new-prosperity-mine-101023

The Crees: Hydro-Quebec's Electric Dreams

The Cree and Quebec (Southern) Inuit had adapted to their world of forest, flowing water, and marsh since the end of the last ice age about 10,000 years ago. At the end of the 20th century on Europe's clock, Hydro-Quebec proposed to alter the entire ecosystem and destroy large parts of it to provide electricity to urban areas in more temperate reaches. During the 1970s, planners and engineers at Hydro-Quebec indulged in dreams of an electric empire built on the lands of the Cree that would make their utility the biggest supplier of electricity in the world. The utility planned to harness dozens of rivers flowing into James Bay, reshaping the ecology of an area the size of Iowa in the service of electrical generation. At first, the planners at Hydro-Quebec paid very little attention to what might become of the flora and fauna of the James Bay region during what they envisaged as the largest earth-moving project in the history of humankind. Although it is a public entity (a "Crown corporation" in Canada), Hydro-Quebec found itself unrestrained even by a public board of directors. Hydro-Quebec's electric dreams met problems other than the Crees' resistance. In 1990, by the time "Phase I" had been completed, the utility was $26 billion in debt, mainly due to expenses associated with planning and construction of earlier James Bay projects.

Commented one observer:

> Hydro projects could have far-reaching and negative impacts if, for example, breeding waterfowl habitat in Quebec river estuaries was damaged, thereby affecting migratory bird populations wintering in the eastern and southern United States. . . . Approximately 75 percent of the global population of Atlantic brant geese are concentrated on the eel grass beds of the Quebec coast and parts of the Ontario coast of James Bay, and almost the entire North American population (up to 320,000) of black scoters use southern James Bay as a staging area. Other waterfowl species that utilize inshore, inter-tidal and brackish coastal habitats in the Hudson Bay/James Bay bio-region include black duck, pintail, mallard, wigeon, green-winged teal, and scaup. Mergansers and loons make extensive use of offshore water for feeding, and a significant number of common eider pass the winter in James Bay and the Belcher Islands. ("Sustainable Development," n.d.)

The James Bay projects did not envisage the construction of traditional dams in fast-flowing waterways bordered by mountains, the usual situation in the North American West. The plan was to rework the dozens of rivers that traverse rolling countryside on their way into James Bay into a network of short dams and shallow reservoirs. In 1971, at its inception, Quebec prime minister Robert Bourassa called Hydro-Quebec's designs for the James Bay region "the project of the century," as he bemoaned the fact that "every day, millions of potential kilowatt hours flow downhill and out to sea. What a waste!" (Biegert, 1995, n.p.). Bourassa made his support of Hydro-Quebec a matter of provincial pride, and sometimes questioned the patriotism of the project's opponents. He dreamed out loud that northern Quebec would become a perfect location for magnesium and aluminum smelters that would draw on the newly generated power.

In replies to Bourassa and Hydro-Quebec, the Crees (often through their spokesman, Cree grand chief Mathew Coon-Come) asserted: "Beavers are the only ones who should be allowed to build dams in our territory" (Biegert, 1995, n.p.). The Crees came to this conclusion as scientists from Quebec's health ministry warned everyone (especially women of childbearing age) not to eat local fish, which were becoming contaminated with methyl mercury. Predatory fish, such as the pike, had been accumulating a great deal of methylmercury in their bodies since Hydro-Quebec began its ambitious plans to reduce the natural landscape of northern Quebec into a shape and a function suitable for generating electricity. Until then, fish had been a major constituent of the Cree diet for thousands of years.

Said Coon-Come: "Nobody asked us or told us, but three or four times from 1670 on, our people and our lands were handed between kings and companies and countries. We found out about all of this when they came to build the dams and when the courts told us that we did not have any rights, that we were squatters on our own land" (Coon-Come, 1994).

Coon-Come recalled: "In the early 1970s, I was a young student in Montreal when I read in the newspaper that Hydro-Quebec . . . was going to build a hydroelectric mega-project of the century in our territory, by diverting and damming the rivers and flooding our traditional lands. I looked at a map and saw that my family's trap-line and our community was going to be underwater! I immediately returned home, and as a result of a speech I made from the back of a community hall I was launched on my political career" (Coon-Come, 1994).

"Twenty-five years later," Coon-Come recalled in the year 2001, "our people know that the treaty we signed was more broken than honored. Many of the most important promises, such as for economic involvement and development, for protection of the environment and our traditional economy and way of life, and for housing, community development, and

Cases: Canada

infrastructure have been twisted, ignored, or broken" (Coon-Come, 1994).

The James Bay I project involved nine dams, 206 dikes, five major reservoirs, and the diversion of five major rivers over an area roughly the size of Connecticut. Rotting vegetation in the area had released about 184 million tons of carbon dioxide and methane into the atmosphere by 1990, adding to global warming. In the meantime, James Bay I had saddled each of Hydro-Quebec's ratepayers with an average of $3,500 in debt (LaDuke, 1993, A-3). James Bay I uprooted 2,000 Cree from Chisasibi Island (also known as Fort George Island). "It's painful to look at young people caught between two worlds. I've seen their faces, knowing that their heritage is under water. It was a whole disintegration of the spirit—all that was drowned," said Coon-Come ("Canadian Indians," 1990, A-2).

An Unwelcome Guest Comes to Stay

The James Bay area is home to 10,000 Cree and 6,000 Inuit people who were not consulted before construction began on James Bay I. James Bay hydroelectric development was first interjected into the Crees' lives on April 30, 1971, when Quebec premier Robert Bourassa (after whom part of the complex later was named) announced its inception to the people of the province.

The Cree occupy the southern part of the region in Manitoba, Ontario, and northern Quebec as far north as Whapmagoostui. Inuit communities dot the eastern shores of Hudson Bay in Quebec, north from Kuujjuarapik to Ivujivik and Salluit. In the Northwest Territories, Inuit communities extend from Arviat on the western shore of Hudson Bay to Coral Harbour on Southampton Island. The Inuit community of Sanikiluaq is located on the Belcher Islands in southeastern Hudson Bay, about 100 kilometers from the mouth of the Great Whale River.

Hunting and fishing comprise the heart of the Cree and Inuit economies. The Cree have traditionally hunted migratory birds, particularly during the spring, as well as terrestrial mammals such as moose. The Cree fish the rivers in the region and trap fur-bearing mammals such as muskrat and beaver. Traditionally, Inuit harvested fish and marine mammals such as seals, walrus, and whales. Some communities also depend heavily on caribou.

The Cree and Inuit, who at first were scarcely even recognized as long-time occupants of the land by Hydro-Quebec, soon found themselves challenging the construction project in court. It was a matter of life and death not only for traditional cultures, but also for the peoples themselves. The construction ruined many traditional hunting areas and replaced them with poisoned earth laced with life-threatening mercury compounds.

The Cree and Inuit of northern Quebec signed a comprehensive claims agreement (formally named the James Bay and Northern Quebec Agreement) with the Canadian federal and Quebec provincial governments in 1975. The Cree entered agreements (in essence, treaties) with the governments of Quebec and Canada, but they found the terms of these treaties being violated by the ecological consequences of hydroelectric construction.

The 1975 agreement provided the Cree $22 million (Canadian) and the right to continue to hunt, fish, and trap in their usual territories. Not even Hydro-Quebec anticipated that its plans would make a significant portion of the territory unsustainable for any of those activities. Hydro-Quebec's lawyers were more interested in other stipulations of what came to be called a "treaty" between the Cree and Quebec: the clauses that gave their clients the right to undertake construction of the James Bay project's first phase. In 1979, the first of four projected power stations at La Grande (in Hydro-Quebec shorthand, LG-1) came on line. With its advent, roughly 4,200 square miles of Cree hunting and trapping grounds were flooded. Three hundred black bears drowned as the reservoirs filled (Biegert, 1995, n.p.). Ignoring natural seasonal cycles, Hydro-Quebec's engineers filled their reservoirs just after the bears had put themselves to sleep for the winter, drowning them. The fact that the black bear is the most sacred animal in Cree mythology did not bother them.

Transformation of the Crees' Homeland

During the James Bay project's first phase, large areas of the Crees' homelands were radically transformed. Rivers that once had spawned large numbers of fish were reduced to trickles or stopped entirely by the creation of reservoirs behind energy-generating dams. Forests were clear-cut and burned, adding greenhouse gases to the atmosphere. More than 10,000 caribou drowned after Hydro-Quebec's rearrangement of the landscape spilled deep water across their migration routes. Hydro-Quebec called the deaths an "act of God" (Biegert, 1995, n.p.). This incident was yet another reminder that while hydroelectricity is often touted as "clean" energy that does not emit pollution or directly increase the atmosphere's overload of greenhouse gases, it is not environmentally benign.

Hydro-Quebec's James Bay II proposed to dam eight major rivers in northern Quebec at a cost of more than $170 billion to provide electricity

Cases: Canada

to urban Canada in the Saint Lawrence Valley, and to several cities in the northeastern United States. Little is said these days of the original James Bay project's third proposed stage, the most ambitious electric dream of all. As originally envisaged by the engineers of Hydro-Quebec, the project's second phase (which was successfully impeded by the Cree) was to be followed by an even more ambitious "Phase Three," a $100 billion proposal to build a 100-mile dike across the mouth of James Bay, "separating it from Hudson Bay so that the now fresh water from James Bay can be pumped (possibly using nuclear-powered pumps) to the Great Lakes and thence to the Midwestern and Southwestern United States" (Native Forest, 1994). Given free range, the empire-builders of Hydro-Quebec were planning to create a utility that would become a power merchant not only to Quebec, Ontario, and New England, but the eastern half of the United States as well, with the raw material, electricity, provided by "clean" hydroelectric energy.

Formally called the "Grand Canal," or "Great Recycling and Northern Development" proposal, Phase III of the James Bay Project would have transformed James Bay into a gigantic freshwater lake.

According to now-abandoned plans, once Phase II was completed, Hydro-Quebec estimated that its generating capacity would rise to 27,000 megawatts, as much electricity as would be made available by fully harnessing the power of Niagara Falls (on both sides of the U.S.-Canadian border) 13 times ("Sustainable Development," n.d.). Following construction of the James Bay project's first phase, Hydro-Quebec was generating one-quarter of the electricity consumed in the United States and Canada. Hydro-Quebec engineers estimated that, by the time James Bay itself was dammed at the end of Phase III, their utility would be able to meet the demands of two-thirds of the same market.

The Toll of Methylmercury

Just as Hydro-Quebec's electric dreams reached a point of ecocidal fantasy, the Cree and Inuit peoples got in the way. In a very basic way, the Crees were called to protest the James Bay project as a matter of life and death, as they faced methylmercury contamination caused by the earth-moving of the James Bay project's first phase during the 1980s.

Mercury contamination occurs when vast areas of land are disrupted. Plant decay associated with the James Bay's project's earthmoving caused large amounts of ordinary mercury to become methylmercury, a bioaccumulative poison. Rotting vegetation accelerated microbial activity that converts elemental mercury in previously submerged glacial rocks to toxic methylmercury. By 1990, many Crees were carrying in their bodies 20 times the level of methylmercury considered safe by the World Health Organization. Hydro-Quebec did not anticipate the accelerated release of methylmercury into the waters of the region, contaminating the entire food chain for the Cree, Inuit, birds, fish, and other animals. This type of mercury poisoning can cause loss of vision, numbness of limbs, uncontrollable shaking, and chronic brain damage. By the late 1980s, the Quebec government's health ministry was telling the Cree not to eat fish from their homeland.

Fishing represents more than sustenance for the Cree. Fishing activities are important in knitting together family and community. Mercury contamination thus disrupted an entire way of life. Before 1978, concentrations of mercury in a 700-millimeter-long pike was approximately 0.6 microgram per kilogram. After completion of Phase I, the concentrations increased gradually. In 1988 concentrations were 3 milligrams per kilogram, five times the original concentration and six times the maximum permissible concentration for commercial fish (e.g., for human consumption) in Canada (Dumont, 1995).

By 1984, the concentration of mercury in the hair of Crees of all ages was much higher than in surveys conducted during the 1970s. During 1993 and 1994, the Cree Board of Health completed an assay of mercury levels in the hair of the Cree. This survey revealed a wide variation in exposure levels between different communities. "If the 6 mg/kg maximum hair concentration recommended by the World Health Organization is used, at least half of the population of several communities is over that limit. In 1984, when Whapmagoostui (Great Whale) was tested, 98 percent of the population surveyed had mercury concentrations above 6 mg/kg" (Dumont, 1995). Mercury levels increased, generally, with a person's age. Trappers consistently tested far higher than usual mercury concentrations. "During the past ten years, the number of individuals with high mercury concentrations has decreased considerably," due in large part to programs persuading the Cree to avoid eating tainted fish (Dumont, 1995). In 1984, two of every three people in Chisasibi, a community of 2,500 at the mouth of the La Grande River, had unhealthy levels of mercury in their bodies; some elders who exhibited symptoms of mercury poisoning had 20 times the usual levels ("Sustainable Development," n.d.).

The Crees, wrote Charles Dumont, have expressed great concern for the effects of mercury on the coming generations: "Mercury is presumably toxic at lower doses on the fetus and can cause delays in walking and speaking, and abnormal reflexes. Boys are probably more sensitive than girls. In higher doses it can cause cerebral palsy" (Dumont, 1995). Dumont and colleagues examined changes in mercury levels within the Cree population between 1988 and 1993–1994. Hair-sample assays for mercury content were taken by the Cree Board of Health and Social Services during 1988 and again during 1993 and 1994 in all nine Cree communities of northern Quebec. The studies found that the proportion of the Cree population with mercury levels above 15.0 milligrams per kilogram declined from 14.2 percent in 1988 to 2.7 percent in 1993 and 1994. Dumont wrote, "There was a correlation between the mercury level of the head of the household and that of the spouse. . . . Mercury levels in the Cree of James Bay have decreased in the recent past. Nevertheless, this decrease in mercury levels may not be permanent and does not necessarily imply that the issue is definitively resolved" (Dumont, 1998).

The Crees Organize Against James Bay II

When James Bay II was proposed, the Cree and other Native American peoples living in the area not only took the case to court, but also sought to organize the customers of the electric utilities that would receive the power, mostly in eastern Canada and New England. This activism ultimately convinced an activist nucleus of customers to pressure their utilities to refuse Hydro-Quebec's power on moral grounds.

The Crees became very effective at addressing public forums in New York and Vermont, where a large part of the electricity would be sold, to tell people that they shared complicity with Hydro-Quebec in the devastation of northern Quebec. The Crees also urged electricity consumers and utilities to conserve, and to consider other sources of supply. Several non-Indian environmental groups joined with the Grand Council of the Cree against the James Bay projects. In New York and New England, electricity users were urged to conserve energy to eliminate a need for more generating capacity.

In addition to its toll on the Cree, hydroelectric development ruined wetlands and coastal marshes that were important staging grounds for migratory water fowl, including several species of duck, teal, and goose. The area also was home to rare and endangered species of freshwater seals, beluga whales, polar bears, and walruses. Anadromous fish such as the brook trout and lake whitefish entered the waters of James Bay to spawn from rivers that would have been disrupted or destroyed by additional extensive hydroelectric development under James Bay II. Local estuaries, heath-covered islands, salt marshes, freshwater fens, subtidal eelgrass beds, and ribbon bogs in and near James Bay nourish very large flocks of geese, ducks, and loons. Tundra provides habitat for caribou, moose, otter, muskrat, beaver, lynx, and polar bear. This wildlife also feeds traditional Cree trappers, fishing people, and further north, Inuit and Naskapi. All of this is the Crees' garden.

For several years during the early and middle 1990s, Cree leaders and elders utilized the lecture circuit with the story of how Hydro-Quebec's plans would damage their world. Bill Namagoose, a James Bay Cree, was quoted as saying (during July 1993): "We're up against the perception that Hydro-Quebec is the engine [of progress] and they've used it to whip up the nationalism of Quebecers against the Cree and the Inuit. [However], if you cut off the market there's no point in doing the financing. If there is no financing there is no construction. And so far we have managed to cancel two American contracts. There is no economic justification for the project, no environmental, no energy reason why these projects should be built. We've been living up there in harmony with the environment. But when the invasion began in 1970, we were totally overwhelmed. . . . We've survived as a nation for many thousands of years and we [would] like to arrive in the future on our own terms and traditions . . . living on an environmentally sound land, with all of our rivers intact for thousands and thousands of years. Two-fifths of our land has already been impacted by the first phase. We know what it's like to live in the middle of a megaproject. That's why we're trying so hard to protect the parts of our lands we still have left" (Vance and Shafer, 1995).

Albert Meascum, a Cree trapper living in the village of Ouje-Bougoumou, said that he had asked the company not to cut certain parts of his trapping territory, but they paid no attention. "Before the forest companies came," he said, "there was lots of game. By cutting down the trees they have chased away the animals." The companies also pollute, he said, as they spill oil and gas on the land and poison the young willows that feed the moose. "When the snow melts," he said, "the gas and oil go into the lakes and pollute the water and the fish" (Native Forest, 1994).

The future of the James Bay project was litigated for several years. During September 1991, a Canadian federal judge in Ottawa ordered a new assessment of the James Bay II project under a process that could give federal authorities the right to stop it. "I conclude that the Crees' right to an independent parallel federal review must be honored," wrote Justice Paul Rouleau ("Cree Indians," 1991, 4). At the time, the total cost of James Bay I and II was estimated to be $62 billion.

During February 1994, the Supreme Court of Canada ruled that the National Energy Board had the right to examine the environmental effects of the Great Whale Project, essentially the same issue that had been decided by Judge Rouleau two and a half years earlier. Armand Couture, president of Hydro-Quebec, denied at the time that the court's order would have any impact on plans to throw the switch on Great Whale II by the year 2003.

In the meantime, the Crees continued to stoke popular pressure against Hydro-Quebec's efforts to market power from the James Bay projects. Ten Cree and Inuit activists paddled a 25-foot combination kayak-canoe from Ottawa to New York City during the spring of 1990. They crossed the Quebec-Vermont border at the northern end of Lake Champlain and timed their arrival in Central Park to coincide with Earth Day. During the first week of October, 1991, Cornell University's American Indian Program organized a forum on James Bay development, with Mathew Coon-Come, grand chief of the Crees, as keynote speaker. In mid-April 1993, Native leaders and their supporters bought a full-page advertisement opposing James Bay II in the *New York Times*. Robert Kennedy Jr. and Coon-Come held a joint press conference, also in New York City, yet another high-profile action that turned more New Yorkers against the project. New York State then yielded to growing consumer protests and canceled a $17 billion export contract with Hydro-Quebec.

On November 18, 1994 (not too many months after Hydro-Quebec's president Armand Couture had asserted that electricity would begin to flow from James Bay II in 2003), Quebec premier Jacques Parizeau said that the project was being shelved "indefinitely." He told the press: "We're not saying never, but that project is on ice for quite a while" ("Quebec Will Shelve," 1994, 7). The decision was made after two governmental review committees said that Hydro-Quebec "would have to go back to the drawing board to correct 'major inadequacies' in its environmental assessment of the project." Hydro-Quebec had been stopped by a blizzard of paper; company officials complained that its environmental-impact study, which ran to 5,000 pages and took 11 years to compile, had cost $190 million ("Quebec Will Shelve," 1994, 7).

Great Whale Redux

The Great Whale (James Bay II) hydroelectric project was revived on a reduced scale during 2001 after having been shelved seven years earlier. The project was revived with a new twist: a proposal that the Crees, who had played a large role in opposing the project, would eventually become its sole owners. The idea was proposed to the Crees by Toronto-based Amec Inc., a large engineering and construction firm that had worked on Hydro-Quebec's original James Bay hydroelectric project, as well as

China's Three Gorges dam and Colombia's Urra dam (The company's name was Agra Inc. It was later bought by Amec PLC, a British-based conglomerate with 50,000 employees in 40 countries.) (Roslin, 2001).

The band councils of Whapmagoostui (the Cree name for the community of Great Whale) and neighboring Chisasibi held quiet discussions addressing the idea of reviving Great Whale in 2001. "It's just an idea, it's not official," said David Masty, a chief at Whapmagoostui. "It's at the discussion stage. We haven't taken a position on it as a community." He continued: "Some Cree officials are furious that the talks have gone on with virtually no community involvement. They say the discussions are a slap in the face to those who fought to kill the earlier variants of the project. They also point out that Crees have repeatedly voted—in regional assemblies, band-council votes and a community referendum—against new hydro projects" (Roslin, 2001).

The new proposal involved diversion of the Great Whale River at its headwater, Lac Bienville. At an estimated cost of $350 million, the river's water would be redirected through 10 kilometers of canals into Hydro-Quebec's La Grande hydroelectric complex, increasing the water flow through the turbines. In 1997, Hydro-Quebec had proposed to divert the Great Whale and, for the first time, sought the Crees' consent and offered a minority partnership in the project. This proposal was shelved after 92 percent of Whapmagoostui Crees voted against any development projects on the river (Roslin, 2001). The new proposal retained the diversion idea, but proposed that the Crees would own the facility once its debt was paid off. Amec would design the facility, arrange financing, and retain an ownership share while the debt was being paid off.

Hydro-Quebec, which earned a net profit of more than $1 billion in 2000, wanted to construct the dams to increase its profits by selling surplus power outside Quebec, which already produced enough power to meet its own needs. Hydro-Quebec planned to allow small private energy producers to build and operate the dams. In turn, the owners of the smaller dams would sell their electricity to Hydro-Quebec. According to an account in the *Cleveland Plain Dealer*, "Quebec has turned its back on the environment, suggesting that even the Rouge River in the beautiful Laurentians could be a site for a dam. Thousands visit the area every year to paddle the white water rapids and pristine pools" (Egan, 2001, D-15).

The Quebec government and Natives in the James Bay region signed an agreement in principle October 23, 2001, to end a bitter legal dispute over hydroelectric development in the area and open the door to further resource development in northern Quebec. Under the agreement, the Cree will receive Canadian $3.5 billion (roughly U.S. $2.2 billion) worth of natural resources royalties from the province over 50 years in return for giving up all legal action against a major power project in the region. "This agreement constitutes, I am sure, the basis of a great peace between Quebec and the Crees," Quebec premier Bernard Landry said before a signing ceremony with Cree grand chief Ted Moses. "This is an historic turning point and a truly profound revolutionary vision for the Cree and aboriginal peoples generally," Moses said (White, 2001). The project, which had been on hold for several years because of opposition from the Cree, produced 1,300 megawatts, or about 15 percent of the power from the entire James Bay area, and created about 8,000 jobs during six years of construction.

The agreement, which was later ratified by the Cree communities of northern Quebec, allowed the 15,000 Natives an annual revenue flow and direct participation in any future economic development on Native land in northern Quebec. The agreement pledged to pay the Cree $70 million a year for 50 years. It also included Hydro-Quebec jobs for Crees, an important issue in communities where more than 80 percent of the young people under 25 years of age were unemployed. The agreement also promised remediation of mercury contamination, funding for startup business programs, job training, health and social services, electricity, sanitation, and fire services for Cree communities (Matteo, 2002).

In return, the Crees promised access to resources (including diversion of the Rupert River for hydroelectric development) and cession of $3.6 billion in environmental lawsuits. The proposed diversions of the Rupert River are subject to environmental-impact reviews, but the government of Quebec is allowed to make the final decisions. "In effect," according to one analysis, "the Cree will not be able to protest, stop, inhibit, or litigate" environmental outcomes, including the anticipated drying up of parts of the Eastman River and the flooding of trap lines (Matteo, 2002).

The Cree agreed to drop their environmental lawsuits in part because legal fees were costing them $9 million a year, but also because many of the cases were faring badly in the Canadian court system. Courts in Quebec had ruled against the Cree on forestry issues, as well as their opposition to hydroelectric development on the Eastman River (Matteo, 2002). The agreement saves roughly 8,000 square kilometers of land from being flooded, according to Coon-Come. "We want jobs," he said after the new agreement was negotiated. "We want a say in where development takes place [and] what happens in our own backyard" (Matteo, 2002). "It isn't a blank check," said chief Cree negotiator Abel Bosum. "Quebec is taking a big risk here," Bosum said. "We consent to Eastmain-Rupert but there is no guarantee that it will be approved." He explained that the project must pass impact studies by Quebec, Ottawa, and the Crees. "It's not a done deal," he said (Dougherty, 2001).

Cree spokesman Romeo Saganash recalled that in 1975 the original James Bay agreement also was greeted with hope. Instead, the Crees faced 26 years of frustration, fighting Quebec and Ottawa in the courts. "Today my only hope is that my children will not be in front of your children in 25 years' time saying: 'Here's another agreement. After 25 years of frustration, we couldn't implement the deal we signed in 2001'" (Dougherty, 2001).

During late January 2002, Quebec Crees voted in favor of the $3.4 billion deal with the provincial government. Of the 6,500 eligible voters, 69.35 percent, or 3,106, voted in favor of the deal, with 30.65 percent, or 1,373, against. The decision, which Cree grand chief Ted Moses called historic, meant that the Cree nation was ready to complete a process it started in October when it signed an agreement in principle with Premier Bernard Landry to allow hydro installations along the Eastmain and Rupert Rivers subject to environmental approval (Authier, 2002). One Cree leader, George Wapachee, said the Cree who oppose hydroelectric development have sat on the fence too long while the world passes them by. In his community, the population has jumped to 500 and will hit 1,000 in 20 years. The land can only support so much traditional trapping and logging activity, he said. "There's a lot of young people who have nothing to do," said Wapachee. "We have to look forward, move ahead. That's the way life is" (Authier, 2002).

As Cree grand chief Ted Moses and Quebec premier Bernard Landry signed the hydroelectric power deal in the Cree village of Waskaganish on February 7, 2002, an elderly Cree chief, Henry Diamond, broke into the assembly hall, shouting his objections. He was tackled by seven police officers and hauled away, bleeding from the head, to be charged with disturbing the peace and resisting arrest. Another dissident, Chisasibi Band councilor Larry House, tried to voice his objections at a press conference following the signing. He was arrested for shoving an officer and impeding pedestrian traffic, for which he was fined $25 (Taylor, 2002). Opposition to the agreement was centered in the Chisasibi community, which sits at the foot of a reservoir that has been plagued with technical problems. The reservoir will rise at least six feet once the Rupert River is diverted, causing floods.

"Today," said Cree deputy chief Matthew Mukash, "Native communities across Canada are calling us sellouts." Mukash believes that the deal is a major mistake that will eventually lead to "the gradual and progressive takeover of the Cree by Canada and Quebec" (Matteo, 2002). He pointed out that while 72 percent of the Cree who voted supported the agreement, only 53 percent of those eligible to vote did so. Many who did not vote "no" did so from fear, Mukash believes (Matteo, 2002).

Nevertheless, Hydro-Quebec by 2002 was preparing to pursue its electric dreams once again, although on a much-reduced scale from a decade earlier, when a gaggle of corporate engineers had nearly forgotten that the Crees and their natural home existed.

Further Reading

Authier, Philip. "Cree Pact Clears Final Hurdle." Montreal *Gazette*, February 5, 2002. http://www.canada.com/montreal/montrealgazette/story.asp?id= {43F9B38E-7577-4579-AEED-90A8F9638936}. In Bruce E. Johansen, *Resource Exploitation in Native North America: A Plague upon the Peoples.* Santa Barbara, CA: ABC-CLIO, 2016, 70.

Biegert, Claus. "A People Called Empty." In Rainer Wittenborn and Biegert, "Amazon of the North: James Bay Revisited." Program for Show, Santa Fe Center for Contemporary Arts, August 4 through September 5, 1995, unpaginated.

"Canadian Indians Paddle to New York City to Protest Quebec Power Plant." *Syracuse Post-Standard*, April 5, 1990, A-2.

Coon-Come, Matthew. Remarks at Goldman Environmental Prize Awarda, 1994. https://www.goldmanprize.org/recipient/matthew-coon-come/

"Cree Claim Victory in Hydro Hearings." Canadian Broadcasting Corporation, December 1, 2000. In Johansen, *Resource Exploitation*, 2016, 72.

"Cree Indians Win Battle in Their Struggle to Stop Canadian Hydropower Plant." *Omaha World-Herald*, September 12, 1991, 4.

Dougherty, Kevin. "Deal Is No Blank Cheque, Crees Say." *Montreal Gazette*, October 24, 2001, In Johansen, *Resource Exploitation*, 2016, 69.

Dumont, C. Proceedings of 1995 Canadian Mercury Network Workshop. Mercury and Health: The James Bay Cree. Cree Board of Health and Social Services. Montreal, 1995. http://www.cciw.ca/eman-temp/reports/publications/mercury95/part4.html

Dumont, Charles, Manon Girard, François Bellavance, and Francine Noël. "Mercury Levels in the Cree Population of James Bay, Quebec, from 1988 to 1993/94." *Canadian Medical Association Journal* 158 (June 2, 1998): 1439–1445.

Egan, D'Arcy. "Dam the Ecology if Quebec Goes Full-Speed Ahead." Cleveland *The Plain Dealer*, July 29, 2001, D-15.

"Hydroelectric Production Is Anything but Cheap." *Virtual Circle: First Nations' Chronicles*, 2001. In Johansen, *Resource Exploitation*, 2016, 71.

Johansen, Bruce E. *Resource Exploitation in Native North America: A Plague upon the Peoples.* Santa Barbara, CA: Praeger, 2016.

LaDuke, Winona. "Tribal Coalition Dams Hydro-Quebec Project." *Indian Country Today*, July 21, 1993, A-3.

Matteo, Enzo di. "Damned Deal: Cree Leaders Call Hydro Pact Signed in Secret a Monstrous Sellout." *Now Magazine* [Toronto], February 2002. In Johansen, *Resource Exploitation*, 2016, 71.

Native Forest Network. "Quebec-Hydro Project May Destroy James Bay." Friends of the Earth, Victoria, British Columbia, 1994, n.p.

"Quebec Will Shelve Huge Hydroelectric Project Indefinitely." *Omaha World-Herald*, November 19, 1994, 7.

Roslin, Alex. "Crees Revive Hydro Project." *Montreal Gazette*, January 21, 2001. In Johansen, *Resource Exploitation*, 2016, 67.

"Sustainable Development in the Hudson Bay: James Bay Bio-region Canadian Arctic Resources Committee." Environmental Committee of Sanikiluaq, Rawson Academy of Aquatic Science, n.d. In Johansen, *Resource Exploitation*, 2018, 71.

Taylor, Robert. "Cree Leaders Jailed in Protest over Power Deal." *Indian Country Today*, February 17, 2002. http://www.indiancountry.com/?101395 5409.

Vance, Chris, and John Shafer. "Voices of Resistance." Radio transcript, CFUV 102 FM, [community radio station, University of Victoria, British Columbia], 1995; transcribed in 1995 and reprinted as the magazine *All That's Left Is Struggle*. http://sisis.nativeweb.org/sov/main.html

White, Patrick. "Quebec, Cree Reach [Canadian] $3.5 Billion Land-Claim Settlement." Reuters, October 23, 2001.

The Lubicon Cree: Land Rights and Resource Exploitation

Despite the fact that more than $20 million worth of oil has been pumped out of their land since 1980, the 500-member indigenous Lubicon Cree community of Little Buffalo, in far northern Alberta, has no running water, inadequate housing, no sewage system, and no public infrastucture (Green, n.d.). The Lubicons have been faced with a choice: rely on an overtly hostile provincial government or move in with another First Nation that can offer them social services. In the words of Chief Bernard Ominayak, the proposed change could "tear our people apart" ("Unions," 2000). In 1990, after six years of deliberation, the United Nations charged Canada with human rights violations under the International Covenant on Civil and Political Rights, stating that "recent developments threaten the way of life and culture of the Lubicon Lake Cree and constitute a violation of Article 27 so long as they continue" (Lubicon, n.d.).

The Lubicons' land claim remains outstanding, as the government of Alberta continued to lease Lubicon territory to multinational corporations that exploited and contaminated the land. The toll on people's health is startling. In 1985 and 1986, of 21 Lubicon pregnancies, 19 resulted in stillbirths or miscarriages.

In 1971, the province of Alberta announced plans for constructing an all-weather road into the Lubicons' traditional territory to provide access for oil exploitation and logging. Road-building plans were undertaken without Lubicon consent and resisted by the Native band in Canadian courts. At one point, the federal government asserted that the Lubicons were "merely squatters on Provincial crown land with no land rights to negotiate" (Lubicon, n.d.).

Having cleared legal challenges, Alberta built the all-weather road into Lubicon territory in 1979. Construction of the road was followed by an explosion of resource-exploitation activity that drove away moose and other game animals, causing the Lubicons' traditional hunting and trapping economy to collapse. Within four years, by 1983, more than 400 oil wells had been drilled within a 15-mile radius of the Lubicons' community. From 1979 to 1983, the number of moose killed for food dropped 90 percent from 219 to 19, as trapping income also dropped 90 percent from $5,000 to $400 per family. At the same time, the proportion of Lubicon Cree on welfare shot up from less than 10 percent to more than 90 percent. "In essence the Canadian government has offered to build houses for the Lubicon people and to support us forever on welfare—like animals in the zoo who are cared for and fed at an appointed time," said Chief Bernard Ominayak (Saladin and Çali, 2006, 159).

The Lubicons: A Long Search for a Land Base

The Lubicon Lake Cree have a claim to about 10,000 square kilometers of land in northern Alberta, east of the Peace River and north of Lesser Slave Lake. The land was regarded as so remote in 1900 that Canadian officials seeking to negotiate treaties completely ignored it. The Lubicons did not sign Treaty 8, which was negotiated in 1899 and 1900, providing the band no legal title to its land—title they were still seeking to negotiate with Canadian officials more than a century later.

During the century that the Lubicons have sought legal title to their land base, it has been scarred by oil and gas production, as well as industrial-scale logging. While Canadian officials have refused to set aside land for the Lubicons, large oil and gas, pulp and paper, and logging companies have moved into the area to exploit its natural wealth (Green, n.d.).

The Lubicons were first promised a reserve by the Canadian federal government in 1939, before oil was discovered under their lands. Oil companies flooded into the area in the 1970s, all but destroying the

Lubicon society and economy. The story of the Lubicons is a case study of how modern resource exploitation can ruin a natural setting and the indigenous people who once lived there.

The Lubicons engaged in negotiations with the federal and provincial governments three times during the 1990s, but the talks broke off because the two sides failed to agree on the size of the land mass and monetary compensation that should be allotted to the Lubicons (Green, n.d.). "It is very worrisome when you are at the table year in, year out . . . with government sponsored and supported resource development . . . subverting the rights you are at the table to negotiate. You have to wonder if there is any sincerity about achieving a settlement," said band adviser Fred Lennarson (Guerette, 2001).

During the mid-1980s, after the provincial government enacted retroactive legislation to prevent the Lubicon from filing legal actions to protect their traditional territory from booming oil and gas development, the Lubicon launched a protest campaign against petroleum companies sponsoring the 1988 Calgary Olympics (Guerette, 2001). On the eve of the international Olympic event Premier Don Getty established a personal dialogue with Lubicon chief Bernard Ominayak, which led to the Grimshaw Accord, an agreement committing the province to transfer to Canada the 95-square-mile reserve the Lubicon had been seeking (Guerette, 2001).

Oil and gas revenues from Lubicon ancestral lands continued at about $500 million a year. Not a penny went to the Lubicons. During 1988, after 14 years of getting nowhere in the courts, the Lubicons asserted active sovereignty over their land. A peaceful blockade of access roads into their traditional territory stopped all oil activity for six days. The barricades later were forcibly removed by the Royal Canadian Mounted Police. Alberta premier Don Getty then met with Lubicon leaders in Grimshaw, Alberta; the result is an agreement on a 243-square-kilometer (95.4-square-mile) reserve area called the Grimshaw Accord.

Twelve years later, the provincial government abandoned the agreement. In the meantime, environmental assessments disclosed that more than 1,000 oil and gas well sites had been established within a 20-kilometer radius of Lubicon Lake, on land that had been promised to the indigenous people. During 2001, Marathon Canada announced plans for a natural gas compressor and pipeline in the area.

Logging on the Lubicons' Land

Forest-industry companies by 2001 held concessions from the provincial government that covered nearly all of the land claimed by the

Lubicon not already leased for oil and gas production. The first of the industrial loggers, the Japanese paper company Daishowa, began logging Lubicon land during the 1980s. In 1988, Daishowa announced plans for a pulp mill near the proposed Lubicon territory that would have processed lumber equaling the area of 70 football fields daily. The province of Alberta also granted Daishowa timber rights to an area that included the entire Lubicon traditional territory.

An international boycott of Daishowa was launched to protest the company's clear-cutting of Lubicon land. In response, Daishowa stayed off Lubicon land during the 1991–1992 winter logging season. Logging later resumed, as the company sought to lift the boycott by suing the Lubicons' non-Native allies in Canadian courts. Daishowa's legal action was thrown out of court during the late 1990s, as the boycott intensified. Daishowa, which manufactures paper bags, newsprint, and other paper products, retracted its plans to log Lubicon land only after the boycott began to reduce its revenues. Daishowa then again pledged to stay out of Lubicon forests until the Natives' land rights were delineated. At this point, the boycott ended. The company asserted that the boycott had cost it $20 million in lost sales (Guerette, 2001).

Conflicts over Resources Continue

During May 2011, the Lubicon village of Little Buffalo was hit by the largest oil spill in Alberta since 1975 when more than 28,000 barrels leaked from an aging pipeline and contaminated rivers and the water table. The Forum on Religion and Ecology at Yale reported: "Members of the Lubicon community are reporting illnesses as a result of the stench of oil in the air, and . . . the company involved is not providing clear information. . . . . Some 20 local people have been hired to help with the 24-hour a day cleanup operation, but the spill has brought into sharp focus some of the long-standing ills that afflict Little Buffalo. The community has no running water; instead, water is trucked in, and people hand-carry it into their houses from 45-gallon oil drums. With no plumbing, people rely on outhouses. Showers are available at the school, but many wash using sponge baths" ("Oil Spill," 2011).

By 2014, Lubicon Cree dissidents were maintaining a campaign against fracking on their land, with signs such as "Frack Off! This is Lubicon Land!" As most people at Little Buffalo went without running water, one chief received Canadian $1.5 million through the Cree Development Corporation (CDC), which is technically nonprofit, but generates millions of dollars through contracts with the energy industry. It was not clear, due to sloppy accounting, whether these were payments for personal use, or if, as Chief Billy Joe Laboucan said, they were "issued because the directors were buying construction equipment so they could bid on jobs" ("Lubicon Chief," 2014).

"Our infrastructure is basically nonexistent," said Laboucan. A Canadian Broadcasting Corp. report said that "Laboucan was voted in as chief of the Lubicon Lake band in 2013, in the first federally recognized election for the band. He commissioned an audit to find out where all the revenue generated by CDC went. The auditor went through thousands of cheques and bank records and found that over a four-year period the directors of the CDC paid themselves close to $3 million. One of those directors was former chief and longtime leader Bernard Ominayak, who received 99 payments totaling $1.5 million" ("Lubicon Chief," 2014). The report said that "living conditions are deplorable" in Little Buffalo.

Cheryl Ominayak, who has lived in Little Buffalo, a village of about 500 people, for 28 years, said she draws water from a barrel and uses an outhouse. "Summer bugs are bad but you have to use it—no running water," Ominayak said of the outhouse. "We are probably about the only community in northern Alberta that doesn't have running water" ("Lubicon Chief," 2014). The assertion that the money was used for business expenses was received with skepticism by many community members, the CBC reported. "Shame on them, shame on them. I think everyone around this community deserves an apology," said community member Denise Ominayak. Cheryl Ominayak also wanted answers. "Where did they [members of the CDC] put the money? They obviously didn't give it to us community members because we all live in old moldy, rotten houses" ("Lubicon Chief," 2014). In a rare move, Alberta's government provided trailers with water tanks and septic systems.

Further Reading

Green, Sara Jean. "Fighting a GIANT." *Windspeaker*, n.d. Accessed October 22, 2005.

Guerette, Deb. "No Clear-Cut Answer: Timber Rights Allocation on Lubicon Land a Worrisome Development." Grande Prairie *Daily Herald-Tribune*, March 5, 2001, n.p.

"Lubicon Chief Collected $1.5M, While Community Had No Running Water: Audit." Canadian Broadcasting Corporation (CBC), September 12, 2014. http://www.cbc.ca/news/indigenous/lubicon-chief-collected-1-5m-while-community-had-no-running-water-audit-1.2763972

Lubicon Lake Indian Land Struggles: Background. Lubicon Cree Nation, Alberta, Canada, n.d. https://www.lubiconlakenation.ca "Oil Spill in Lubicon

Lake Cree Nation, Alberta: KAIROS Urgent Action." May 6, 2011. KAIROS Canadian Ecumenical Justice Initiatives. The Forum on Religion and Ecology at Yale. http://fore.yale.edu/news/item/oil-spill-in-lubicon-lake-cree-nation-alberta-kairos-urgent-action/

Saladin, Meckled-García, and Basak Çali, eds. *The Legalization of Human Rights: Multidisciplinary Perspectives on Human Rights and Human Rights Law.* New York: Routledge, 2006.

"Unions Back Lubicons." Indian Country Today Media Network, November 27, 2000. http://indiancountrytodaymedianetwork.com/article/turtle-mountain-tribal-council-bans-fracking-64866

The Dene: Killed by the "Money Rock"

At the dawn of the nuclear age, Paul Baton and more than 30 other Dene hunters and trappers who were recruited to mine uranium called it the "money rock." Paid $3 a day by their employers, the Dene hauled burlap sacks of the grimy ore from one of the world's first uranium mines at Port Radium across the Northwest Territories to Fort McMurray. While mining, "many Dene slept on the ore, ate fish from water contaminated by radioactive tailings and breathed radioactive dust while on the barges, docks, and portages. More than a dozen men carried sacks of ore weighing more than 45 kilograms for 12 hours a day, six days a week, four months a year. . . . Children played with the dusty ore at river docks and portage landings. And their women sewed tents from used uranium sacks" (Nikiforuk, 1998, A-1). Within half a century, uranium mining in northern Canada had left behind more than 120 million tons of radioactive waste, enough to cover the Trans-Canada Highway across Canada two meters deep. By 2000, production of uranium waste from Saskatchewan alone occurred at the rate of over 1 million tons annually (LaDuke, 2011, 376–377). According to an account by Andrew Nikiforuk in the *Calgary Herald*, at least 14 Dene who worked at the mine between 1942 and 1960 died of lung, colon, and kidney cancers, according to documents obtained through the Northwest Territories Cancer Registry. The Port Radium mine supplied the uranium to fuel some of the first atomic bombs.

A Plague of Cancer

Dene Cindy Gilday said that uranium mining there beginning during the 1940s devastated her hometown of Deline, near Great Bear Lake. Beginning at that time, young Dene men were hired "to carry uranium in sacks from the mines onto barges. The men had no knowledge of the toxic qualities of their loads. . . . It was the first time people at Great Bear Lake started to die of lung, bone, stomach, brain and skin cancer" (Knight, 2013, 16). Since 1975, following a 30-year latency period after uranium mining began in the area, hospitalizations for cancer, birth defects, and circulatory illnesses in northern Saskatchewan had increased between 123 and 600 percent. In other areas impacted by uranium mining, cancers and birth defects have increased, in some cases, to as much as eight times the Canadian national average.

"Before the mine, you never heard of cancer," said Baton, age 83. "Now, lots of people have died of cancer" (Nikiforuk, 1998, A-1). Declassified documents have revealed that the U.S. government, which bought the uranium, and the Canadian federal government, at the time the world's largest supplier of uranium outside the United States, withheld health and safety information from the native miners and their families.

While many of the Dene blame uranium mining and its waste products for their increased cancer rates, some Canadian officials compiled statistics indicating only marginal increased mortality from uranium exposure. André Corriveau, chief medical officer of health for the Northwest Territories, noted that high cancer rates among the Dene do not differ significantly from the overall territorial profile. He said that the death rate was skewed upward by high rates of smoking. The Dene, in the meantime, maintain that the fact that almost half the workers in the Port Radium mine (14 of 30) died of lung cancer cannot be explained by smoking alone.

Until his death in 1940, Louis Ayah, one of the North's great aboriginal spiritual leaders, repeatedly warned his people that the waters in Great Bear Lake would turn a foul, dirty yellow. According to "Grandfather," the yellow poison would flow toward the village, recalled Madelaine Bayha, one of a dozen scarfed and skirted "uranium widows" in the village (Nikiforuk, 1998, A-1).

The first Dene to die of cancer, or what elders still call "the incurable disease," was Old Man Ferdinand in 1960. He had worked at the mine site as a logger, guide, and stevedore for nearly a decade. "It was Christmastime and he wanted to shake hands with all the people as they came back from hunting," recalled Rene Fumoleau, then an Oblate missionary working in Deline. After saying good-bye to the last family that came in, Ferdinand declared, "'Well, I guess I shook hands with everyone now,' and he died three hours later" (Nikiforuk, 1998, A-1).

"A Vicious Example of Cultural Genocide"

According to Nikiforuk's account, others died during the next decade. Joe Kenny, a boat pilot, died of colon cancer. His son, Napoleon, a

Cases: Canada

deckhand, died of stomach cancer. The premature death of so many men has not only left many widows but also interrupted the transmission of culture. "In Dene society it is the grandfather who passes on the traditions and now there are too many men with no uncles, fathers or grandfathers to advise them," said Cindy Gilday, Joe Kenny's daughter and chair of Deline Uranium Committee (Nikiforuk, 1998, A-1).

"It's the most vicious example of cultural genocide I have ever seen," Gilday said. "And it's in my own home." According to Nikiforuk, "Watching a uranium miner die of a radioactive damaged lung is a job only for the brave." He described Al King, an 82-year-old retired member of the United Steelworkers union in Vancouver, British Columbia, who has held the hands of the dying. King described one retired Port Radium miner whose chest lesions were so bad that they had spread to his femur and exploded it. "They couldn't pump enough morphine into him to keep him from screaming before he died," said King (Nikiforuk, 1998, A-1).

In exchange for their labors in the uranium mines, the Dene received a few sacks of flour, lard, and baking powder. "Nobody knew what was going on," recalled Isadore Yukon, who hauled uranium ore for three summers in a row during the 1940s. "Keeping the mine going full blast was the important thing" (Nikiforuk, 1998, A-1).

The Dene town of Deline was described by one of its residents as

> practically a village of widows. Most of the men who worked as laborers have died of some form of cancer. The widows, who are traditional women, were left to raise their families with no breadwinners, supporters. They were left to depend on welfare and other young men for their traditional food source. This village of young men, are the first generation of men in the history of Dene on this lake, to grow up without guidance from their grandfathers, fathers and uncles. This cultural, economic, spiritual, emotional deprivation impact on the community is a threat to the survival of the one and only tribe on Great Bear Lake. (Gilday, n.d.)

The Conflict Continues

The Dene protested uranium's effects as soon as they became obvious, but on a singular basis. Few non-Dene seemed to be listening. The companies always had a ready rationale (such as blaming smoking for the cancers). During and after 2014, many Dene continued to protest uranium mining on their lands, but in a more organized fashion, to the point of setting up blockades against industrial traffic aiming to open one of the largest uranium mines in North America. Fission Uranium Corp. filed applications to develop a high-grade uranium mine that could become one of the largest on Earth, extending a 150-mile long "integrated uranium corridor," which already hosts "the largest high-grade uranium mines and mills in the world, with their own stockpiles of radioactive tailings and a decades-long history of radioactive spills" (Toledano, 2015). As of 2019, this ambitious plan remained on the shelf.

Organized as the Northern Trappers Alliance, the Dene organized a blockade in reaction to a rise in cancer rates in their community, as well as industrial development that drives away game on which they depend for income, food, and sustenance of traditional culture. The blockade began on November 22, 2014. It was "forcibly dismantled" by officers of the Royal Canadian Mounted Police on December 1 (Toledano, 2015). Eighty days later, wrote Michael Toledano in *Vice*, "The [Dene] remain[ed] camped on the side of the highway in weather that has routinely dipped below −40 [degrees] C. They are constructing a permanent cabin on the site that will be a meeting place for Dene people and northern land defenders."

> "We want industry to get the hell out of here and stop this killing," said Don Montgrand, who has been at the encampment since day one and was named as one of its leaders on the police injunction. "We want this industry to get the hell out before we lose any more people here. We lose kids, adults teenagers." "They're willing to stay as long as it takes to get the point across that any of this kind of development is not going to be welcomed," said Candyce Paul, the alliance's spokesperson and a member of the anti-nuclear Committee for the Future Generations. "It's indefinite." "We don't want to become a sacrifice zone. That's where we see ourselves heading." (Toledano, 2015)

The new mine is scheduled to be built upon the ruins of earlier mines that killed many Dene in earlier generations. "Abandoned and decommissioned uranium mines already host millions of tons of radioactive dust (also known as tailings) that must be isolated from the surrounding environment for millennia, while no cleanup plans exist for the legacy of severe and widespread watershed contamination that is synonymous with Uranium City, Saskatchewan" (Toledano, 2015). More than 85 percent of the people in this area (northern Saskatchewan) are aboriginal. They are fighting exploratory mining that could increase in scale in coming years, a new neighbor to the open-pit tar sands mines further south that have turned indigenous lands into "moonscapes."

"When they spew the pollution, it affects our water, lakes, fish—any kind of species. Our traditional life [is] destroyed with these oil mines around us," said Kenneth, one of the protesters. "We're in the middle of these oil mines and the government's still not listening." "We know our water isn't as good as it used to be," said Paul. "You see more fish with lesions" (Toledano, 2015).

Further Reading

Gilday, Cindy Kenny. "A Village of Widows." *Arctic Circle*, n.d. Accessed October 25, 2015. http://arcticcircle.uconn.edu/SEEJ/Mining/gilday.html

Knight, Danielle. "Native Americans Denounce Toxic Legacy." Third World Network, June 14, 2013. In Johansen, *Resource Exploitation*, 2016, 16.

LaDuke, Winona. "The Indigenous Women's Network: Our Future, Our Responsibility." Statement of Winona LaDuke, Co-Chair Indigenous Women's Network, Program Director of the Environmental Program at the Seventh Generation Fund, at the United Nations Fourth World Conference on Women, Beijing, China, August 31, 1995. In Kathlyn Gay, *American Dissidents: An Encyclopedia of Activists, Subversives, and Prisoners of Conscience*. Santa Barbara, CA ABC-CLIO, 2011, 376–377. https://books.google.com/books?id=ZzQVpPvlVMcC&pg=PA376&lpg=PA376&dq=LaDuke,+Winona.+"The+Indigenous+Women

LaDuke, Winona. 2001. "Insider Essays: Our Responsibility." Electnet/Newswire, October 2, 2001. http://www.electnet.org/dsp_essay.cfm?intID=28

Nikiforuk, Andrew. "Echoes of the Atomic Age: Cancer Kills Fourteen Aboriginal Uranium Workers." *Calgary Herald*, March 14, 1998. A-1, A-4. http://www.ccnr.org/deline_deaths.html

Toledano, Michael. "Indigenous Canadians Are Fighting the Uranium Mining Industry: A Group of Remote Northern Dene Trappers Are Fighting to Preserve Some of Their Traditional Land from Exploitation." *Vice*, February 11, 2015. https://www.vice.com/en_us/article/jmbwx8/a-dene-alliance-formed-to-resist-uranium-and-tar-sands-mining-in-saskatchewan-892

The Inuit: Mother's Milk Is Toxic

To environmental toxicologists, the Arctic by the 1990s was becoming known as the final destination for a number of manufactured poisons, including, most notably, dioxins and polyvinyl biphenyls (PCBs), which accumulate in the body fat of large aquatic and land mammals (including human beings), sometimes reaching levels that imperil their survival. Thus the Arctic, which seems so clean, has become one of the most contaminated places on Earth—a place where mothers think twice before breast-feeding their babies, and where a traditional diet of "country food" has become dangerous to the Inuits' health.

Most of the chemicals that now afflict the Inuit are synthetic compounds of chlorine; some of them are incredibly toxic. For example, one millionth of a gram of dioxin will kill a guinea pig (Cadbury, 1997, 184). To a tourist with no interest in environmental toxicology, the Inuits' Arctic homeland may seem as pristine as ever during its long, snow-swept winters. Many Inuit still guide dogsleds onto the pack ice surrounding their Arctic-island homelands to hunt polar bears and seals. Such a scene may seem pristine, until one realizes that the polar bears' and seals' body fats are laced with dioxin and PCBs.

Welcome to ground zero on the road to environmental apocalypse: a place, and a people, who never asked for any of the travails that industrial societies to the south have brought to them. The bevy of environmental threats facing the Inuit are entirely outside their historical experience.

"We are the miner's canary," said Sheila Watt-Cloutier. "It is only a matter of time until everybody will be poisoned by the pollutants that we are creating in this world. At times," said Watt-Cloutier, "we feel like an endangered species. Our resilience and Inuit spirit and of course the wisdom of this great land that we work so hard to protect gives us back the energy to keep going" (Johansen, 2000, 27).

The toxicological due bills for modern industry at the lower latitudes are being left on the Inuits' table in Nunavut. Native people whose diets consist largely of sea animals (whales, polar bears, fish, and seals) have been consuming a concentrated toxic chemical cocktail. Abnormally high levels of dioxins and other industrial chemicals are being detected in Inuit mothers' breast milk.

Feeding Babies a Chemical Cocktail

"As we put our babies to our breasts we are feeding them a noxious, toxic cocktail," said Watt-Cloutier, a grandmother who also has been Canadian vice president of the Inuit Circumpolar Conference (ICC). "When women have to think twice about breast-feeding their babies, surely that must be a wake-up call to the world" (Johansen, 2000, 27).

Watt-Cloutier was raised in an Inuit community in remote northern Quebec. Unknown to her at the time, toxic chemicals were being absorbed by her body, and those of other Inuit in the Arctic. As an adult, Watt-Cloutier traveled between her home in Iqaluit (pronounced "Eehalooeet," capital of the semi-sovereign Nunavut Territory) to and from Montreal, New York City, and other points south, doing her best to alert the world to toxic poisoning and other perils faced by her people. The ICC represents the interests of roughly 140,000 Inuit who live around the North

Pole from Nunavut (which means "our home" in the Inuktitut language) to Alaska and Russia. Nunavut itself, a territory four times the size of France, has a population of roughly 25,000, 85 percent of whom are Inuit. Some elders and hunters in Iqaluit reported abnormalities affecting the seals they had caught. Some seals had no fur; seals and walruses also had burning holes in their skins.

Persistent organic pollutants (POPs) have been linked to cancer, birth defects, and other neurological, reproductive, and immune system damage in people and animals. At high levels, these chemicals also damage the central nervous system. Many of them also act as endocrine disrupters, causing deformities in sex organs as well as long-term dysfunction of reproductive systems. "POPs" also can interfere with the function of the brain and endocrine system by penetrating the placental barrier and scrambling the instructions of the naturally produced chemical messengers. The latter tell a fetus how to develop in the womb and postnatally through puberty; should interference occur, immune, nervous, and reproductive systems may not develop as programmed by the genes inherited by the embryo.

Pesticides from the United States

Pesticide residues in the Arctic today may include some used decades ago in the southern United States. The Arctic's cold climate slows the natural decomposition of these toxins, so they persist in the Arctic environment longer than at lower latitudes. The Arctic acts as a cold trap, collecting and maintaining a wide range of industrial pollutants, from PCBs to toxaphene, chlordane to mercury, according to the Canadian Polar Commission (PCB Working Group, n.d.). As a result, "Many Inuit have levels of P.C.B.s, several forms of D.D.T., and other persistent organic pollutants in their blood and fatty tissues that are five to ten times greater than the national average in Canada or the United States" (PCB Working Group, n.d.).

During the late 1990s, ecologist Barry Commoner and his colleagues used a computer model to track dioxins released from each of their 44,091 sources in North America, a list that includes trash-burning facilities and medical waste–burning plants. For one year, the scientists followed dioxins as weather patterns scattered them from their sources. Winds took some of the pollution north in a hurry. Riding strong air currents, dioxin molecules can travel 400 kilometers in one day, according to Mark Cohen, an atmospheric scientist who adapted the model for the study, who works at the National Oceanic and Atmospheric Administration in Silver Spring, Maryland (Rozell, 2000).

Dioxins can travel from a smokestack in Indiana, for example, to the breast milk of a woman in Coral Harbour, Nunavut. After riding air currents northward, dioxins drop with snowflakes into Hudson Bay. During the summer, heat may promote evaporation of pesticides in the fields of the U.S. South, feeding a "molecular trickle" of toxaphene, chlordane, and other compounds that makes its way to the Arctic, then condenses and falls to Earth. In water, algae absorb the dioxins. A fish eats the algae; a bearded seal eats the fish, and dioxins build up in the animal's fatty tissue. The woman in Coral Harbour eats the seal meat, and her body transfers the dioxins to the fatty molecules of her breast milk (Rozell, 2000; Schneider, 1996, A-15). "The Arctic is more than myth and dreams. . . . The fish and whales carry scary amounts of contaminants," Canadian environment minister Sergio Marchi said (Schneider, 1996, A-15). "This is an important issue for indigenous people in the Arctic," Commoner said. "There's no way of protecting [areas from dioxin fallout]. You can't put an umbrella over Nunavut" (Rozell, 2000).

Persistent organic pollutants have been taking a toll on Arctic peoples in Russia as well as in Canada. With regard to persistent organic pollutants, "The peoples of the Arctic of Russia are at the edge of an abyss, physical disappearance," said Yeremei Danilovich, president of an association representing the more than two dozen Native groups in Russia's Arctic. "The reforms have mercilessly hit the people of the North. The oil and gas companies, the logging companies, the gold and silver companies, have given nothing to the indigenous people. . . . I hope the world understands how important this entire area is" (Schneider, 1996, A-15).

One may scan the list of scientific research funding around the world and add up what ails the Arctic. In addition to a plethora of studies documenting the spread of persistent organic pollutants through the flora and fauna of the Arctic, many studies aim to document the saturation of the same area by levels of mercury, lead, and nuclear radiation in fish and game ("PD 2000 Projects," 2001). Following is a sampling of titles of research projects directed at documenting ongoing ecological troubles in the Arctic. The listed studies have been generated by scientists in the United States, Canada, Sweden, Norway, and Russia.

"Assessment of Organochlorines and Metal Levels in Canadian Arctic Fox"

"Concentrations and Patterns of Persistent Organochlorine Contaminants in Beluga Whale Blubber"

"Contaminants in Greenland Human Diet"

"Effects of Metals and POPs on Marine Fish Species"

"Effects of Prenatal Exposure to Organochlorines and Mercury in the Immune System of Inuit Infants"

"Effects and Trends of POPs on Polar Bears"

"Endocrine Disruption in Arctic Marine Mammals"

"Estimation of Site Specific Dietary Exposure to Contaminants in Two Inuit Communities"

"Follow-up of Pre-School Aged Children Exposed to PCBs and Mercury Through Fish and Marine Mammal Consumption"

"Heavy Metals in Grouse Species"

"Lead Contamination of Greenland Birds"

"Metals in Reindeer"

"New Persistent Chemicals in the Arctic Environment"

"Persistent Toxic Substances, Food Security, and Indigenous Peoples of the Russian North"

"Retrospective Survey of Organochlorines and Mercury in Arctic Seabird Eggs"

"Temporal Trends of Persistent Organic Pollutants and Metals in Ringed Seals of the Canadian Arctic"

"Ultraviolet (UV) Monitoring in the Alaskan Arctic"

"UV-Radiation and Its Impact on Genetic Diversity, Population Structure, and Foodwebs of Arctic Freshwater"

The bodies of some Inuit on the northernmost islands of Nunavut, thousands of miles from sources of pollution, have the highest levels of PCBs ever found, except for victims of industrial accidents. Some Native people in Greenland have several dozen times as much of the pesticide hexaclorobenzene (HCB) in their bodies as temperate-zone Canadians.

Generation of POPs has become an issue in Watt-Cloutier's present residence, Iqaluit, on Baffin Island, where the town dump burns wastes that emit dioxins. The dump's plume provides only a small fraction of Iqaluit residents' POP exposure, but it has become enough of an issue to provoke a three-month shutdown of the dump that caused garbage to pile up in the town. The dump was reopened after local public health authorities warned that the backlogged garbage could spread disease; that "the hazard posed by the rotting piles of garbage outweighed the risks of burning it" (Hill, 2001, 5). In 2001, Iqaluit's government was asking residents to separate plastics and metals from garbage that can be burned without adding POPs to the atmosphere.

Inuit Infants: "A Living Test Tube for Immunologists"

Eric Dewailly, a Laval University scientist, accidentally discovered that the Inuit were being heavily contaminated by PCBs. During the middle 1980s, Dewailly first visited the Inuit as he sought a pristine group to use as a baseline with which to compare women in southern Quebec who had PCBs in their breast milk. Instead, Dewailly found that Inuit mothers' PCB levels were several times higher than those of the Quebec mothers in his study group.

Dewailly and colleagues then investigated whether organochlorine exposure is associated with the incidence of infectious diseases in Inuit infants from Nunavut (1993a, 1993b, 1994, 2000). Dewailly and his colleagues reported that serious ear infections were twice as common among Inuit babies whose mothers had higher than usual concentrations of toxic chemicals in their breast milk. More than 80 percent of the 118 babies studied in various Nunavut communities had at least one serious ear infection in the first year of their lives. The three most common contaminants that researchers found in Inuit mothers' breast milk were three pesticides (dieldrin, mirex, and DDE) and two industrial chemicals, PCBs and hexachlorobenzene. The researchers could not pinpoint which specific chemicals were responsible for making the Inuit babies more vulnerable to illnesses because the chemicals' effects may amplify in combination.

Inuit infants have provided what one observer has called "a living test tube for immunologists" (Cone, 1996, A-1). Due to their diet of contaminated sea animals and fish, Inuit women's breast milk by the early 1990s contained six times more PCBs than women in urban Quebec, according to Quebec government studies. Their babies have experienced strikingly high rates of meningitis, bronchitis, pneumonia, and other infections compared with other Canadians. One Inuit child out of every four has chronic hearing loss due to infections. Born with depleted white blood cells, the children suffer excessive bouts of diseases, including a 20-fold increase in life-threatening meningitis compared to other Canadian children. These children's immune systems sometimes fail to produce enough antibodies to resist even the usual childhood diseases.

"In our studies, there was a marked increase in the incidence of infectious disease among breast-fed babies exposed to a high concentration of contaminants," said Dewailly (Cone, 1996, A-1). A study published on September 12, 1996, in the *New England Journal of Medicine* confirmed that children exposed even to low levels of PCBs in the womb grow up with low IQs, poor reading comprehension, difficulty paying attention, and memory problems (Jacobson and Jacobson, 1996, 783–789).

According to the Quebec Health Center, a concentration of 1,052 parts per billion of PCBs has been found in Arctic women's milk fat. This compares to a reading of 7,002 ppb in polar bear fat, 1,002 ppb in whale blubber, 527 ppb in seal blubber, and 152 ppb in fish. The U.S. Environmental Protection Agency safety standard for edible poultry, by contrast, is 3 ppb, and in fish, 2 ppb. At 50 ppb, soil is often classified as hazardous waste by the U.S. Environmental Protection Agency. Research by the Canadian federal Department of Indian and Northern Affairs indicates that Inuit women throughout Nunavut experience DDT levels that are nine times the average of women in Canadian urban areas. The milk of Inuit women of the eastern Arctic has been found to contain as much as 1,210 ppb of DDT and its derivative, DDE, while milk from women living in southern Canada contains about 170 ppb (Suzuki, 2000).

The Arctic Monitoring and Assessment Programme, a joint activity of the Arctic nations and organizations of indigenous Arctic people, found in its study *Pollution and Human Health* that "PCB blood levels, while highest in Greenland and the eastern Canadian Arctic, were high enough (over 4 micrograms of PCBs per liter of blood) that a proportion of the population would be in a risk range for fetal and childhood development problems" (PCB Working Group, n.d.).

"The last thing we need at this time is [to] worry about the very country food that nourishes us, spiritually and emotionally, poisoning us," Watt-Cloutier said. "This is not just about contaminants on our plate. This is a whole way of being, a whole cultural heritage that is at stake here for us" (Mofina, 2000, A-12). "The process of hunting and fishing, followed by the sharing of food—the communal partaking of animals—is a time-honored ritual that binds us together and links us with our ancestors," said Watt-Cloutier (PCB Working Group, n.d.).

Further Reading

Cadbury, Deborah. *Altering Eden: The Feminization of Nature.* New York: St. Martin's Press, 1997.

Cone, Marla. "Human Immune Systems May Be Pollution Victims." *Los Angeles Times*, May 13, 1996, A-1.

Dewailly, E., P. Ayotte, S. Bruneau, S. Gingras, M. Belles-Isles, and R. Roy. "Susceptibility to Infections and Immune Status in Inuit Infants Exposed to Organochlorines." *Environment Health Perspectives* 108 (2000): 205–211.

Dewailly, E., S. Bruneau, C. Laliberte, M. Belles-Iles, J.-P. Weber, and R. Roy. "Breast Milk Contamination by PCB and PCDD/Fs in Arctic Quebec. Preliminary Results on the Immune Status of Inuit Infants." *Organohalogen Compounds* 13 (1993a): 403–406.

Dewailly, E., S. Dodin, R. Verreault, P. Ayotte, L. Sauve, and J. Morin. "High Organochlorine Body Burden in Breast Cancer Women with Oestrogen Receptors." *Organohalogen Compounds* 13 (1993b): 385–388.

Dewailly, E., J. J. Ryan, C. Laliberte, S. Bruneau, J.-P. Weber, S. Gringras, and G. Carrier. "Exposure of Remote Maritime Populations to Coplanar PCBs." *Environmental Health Perspectives* 102 suppl. 1 (1994): 205–209.

Hill, Miriam. "Iqaluit's Waste Woes Won't Go Away; City Sets Up Bins Where Residents Can Dump Plastics, Metal." *Nunatsiag News*, July 27, 2001, 5.

Jacobson, Joseph L., and Sandra W. Jacobson. "Intellectual Impairment in Children Exposed to Polychlorinated Biphenyls in Utero," *New England Journal of Medicine* 335, no. 11 (September 12, 1996): 783–789.

Johansen, Bruce E. "Pristine No More: The Arctic, Where Mother's Milk Is Toxic." *The Progressive*, December 2000, 27–29.

Mofina, Rick. "Study Pinpoints Dioxin Origins: Cancer-Causing Agents in Arctic Aboriginals' Breast Milk Comes from U.S. and Quebec." Montreal *Gazette*, October 4, 2000, A-12.

PD 2000 Projects, 2001. PCB Working Group, IPEN. "Communities Respond to P.C.B. Contamination," n.d. Accessed November 22, 2015. http://www.rst2.org/ties/pcbs/university/pdfs/ipen-pcb.pdf

Rozell, Ned. "Alaska Science Forum: Dioxins: Another Uninvited Visitor to the North." Geophysical Institute, University of Alaska Fairbanks. November 9, 2000. https://www.gi.alaska.edu/alaska-science-forum/dioxins-another-uninvited-visitor-north

Schneider, Howard. "Facing World's Pollution in the North." *Washington Post*, September 21, 1996, A-15. http://www.washingtonpost.com/wp-srv/inatl/longterm/canada/stories/pollution092196.htm

Suzuki, David. "Science Matters: POP Agreement Needed to Eliminate Toxic Chemicals." December 6, 2000. http://www.davidsuzuki.org.

Who Is Liable for Ruining a Culture? The Inuit Sue the United States of America

The debate over global warming now turns more frequently to legal liability—which individuals, corporations, and governments are responsible, and how should they be held to account? The Inuit Circumpolar Conference filed a petition and obtained a hearing March 1, 2007, before the Inter-American Commission on Human Rights, created in 1959 by the Organization of American States, based in Washington, D.C., to safeguard personal freedom and security among the citizens of member states. The Inuit in this case are very conscious of their pivotal role in a natural world that will not survive climatic business as usual. The Inuit petition seeks to establish a legal basis for legal responsibility in world forums for countries' violation of human rights because of their contributions to rapid warming in the Arctic.

The ICC represents the interests of roughly 150,000 Inuit spread around the North Pole from Nunavut (which means "our home" in the Inuktitut language) to Alaska and Russia. Nunavut itself, a territory four times the size of France, has a population of roughly 27,000, 85 percent of whom are Inuit. From the top of the world, having been exposed to atmospheric perils from toxic chemicals and global warming, the Inuit find themselves in an unwilling but necessary position of international arbiters in an emerging "law of the air" that will eventually govern our shared atmospheric commons.

The OAS responded affirmatively early in 2007 to a request by Sheila Watt-Cloutier (president until 2006 of the ICC) and two environmental law organizations, Earthjustice and the Center for International Environmental Law. The petition sought a declaration from the commission that emissions of greenhouse gases from the United States—the source of more than 25 percent of the world's greenhouse gases during the last century—are violating Inuit human rights as outlined in the 1948 American Declaration on the Rights and Duties of Man. As of this writing, such a declaration has not been issued.

The Inuit petition (Petition, 2005) cites frequently from an extensive report, *The Arctic Climate Impact Assessment* (2004), which demonstrates that the Arctic is currently experiencing some of the most rapid and severe climate change on earth. Two of its key findings are (1) that marine species dependent upon sea ice, including polar bears, seals, walrus, and various species of birds, are declining and could face extinction, and (2) that the Inuit culture, which is heavily dependent upon sea ice and these species, will experience severe disruption (Tsosie, 2007). Watt-Cloutier said that the petition had been filed in a commitment to cultural survival: "Inuit are an ancient people. Our way of life is dependent upon the natural environment and the animals. Climate change is destroying our environment and eroding our culture. But we refuse to disappear. We will not become a footnote to globalization" (Press Release, 2005).

The Inuits' Central Role in World Context

The petition does not seek monetary damages. Instead, it seeks cessation of U.S. actions that violate Inuit rights to live in a cold environment—not a small task, since such action will involve major restructuring of the economic base to sharply curtail emissions of greenhouse gases. The petition anticipates the types of actions that will have to take place on a worldwide scale, including the rapidly expanding economies of China and India, to preserve the Inuit way of life, as well as a sustainable worldwide biosphere. The Inuit in this case are very conscious of their pivotal role in a natural world that will not survive climatic business as usual. The Inuit request U.S. leadership in an international effort involving sharp reductions in greenhouse-gas emissions to avoid destruction of the order of nature that has sustained them for many thousands of years.

The ICC's 167-page petition alleges violations of fundamental human rights among Arctic peoples who ring the Arctic Ocean from Nunavut (a semisovereign Inuit province of Canada), to Greenland, Russia, and Alaska. The petition, which was compiled in defense of Inuit rights as a people within evolving international human rights law, asks that members of the commission visit the Arctic to learn firsthand the effects of climate change on the environment and Inuit people.

Inuits' Rights to Culture and Life

The petition asserts that practice of the Inuits' rights to culture, life, health, physical integrity and security, property, and subsistence have been imperiled by global warming. With accelerating loss of ice and snow, hunting, travel, and other subsistence activities have become more dangerous, and in some cases impossible, the Inuit assert. In addition, their drinking-water sources have been threatened. Some coastal communities may be forced to move to escape rising waters provoked by rising seas and increasing storminess.

The petition begins by establishing that global warming is harming "every aspect of Inuit life and culture" (Petition, 2005, 13–19). It next associates warming with human-provoked emissions of greenhouse gases (Petition, 2005, 20–34). Detail then follows regarding the specific perils faced by Inuit people, including dangers to hunters and others who need to travel and obtain food from the land, dangers of melting permafrost, harm to animals in the Arctic, coastal erosion and storm surges, and heat-related health problems (Petition, 2005, 35–67). Next, the petition establishes that the United States of America historically has been the world's greatest national source of greenhouse gases (Petition, 2005, 68–69). Because carbon dioxide, the major greenhouse gas, may reside in the atmosphere for a century or longer, the burden is cumulative, so while China passed the United States in present-day emissions in 2007 (and reached 200 percent

Cases: Canada

of its emissions by 2017), the United States remains by far the largest source of the historical burden, at about 27.5 percent of the worldwide total.

The petition then documents violations of international law, especially the American Declaration (Petition, 2005, 95–97). Combining traditional knowledge of hunters and elders with wide-ranging peer-reviewed science, the petition alleges that Inuit human rights are being violated in several ways, including:

1. The right to life and physical security;
2. The right to personal property;
3. The right to health;
4. The right to practice indigenous culture;
5. The right to use traditionally occupied land; and
6. The right to traditional means of subsistence. (Petition, 2005, 70–102, 111–14)

According to Watt-Cloutier, the ICC petition illustrates three basic messages that arise from Inuit experience in the Arctic:

1. Dangerous climate change already is occurring;
2. Climate change in the Arctic is quickly going to become worse; and
3. Climate change in the Arctic is important globally. (Watt-Cloutier, 2005)

The United States' Liability

The petition alleges that the United States has "consistently denied, distorted, and suppressed scientific evidence of the causes, rate, and magnitude of global warming" (Petition, 2005, 109) as it reiterates that many of the dangers currently facing the Inuit, including the retreat of protective sea ice, impaired access to vital resources, and loss of homes and other infrastructure, are a direct result of human rights violations committed by the United States, which should be held to account (Petition, 2005, 103–110). The petition then concludes by documenting a lack of remedies within the U.S. legal system, as well as that country's lack of cooperation under international law in this venue under the administration of George W. Bush (Petition, 2005, 112–116).

The ICC and its co-petitioners acknowledge that the declaration they seek from the commission will not be legally enforceable, but that it would have great moral value. The petition is intended to educate and encourage the United States to join the community of nations in a global effort to combat climate change. The focus has been placed on the United States because of its refusal to join in the Kyoto Protocol and other diplomatic efforts to reduce greenhouse-gas emissions.

Summarizing, the petition asks the commission to recommend that the United States:

1. Adopt mandatory measures to limit its emissions of greenhouse gases in cooperation with the community of nations;
2. Take into account the impact of U.S. greenhouse gas emissions on the Arctic and Inuit before approving all major government actions;
3. In consultation with the Inuit, develop a plan to protect Inuit culture and the Arctic environment and to mitigate any harm caused by U.S. greenhouse gas emissions; and
4. In coordination with Inuit, develop a plan to help Inuit adapt to unavoidable climate change. (Watt-Cloutier, 2005)

The petition also asks the commission to declare that the United States of America has an obligation to take into account the impact of its emissions on the Arctic and Inuit people in all major government actions (Petition, 2005, 109).

International Legal Context

In addition to detailed documentation of the perils faced by Inuit people as a result of global warming, the ICC petition also contains an extensive legal justification making a case that international law is a proper forum for this dispute, given that one of the fundamental norms of customary international law establishes every state's obligation not to knowingly allow its territory to be used for acts contrary to the rights of other states. Because the emission of greenhouse gases in one state causes harm to others, this norm provides context for assessing states' human rights obligations with respect to global warming. Under international law, a strong presumption exists compelling nations to work within the international framework to correct human-rights violations.

The United States has not replied to this legal initiative, and the Inuit have received no "relief," in legal jargon, for harms inflicted. In the future, however, the Inuit petition may be perceived as an initial "shot across the bow" in a new genre of law that ultimately will penalize the destruction of the global atmospheric commons. The legal world just must catch up with the Inuit, whose lives have been afflicted first and most harshly by a warming atmosphere.

Further Reading

Petition to the Inter-American Commission on Human Rights Seeking Relief from Violations Resulting from Global Warming Caused by Acts and Omissions of the United States. Submitted by Sheila Watt-Cloutier with the Support of the Inuit Circumpolar Conference, on Behalf of All Inuit in the Arctic. December 7, 2005. Iqualuit, Nunavut. http://climate-casechart.com/non-us-case/petition-to-the-inter-american-commission-on-human-rights-seeking-relief-from-violations-resulting-from-global-warming-caused-by-acts-and-omissions-of-the-united-states/

Press Release. "Inuit Circumpolar Conference, Inuit Petition Inter-American Commission on Human Rights to Oppose Climate Change Caused by the United States of America." December 7, 2005. http://www.inuitcircumpolar.com/index.php?ID=316&Lang=En

Tsosie, Rebecca. "Indigenous People and Environmental Justice: The Impact of Climate Change." *University of Colorado Law Review* 78 (2007): 1,625–1,677.

Watt-Cloutier, Sheila. "The Climate Change Petition by the Inuit Circumpolar Conference to the Inter-American Commission on Human Rights: Presentation by Sheila Watt-Cloutier, Chair, Inuit Circumpolar Conference [at the] Eleventh Conference of Parties to the UN Framework Convention on Climate Change." December 7, 2005. Montreal. https://earthjustice.org/news/press/2005/inuit-human-rights-petition-filed-over-climate-change

Selected Bibliography

Alston, Dana. "Transforming a Movement: People of Color Unite at Summit against Environmental Racism." *Sojourner* 21 (1992): 30–31.

Anderton, Douglas L., Andy B. Anderson, John Michael Oakes, and Michael R. Fraser. "Environmental Equity: The Demographics of Dumping." *Demography* 31, no. 2 (1994): 229–248.

Austin, Regina, and Michael Schill. "Black, Brown, Poor, and Poisoned: Minority Grassroots Environmental and the Quest for Eco-Justice." *Kansas Journal of Law and Public Policy* 1 (1991): 69–82.

Baibergenova, Akerke, Rustam Kudyakov, Michael Zdeb, and David O. Carpenter. "Low Birth Weight and Residential Proximity to PCB Contaminated Waste Sites." *Environmental Health Perspectives* 111, no. 10 (2003): 1352–1357.

Been, Vicki. "Locally Undesirable Land Uses in Minority Neighborhoods: Disparate Siting or Market Dynamics?" *Yale Law Journal* 103, no. 6 (1994): 1383–1422.

Been, Vicki. "Analyzing Evidence of Environmental Justice." *Journal of Land Use & Law* 11, no. 1 (1995): 1–36.

Been, Vicki, and Francis Gupta. "Coming to the Nuisance or Going to the Barrios? A Longitudinal Analysis of Environmental Justice Claims." *Ecology Law Quarterly* 24, no. 1 (1997): 1–56.

Blackford, Mansel G. "Environmental Justice, Native Rights, Tourism, and Opposition to Military Control: The Case of Kaho'olawe." *Journal of American History* 91, no. 2 (2004): 544–571.

Brook, Daniel. "Environmental Genocide: Native Americans and Toxic Waste." *American Journal of Economics and Sociology* 57, no. 1 (1998): 105–113.

Bryant, Bunyan. *Michigan: A State of Environmental Justice?* New York: Morgan James Publishing, 2011.

Bryant, Bunyan, and Paul Mohai, eds. *Race and the Incidence of Environmental Hazards: A Time for Discourse.* Boulder, CO: Westview Press, 1992.

Bullard, Robert D. "Solid Waste Sites and the Black Houston Community." *Sociological Inquiry* 53 (Spring 1983): 273–288.

Bullard, Robert D. "Invisible Houston: The Black Experience in Boom and Bust." College Station, TX: Texas A&M University Press, 1987.

Bullard, Robert D. *Dumping in Dixie: Race, Class, and Environmental Quality.* Boulder, CO: Westview Press, 1990.

Bullard, Robert D. "Race and Environmental Justice in the United States." *Yale Journal of International Law* 18 (Winter, 1993): 319–335.

Bullard, Robert D. "The Threat of Environmental Racism." *Natural Resources & Environment* 7 (Winter 1993): 23–26.

Bullard, Robert D. "Environmental Racism and Land Use." *Land Use Forum: A Journal of Law, Policy & Practice* 2 (Spring 1993): 6–11.

Bullard, Robert D. "Anatomy of Environmental Racism and the Environmental Justice Movement." In *Confronting Environmental Racism: Voices from the Grassroots*, ed. Robert D. Bullard. Boston: South End Press, 1993.

Bullard, Robert D. "Dismantling Environmental Racism in the USA." *Local Environment* 4 (1999): 5–19.

Bullard, Robert D., ed. *The Quest for Environmental Justice.* Berkeley, CA: Counterpoint, 2005.

Bullard, Robert D. "The 'Poster Child' for Environmental Racism in 2007: Dickson County, Tennessee." In Robert D. Bullard, Paul Mohai, Robin Saha, and Beverly Wright, *Toxic Wastes and Race at Twenty: 1987–2007.* United Church of Christ Justice and Witness Ministries. March 2007, 134–151. http://www.ucc.org/environmental-ministries_toxic-waste-20

Bullard, Robert D., Glenn S. Johnson, and Angel O. Torres. *Environmental Health and Racial Equity.* Washington, D.C.: American Public Health Association, 2011.

Bullard, Robert D., Paul Mohai, Robin Saha, and Beverly Wright. *Toxic Wastes and Race at Twenty: 1987–2007.* United Church of Christ Justice and Witness Ministries. March 2007. http://www.ucc.org/environmental-ministries_toxic-waste-20

Bullard, Robert D., and Beverly Hendrix Wright. "Blacks and the Environment." *Humboldt Journal of Social Relations* 14, no. ½ (1987): 165–184.

Burns, Shirley Steward. *Bringing Down the Mountains: The Impact of Mountaintop Removal Surface Coal Mining on Southern West Virginia Communities, 1970–2004 (West Virginia and Appalachia).* Morgantown: West Virginia University Press, 2007.

Camacho, David E., ed. *Environmental Injustices, Political Struggles: Race, Class, and the Envirionment.* Durham, NC: Duke University Press, 1998.

Checker, Melissa. *Polluted Promises: Environmental Racism and the Search for Justice in a Southern Town.* New York: New York University Press, 2005.

Checker, Melissa. "Withered Memories: Naming and Fighting Environmental Racism in Georgia." In *New Landscapes of Inequality: Neoliberalism and the Erosion of Democracy in America*, eds. Jane L. Collins, Micaela di Leonardo, and Brett Williams. Santa Fe, NM: School for Advanced Research Press, 2008, 122–123.

Chiles, Nick. "8 Horrifying Examples of Corporations Mistreating Black Communities with Environmental Racism." *Atlanta Black Star*, February 12, 2015. http://atlantablackstar.com/2015/02/12/8-horrifying-examples-of-corporations-mistreating-black-communities-with-environmental-racism/

Clark, Brett. "The Indigenous Environmental Movement in the United States." *Organization & Environment* 15, no. 4 (2002): 410–442.

Cole, Luke W., and Sheila R. Foster. *From the Ground Up: Environmental Racism and the Rise of the Environmental Justice Movement*. New York: New York University Press, 2001.

Colquette, Kelly Michele, and Elizabeth A. Henry Robertson. "Environmental Racism: The Causes, Consequences, and Commendations." *Tulane Environmental Law Journal* 5, no. 1 (1991): 168.

Comer, Krista. "Sidestepping Environmental Justice: 'Natural' Landscapes and the Wilderness Plot." *Frontiers: A Journal of Women Studies* 18, no. 2 (1997): 73–101.

Corburn, Jason. *Street Science: Community Knowledge and Environmental Health Justice*. Cambridge, MA: MIT Press, 2005.

Faber, Daniel R., and Eric J. Krieg. *Unequal Exposure to Ecological Hazards: Environmental Justice in the Commonwealth of Massachusetts*. Boston: Northeastern University, 2001.

Gedicks, Al. *The New Resource Wars: Native and Environmental Struggles Against Multinational Corporations*. Boston: South End Press, 1993.

Godsil, Rachel D. "Remedying Environmental Racism." *Michigan Law Review* 90 (1991): 394–427.

Goldman, Benjamin, and Laura Fitton. *Toxic Wastes and Race Revisited*. Washington, D.C.: Center for Policy Alternatives, 1994.

Gottlieb, Robert. *Forcing the Spring: The Transformation of the American Environmental Movement*. New York: Island Press, 2005.

Grinde, Donald A., Jr., and Bruce E. Johansen. *Ecocide of Native America: Environmental Destruction of Indian Lands and Peoples*. Santa Fe, NM: Clear Light Publishers, 1995.

Grossman, Zoltán. *Unlikely Allies: Native American and White Communities Join to Defend Rural Lands*. Seattle: University of Washington Press, 2017.

Hansen, Terri. "Major Environmental Disasters in Indian Country." Indian Country Today Media Network, October 8, 2013. http://indiancountrytodaymedianetwork.com/2013/10/08/7-major-industrial-environmental-disasters-indian-country-151661

Holifield, Ryan. "Defining Environmental Justice and Environmental Racism." *Urban Geography* 22 (2001): 78–90.

Hooks, Gregory, and Chad L. Smith. "The Treadmill of Destruction: National Sacrifice Areas and Native Americans." *American Sociological Review* 69, no. 4 (2004): 558–575.

Johansen, Bruce E. *The Dirty Dozen: Toxic Chemicals and the Earth's Future*. Westport, CT: Praeger, 2003.

Johansen, Bruce E. "The High Cost of Uranium Mining on Navajoland." *Akwesasne Notes New Series* 2, no. 2 (Spring 1997): 10–12.

Johansen, Bruce, and Roberto Maestas. *Wasi'chu: The Continuing Indian Wars*. New York: Monthly Review Press, 1979.

Kimmelman, Michael. "Lessons from Hurricane Harvey: Houston's Struggle Is America's Tale." *New York Times*, November 11, 2017. https://www.nytimes.com/interactive/2017/11/11/climate/houston-flooding-climate.html

Klein, Naomi. "Why #BlackLives Matter Should Transform the Climate Debate." *The Nation*, December 12, 2014 https://www.thenation.com/article/what-does-blacklivesmatter-have-do-climate-change/

Kohlhoff, Dean. *Amchitka and the Bomb: Nuclear Testing in Alaska*. Washington: University of Washington Press, 2003.

Krajicek, David J. "7 Toxic Assaults on Communities of Color Besides Flint: The Dirty Racial Politics of Pollution." Alternet. January 23, 2016. https://www.alternet.org/environment/7-toxic-assaults-communities-color-besides-flint-dirty-racial-politics-pollution

Kuletz, Valerie L. *The Tainted Desert: Environmental and Social Ruin in the American West*. New York: Routledge, 1998.

LaDuke, Winona. "A Society Based on Conquest Cannot Be Sustained: Native Peoples and the Environmental Crisis." In *Toxic Struggles: The Theory and Practice of Environmental Justice*, ed. Richard Hofrichter. Philadelphia: New Society Publishers, 1993, 98–106.

LaDuke, Winona. *All Our Relations: Native Struggles for Land and Life*. Cambridge, MA: South End Press, 1999.

Lavelle, Marianne, and Marcia Coyle. "Unequal Protection." *National Law Journal*, September 21, 1992, S1–S2.

Lerner, Steve. *Diamond: A Struggle for Environmental Justice in Louisiana's Chemical Corridor (Urban and Industrial Environments)*. Cambridge, MA: MIT Press, 2005.

Linzey, Thomas. "'We've Broken the Planet': A Case for Liberation Ecology and the Rights of Nature." *In These Times*, June 16, 2016. http://inthesetimes.com/rural-america/entry/19222/linzey-celdf-community-rights-13-breaking-the-planet

Miller, Todd. *Storming the Wall: Climate Change, Migration, and Homeland Security*. San Francisco: City Lights/Open Media Series, 2017.

Mohai, Paul. "The Demographics of Dumping Revisited: Examining the Impact of Alternate Methodologies in Environmental Justice Research." *Virginia Environmental Law Journal* 14 (1995): 615–653.

Mohai, Paul, and Robin Saha. "Reassessing Racial and Socioeconomic Disparities on Environmental Justice Research." *Demography* 43, no. 2 (2006): 383–389.

Morello-Frosch, Rachel, Manuel Pastor Jr., Carlos Porras, and James Sadd. "Environmental Justice and Regional Inequality in Southern California: Implications for Future Research." *Environmental Health Perspectives* 110, suppl.

2 (April 2002): 149–154. https://www.ncbi.nlm.nih.gov/pmc/articles/PMC1241158/

Moseley, William, Eric Perramond, Holly Hapke, and Paul Laris. *An Introduction to Human-Environmental Gerography*. London, U.K.: Wiley Blackwell, 2014.

Motavalli, Jim. "Toxic Targets: Polluters That Dump on Communities of Color Are Finally Being Brought to Justice." 1998. *[E]-Environment* [magazine]. http://www.ejnet.org/ej/Estory.html

Murillo, Mario. *Island of Resistance: Vieques, Puerto Rico, and U.S. Policy*. New York: Seven Stories Press, 2001.

Nixon, Rob. *Slow Violence and the Environmentalism of the Poor*. Cambridge, MA: Harvard University Press, 2013.

Oakes, John Michael, Douglas L. Anderton, and Andy B. Anderson. "A Longitudinal Analysis of Environmental Equity in Communities with Hazardous Waste Facilities." *Social Science Research* 25 (1996): 125–148.

Okonta, Ike, and Oronto Douglas. *Where Vultures Feast: Shell, Human Rights, and Oil*. New York: Verso, 2003.

Pastor, Manuel, Jr., Jim Sadd, and John Hipp. "Which Came First? Toxic Facilities, Minority Move Ins, and Environmental Justice." *Journal of Urban Affairs* 23, no. 1 (2001): 3.

Pello, Davis Naguib. *Garbage Wars: The Struggle for Environmental Justice in Chicago*. Cambridge, MA: MIT Press, 2002.

Pulido, Laura. "Rethinking Environmental Racism: White Privilege and Urban Development in Southern California." *Annals of the Association of American Geographers* 90, no. 1 (2000): 12–40.

Pulido, Laura, Steve Sidawi, and Robert O. Vos. "An Archaeology of Environmental Racism in Los Angeles." *Urban Geography* 17, no. 5 (1996): 419–439.

Reith, Charles C., and Bruce M. Thomson. *Deserts as Dumps? The Disposal of Hazardous Materials in Arid Ecosystems*. Albuquerque: University of New Mexico Press, 1992.

Ringquist, Evan J. "Assessing Evidence of Environmental Inequities: A Meta-analysis." *Journal of Policy Analysis and Management* 24, no. 2 (2005): 223–247.

Rothman, Hal. *On Rims and Ridges: The Los Alamos Area Since 1880*. Lincoln: University of Oklahoma Press, 1992.

Russell, Dick. "Environmental Racism." *The Amicus Journal* 11 (Spring 1989): 22–32.

Sachs, Noah. "The Mescalero Apache Indians and Monitored Retrievable Storage of Spent Nuclear Fuel: A Study in Environmental Ethics." *Natural Resources Journal* 36 (1996): 881–912.

Saha, Robin, and Paul Mohai. "Historical Context and Hazardous Waste Facility Siting: Understand Temporal Trends in Michigan." *Social Problems* 52, no. 4 (2005): 618–648.

Sandler, Ronald D., and Phaedra C. Pezzulo. *Environmental Justice and Environmentalism: The Social Justice Challenge to the Environmental Movement.* Cambridge, MA: MIT Press, 2007.

Schecter, Arnold, Le Cao Dai, Olaf Papke, Joelle Prange, John D. Constable, Muneaki Matsuda, Vu Duc Thao, and Amanda L. Piskac. "Recent Dioxin Contamination from Agent Orange in Residents of a Southern Vietnamese City." *JOEM* (*Journal of Occupational and Environmental Medicine*) 43, no. 5 (May 2001): 435–443.

Sovacool, Benjamin K. "Don't Let Disaster Recovery Perpetuate Injustice." *Nature* 549 (September 27, 2017): 433.

Stretesky, Paul, and Michael J. Hogan. "Environmental Justice: An Analysis of Superfund Sites in Florida." *Social Problems* 45 (May 1998): 268–287.

Swart, Betsy. "The Passion of Aurora Castillo and the Militant Mothers of East L.A.: Latina Women Demand a Safe Environment for Their Children." *On the Issues: A Magazine of Feminist, Progressive Thinking,* Spring 1992. http://www.ontheissuesmagazine.com/1992spring/swart_spring1992.php

Swift, James A. "It's Not Just Flint: Environmental Racism Is Slowly Killing Blacks across America." *The Grio,* January 24, 2016. http://thegrio.com/2016/01/24/flint-water-environmental-racism-blacks/

Targ, Nicholas. "The States' Comprehensive Approach to Environmental Justice." In David Naguib Pellow and Robert J. Brulle, eds., *Power, Justice, and the Environment: A Critical Appraisal of the Environmental Justice Movement.* Cambridge, MA: MIT Press, 2005, 171–184.

Taylor, Dorceta E. "Mobilizing for Environmental Justice in Communities of Color: An Emerging Profile of People of Color Environmental Groups." In Jennifer Aley, William R. Burch, Beth Canover, and Donald Field, eds., *Ecosystem Management: Adaptive Strategies for Natural Resource Organizations in the Twenty-first Century.* Philadelphia: Taylor & Francis, 1998, 32–67.

The Third Citizens' Conference on Dioxin and Other Synthetic Hormone Disrupters. March 15–17, 1996, Baton Rouge, Louisiana. http://www.americanhealthstudies.org/wastenot/wn354.htm

United Church of Christ Commission for Racial Justice. *Toxic Wastes and Race in the United States.* New York: Commission for Racial Justice, 1987.

U.S. Environmental Protection Agency. *Environmental Equity: Reducing Risks for All Communities.* EPA 230-R-92-008. Washington, D.C.: U.S. Environmental Protection Agency, 1992.

Vandenbosch, Robert, and Susanne E. Vandenbosch. *Nuclear Waste Stalemate.* Salt Lake City: University of Utah Press, 2007.

Waugh, Charles. "'Only You Can Prevent a Forest': Agent Orange, Ecocide, and Environmental Justice." *Interdisciplinary Studies of Literature and the Environment* 17, no. 1 (2010): 113–132. http://digitalcommons.usu.edu/english_facpub/791

Wernette, D. R., and L. A. Nieves. "Breathing Polluted Air: Minorities Are Disproportionately Exposed." *EPA Journal* 18 (March/April 1992): 16–17.

Westra, Laura, Bill E. Lawson, and Peter S. Wenz. *Faces of Environmental Racism: Confronting Issues of Global Justice*, 2nd ed. Lanham, MD: Rowman & Littlefield, 2001.

Williams, Teresa. "Pollution and Hazardous Waste on Indian Lands: Do Federal Laws Apply and Who May Enforce Them?" *American Indian Law* Review 17 (1992): 269–290.

Index

Page numbers followed by *t* indicate tables.

Aamjiwnaang First Nation, 302–306
Acuna, Rodolfo, 228
African Americans: asthma, 16; "Cancer Alley" (Louisiana), 132, 204–211; Hurricane Katrina, 212–217; lead contamination (Indiana), 45–48; lead contamination (Nebraska), 44–45; oil refinery pollution (California), 222, 238–242; PCB contamination (Alabama), 132, 138–142; pig manure spraying (North Carolina), 131, 147–154; toxic dumping (Alabama), 184–187; toxic dumping (Illinois), 162–166; toxic dumping (New York), 166–171; toxic dumping (North Carolina), 172–176; toxic dumping (Pennsylvania), 131, 158–161; toxic dumping (Tennessee), 132, 143–146; toxic dumping (Texas), 59–61, 133–137; toxic water (Michigan), 39–42
African Canadians, toxic dumping (Nova Scotia), 306–310

Africville, Nova Scotia, 306–310
Afton, North Carolina, 172–176
Agent Orange, 29, 78–79; deformed births, 79–81; effects on succeeding generations, 82–83; effects on Vietnamese children decades later, 83–84; and environmental racism, 84–87; risk of diseases, 81–82
Ahnassay, James, 66
air pollution: Ontario, 302–306
Akwesasne, New York, 131, 195–203
Alabama: coal ash pollution, 8; PCB contamination, 132, 138–142; toxic dumping, 184–187
Alaska: climigration, 118–119; global warming, 249–254; gold mining, 8; ice thaws, 113–115; Iditarod and reduced snow, 125–127; land erosion, 115–118, 119–121, 121–123; nuclear weapons, 7, 221, 254–259; permafrost thaws, 123–125; salmon spawning and toxic waste, 221, 243–248

Alaskan Natives: global warming, 249–254; ice thaws, 113–115; Iditarod and reduced snow, 125–127; land erosion, 115–118, 119–121, 121–123; nuclear weapons (Point Hope), 221, 254–259; permafrost thaws, 123–125; salmon spawning and toxic waste (Bristol Bay), 221, 243–248. *See also* Native peoples
Alberta: land rights, 296, 330–334; tar sand mining, 62–71
algae, 55–59
Allen, John, 225–226
Allen, Paula Gunn, 269
Allen, Shantel, 47
Alphonse, Joe, 311–312
Altgeld Gardens, 162–164
Aluminum Company of America (Alcoa), 197, 202
American Bar Association Special Committee on Environmental Justice, 4
American Ecology, 60
American Smelting and Refining Company (ASARCO), 44–45
Anaconda Minerals Co., 267–268, 269, 270–271
Anderson, Donald M., 57
Anderson, William, 290–291, 292
Anglo American (mining conglomerate), 244
Anniston, Alabama, 132, 138–142
Antone, Wally, 286
Arctic, 26–27, 295–296, 339–345, 347, 348, 349, 350
Aronofsky, Darren, 71
Arrowhead Landfille (Uniontown, AL), 3–4
arsenic contamination, 234–235
Assiniboine, 221, 222–226
asthma, 16
Atleo, Shawn A-in-chut, 298–299
Ayah, Louis, 336

Bad River tribe, 33, 35
Badoni, Gilbert, 274
Baptiste, Marilyn, 311
Baraka, Ras, 48
Barrow, Alaska, 250
Barton, Demetri, 235–236
Basu, Niladri, 303
Baton, Paul, 335, 336
Bear, Leon, 265–266
bees, 107
Bell-Jefferson, Jackie, 274
Benjamin, Craig, 300
Bienkowski, Brian, 303
bison. *See* buffalo
Blackburn, Jim, 194
Blum, Elizabeth, 169–170
Blumenfeld, Jared, 281, 282
Booker, Cory, 151
Bosum, Abel, 327–328
Bourassa, Robert, 318, 319
Boyle, Barb, 291
breast milk, toxic, 339–345
Breitburg, Denise, 58–59
Bridgeport, Connecticut, 131, 154–157
Bristol Bay, Alaska, 221, 243–248
British Columbia: mining, 311–315; pipeline protests, 74–75
Bronen, Robin, 118–119
buffalo: and European immigration, 106–107; extermination of, 103, 108–111; history of, 103–104; hunt customs and protocols, 104–106; modern status of, 111–112; taboos against waste, 108
Bullard, Robert D.: and Dickson County, Tennessee, toxic garbage dumps, 132, 143, 145; environmental justice, 2, 3, 6, 10, 14; and Flint, Michigan, water crisis, 16–17; and Houston, Texas, garbage dumps, 133–135, 137
Burns, Robert, 173
Bush, George W., 16, 216–217

Index

California: nuclear dump, 285–287; oil refinery pollution, 222, 238–242; toxic incineration, 221, 227–232
Calley, William, 86
Canada. *See* Alberta; British Columbia; Northwest Territories; Nunavut; Ontario; Quebec
"Cancer Alley" (Mossville, LA), 132, 204–211
Carpenter, David, 198, 199
Carson, Rachel, 32, 185
Castillo, Aurora, 230, 231–232
census ethnic categories, 14
Chamberlin, Bob, 314–315
Chávez, César, 92–93
Chavis, Benjamin, 1, 4
ChemClear, 230–231
chemical disasters, 15–16
Chester, Pennsylvania, 131, 158–161
Chevron, 222, 238–242
Chicago, Illinois, 162–166
Chilcotin, 311–315
chlorpyrifos, 93–94, 96–98
Chythlook-Sifsof, Callan J., 244–245
Citizens for a Clean Environment, 165
Clark, Henry, 239–240
climigration, 118–119
Clinton, Bill, 26
coal pollution: Nevada, 289–293
coal-fired power plants, 2–4, 15
Coalition for Navajo Liberation (CNL), 275, 276
Cohn, Gary, 77
Colorado: smelting pollution, 221–222, 233–237
Colorado Fuel & Iron (CF&I) Steel, 221–222, 233–234
Commoner, Barry, 341, 342
Connecticut, industrial waste in, 131, 154–157
Contrada, Carol, 56
Coon-Come, Mathew, 318–319, 325

Copeland, Anthony, 46, 47
Covenant, Louisiana, 206–207, 208–209
Crees, 12, 296, 317–329
Cromer-Campbell, Tammy, 60
Cruz, Carmen Yulín, 181
cyanide poisoning: Montana, 221, 222–226

Da Silva, Judy, 301
Daishowa, 333
Dakota Access pipeline, 73
Daniels, Heather, 236–237
Danilovich, Yeremei, 342
Davis, Kenneth, 240
DDT, 184–187
Delgado, Lucy, 228
Deline, Northwest Territories, 335–339
Dene, 335–339
Devine, Jon, 58
Dewailly, Eric, 344
Diamond, Henry, 328
Diaz, Alina, 94–95
DiCaprio, Leonardo, 71
Dickson, Tennessee, 132, 143–146
Dietrich, Kim, 43
dioxins, 10, 132, 204–211
Dixon, Jimmy, 151–152
Dodge, Irving Richard, 104
Donahue, William, 67
Dow AgroSciences, 97
Dow Chemical, 206, 209, 210
DowDuPont, 93–94
Dryden Chemical Co., 298, 299

East Chicago, Indiana, 45–48, 165–166
East Los Angeles, California, 221, 227–232
Ecojustice, 304–306, 315
Ecology Action Center, 309–310
Edwards, Marc, 55
Eichstaedt, Peter, 275, 276

electricity, impact of in Quebec, 296, 317–329
Emanuel, Kerry, 191
Emmett, Ed, 194
ENRICH Project (Environmental Noxiousness, Racial Inequities, and Community Health), 307–310
environmental disasters, 11–17
environmental discrimination, types of, 6–10
environmental justice, 1–5
Environmental Protection Agency, 26
Environmental Protection Agency Water Committee, 50–52
environmental racism: challenges and solutions, 18–23; and environmental justice, 1–5; future outlook, 23–27
Erasmus, Bill, 66–67
erosion, 251–252
ethylene dichloride (EDC), 205, 207, 209
Ewall, Mike, 161
Exxon, 33–34, 35

farmworkers. *See* pesticides and farmworkers
Fauret, Aurore, 75
Fay, Peter, 112
Ferner, Mike, 56
Ferruccio, Deborah, 174
Ferruccio, Ken, 175
fertility rates, 42–43
fetal deaths, 42–43
Fire Lame Deer, John, 104
Fish Lake, British Columbia, 311–315
Flint, Michigan: lead-tainted water, 4, 16–17; toxic water, 37–44
flooding, 6, 251–252
Fobister, Simon, 297–298, 301
Foster, Clyde, 186
Fugate, W. Craig, 182
Fumoleau, Rene, 336

garbage dumps: Texas, 133–137
Geisinger, Alex, 159–160
General, Rowena, 199–200
General Motors, 196–199, 200–201, 202–203
Gentry, Don, 76, 77
George, Reuben, 74–75
George, Will, 74
George-Kanentiio, Doug, 203
Georgia Gulf, 206
Georgia-Pacific, 206
Gibbs, Lois, 169, 170
Gilday, Cindy, 335–336, 337
glaciers, 251
Glazer, Phyllis, 20, 59–61
global warming, 14–15; Alaska, 249–254; Inuit and the United States, 346–350; Nunavut, 347, 348
Gogebic Taconite (GTAC), 35–36
gold mining, in Montana, 221, 222–226
Goldtooth, Tom, 286, 287
Gómez, Hernán, 43
Goshutes, 263–267
Grants, New Mexico, 272–277, 279
Grassy Narrows, Ontario, 296–297, 297–301
Grassy Narrows First Nation, 296–297, 297–301
Great Sioux Uprising, 110
Greenpeace, 205, 206–211
Griffiths, Jeffrey K., 50, 51
Gros Ventre, 221, 222–226

Halifax, Nova Scotia, 306–310
Hallbauer, Russell, 311, 312, 315
Hanford (WA) Nuclear Reservation, 287–289
Hanna-Attisha, Mona, 37–38, 41, 43
Hansen, James, 65
Harney, Corbin, 260–261, 263
Harper, Stephen, 63, 70, 312
Harriott, Nishelle, 98
Harris, Walter J., 173

Hartnell, Anna, 214–215
Hasselman, Jan, 74
hazmat sites, 18–19
Helgeson, Gus, 223–224
Herman, Harvey, 189, 190
Hicks-Hudson, Paula, 58
Highfield, Wes, 192
Hispanic Americans. *See* Latino Americans
Holt family, 144–146
Homer-Dixon, Thomas, 64
Hoover, Elizabeth, 203
House, Larry, 328
Houston, Texas, 133–137, 190–195
Huichols, 100–101
Hunt, James B., Jr., 173
Hurricane Harvey, 190–195, 215
Hurricane Katrina, 9, 16, 212–217
Hurricane Maria, 177–183
Hydro-Quebec, 296, 317–329

ice thaws, 113–115
Iditarod, and reduced snow, 125–127
Illinois: lead contamination, 45–48; toxic dumping, 162–166
Indiana, toxic dumping in, 165–166
indigenous peoples. *See* Native peoples
industrial waste: Connecticut, 131, 154–157
International Tribunal of Indigenous People and Oppressed Nations, 7
Inuit, 295–296, 317, 319–320, 321, 339–345, 346–350
Inuit Circumpolar Conference, 346–347, 348, 349–350

James Bay, Quebec, 296, 317–329
Jewell, Sally, 292–293
Jock, Ken, 199, 202
Johnson, Hazel, 163, 164
Johnson, Laura, 58
Johnson, Robert, 86

Jones, Lynn, 308–309
Jordan, Keith, 56

Kaktovik, Alaska, 250
Kaleak, Jeslie, 259
Kaplan, Robert A., 46
Kelly, John F., 180
Kennecott Copper Corporation, 34
Kerr-McGee Company, 272
Keystone XL Pipeline, 62–64, 70
Kinder Morgan Trans Mountain pipeline, 73–75
King, Al, 337
King, Stephanie, 45–46
Kirby, Jane, 188–189
Kirchhoff, Jon, 59
Kivalina, Alaska, 115–118
Klamath tribes, 76–77
Kraus, Ezra Jacob, 78
Kynoch, Brian, 313–314

Laboucan, Billy Joe, 70, 334
Lac Courte Oreilles Chippewa, 34
Lac du Flambeau Chippewa, 33
LaDuke, Winona, 7, 269
Laguna, New Mexico, 220, 267–271
Lake Erie water pollution, 55–59
Lamb, Anita, 60–61
Lambrinidou, Yanna, 50–51
land erosion, in Alaska, 119–121, 121–123
land rights, in Alberta, 296, 330–334
Landry, Bernard, 327, 328
Langston, Nancy, 303
Las Vegas, Nevada, 289–293
Latino Americans: industrial waste (Connecticut), 131, 154–157; smelting pollution (Colorado), 221–222, 233–237; toxic dumping (Texas), 59–61
lead contamination: East Chicago, Indiana, 45–48; Nebraska, 44–45; Pueblo, Colorado, 234–237
lead toxicity, 6, 50–52, 52–55

Leavitt, Mike, 264
LeBlanc, Judith, 73
Lee, Vernon, 291
Lennarson, Fred, 332
Lenz, Garth, 66
Lewis, Gloria, 268
Limer, Edgar, 173, 175
Lincoln, Abraham, 110
Lindner, Jeff, 194
Linzey, Thomas, 19
Little Buffalo, Alberta, 296, 330–334
Little Rocky Mountains, Montana, 221, 222–226
Lockridge, Ada, 304, 305
Loeb, Nancy, 193
Lopez, Steve, 286
Lorenzo, June, 268–269
Louie, Ann, 247, 314
Louisiana: "Cancer Alley," 132, 204–211; Hurricane Katrina, 212–217
Love, William, 167, 168
Love Canal, New York, 12, 166–171
Lowry, Jennifer, 48
Lubicon Lake Cree Nation, 69–70, 296, 330–334
Lyon, Nick, 43

MacFarlane, Karla, 297
Mah, Alice, 167, 168–169, 170–171
malathion spraying: South Dakota, 187–190
Mandros, Nick, 56
Mann, Barbara Alice, 14, 269
Marchi, Sergio, 342
Marrismarch, Emma, 76, 77
Masty, David, 326
McCauley, Linda, 98
McClain, Mildred Bahati, 21
McGreevey, James, 19
McKean, Deborah, 236
McKibben, Bill, 64
McLaughlin, Gayle, 222, 242
Meascum, Albert, 324

mercury contamination: Ontario, 296–297, 297–301; Quebec, 321–323
Michigan, lead-tainted water in, 16–17, 37–44
mining, 30–36; British Columbia, 311–315
Mission, South Dakota, 187–190
Mitchell, Kaitlyn, 297, 305–306, 310
Moapa Paiutes, 289–293
Mohai, Paul, 4
Mohawks, 131, 195–203
Molina, Gloria, 228
Monsanto, 139, 140–141
Montana, gold mining and cyanide poisoning in, 221, 222–226
Montgrand, Don, 338
Moretta, John, 227, 229
Morneau, Bill, 75
Moses, Ted, 327, 328
Mossville, Louisiana, 132, 204–211
Mothers of East Los Angeles (MELA), 221, 227–232
Mount Polley Mine, 313–314
Moyers, Bill, 211
Muir, Stewart, 75
Mukash, Matthew, 328–329
Muller, Paul, 185
Murkowski, Frank, 259
Murphy, Wendell, 152

Nagin, Ray, 216
Namagoose, Bill, 324
Native peoples: air pollution (Ontario), 302–306; buffalo, importance of, 103–112; coal pollution (Nevada), 289–293; electricity, impact of (Quebec), 296, 317–329; gold mining and cyanide poisoning (Montana), 221, 222–226; land rights (Alberta), 296, 330–334; lands, 7; malathion spraying (South Dakota), 187–190; mercury contamination (Ontario),

Index   367

296–297, 297–301; and mining, 30–36; mining (British Columbia), 311–315; nuclear dumping (California), 285–287; nuclear weapons (Nevada), 260–263; pipeline protests (Canada), 73–75; pipeline protests (Standing Rock), 73; tar sand mining (Alberta), 65–71; toxic breast milk (Nunavut), 339–345; toxic dumping (New York), 131, 195–203; uranium mining (New Mexico), 272–277; uranium mining (Northwest Territories), 335–339; uranium waste (New Mexico), 278–284; uranium waste (Utah), 263–267. *See also* Alaskan Natives

Navajo Nation, 272–277, 278–284
Nazile, Warner, 65
Nebraska, lead contamination in, 44–45
Nevada: coal pollution, 289–293; nuclear weapons, 260–263
New Jersey, toxic water in, 48
New Mexico: uranium mining, 220, 267–271, 272–277; uranium waste, 278–284
New Orleans, Louisiana, 212–217
New York, toxic dumping in, 131, 166–171, 195–203
Newark, New Jersey, 48
Newtok, Alaska, 119–121
Nez, Bertha, 282–283
Nez Perce, 67–68
Nixon, Richard, 86
North Carolina: PCB disposal landfill, 13–14; pig manure spraying, 131, 147–154; toxic dumping, 172–176
North Richmond, California, 238–242
Northern Dynasty Minerals, 244, 246, 247, 248
Northwest Territories: uranium mining, 335–339

Nova Scotia, toxic dumping in, 306–310
nuclear dump: California, 285–287
nuclear weapons: Alaska, 221, 254–259; Nevada, 260–263
Nunavut: global warming, 347, 348

Oatman, McCoy, 68
Obama, Barack: and Lakota activist, 70; Pebble Mine, Alaska, 8, 221, 243, 246; pesticides and farmworkers, 93; water quality tests, 52
Office of Civil Rights (OCR), 25
Ohio, toxic water in, 55–59
oil refinery pollution, in California, 222, 238–242
Oklahoma, toxic mining in, 31–32
Old Man Ferdinand, 336
Olin Corporation, 184–187
Olson, Erik D., 52
Omaha, Nebraska, 44–45
Ominayak, Bernard, 70, 330, 331, 332, 334
Ominayak, Cheryl, 334
Ontario: air pollution, 302–306; mercury contamination, 296–297, 297–301
Operation Plowshare, 255–257
Operation Ranch Hand, 78, 79, 86
Oregon, pipeline protests in, 76–77

Pacific Connector Gas Pipeline, 76–77
Parizeau, Jacques, 325
Parras, Brian, 137
Parras, Juan, 136–137
Paul, Candyce, 338
PCB contamination, 10; Alabama, 132, 138–142; Arctic, 341; New York, 196–203; North Carolina, 172–176; Nunavit, 343; Ontario, 303; Quebec, 344–345
Pegasus Gold Corp., 224–225

Pennsylvania, toxic dumping in, 19–20, 131, 158–161
People for Community Recovery, 163, 164
Percell, John, 154, 155
Perdue, Sonny, 93
permafrost thaws, in Alaska, 123–125, 250, 252
persistent organic pollutants (POPs), 341, 343
Pesticide Action Network, 91
pesticides and farmworkers, 341–343; chlorpyrifos, 93–94, 96–98; effects on DNA, 98; and elemental sulfur, 98–100; health effects, 89–91; protests, 91–93; and Trump era, 93–96
Phelps Dodge Corporation, 33, 34
Phillip, Stewart, 75, 312
Picher, Oklahoma, 11
Pierrehumbert, Raymond, 64
pig manure spraying, in North Carolina, 131, 147–154
pipeline protests: Canada, 73–75; Oregon, 76–77; Standing Rock, 73
Plain, Ron, 304, 305
Point Hope, Alaska, 123–125, 221, 254–259
polyvinyl chloride (PVC), 205–206
Porter, Tom Sakokwenionkwas, 201
Private Fuel Storage (PFS), 264, 265, 266
Project Carryall, 256
Project Chariot, 255–257
Project Sedan, 256
Pruitt, Scott: appointment of, 26, 31; lead standards, 38; Pebble Mine, Alaska, 8, 221, 248; water quality tests dropped, 52
Pueblo, Colorado, 221–222, 233–237
Pueblo tribe, 220, 267–271
Puerto Rico, Hurricane Maria in, 177–183
Pungowiyi, Caleb, 252–254

Purley, Dorothy, 270–271
PVC, 206–207, 209, 210, 211

Quapaw Indian Reservation (Picher, OK), 11–17, 31–32
Quebec, impact of electricity in, 296, 317–329

radiation dump, in Washington, 287–289
Ramey, Willie T., III, 174, 176
Ramos, Lucy, 229
Rankin, Murray, 74
Ransom, Jim, 198
Redhouse, John, 268, 280
Reid, Harry, 292, 293
Reid Gardner Generating Station, 290–293
Remington Arms, 155, 156
Reynolds, Joel, 247
Reynolds, Ray, 211
Reynolds Metals Company, 197, 200
Richmond, California, 222, 238–242
Rio Puerco, 278–280
Roane County, Tennessee, 3–4
Rock, Tommy, 277
Rogers, Shane, 148
Rosebud Sioux, 187–190
Ross, Dan, 211
Rosse, William, Sr., 261
Rosselló, Ricardo, 179, 180
Rudd, John, 298, 301
Ruiz, Virginia, 93

"sacrifice zones," 135–136
Saeteurn, Sandy, 240
Saganash, Romeo, 328
Saha, Robin, 5
salmon spawning and toxic waste, in Alaska, 221, 243–248
Sangster, Shanon, 277
Sarnia, Ontario, 302–306
Sass, Stephen, 228

Scharper, Stephen Bede, 297
Schecter, Arnold, 83
Schell, Lawrence, 202
Sellars, Bev, 247, 314
Shapiro, Isaac, 213–214
Sharpe, Charles, 61
Shekter-Smith, Liane, 43
Shelly, Ben, 281, 283
Sheridan, Phil, 103, 111
Sherman, Arloc, 213–214
Shintech, 206–207, 208–210
Shishmaref, Alaska, 121–123
Shoshone, 260–261, 263
Silent Spring (Carson), 185
Simmons, Vickie, 290
Simpson, Isobel, 304
Skull Valley, Utah, 263–267
smelting pollution, in Colorado, 221–222, 233–237
Smith, Damu, 210
Snyder, Rick, 39, 41, 43
Sokaogon Chippewa, 33, 35
Solutia, 139, 141
South Dakota, malathion spraying in, 187–190
Spitzer, Eliot, 200–201
Stair, Philip, 40
Standing Rock protests, 73
Steele, Todd, 56–57
Stein, Fernando, 97
Sterner, Robert, 57
Stevens, Ted, 248
Stone, Ward, 196, 201–202
Strategic Lawsuits Against Public Participation (SLAPPs), 20
sulfur, elemental, 98–100
Superfund sites, 6, 7
Swearingen, Terri, 20

Tanaqua Borough, Pennsylvania, 19–20
Tar Creek Superfund, 11–12
tar sand mining, in Alberta, 62–71
tar sands reserves, 13t

Taseko mining company, 311, 312, 315
Teller, Edward, 255–256
Tennessee: coal ash pollution, 8; toxic garbage dumps, 132, 143–146
Texas: garbage dumps, 133–137; toxic dumping, 59–61; toxic flooding, 133, 190–195
Teztan Biny (Fish Lake), British Columbia, 311–315
Theodore Swann Company, 139
Thin Elk, Anna Carol, 189–190
Thompson, Dana Leigh, 197–198, 203
Thompson, Larry, 202–203
Thompson, Loran, 201
Thompson, Marilyn, 199
Thompson, Paul, 197, 199
Thompson, Tommy, 34
Toledo, Ohio, 55–59
Tom, Aletha, 291
Tomlinson, Garrett, 69
Toulouse, Angus, 299
toxic dumping: Alabama, 184–187; Illinois, 162–166; Indiana, 165–166; New York, 131, 166–171, 195–203; North Carolina, 172–176; Nova Scotia, 306–310; Pennsylvania, 131, 158–161; Tennessee, 132, 143–146; Texas, 59–61
toxic flooding, in Texas, 133, 190–195
toxic incineration, in California, 221, 227–232
toxic water, 50–52; Michigan, 37–44; New Jersey, 48; Ohio, 55–59
Treviño-Sauceda, Mily, 95
Triana, Alabama, 184–187
Trump, Donald: appointment of Pruitt, 26, 31; lead standards, 38; liquid natural gas export facility, 77; Pebble Mine, Alaska, 8, 221, 243, 248; pesticides and farmworkers, 93; and Puerto Rico, 177–183; water quality tests dropped, 52

Tsilhqot'in (Chilcotin), 311–315
Tsosie, Kathleen, 270

Ujvagi, Peter, 56
Uniontown, Alabama, 3–4
United Church of Christ (UCC), 21–22
United Farmworkers, 91–93
United States, Inuit, and global warming, 346–350
University of Michigan Environmental Justice Program, 4
uranium mining: New Mexico, 220, 267–271, 272–277; Northwest Territories, 335–339
uranium waste, in New Mexico, 278–284; Utah, 263–267
Utah, uranium waste in, 263–267

Vietnam and Agent Orange, 78–87
vinyl chloride monomer (VCM), 205–206, 207, 209
Violette, Marc, 201
Vulcan Chemicals, 207

Waldron, Ingrid, 307, 308
Walker, Scott, 35–36
Walnut Tree, North Carolina, 2–3
Wapachee, George, 328
Ward Valley, California, 285–287
Warren County, North Carolina, 13–14

Washington, radiation dump in, 287–289
waste disposal, 18
Watt-Cloutier, Sheila, 340, 345, 347, 349
Weaver, Karen, 42, 44
Webb, Dona, 149
Weller, Gunter, 249–250
Wells, Eden, 43
Wells, John, 261
Wenstrom, Michael, 236
West Lake Landfill (MO), 3
Westmoreland, William, 85
white bison, 111–112
White Plume, Debra, 70
Whitman, Silas, 67–68
Williams, Kim, 247, 313
Williams, Mike, 127
Wing, Steve, 148, 149, 150, 151
Winona, Texas, 59–61
Wisconsin, toxic mining in, 32–36
Woody, Carol Ann, 313

Yakama Nation, 287–289
Yazzie, Emma, 219–220
Young, Neil, 70–71
Yukon, Isadore, 337
Yup'ik Eskimos, 115, 119

Zann, Lenore, 307–308
Zortman Mining Inc., 224–225
Zuroweste, Edward, 90

About the Author

Bruce E. Johansen, as a professor of Communication and Native American Studies, taught, researched, and wrote at the University of Nebraska at Omaha from 1982 to 2019, retiring to emeritus status as Frederick W. Kayser research professor. He has published 50 books in several fields: history, anthropology, law, Earth sciences, and many others. Johansen's writing has been published, debated, and reviewed in many academic venues, among them the *William and Mary Quarterly*, *American Historical Review*, *Current History*, and *Nature*, as well as in many popular newspapers and magazines, such as *The New York Times*, *The Nation*, and *National Geographic*.

www.ingramcontent.com/pod-product-compliance
Lightning Source LLC
LaVergne TN
LVHW021558201224
799625LV00001B/32